Venetian Views, Venetian Blinds

English Fantasies of Venice

| 37 | Internationale Forschungen zur
Allgemeinen und
Vergleichenden Literaturwissenschaft |

In Verbindung mit

Dietrich Briesemeister (Friedrich Schiller-Universität Jena) — Guillaume van Gemert (Universiteit Nijmegen) — Joachim Knape (Universität Tübingen) — Klaus Ley (Johannes Gutenberg-Universität Mainz) — John A. McCarthy (Vanderbilt University) — Manfred Pfister (Freie Universität Berlin) — Sven H. Rossel (University of Washington) — Azade Seyhan (Bryn Mawr College) — Horst Thomé (Universität Kiel)

herausgegeben von

Alberto Martino
(Universität Wien)

Redakteure:
Prof. Dr. Norbert Bachleitner. — Doz. Dr. Alfred Noe

Anschrift der Redaktion:
Institut für Vergleichende Literaturwissenschaft, Berggasse 11/5, A-1090 Wien

Venetian Views, Venetian Blinds

English Fantasies of Venice

edited by
Manfred Pfister
and Barbara Schaff

Amsterdam - Atlanta, GA 1999

Cover Design: William Marlow (1740-1813): *Capriccio: St Paul's and a Venetian Canal* (ca. 1795-97), Tate Gallery London

∞ The paper on which this book is printed meets the requirements of "ISO 9706:1994, Information and documentation - Paper for documents - Requirements for permanence".

ISBN: 90-420-0757-5 (bound)
©Editions Rodopi B.V., Amsterdam-Atlanta, GA 1999
Printed in The Netherlands

Table of Contents

Manfred Pfister and Barbara Schaff:
    Introduction   1

Manfred Pfister:
    The Passion from Winterson to Coryate   15

Andreas Mahler:
    Writing Venice: Paradoxical Signification as Connotational Feature   29

Tony Tanner:
    "Which is the Merchant here? And which the Jew?":
    The Venice of Shakespeare's *Merchant of Venice*   45

Jürgen Schlaeger:
    Elective Affinities: Lady Mary Wortley Montagu in Venice   63

Elinor Shaffer:
    William Beckford in Venice, Liminal City:
    The Pavilion and the Interminable Staircase   73

Barbara Schaff:
    Venetian Views and Voices in Radcliffe's *The Mysteries of Udolpho*
    and Braddon's *The Venetians*   89

Werner von Koppenfels:
    Sunset City - City of the Dead: Venice and the 19th Century
    Apocalyptic Imagination   99

Sergio Perosa:
    Literary Deaths in Venice   115

Elisabeth Bronfen:
    Venice - Site of Mutability, Transgression and Imagination   129

Michael Gorra:
    The Venetian Hours of Henry James   147

Ina Schabert:
    An Amazon in Venice: Vernon Lee's "Lady Tal"   155

Erika Fischer-Lichte:
    Theatre as Festive Play: Max Reinhardt's Production of
    The Merchant of Venice in Venice   169

Virginia Richter:
    Tourists Lost in Venice: Daphne du Maurier's *Don't Look Now* and
    Ian McEwan's *The Comfort of Strangers*   181

Sabine Schülting:
    'Dream Factories': Hollywood and Venice in Nicolas Roeg's
    Don't Look Now   195

Indira Ghose:
    Confidential Venice   213

Rosella Mamoli Zorzi:
    Intertextual Venice: Blood and Crime and Death Renewed in
    Two Contemporary Novels   225

Judith Seaboyer:
    Robert Coover's *Pinocchio in Venice*: An Anatomy of a Talking Book   237

Manfred Pfister and Barbara Schaff

Introduction

This collection of essays is the outcome of a symposium inspired by a unique *genius loci* and a powerful, yet benign *spiritus rector*: the Venetian island of San Servolo, since 1997 home of the "Venice International University", which generously hosted our international band of Anglo-Venetian enthusiasts, and Professor Tony Tanner, who agreed to join us in spite of seriously impaired health to grace our meeting with his genial presence and spirited interventions. His *Venice Desired* (1992), that magnificent study of Venetian fantasies and literary representations of Venice from Byron to Thomas Mann, from Ruskin to Proust, proved to be the most significant point of departure and the most frequent point of reference in all the contributions to this volume. This in itself has turned our project, quite unwittingly, into one continued *hommage* to his humane scholarship and critical acumen and wit - and as such it must stand now: Tony Tanner died on 5 December 1998, between the symposium and the publication of its proceedings. It is to his memory that we dedicate our joint efforts in gratitude, affection, admiration and mourning.

The venue of our symposium in March 1998 was a uniquely Venetian place: San Servolo, an island in the lagoon. It had first served, since the 8th century, as a Benedictine monastery, then, in 1725, was turned into a hospital for the insane, for "maniacs of noble family or comfortable circumstances" and opened in 1779, by order of Napoleon, to all mental patients. When Théophile Gautier visited it in 1850, he pointed out "that it had been no great task to adapt the monastic cells' use from monks to madmen" (*Voyage en Italie*, 1852). When we gathered there one and a half century later, we found it recently converted into an academic centre. And again, these cells and halls and the seclusion of the place proved to be as adaptable to the uses of scholars as to those of the madmen and the monks in previous periods of its history. It reminded us how metamorphic Venice is, how easily and ambiguously convents change into madhouses and madhouses into institutions of learning here. And, of course, we were thrilled by the fact that our venue epitomized what our symposium was about: San Servolo, first put on the English literary map in Shelley's poem "Julian and Maddalo" and recently featuring prominently in Jeanette Winterson's novel *The Passion*, underlines how even the remoter parts of Venice have been written over again and again by travellers from abroad, amongst them many English-speaking visitors, and how this has turned Venice into a virtual palimpsest of texts, which have appropriated the place and refashioned it in their own terms throughout the centuries. For having put us into this position by hosting us on the island, we are deeply grateful to Venice International University, in particular to its Dean, Dr. Gianni Toniolo, and its General Manager, Andrea Del Mercato.

Manfred Pfister and Barbara Schaff

The Venice we had come here to discuss lay across a wide stretch of the lagoon, hidden behind the high forbidding walls surrounding the island on all sides and visible only through window openings broken into them, which framed our view of its celebrated skyline. Venice near and distant at the same time, visible and invisible, a panorama framed for viewing and thus always only partially in view - this perspective allegorized for us both our own pursuits and the pursuits of those we pursued in our studies, the travel writers, poets, novelists, painters, film makers and theatre workers representing and performing their views and fantasies of Venice. Both their and our views are always framed and therefore always partial, deleting what is beyond the frame; they are always focused and therefore always blur what is out of focus; they are always constructed and therefore open to deconstruction.

This is also what our punning title *Venetian Views, Venetian Blinds* suggests: Venice, famous *for* its views and *as* a view, self-consciously presenting itself as a gallery of *vedute* or a *thea-tron*, a *Schau-Bühne* for performances, has been represented as such in the texts and images of its visitors from the Early Modern period, the Renaissance, to our postmodern present. This heightened sense of visibility, of being displayed for viewing and framed as a view, highlights at the same time its opposite - blindness, in its double meaning of being deprived of the sense of sight, and being invisible, dark, lacking in lustre. Blindness is the ineluctable shadow of sight; each insight, as Paul de Man has argued on a general hermeneutical level in *Blindness and Insight* (1971), is based upon, and creates, its own blindness. In more concrete terms, the Venetian views are grounded on what they turn a blind eye to, what is faded out and remains hidded behind or beyond the field of vision, and behind or beyond the pre-scribed *videnda*, the pre-scripted sights.

'Venetian blinds', of course, has a more specific application. It refers to the contraption of long, thin, flat bars attached to windows with which one can regulate or shut out the incidence of light - and sight - and which is called *taparelle*, *persiane* or *veneziane* in Italian and *jalousie* in French and German (cf. Andreas Mahler's essay in this volume). There is, actually, an English novel that has it in the title, Ethel Mannin's *Venetian Blinds* (1933). Foreign travellers have noticed, and commented upon, these Venetian blinds particularly in conjunction with that other quintessentially Venetian object, the *gondola* - to the tourist a medium for viewing Venice and its sights as much as a means of transport. In a letter to his wife (23 August 1818), Shelley described their combined features and uses: "These gondolas are the most convenient and beautiful boats in the world. They are finely carpeted and furnished with black, and painted black. The couches upon which you lean are extraordinarily soft, and are so disposed as to be the most comfortable to those who lean or sit. The windows have at will either Venetian plate-glass flowered, or Venetian blinds, or blinds of black cloth to shut out the light." Similarly, Emerson in his journal (3 June 1833) noted that "it is very luxurious to lie on the eider-down cushions of your gondola and read or talk or smoke, drawing to, now the cloth-lined shutter, now the Venetian blind, now the glass window as you

Introduction

please", but promptly turned against them in disenchantment: "yet there is always a slight smell of bilgewater about the thing, and houses in water remind one of a freshet and of desolation, anything but comfort. I soon had enough of it."

Again, the *gondole* and their Venetian blinds allegorise our theme: they frame and construct the expected picturesque views of Venice, control and direct the viewer's gaze upon this moveable feast and aestheticise and de-materialise the city into a *Gesamtkunstwerk*. There is, however, a two-way traffic of glances at stake here - from within to without as well as from without to within. The Venetian blinds do not only serve to shut out excessive light or "turn off", as it were, either a cloying surfeit of Venetian views or unpleasant and unappetising aspects of the city; they also prevent outsiders from looking inside the *tende* of the *gondola* and thus create a private and intimate space that turns the glance inwards towards a fantasised Venice or suggests to the outsider the erotic potential of such intimacy. At this point, the frequently commented upon funereal blackness of the boats comes into play, triggering the kind of fantasies of sexuality and death, of *eros* and *thanatos* inextricably interwoven that trouble and fascinate so many of the texts discussed in the essays of our collection.

Of course, this is by no means the first book dedicated to fantasies and representations of Venice. In contrast to those already extant (and listed in the bibliographies at the end of this introduction and of each essay, we have opted for a broad perspective in our book, which surveys half a millennium of Venetian views, Venetian blinds. With such a wide canvas, we had to be highly selective, allowing ourselves only side glances at already well-treated aspects such as the Venice of the Grand Tourists or Ruskin's Venice and focusing on cases that help to illuminate both continuities in, and disruptions of, traditional ways of perceiving, constructing and performing Venice. Particular emphasis is given to more recent and popular versions of Venice and how they relate to those canonised in the Renaissance, in Neoclassicism and Romanticism. And, more than in other publications, visual images of Venice - drawn, painted, staged or filmed - are taken into account and discussed in their contribution towards setting up Venice as a *Gesamtkunstwerk*.

So how is Venice constituted as a literary topos, what are the discourses of Venice? Venice is the ultimate palimpsest, insists **Manfred Pfister**: it is both unrepresentable and represented over and over again. Jeannette Winterson's postmodernist novel *The Passion* serves as a paradigmatical text, in which all the myths and metaphors of Venice are recycled: the city of mazes, disguises, uncertainty, madness, to name only a few. All these labels belong to discourses of Venice that can be traced back to different historical and literary eras, and Pfister shows their origin and variations spanning from Winterson back to Coryate. The very title of Winterson's book refers to the myth of Venice as *città galante*, the only myth which has been persistently repeated in literary fantasies from the Renaissance to the present day. In Winterson's novel passion, or sexuality, is the aspect which permeates everything else. The topography of Venice turns out to be polymorphous and evasive – a maze, which as a city of the interior, a fluid, exotic and oriental city, is characterized as female. However, Venetian fantasies are almost always also marked by a distinctive gender ambivalence. Gender clearly is at stake and in trouble in this city of theatrical performance, and Venice has always enticed travellers to participate in, comment on or just observe the metamorphoses, masquerades and crossdressings. Winterson's allusions to these tropes reveal not only their continuity, but also fundamental differences: In her novel, sexual identity behind the mask remains ambiguous, the very distinction between self and mask no longer even applies and the difference between performance and reality collapses.

Andreas Mahler, like Pfister, attempts an overall view of the Venetian semantics and sets out to trace the problem of representing Venice and the signature of the Venetian in a systematic rather than historical fashion. *Mahler* takes a literal approach to our title "Views and Blinds" and, taking Donna Leon's *Death at La Fenice* as a paradigm, he shows how texts organize their signs in such a way as to present themselves as "Venetian". Mahler observes that the peculiar position and construction of Venice makes it impossible to have access to a central signifier. Instead, Mahler argues, Venice becomes readable by simultaneously allocating the double meaning of the view and the blind; in other words the semiotics of the masquerade. He establishes this principle of paradoxical signification as a characteristic feature to connote the city's ambiguity. This intrinsic doubleness of Venetian representations is furthermore linked to Foucault's idea of heterotopia, which is defined as a place which is and is not, part of a culture and detached from it, bringing together the incompatible, uniting the heterogeneous. Referring to Henry James' *The Wings of the Dove* and Thomas Mann's *Der Tod in Venedig*, Mahler shows that to construct Venice as a heterotopia means to open up a space where the characters may perform both the imaginary as well as the real at the same time. If one defines fiction simply as the crossing of boundaries between the real and the imaginary, then Venice itself looks very much like fiction. In this structural affinity between Venice and fiction Mahler sees the specific attraction of Venice as a literary topos.

In the chronology of English texts on Venice, Shakespeare's *Merchant of Venice* is albeit not the first, yet certainly the best-known text. Two papers approach the drama from the different angles of text interpretation and performance.

Tony Tanner takes Portia's apparently simple question: "Which is the Merchant here? And which the Jew?" literally, to unfold an intricate play with differences and transactions. This turns out to be far more complicated than it first seems. Tanner establishes the Rialto, Belmont and the Ghetto as the three distinct areas of the play, and argues that the Venetian setting allowed Shakespeare to explore the relationship between the values of a mercantile society and those of a Christian community. He takes a close look at the play's contrastive puns and mercantile metaphors, which hint at a constant inter-involvement of money and body. The recurrent linking of law and flesh (through bonds and rings) interconnect the otherwise separated worlds of Venice – a closed men's world of law, public life and money – and of Belmont – an open

Introduction

women's world of liberty and harmony. Just as Shylock insists on his bond, so does Portia in the last act insist on the letter of the pledge and here Bassanio stands as guilty and helpless before her as Antonio stood before Shylock. Thus, concludes Tanner, the manifold transactions and transformations between the different Venetian worlds eventually undermine the distinct opposition which Portia's question had implied.

Erika Fischer-Lichte depicts how, at the beginning of our century, Max Reinhardt repeatedly produced *The Merchant of Venice*, not to give a new reading of the text, but to exemplify a new concept of theatre as festive play. In his Berlin production of 1905/06 he created a particular atmosphere through the interaction of stage architecture, colours, light, music and movements – particularly by means of a revolving stage - and cast Venice itself as the protagonist and centre of the performance. A new fast style of acting violated established rules of realism and psychology. It focused on the situation and realized a new body concept where the actor's body was used to expose the theatricality of the performance. Max Reinhardt thus redefined theatre in a way where, as Fischer–Lichte pointedly states, the theatricality of the play was more important than the interpretation of the text: the play's performativity outweighs its referentiality. This principle culminated in Reinhardt's last production of *The Merchant of Venice* on the Campo San Trovaso in Venice in 1934. Here he not only put Venice on stage but used the city itself as a stage, where actors as well as spectators took part in the play and Reinhardt fully exploited the possibilities this unique space had to offer. This theatrical performance foregrounded the city's own theatricality: performing Venice here virtually meant to let the city act itself.

As an ambiguous city, whose liminal position between land and water, East and West, obliterates differences as well as puts them into focus, as the city of masquerades where performance is the overall rule, Venice has always been particularly attractive to female authors who have battled in life and letters against restricting gender roles and gendered notions of aesthetic concepts.

Jürgen Schlaeger traces Lady Montagu's affinities with Venice and presents her as an in-between personality, a liminal figure who represented both the aristocratic world of the 17th century and the intellectual enlightened bourgeois world of the 18th century. According to her contemporaries, Lady Montagu freely crossed and re-crossed gender boundaries, propagated masculine ideas in a female voice and created and staged her personality after literary role models. This cosmopolitan intellectual had spent six years of her life in Venice. "Why Venice?", Schlaeger asks and demonstrates how, of all of the foreign places where Montagu had lived, the six years in Venice played a key role in her life. When at forty-seven she fell in love with the young Italian Francesco Algarotti, she chose Venice as the place where she hoped to reconcile her different roles as an aristocratic lady, a woman of letters and a passionate lover. Forever crossing lines, Montagu felt attracted to the city of shifting boundaries, its social fluidity and intellectual excitement. As Schlaeger deduces from her letters, Venice provided her with the free space for role-model-oriented self-fashioning as well as for individual feminine self-assertion.

A particularly rich source of the Gothic imagination, Venice is above all linked up with the writings of William Beckford and Ann Radcliffe. **Elinor Shaffer** considers two architectural images, the oriental pavilion and Piranesi's interminable staircase, as metaphors for Beckford's obsession with entries and the crossing of boundaries. In Beckford's account of his Grand Tour, Venice figures largely as his entry into Italy and a new world, and the city's liminal situation and fantastic architecture fosters his imaginative language of borders, frontiers and modes of transition. Venice is further linked to the even more exotic landscapes of China and the Indies, an imaginary space full of erotic suggestiveness. For Beckford, actual travel became the occasion for mental travelling in which the familiar topoi of the Grand Tour were refashioned into new modes of visual encounter with inner landscapes. He was particularly attracted by the drawings of the Venetian Piranesi, who deeply influenced his visual inventions: the famous interminable staircase is used by Beckford as a metaphor for a Miltonic mental landscape of inner torment.

Two very different fictional heroines from novels about a hundred years apart – Emily St. Aubert from Ann Radcliffe's *The Mysteries of Udolpho* and the Venetian singer Fiordelisa from Mary Elizabeth Braddon's *The Venetians* – are juxtaposed in **Barbara Schaff**'s essay, in order to show that both novels link questions of female authorship and autonomy with the semantics of their Venetian setting. In both novels the image of a singing Venetian woman serves as a positive counter image to – at least in the discourse of the 19th century - traditional feminine dependency. Thus, both the gothic and the sensational novel rework the assumptions of the ideal of the proper feminine. Venice here again is the ambiguous, the real and at the same time the imaginary place, which relates to patriarchal dominance as well as to fantasies of female liberation. A significant feature in both novels is the staging of Venice as a spectacle, which implies a gendered notion of viewing male subject and viewed female object that is represented as well as undermined in both texts. The prominence of the gaze hints at the inherent theatricality of Venice, and the multiplied ways of seeing in these novels refer not only to the Venetian semantics of the masquerade, but in an epistemological way they also refer to the impossibility of objective perception.

Ina Schabert reads Vernon Lee's story "Lady Tal" as a meta-literary narrative, in which the conflicting aesthetic and moral ideals of the *fin de siècle* are negotiated. In this story, aestheticism and self-fashioning subjectivity are attached to the novelist Jervase Marion; moral engagement and social responsibility to the central protagonist Lady Tal. Both Marion and Lady Tal are writers; and the planning and revising of their novels reveal to the reader their different aesthetic views. By opposing a gendered literary and a literal Venice, Schabert shows Lee's acute awareness of different and contradictory representations of Venice. The male artist in her story constructs a well-known patchwork Venice – the city of mazes, masks and madness, which answers the *fin de siècle* cult of self-decentralisation. In his pure and superhuman text, no direct experience or personal involvement of the narrator mars the aesthetic pattern.

Introduction

However, perfection is always closely linked to stagnation and death, and Marion's depiction of Lady Tal, according to avant-garde conceptions of character, completely fails to get to the core of her personality. In contrast to this, Lady Tal's literal Venice is the busy Rialto market, a hospital and her living garden; a setting which is linked to her empathic humanitarian involvement and the revelation of her inner self, which eludes Marion. In the end, Lady Tal resists Marion's efforts to turn her into a script of his own, just as Venice, described in different and contradictory images, resists representation in merely aesthetic terms.

It is not surprising that a book on literary representations of Venice gives a special importance to the romantic and decadent topoi of death and destruction. Novels and poems where people die in this city of decay abound – throughout the 19th century Venice seems to be the perfect place for literary deaths and gloomy visions of doom. Werner von Koppenfels and Sergio Perosa, however, manage to give this obvious aspect of literary Venice a new and acute twist.

Werner von Koppenfels starts with Byron and positions literary Venice within the Romantic European discourse of the ruin, where Venice appears as a metonymy of a doomed and moribund civilisation. Byron, the elegiac observer, "meditates amongst decay" on the vanity of past greatness. His image of the dead city entombing its own glorious past became one of the most forceful icons of 19th century imagination. Von Koppenfels then explores the trope of the Venetian sunset in romantic and decadent European literature, which reflects the observer's present state of mind, and functions similarly as a foreboding of evil things to come. In the novels of Radcliffe and de Stael literary Venice at sunset figures as a premonition of death and separation. The splendour and beauty of the twilight thus turns out to be deceptive, and leads always, as in Shelley's "Julian and Maddalo", to solitary confinement in the darkness of the soul. This trope is carried to further extremes in apocalyptic visions of Venice. Mary Shelley's *Last Man* shows a defaced Venice where the traces of civilization are wiped out and the city is swallowed up by the sea; other apocalyptic visions such as those of Maurice Barrès and James Thompson turn the metropolis into necropolis: after the fall of the City, no New Jerusalem will arrive.

Sergio Perosa conceives the prominent literary conceit of "Death in Venice" in the context of the historic, artistic and moral fall of the Republic. In English views of Venice, the city represents the heroic opposition to the oppressive role of the Italian Church. Romantic poets tried to rescue a textualized Venice from death, or, as one could put it paradoxically, to immortalize dying Venice through literature. It was Ruskin, however, who first portrayed the decadent Venice which *fin de siècle* literature would excessively deploy. For Henry James, Venice as sepulchre is an appropriate setting for death which is inescapable. Perosa gives a general outline of Anglo-American variations on the motif, and shows that the coexistence of beauty and splendour with collapse and decay has, throughout the 19th century, portrayed literary images of death. Perosa further argues that this does not explain the prevalence of so many literary deaths in Venice. He draws an analogy to postcolonial writers such as

Walcott and Naipaul, who have shown that islands have always suffered a series of historical, cultural and artistic incrustations and sedimentations which have produced paradoxical conjunctions of nature and culture. According to Perosa, Venice is the epitome of a deadly construction, where architecture is naturalized and nature is culturized and the boundaries between nature and culture are threateningly blurred. In this architecture of incrustation and interpolation one runs the risk of a loss of identity and historical memory, which is why this hybrid city is the perfect stage for so many literary deaths - but, Perosa adds, this turns out to be the typical and exclusive projection of the foreigner. Venetian writers, who have an inside view, do not share this obsession with death and dying.

Elizabeth Bronfen and Michael Gorra both turn to Henry James as the writer who has persistently coined Venice's image at the turn of the century.
Elizabeth Bronfen extracts from Melville's *Pierre* the notion that love is founded on secrets as well as an analogy between love's secrets and Venice's imaginary construction, in order to constitute a frame for her analysis of James' *The Wings of the Dove*. This novel, Bronfen suggests, traces a communicative situation, in which the psychic reality shared by the various characters, is held together by the shared bond of a committed crime. Venice here has a double function: as a cryptophoric site, where the shared clandestine knowledge of the protagonists can fantasmatically be staged, and also as Milly Theale's crisis heterotopia; a site of illusion, sexual transgression and betrayal. Bronfen points to the analogous construction of Venice and the novel's protagonists and further shows that Venice is not only configured as the topographical equivalent of the dying heroine in its liminality, but also as the site performing the fault line between beauty, decay and chance. This is, after all, what fiction is about: to resolve the crucial contradiction between the traumatic knowledge of contingency and one's conviction to possess agency. Staging the fluidity of undecidability to irritating perfection, concludes Bronfen, James' novel both supports and undercuts its own narrative desire.
Michael Gorra analyses James' travel essays, and states that the conventional ideas of Venice as a city of treachery and masquerades do not figure in them at all. Instead, James invests Venice with a marked sense of splendour. Whereas Rome serves in his writings as a trope for immense and endless suffering, Venice is the city of joy; a kind of permanent celebration of the senses, albeit the city's glory belongs to the past. Gorra is particularly interested in the way James shaped the language in his Italian travel writing and draws an analogy to the rhetoric of Empire. He lists the imposition of power, aestheticisation, appropriation, surveillance, negation and insubstantialisation as the strategies by which James' Italy is depicted - an above all picturesque Italy, scenery without life or people. When it came to describing Venice, however, Gorra observes that James tried to have it both ways - to preserve the picturesque quality and at the same time pursue "the inner springs of the subject". In his early essays James states that Venice for him is a place, where nothing is left to discover or describe, a city which has lost its sense of the mysterious. Gorra's analysis of James' description of

Introduction

Venetian paintings demonstrates, how James established a double mode of seeing and not seeing at the same time as a key concept in his representations of Venice. Gorra reads the descriptions of Venetian paintings as metonymies of the city itself – paintings to which time has added beauty and significance such as Bellini's "Madonna Enthroned" or paintings such as the Tintorettos, blackened by age, which are substantially there and yet cannot be fully perceived. Similarly, James depicts a secretive Venice whose secrets he is not willing to share with his readers. The more intimately he knows a place, concludes Gorra, the less willing he is to speak about it.

Towards the end of the millennium, Venice seems to be becoming popular again in contemporary fiction. Some of the well-known agonies and obsessions which haunted the romantic and *fin de siècle* images of Venice, seem to be again relevant at the turn of our century. But the order of stable dichotomies now gives way to multiple shifts of meaning - postmodernist representations of Venice give full credit to the city's potential of unstable and stratified meanings.

So far our essays have not yet put great emphasis on the fact that Venice is not only a city explored by writing travellers or travel writers, but that it is, especially in the 20th century, above all a city of and for tourists. **Virginia Richter** considers this aspect and connects her reading of Daphne du Maurier's "Don't Look Now", a story about second sight, and Ian McEwan's *The Comfort of Strangers* with a psychoanalytical and sociological analysis of the tourist condition. She defines the role of the tourist as of a transitional status and asks, in which way this relates to the representation of Venice and the male traveller's final death. Richter establishes as her theoretical frame of reference a structural analogy between fantasy and tourism, which both share the liminal experience and the ability to transform objects of the real into a larger imaginary syntax. Travelling is defined as a crossing into a realm with a different reality status. Other than border-crossing in literature, which always implies irreversible transformation, the tourist's experience is an event without a risk, with the return included in the package. Just this very question of boundary crossing or the tourist's possible danger of no return is at stake in "Don't Look Now" and *The Comfort of Strangers*. Viewing Venice in "Don't Look Now" is interlocked with the vital importance of cognition and the male protagonist's fear of transgression – of gender categories as well as of the boundaries between life and death - leads to his fatal cognitive failure and death. Both texts refer to Venice as a deceptive and highly ambiguous city; a paradigmatical location where literature, fantasy and tourism interlock. But whereas du Maurier's text has all the stereotypical references to Venice, McEwan's Venice is radically emptied of referentiality – it is an alienating counterspace, where binary oppositions collapse and the received touristic stance is utterly deconstructed.

In the 20th century, Venice is, of course, one of the most important settings for films. Cinematic representations continue to produce fantasies around Venice very often as adaptations of literary texts. **Sabine Schülting** argues that in Nicholas Roeg's adaptation of "Don't Look Now", Venice's ability to dissolve differences and identities provides the means to insert meta-cinematic elements into the film. Roeg here breaks the rules and conventions of classical Hollywood cinema, he violates the corresponding habits of seeing, and tries to overcome the pattern of a classical narrative. Schülting positions Roeg's film at the historical moment, when classical Hollywood film aesthetics were being questioned and reconsidered. Vision and chronology is problematized in this film to the extreme –nothing is what it seems; present, past and future are juxtaposed just as are reality and fantasy. There is no reliable narrational agency. Following Deleuze's theory of the "crystalline regime" – an avant-garde cinema aesthetics, Schülting demonstrates that Roeg's film constantly deconstructs traditional beliefs in coherent subjectivity as the source of action and narration: a fundamental critique of the concepts of truth and authenticity. By analysing Roeg's camera techniques, his subtle way of playing with views, gazes and perspectives, Schülting shows that the gaze in Roeg's film no longer guarantees subjectivity. In this respect Venice functions in a much more complicated way than just as a setting. Almost all the Venetian shots play with the problem of vision using a combination of light and reflection. Roeg turns Venetian space into an empty surface on which images are ceaselessly projected, thus showing montage as the basic cinematic technique.

Indira Ghose takes Michael Dibdin's novel *Dead Lagoon* as a paradigmatic text of the detective novel set in Venice, and foregrounds the representation of Venice and the delineation of the authentic Venetian. In contrast to the Brunetti novels by Donna Leon, where Venice is an aestheticized Disneyland represented with the rhetoric of the picturesque, Dibdin's Venice is a bleak city of decay and corruption. It is a city haunted by the ghosts of the past and the spectre of an ominous future: two wars, World War II and the Balkan War, make the historical background for the plot. These two different discursive constructs also relate to the figure of the detective: In Leon's novels Brunetti is constructed as a domesticated male, an insider, and, most important, as an "authentic" native, or, as Ghose acutely puts it, as a "tourist in drag" who serves as a model for the reader's narcissistic identification. Dibdin's Aurelio Zen, albeit a Venetian by birth, oscillates between the position of outsider and insider. A highly ambivalent character – and thus in accordance with an elusive, unstable Venice of shifting appearances - Zen is the eternal stranger as well as the permanent wanderer. Dibdin thus radically deconstructs the myth of the authentic native as well as an essentialist concept of identity.

Contemporary fantasies of Venice cannot take into account the many already existing literary and visual representations, accumulated over the centuries, which have established the image of a virtual Venice that is quite independent of the real city. Venice, claims **Rosella Mamoli Zorzi**, would still continue to be reproduced in texts, even if the real city had vanished. Mamoli Zorzi analyses two recent novels which refer to the tradition of "Dark Venice" as it is epitomized in William Etty's famous painting "The Bridge of Sighs". In his time-travelling novel *The Nature of Blood*, Caryl Phillips weaves the different lives and circumstances of a Jewish woman from World War II Germany, a Jewish community from fifteenth-century Venice and Othello into

Introduction

one theme: the nature of racism. Here again, Venice is represented ambiguously: On the one hand, Venice is the real place where Jews are persecuted and killed, on the other hand it is deprived of its cliché-like characteristics and acts as a stage, where human intolerance and hatred are displayed. The tradition of death and dying in Venice is taken up by Robert Dessaix in his novel *Night Letters*, where the narrator, obviously suffering from AIDS, decides to spend the rest of his life in Venice. In this rich intertextual fabric, where literary cross-references abound, and the topographical allusions mainly refer to traditions of literary representation - to Venice as the city of eros and crime, adventure and commerce - the city once more is a literary city, a "City of Words" (Tony Tanner) rather than an existing one.

Writing Venice, as **Judith Seaboyer** also insists, means relating oneself to the rich intertextual background of Venetian fiction; writing the city, in a broader sense, means shaping and interpreting culture. Robert Coover's novel *Pinocchio in Venice* is a paradigmatic text in this respect, as it is an overt response to Mann's *Death in Venice* as well as the postmodernist answer to the ultimate modernist city novel: *Ulysses*. Devised as a retelling of, and sequel to Collodi's classical children's story, Coover takes up the familiar Venetian leitmotif of metamorphosis and structures his text in terms of Menippean satire and Bakhtinian dialogism and his theory of the carnivalesque. Both Venice and Pinnochio undergo a metamorphosis in this text: Venice eventually returns to its swampy origins, and Pinocchio, whose former metamorphosis from wood into a human subject is heavily satirized by Coover, will be redeemed by again becoming a bundle of sticks. For Coover's text, which is a collage of the canon of European literature, where heterogeneous literary voices are forced into dialogical collision, Venice is the perfect setting – it represents after all, argues Seaboyer, in San Marco as its metonymy the constructive principle of disparate bits and pieces from East and West moulded into one. Pinnochio becomes a multivoiced personality, through whom the protagonists from Dante to Joyce speak, the ultimate "talking book", where the endless dialogue of literature will be incorporated and revivified. And which city could be more appropriate for this than Venice?

The editors wish to thank all contributors for their dedication to this joint venture and Frau Barbara Manzke, Frau Ina Eichhorn, M.A. and Herrn Symon Nicklas for their painstaking paper work of typing, wordprocessing, layouting and proofreading.

Bibliography

Anicetti, Luigi: *Scrittori inglesi e americani a Venezia (1816-1960)*. Treviso 1968.
Battilana, Marilla: *Venezia fondo e simbolo nella narrativa di Henry James*. Milano 1971.
Battilana, Marilla (ed.): *English Writers in Venice, 1350-1950. An Anthology of Texts in the Original Language*. Venezia 1981.
Belsey, Catherine: "Love in Venice". *Shakespeare Survey* 44 (1992), 41-53.
Bettagno, Alessandro (ed.): *Venezia da stato a mito*. Venezia 1997.

Brilli, Attilio: *Il viaggio in Italia*. Milano 1987; German translation: *Reisen in Italien. Die Kulturgeschichte der klassischen Italienreise vom 16. bis 19. Jahrhundert*. Köln 1989.
Clegg, Jeanne: *Ruskin and Venice*. London 1981.
Corbineau-Hoffmann, Angelika: *Paradoxie der Fiktion. Literarische Venedig-Bilder 1797-1984*. Berlin 1993.
Cosgrave, Denis: "The Myth and the Stones of Venice". *Journal of Historical Geography* 8/2 (1987), 145-169.
Dieterle, Bernard: *Die versunkene Stadt. Sechs Kapitel zum literarischen Venedig-Mythos*. Frankfurt/M. 1995.
Gaeta, Franco: "Alcune considerazioni sul mito di Venezia". *Bibliothèque d'humanisme et Renaissance* 23 (1961), 58-75.
Hale, John Rigby (ed.): *Renaissance Venice*. London 1973.
Hewison, Robert: *Ruskin and Venice*. London 1978.
Honour, Hugh/Fleming, John: *The Venetian Hours of Henry James, Whistler and Sargent*. London 1991.
Ingamells, John: *Dictionary of British and Irish Travellers in Italy. 1701-1800*. New Haven/Conn. 1997.
Jeffery, Violet M.: "Shakespeare's Venice". *Modern Language Review* 27 (1932), 24-35.
Jones-Davies, M. T. (ed.): *L'image de Venise au temps de la Renaissance*. Paris 1989.
Kanceff, Emanuele/Boccazzi, Gaudenzio (eds.): *Voyageurs étrangers à Venezia*. 2 vls. Genève 1981.
Keller, Luzius: "Postmoderne Venedig-Bilder". In: Schulz-Buschhaus, Ulrich/Stierle, Karlheinz (eds.): *Projekte des Romans nach der Moderne*. München 1997, 173-193.
Korg, Jacob: *Browning and Italy*. Athens/Ohio 1983.
Kraft, Quentin G.: "Life Against Death in Venice". *Criticism* 8.1 (Winter 1965), 217-223.
Levith, Murray J.: *Shakespeare's Italian Settings and Plays*. London 1989, 12-39.
Littlewood, Ian: *Venice. A Literary Companion*. London 1992.
Mahler, Andreas: "Referenzpunkt oder semantischer Raum? Zur Funktion der italienischen Stadt im englischen Drama am Beispiel Venedigs". In: Dirscherl, Klaus (ed.): *Die italienische Stadt als Paradigma der Urbanität*. Passau 1989, 85-103.
Mamoli Zorzi, Rosella (ed.): *Ezra Pound a Venezia*. Firenze 1985.
Mamoli Zorzi, Rosella (ed.): "Lord Byron e Venezia". *Ateneo Veneto* 175 (1988), 243-255.
Mamoli Zorzi, Rosella (ed.): "The Text in the City: TheRepresentation of Venice in Two Tales by Irving and Poe and a Novel by Cooper". *RSA* 6 (1990), 285-300.
Marrapodi, Michele/Hoenselaars, A. J./Cappuzzo, Marcello/Santucci, L. Falzon (eds.): *Shakespeare's Italy. Functions of Italian Locations in Renaissance Drama*. Manchester 1993, 143-209.
McCarthy, Mary: *The Stones of Florence and Venice Observed*. Harmondsworth 1972.
McPherson, David C.: *Shakespeare, Jonson, and the Myth of Venice*. Newark/N.Y. 1990.
Morris, Jan: *Venice*. London 1960.
Motyka, Gereon: *Venedig im Spiegel viktorianischer Reiseliteratur*. Frankfurt/M. 1990.
Parks, George B.: *The English Traveler in Italy*. 2 vls. Roma 1954.
Pemble, John: *Venice Rediscovered*. Oxford 1995.
Perosa, Sergio (ed.): *Henry James a Venezia*. Firenze 1987.
Perosa, Sergio (ed.): *Hemingway a Venezia*. Firenze 1988.
Perosa, Sergio (ed.): *Browning a Venezia*. Firenze 1991.
Pfister, Manfred (ed.): *The Fatal Gift of Beauty: The Italies of British Travellers. An Annotated Anthology*. Amsterdam 1996, 337-355.

Introduction

Pine-Coffin, R. S.: *Bibliography of British and American Travel in Italy to 1860.* Florence 1974.

Praz, Mario: "Ben Jonson's Italy". In: M.P.: *The Flaming Heart: Essays on Crashaw, Machiavelli, and Other Studies in the Relations between Italian and English Literature from Chaucer to T.S. Eliot.* New York 1958, 168-185.

Redford, Bruce: *Venice & the Grand Tour.* New Haven/Conn. 1996.

Ross, Michael: *Storied Cities: Literary Imaginings of Florence, Venice and Rome.* Westport/Conn. 1994.

Schenk, Christian: *Venedig im Spiegel der Décadence-Literatur.* Frankfurt/M. 1987.

Stainton, Lindsay: *William Turner in Venice.* London 1985.

Tanner, Tony: *Venice Desired.* Oxford 1992.

Unrau, John: *Ruskin and St. Mark's.* London 1984.

Wilson, Milton: "Travellers' Venice: Some Images for Byron and Shelley." In: *University of Toronto Quarterly* 43 (1974), 93-120.

Manfred Pfister

The Passion from Winterson to Coryate

1. Venice Recycled

Venice is both unrepresentable - beyond representation, as many of those trying to represent it have claimed - and one of the most frequently and "thickly" represented places on this earth. Nothing in Venice has not been written about, and written over, again and again; everything is a palimpsest. The quality of excess that has been so often ascribed to Venice in these representations, seems to spread to the representations themselves in an excess of *topoi* and *tropoi*.

Mary McCarthy highlights this when she opens her *Venice Observed* (1961) with a *florilegium* of literary responses from Montaigne to Henry James and D.H. Lawrence. The demonstration of the *déjà lu*, the *déjà vu*, ends in dismay: "Sophistication., that modern kind of sophistication that begs to differ, to be paradoxical, to invert, is not a possible attitude in Venice." Even her hope to find in the cats of Venice a subject as yet untouched by writer or artist, founders when she promptly discovers two books with whole chapters dedicated to the feline Venetians.[1]

Everything in Venice is a palimpsest - down to its cats and down to the minor islands in the lagoon. Even San Servolo, the madhouse island off the Giudecca, on which Jeanette Winterson has her Venetian novel, *The Passion* (1987), culminate, is not her literary discovery.[2] The once Benedictine monastery, then hospital for the insane and now academic centre had already been prominently put on the map of English literature by Shelley in 1819 in his conversational poem "Julian and Maddalo": here, the "windowless, deformed and dreary pile", "such a one / As age to age might add, for uses vile" (99-101), casts a chill upon the two friends who, amidst the "fierce yells and howlings and lamentings keen" listen to the story of a nameless "Maniac", a mysterious tale of love and madness, indeed a tale that would merit Winterson's title *The Passion*.[3] No need, therefore, for Winterson to explicitly connect her story with Shelley's: the similarity in kind suffices - plus the fact that her Henri and Shelley's Maniac, who both tell their stories on the island, might have told them to each other, being co-inmates of the asylum in the same years.[4]

---

[1] McCarthy 1972, 181. Cf. Pfister 1993, 115f.

[2] Winterson 1987.

[3] Shelley 1977, 112-127. - Winterson's attention may have been drawn to San Servolo - or Servelo, as she misspells it - and Shelley's poem by Jan Morris's popular guide; at least, there is no information on Venice in Winterson's novel that cannot be found in Morris's guide, down to details like the four churches destroyed to make the Public Gardens (Winterson, 52 and 112 - Morris, 76) or Paolo Sarpi's bonmot about lies (Winterson, 70 - Morris, 39); cf. Morris 1993, 279f.

[4] With all its fantasy elements, there is sufficient historical chronology to *The Passion* to affix a date to Henri's sojourn on the island: between 1813/14 (see p. 143) and ca. 1825, when Henri narrates the end of his story (see p. 160).

San Servolo epitomises what is writ large in the title: the story of Henri and Villanelle and the Queen of Spades is just the kind of story that has been told about Venice over the centuries. *The Passion* might be the title or subtitle of almost any fiction localised in Venice ever since the Renaissance: the Venetian episode in Thomas Nashe's *Unfortunate Traveller* and Shakespeare's *Merchant of Venice* and *Othello*, Thomas Otway's *Venice Preserved* and Ann Radcliffe's *Mysteries of Udolpho*, Byron's *Marino Faliero* and Henry James's *Wings of the Dove*, Hugo von Hofmannsthal's *Andreas* and Thomas Mann's *Tod in Venedig*, Ian McEwan's *Comfort of Strangers* and John Berger's *To the Wedding* - they are all stories of passion, passion in a sense that, as in Jeanette Winterson's novel, comprises both the *passio* of suffering and erotic desire. Even the travel writers often go out of their way to insert such passionate narratives into their otherwise topographic and apodemic accounts of Venice - Thomas Hoby, for instance, in his mid-sixteenth century *Travels* tells the story of "lusty young Duke Ferradin" slain during "a masquery after the Turkish manner" for courting the wife of a Venetian patrician,[5] and Hester Lynch Piozzi in the eighteenth century similarly interrupts her account with the story of a "martyr of love".[6]

Such stories construct Venice as a place of ardent and illicit, or transgressive, passions, of *eros* and *thanatos*, of love and madness, of sensuality, licentiousness, prostitution and sexual perversion - as an Other that exceeds and endangers the symbolic order of the Self. And, indeed, these are not stories that the Venetians tell about themselves and to themselves, but stories written about them by foreigners and, more often than not, also crucially involving foreigners. As Tony Tanner has acutely observed, there is no Venetian writer that would have written his or her city for us the way Dickens wrote London, Joyce Dublin, Balzac Paris, Döblin Berlin or Musil Vienna.[7] There is a one-way traffic of representations, fantasies and projections at work in the case of Venice that reminds one of the colonialist and Orientalist discourses writing the non-European Other and seems to be rather unique with conditions within Europe. This may also go some way towards accounting for the equally unique stability of these fantasies across the centuries.

Fantastically strange as Winterson's Venice is, it is also strangely familiar. It recycles quite demonstratively and with self-conscious flamboyance the accumulated myths and metaphors of Venice. All the labels which she sticks upon her Venice so insistently - "city of mazes", "of the interior", "of disguises", "of uncertainty", "of madmen", "of chances", "of destiny" - and all the adjectives with which she defines it - "unusual", "enchanted", "living", "mercurial" or "changeable" - belong to discourses of Venice that can be traced back to the *fin de siècle*, to Romanticism, to the seventeenth and eighteenth centuries of the Grand Tour, some even to the Renaissance.

I am not saying, of course, that the discourses of Venice have not changed at all from the Renaissance to the present: there has been change due to the changing fortunes of Venice and, even more so, due to the changing expectations of the visitors,

---

[5] Pfister 1996, 256.
[6] Piozzi 1967, 84f.
[7] Tanner 1992, 4.

but the changes have remained within a recognisable matrix. Of the four myths of Venice current throughout Early Modern Europe - Venice the Rich, Venice the Wise, Venice the Just and Venice, *città galante*[8] - two have survived and two have disappeared altogether or are remembered only as things of the past, against which the present is measured as fallen or decadent. Venice the Wise and Just vanished with the Venetian republic and its unique constitution in 1797, when it lost its celebrated millennial autonomy to the French and then the Austrians. Venice has, however, remained the Rich, even if, with its increasing economic decline from the sixteenth century already, its riches have been redefined in terms of the wealth of its artistic and cultural heritage. Venice as *città galante*, finally, has survived almost intact in the literary fantasies of Venice, with *galanteria* oscillating in its evaluations between depraved licentiousness and refined erotic pleasures, between degrading lust and high romantic passion.

Winterson's *The Passion*, which is, among other things, also a historical novel, situates its plot just after the fall of the Serenissima. The Venice in which Villanelle meets her mysterious Queen of Spades is already under Napoleon's yoke - "Since Bonaparte captured our city of mazes in 1797, we've more or less abandoned ourselves to pleasure." (52) - and the Venice to which she returns together with Henri in 1813 (109), after having defected from Napoleon's disastrous Russian campaign, is about to fall into Austrians hands again. Venice the Wise and the Just is, therefore, a thing of the past in Winterson's *Venice*, and with that the tension between the political myths of Venice's magisterial liberty and the sexual myths of its erotic licence that had riddled so many of the Renaissance representations and Grand Tour accounts is defused. What upstages everything else in Winterson's staging of Venetian fantasies is thus the *città galante* myth - is the sexual that is made to permeate every other aspect here. Everything - from politics to religion, from the topography of Venice to its history, from gambling to story-telling, from collecting to masquerading - is presented *sub specie eroticorum*, is presented as spilt sexuality.

Winterson's eroticized Venice is, of course, not a novelty in itself; it is inscribed into a history of eros-heady fantasies of Venice. Here as well, she need not and does not work against tradition, but can freely draw upon it in her attempt to exceed the traditional erotic metaphors and metamorphoses of Venice and to tease new twists and frictions from them. How she does that, and to what effect, will be my concern in the following sections which focus on three related aspects: mapping Venice, Venice as performance, and Venetian gender trouble.

2. Mapping Venice

When Thomas Coryate reached Venice in 1608, one of the first things he did was scale the campanile of San Marco to gain and enjoy "the fairest and goodliest prospect [...] in all the world".[9] The city being so labyrinthine and amphibian, such a "synopsis" of

---

[8] McPherson 1990, 27-50; cf. also Levith 1989 and Marrapodi et al. 1993.
[9] *Coryate's crudities* (London 1611), 183-185; quoted from Pfister 1996, 337.

"the whole model and form of the city *sub uno intuitu*" is particularly helpful in establishing one's bearings, together with the systematic account of the topography of Venice, its *sestieri* and its outlying islands in the lagoon, with which Coryate prepares the reader for this bird's eye view. The ascent of the campanile and the view from above, which turns the city into its own map, will become a standard element of Venetian travelogues, offering a number of metaphors to sum up the city's shape - a ship, for instance, or a lute.[10]

In *The Passion*, we are never granted such a view from above; we are always in the maze and its overall *gestalt* remains a mystery. Winterson's Venice is beyond mapping (113), and a compass is of no use in this "city of mazes" (49, 52, 103). Some of the expected landmarks are there, San Marco, the Canal Grande and the Rialto, but what lies between them is too convoluted and polymorphous to be represented in a coherent map - quite unlike the Cartesian geometry and topography of Napoleon's roads and campaigns and the "regimental pines" he had planted to create the Giardino Pubblico (112). "This city enfolds upon itself" (113), the way the poetic form of the villanelle does, whose name the quintessentially Venetian heroine bears, and its criss-crossing canals and alleyways end up in *cul-de-sacs* or in amorphous slime (54, 114). The changeability of this "mercurial city" (49), this "watery city that is never the same" (99), defies the mapmaker's fixative art, as do the cities within the city in this city of the interior: such "cities of the interior are vast and do not lie on any map", as both Villanelle and Henri assert (114, 150, 152).

In short - and in vaguely Freudian and Lacanian terms - Winterson's mercurial and fluid, labyrinthine and amphibian city of the interior is like the female body, and Winterson's circulating and spiraling prose, in which the voices of Henri and Villanelle flow and merge into each other, performs in its self-conscious *écriture féminine* the mysteries of this female body that is Venice.[11]

The only maps that account for anything in Winterson's Venice are the maps that the husband of Villanelle's lover collects, "ancient maps that showed the lairs of griffins and the haunts of whales" and "the whereabout of the Holy Grail" (67; cf. also 144). They link Venice not with Italy and Europe, but with a fabulous East and South and contribute towards constructing Venice as the inner-European Orient. Again, Winterson draws upon conventional discourses here: as she was not the first to make much of Venice's amphibious and labyrinthine topography, so she did not have to orientalize it. Mandeville had already likened it to Cathay, and for crusaders and pilgrims it was - a European Constantinople or Jerusalem - half-way to the Holy Land. Coryate visited the exotic Jews of the East in their ghetto;[12] John Evelyn was intrigued by the "strange variety of the several nations", Jews, Turks, Armenians, Persians, Moors, Greeks;[13] Hester Lynch Piozzi enthused over "the swarthy Moor, the soft

---

[10] Cf. Lassels 1670, II, 362, 365.
[11] The 'genderedness' of Winterson's Venetian topography has been illuminatingly commented upon in Maassen 1993, here 60f; Morrissey 1994; Schmid 1996; Quadflieg 1997.
[12] Pfister 1996, 199f.
[13] Pfister 1996, 338f.

Circassian maid" and linked "our luxurious Lady Mary" Wortley Montagu in Venice with "the still more dissolute Turks"[14]; William Beckford ventured "into the most curious, and musky quarters of the city, in search of Turks and Infidels";[15] Byron combined his sexual exploits with Armenian studies, "seeking some form of extreme otherness, both sexual and linguistic",[16] and right down to Proust Venice is very much an Arabian Nights' city, "saturated with oriental splendour".[17]

Thus, from the beginning, Venice has appeared to the foreign traveller as liminal to Italy, as the place where Italy, and with it Europe, intermingles with its Oriental and African Other. At one and the same time, however, the *Serenissima* has also been constructed as *Italianissima* - that is, not only *of* and *in* Italy, but its very epitome. In Winterson's representation of Venice, in contrast, this balance is now decidedly shifted towards the exotic and Oriental. At the heart of her Venice lies the palace where Villanelle's heart - quite literally - lies, the palace of the Queen of Spades and her husband, oriental travellers both, and at the heart of their palace are cabinets of Oriental curiosities, decorated with "Chinese ornaments" (66, see also 119f). The public collections of exotic curiosities, from Oriental jewellery and tapestry to the horns of rhinoceroses or unicorns, which many of the travellers have admired and catalogued in their descriptions of Venice, are here turned private and intimate and are, to that extent, eroticized and sexualized in the heady style of *fin de siècle* Orientalism. Their two most precious holdings are Villanelle's heart, magically beating in an indigo jar wrapped in a silk shift (120), and, equally magical, her unfinished tapestry picture, the completion of which would have made her "a prisoner for ever" (121). Villanelle, whose name chimes with that of Venice, is at the centre of the orientalized city, Oriental herself in the infinite variety of her sensuous and sensual allure.

3. Performing Venice

Italy in general, and Venice in particular, have always been experienced and described by travellers as a performance, spectacular and theatrical, and, more recently, scholars have characterised Early Modern Italian and Venetian society as a *società spettacolo* "in which face and facade play an important role in interpersonal communication".[18] Many of the visitors actually came for the spectacle, timing their visits to coincide with Carnival, with the *Festa della Sensa*, that is Ascension Day and its spectacular ceremony of the Doge's *Sposalizio al Mar* and the following fair, and with Corpus Christi and its magnificent procession.[19] Then there were, of course, the theatre and opera performances themselves, to which Venetians and foreign visitors often repaired

---

[14] Piozzi 1967, 112, 82.
[15] Mavor 1986, 61.
[16] Tanner 1993, 25.
[17] Proust 1984, III, 376.
[18] Mahler 1993, 53; the term was coined by V. Titone and is used in Burke 1987.
[19] The recent *Dictionary of British and Irish Travellers in Italy. 1701-1800*, compiled from the Brinsley Ford Archive by John Ingamells (New Haven 1997) substantiates this for hundreds of travellers to Venice.

in masquerade - thus not only saving the "trouble in dressing, or forms of any kind", as practically-minded Lady Montagu commented,[20] but blurring the distinction between actors and spectators and extending the theatre into reality.

The travellers' accounts and fictions throughout half a millennium seem to merge into one text on this point: the strange cosmetics and costumes of the Venetians, the splendid buildings and their sophisticated interiors, the cunning trading and gambling, the liturgical pomp and the elaborate political rituals, the dignified patricians at their *broglio*, the mountebanks and *ciarlatani* in the streets,[21] the volubly gesticulating lawyers[22] - they all turn Venice into one theatrical performance, or into a carnival that cannot be contained within established spatial and temporal bounds. Where they differ is whether the foreigner remains a distant - and then often unsympathetic - observer, or whether he or she realises that even as spectators they are part of the spectacle, as for instance Piozzi does,[23] or whether they themselves join the histrionic show with zest, become part of the carnival and emulate the Venetians in their "noble art of mimicking".[24] In the latter case, the travellers do not only witness and represent Venice as a performance; they become performers of Venice themselves, performing Venice in the *piazze* and *casine* as well as in their texts. Lord Byron is, of course, the most prominent and the most brilliant example here, representing his life in Venice in careful self-stylisation as a carnival, in which all distinctions of class and gender collapse, as a comedy, which allows him to act out ever new roles.

Winterson's Henri, the timid Frenchman, obviously is no Lord Byron. This is why he dreams of returning to his unspectacular native village and refuses to return from the island of real madmen to the staged derangements of reason and the senses in carnivalesque Venice. He remains the undisguised in this "city of disguises" (56, 92, 100, 150), which is Villanelle's city. Her Venice is not unlike the *città spettacolo* of the traditional fictions and fantasies: she works at the Casino, a place of subtle make-believe and deception; she participates in the celebrations of Bonaparte's birthday and New Year's Eve, that turn night into day (54ff, 74ff), in the fabulously histrionic funerals (58) and the fairs with their acrobats and their women "who are not all of them [...] women" (58); she "basks" in the theatricality of staged religion (71f). Most importantly, her gambling and thieving involve staging her body in ever changing masquerades, particularly in cross-dressing, which masks her sex or heightens its ambiguous allure: "It was part of the game, trying to decide which sex was hidden behind tight breeches and extravagant face-paste..." (54)[25]

---

[20] *Letters from the Right Honourable Lady Mary Wortley Montagu. 1709 to 1762*, introd. by Johnson 1906, 275. - A particularly vivid account of how pervasive this custom was in the 17th century already, can be found in the diaries and letters of Colonel Bullen Reymes; cf. Kaufman 1962, 121ff.
[21] Cf., for instance Lassels 1670, II, 401, 404.
[22] For the lawyers cf. Spence 1975, 95 and Sharp 1766, 32f.
[23] Piozzi 1967, 79.
[24] Spence 1975, 95.
[25] Masquerade and transvestism has recently become a central concern in gender studies; cf. Castle 1986; Garber 1992; Bettinger/Funke 1995.

Here, again, we seem to be in the world of the Grand Tourists who frequently comment upon, or even participate in transvestite masquerades - or, if it comes to that, in the world of Shakespeare's Italianate comedies with their cross-dressed heroines. There is, however, a crucial difference: behind Villanelle's cross-dressing and masquerades there is no longer an apparently unambiguous sexual identity that would reveal itself at the end. The difference between performance and reality collapses; she does not only stage herself as male and female, her very soul is "Siamese" (57). And even when, at the end, she gives up masquerading - "I don't dress up any more." (150) -, she re-enacts it in the text she shares with Henri.

4. Venetian Gender Trouble

The core of Coryate's Venetian narrative is his encounter with "one of the courtesans of Venice famoused over all Christendom". Its centrality is highlighted by the detailed account he gives of it, and reinforced by an illustration which shows him together with Margarita Emiliana - one of the few illustrations in his book and the first image of an encounter between an Englishman and an Italian we have.[26] There were some twenty thousand courtesans in Venice, as Coryate maintains, and the highly visible and histrionic presence of these votaresses of Venus defined Venice for many travellers as "Paphos, Cnidos, or Cythera" transmigrated.[27]

'Venice' and 'Venus' were actually seen as etymologically related, and many a text punned upon the phonetic closeness of the two names. "*Venus* and *Venice* are Great Queens", wrote Howell in his *Survey of the Signorie of Venice* (1651), topping the Venus/Venice quibble with another pun: 'queen' as ruler and 'quean' as whore.[28] A hundred years later, Piozzi forged an even more fanciful etymological link between Venice and its prostitutes: she hears the name of the city in the cry "*Veni etiam*", with which these "permitted professors of the inveigling arts" allure their clients. Reminding us that this was also the cry of their ancestors as they escaped from the Goths onto the islands of the lagoon to maintain their freedom, she, like Howell, demonstrates the unstable boundary between political liberty and sexual licence, between Venice as *stato di libertà* and *città galante*.[29]

It was, however, not only the prostitutes who inflamed the erotic fantasies and passions and stirred the sexual anxieties of the foreign visitor: carnival licence and transvestite masquerade, effeminacy and homosexuality in men, the liberties the ladies took in exposing their "naked necks and breasts" and flirting with their *cicisbei* or *cavalieri serventi*,[30] the "gay voluptuousness" of the nuns in the conservatories and

---

[26] Pfister 1996, 256-259 and Ill. 1. - Bullen Reymes even provides us with an impressive list of the courtesans he visited together with the English ambassador; cf. *Conscientious Cavalier*, 135f.

[27] Pfister 1996, 257. Cf. also Sharp 1766, who regards "this Republick a second *Cyprus*, where all are votaries to *Venus*" (20).

[28] Howell 1651, Sig B4v; cf. Redford 1996, 54f.

[29] Piozzi 1967, 89.

[30] Moryson 1907, IV, 220.

convents[31] - they all suggested to the visitor an Oriental sophistication and excess of erotic pleasures. Howell was not alone in accounting for it in terms of a disease, an "infection" caught "from the *Greek* and the *Turk* Her Neighbors",[32] and Byron was only putting into a mythological nutshell what others had expounded upon at great length when he has Marino Faliero, about to be executed, address Venice as "thou sea-Sodom".[33]

This projection of Venice as Scarlet Woman contrasts with the self-image of Venice as a maiden or virgin city, which was also picked up by many a foreigner. Lewis Lewkenor even links the image of unravished Venice, who has preserved her free autonomy and Christian religion throughout the centuries, with Elizabeth, the Virgin Queen, in his 1599 translation of Gasparo Contarini's *De Magistratibus et Republica Venetorum*[34]. In both images, Venice is a woman, and the co-presence of the two images in many of the texts suggests the myth of a Fall from innocence to vice and decadence. In the writings of Ruskin this particular myth of Venice as a Fallen Woman was to become so powerful an obsession that he finally erased the city from his carefully monitored autobiography, the *Praeterita*, altogether.

Venice has, however, not only been fantasised in unambiguously female terms. There has always been a certain gender ambivalence to the writing of Venice, and the female images of Virgin Maid and Fallen Women have always been overwritten with the male image of Venice as powerful and potent master. The Doge's *Sposalizio al Mare*, after all, which fascinated so many visitors, enacted in a ritual performance "the coupling of a powerful male force with an acquiescent female Adriatic in order to beget and perpetuate empire".[35] Venice here is staged not as the goddess Venus, but, according to Lassels, as "*Neptune* himself" wedding "some Nereide", or as a husband "who hath power over his wife".[36] The gender ambiguity which underlies these conflicting myths and representations occasionally inscribes itself as an oscillation between genders into one and the same text - for instance in Byron's *Childe Harold's Pilgrimage*, canto IV, where stanza 31 begins with "the spouseless Adriatic" mourning "her Lord" and ends with Venice as "a queen with an unequalled dower",[37] or in Charles Dickens' *Pictures from Italy*, where Venice appears not as master, but as "mistress" of the Adriatic waters of the lagoon, which in turn fluctuate strangely between the male and the female.[38] This male image of Venice implied its own myth of a Fall - a Fall from potency to impotence or, even more disturbing, from masculinity to effeminacy or downright homosexuality. Clearly, gender is at stake in Venice, and gender is in trouble - particularly that of the young, male, and Protestant Briton.

---

[31] Cf., amongst many other voices, Addison 1890, I, 391f. Piozzi 1967, 90 - speaks of the "gay voluptuousness" of these "pretty syrens".
[32] Howell 1996, Sig. Ee.
[33] *Marino Faliero, Doge of Venice* (5.3.99). In: Byron 1945, 452.
[34] Lewkenor 1599, Sig. A4.
[35] Redford 1996, 7.
[36] Lassels 1670, II, 414.
[37] Cf. Tanner 1992, 35 and Redford 1996, 121f.
[38] Dickens 1988, 77.

Thomas Coryate meeting a Venetian courtesan
(from: *Coryat's Crudities*, London 1611, 261)

Coryate, in the account of his visiting Margarita Emiliana in her "chamber of recreation", tries to persuade the reader at great length that the motivation that took him to her was entirely ethnological (Ill.). The tale he tells is a cautionary one, and he sounds like Roger Ascham and Thomas Nashe before him in warning of these Circes and Sirens and the metamorphoses they will work upon the unwary British youth.[39] Metamorphic, mercurial Venice is the cause of metamorphoses in those who come into too close a contact with her - metamorphoses that, more than anything else, endanger the traveller's gender identity, his masculinity and masculine self-control. Over-exertion of his sexual passions and venereal diseases will sap his virile strength and turn him into one of those *castrati*, whose soft singing first stimulated his erotic fancies; imitation of the Italian manners will make a *macaroni* or *androgyne* of him, that is, an eighteenth-century parlance, an emasculated and effeminate fellow;[40] and decadent sexual sophistication will teach him, in Nashe's kersey Elizabethan, "the art of sodomitry".

Now, Winterson's *The Passion* quite obviously takes up many of these fantasies of a sexually transgressive and metamorphic Venice. Here, too, erotic desire cannot be contained within the social code and symbolic order of binary gender divisions; it is as fluid, instable, labyrinthine and amphibious as the city itself. Neither is Henri, smallish, passive, shy, and introvert, a paradigm of potent and self-asserting masculinity, nor is Villanelle unambiguously a woman. Her magically webbed feet (49) mark her as a man rather than a woman and so do her, for a Venetian woman, unusual tallness and the smallness of her breasts (56).[41] She seems to quite naturally take to cross-dressed masquerades, in which her androgynous charm makes her attractive as a lover and as a prostitute to both male and female suitors, and she in turn is attracted to both and has "taken [her] pleasure with both men and women" (57f) - particularly with men who, like Henry, are not imposingly male, and women, who, like the Queen of Spades, are bi-sexual like herself. Villanelle's lesbian desire for her, whose ominous name suggests the conjunction of male and female, *eros* and *thanatos*, is, however, the overruling passion of her polymorphous romance; with her, as with Bellinda in Pope's *Rape of the Lock* (III, 46), "Spades" is "Trumps", indeed.

There is a religious intensity to her passion, and one of the leitmotifs actually situates religion and passion between "fear and sex" (55, 62, 68, 74, 76). This blurs the borderline between religious and sexual intensity, between religion and sex, in a way that is not unprecedented in the narratives and fictions of the travellers to Venice: Coryate's courtesan already is shown in an ambience conflating religious and erotic devotion, "with the picture of our Lady by her bedside, with Christ in her arms". A generation later, John Evelyn grants us a glimpse of the same Margarita Emiliana as the builder and foundress of a convent,[42] and we know already how Venetian convents,

---

[39] For Ascham cf. Pfister 1996, 78f; for Thomas Nashe cf. Steane 1972, 345.
[40] Cf. Redford 1996, 24.
[41] Cf. for the cliché of the Venetian ladies' shortness Lassels 1670, II. 380 and Piozzi 1967, 93f.
[42] Pfister 1996, 258; Evelyn 1946, 210.

like Hamlet's nunnery, have come to be considered as places that signify erotic as well as religious passions.

Drawing such comparisons between earlier fantasies and representations of Venice and what Winterson makes of them does, however, not only reveal similarities and the continued appeal of the traditional *topoi* and *tropoi* of Venice. It also reveals difference and discontinuity. This is less a matter of a difference between exorcising or celebrating an Other that exceeds and undermines the symbolic order of the self; some of the earlier representations - those of William Beckford, for instance, of Lord Byron and Marcel Proust - have done that already and have celebrated Venice for its confusions of gender and, with gender, of other fundamental divisions. The crucial difference resides rather in a different conception of the self. Where the older confusion of the religious and the erotic could always be disentangled in terms of a religious hypocrisy that masks a real sexual licentiousness, with Winterson's Villanelle the passionate self is unentwinably sexual and religious at one and the same time. Where, in the traditional representations, Venice was male primarily in political contexts and female as the *città galante*, Winterson's tropes define it as irresolvably androgynous. Where the transvestite masquerades observed, or engaged in, by the Grand Tourist were seen as a deviancy from the true self and its true gender identity, with Villanelle the distinction between self and mask does no longer apply. "And what [is] myself?", she asks (66), and the answer the novel suggests is that it is neither her "breeches and boots self" nor her "garters". One is as much a masquerade as the other, and her gender identity is as indeterminate as the masquerade in which she constantly re-defines it. In other words - not her own, but Judith Butler's: her self and her gender identity enact and define themselves in her performances: they are not stable essences but essentially and passionately performative.[43] And so is Winterson's text which, in its interweaving of Henri's and Villanelle's voices and narrations, performs a subjectivity beyond binary divisions. And so is, finally, her Venice: all staged performances that, together, act out and explore the indeterminacies of in-betweenness - in between:

    water and land > *amphibiousness*
    East and West > *inner-European orientalism*
    past, present and future > *metamorphosis*
    structure and chaos > *labyrinth*
    freedom and destiny > *gambling*
    contradictory opposites > *paradox*
    reality and dream > *fantasy*
    male and female > *androgyny*
    religion and sexuality > *passion*

---

[43] Butler 1990.

Bibliography

Addison, Joseph: *Remarks on Several Parts of Italy*. In: Hurd, Richard (ed.): *The Works*. London 1890.
Bettinger, Elfi /Julia Funke (eds.): *Maskeraden. Geschlechterdifferenz in der literarischen Inszenierung*. Berlin 1995.
Burke, Peter: *The Historical Anthropology of Early Modern Italy*. Cambridge 1987.
Butler, Judith: *Gender Trouble. Feminism and the Subversion of Identity*. New York 1990.
Byron, Lord: *The Poetical Works of Lord Byron*. London 1945.
Castle, Terry: *Masquerade and Civilisation. The Carnivalesque in Eighteenth-Century Culture and Fiction*. Standford 1986.
Dickens, Charles: *Pictures from Italy*. New York 1988.
Dictionary of British and Irish Travellers in Italy. 1701-1800, compiled from the Brinsley Ford Archive by John Ingamells. New Haven 1997.
Evelyn, John: *The Diary of John Evelyn*, ed. William Bray, prefaced by G.W.E. Russel. London 1907, repr. 1946.
Garber, Marjorie: *Vested Interests. Cross-Dressing and Cultural Anxiety*. New York 1992.
Howell, James: *S.P.Q.V. A Survay of the Signorie of Venice*. London 1651.
Kaufman, Helen Andrews: *Conscientious Cavalier. Colonel Bullen Reymes, M.P., F.R.S. 1613-1772*. Cambridge/Mass. 1962.
Lassels, Richard: *The Voyage of Italy*. II. London 1670.
Levith, Murray J.: *Shakespeare's Italian Settings and Plays*. London 1989.
Lewkenor, Lewis: *The Commonwealth and Government of Venice*. London 1599.
Maassen, Irmgard: "*Fantasy* und Feminismus: Jeanette Winterson und die weibliche Postmoderne". *Hard Times* 50 (1993), 56-62.
Mahler, Andreas: "Italian vices: cross-cultural constructions of temptation and desire in English Renaissance drama". In: Marrapodi et al. (eds.): *Shakespeare's Italy*. Manchester 1993, 49-68.
Marrapodi, Michele/A.J. Hoenselaars/Marcello Cappuzzo/L. Falzon Santucci (eds.): *Shakespeare's Italy*. Manchester 1993.
Mavor, Elizabeth (ed.): *The Grand Tour of William Beckford*. Harmondsworth 1986.
McCarthy, Mary: *The Stones of Florence and Venice Observed*. Harmondsworth 1972.
McPherson, David C.: *Shakespeare, Jonson, and the Myth of Venice*. Newark 1990.
Montagu, Mary Wortley: *Letters from the Right Honourable Lady Mary Wortley Montagu. 1709 to 1762*, introd. by R. Brimley Johnson. London 1906.
Morris, Jan: *Venice*, new and revised ed. Harmondsworth 1993.
Morrissey, Thomas J.: "Landscape He-Scape, Sea-scape, She-Scape: Are the Tropes of Utopia Nowhere to be Found?". In: Kleist, Jürgen/Bruce A. Butterfield (eds.): *Re-Naming the Landscape*. New York 1994, 121-131.
Moryson, Fynes: *An Itinerary*. Glasgow, repr. 1907 (first 1617).
Pfister, Manfred: "Intertextuelles Reisen: oder der Reisebericht als Intertext". In: *Tales and "their telling difference". Zur Theorie und Geschichte der Narrativik. Festschrift zum 70. Geburtstag von Frank K. Stanzel*, Foltinek, Herbert/Wolfgang Riehle/Waldemar Zacharasiewicz (eds.). Heidelberg 1993, 109-132.
Pfister, Manfred: *The Fatal Gift of Beauty: The Italies of British Travellers. An Annotated Anthology*. Amsterdam 1996.
Piozzi, Hester Lynch: *Observations and Reflections Made in the Course of a Journey Through France, Italy and Germany*, ed. Barrows, Herbert. Ann Arbor 1967.

Proust, Marcel: *Remembrance of Things Past*, transl. C.K.S. Moncrieff/T. Kilmartin. Harmondsworth 1984.

Quadflieg, Helga: "Feminist Stories Told on Waste Waters: Jeanette Winterson". In: Maassen, Irmgard/Anna Maria Stuby (eds.): *(Sub)Versions of Realism - Recent Women's Fiction in Britain*. Heidelberg 1997, 97-110

Redford, Bruce: *Venice & the Grand Tour*. New Haven 1996.

Schmid, Susanne: *Jungfrau und Monster. Frauenmythen im englischen Roman der Gegenwart*. Berlin 1996.

Sharp, Samuel: *Letters from Italy*. London 1766.

Shelley, Percy Bysshe: *Shelley's Poetry and Prose*, ed. Reiman, Donald H./Sharon B. Powers. New York 1977.

Spence, Joseph: *Letters from the Grand Tour*, ed. Slava Klima. Montreal 1975.

Steane, J.B. (ed.): *The Unfortunate Traveller and Other Works*. Harmondsworth 1972.

Tanner, Tony: *Venice Desired*. Oxford 1992.

Winterson, Jeanette: *The Passion*. London 1987.

Andreas Mahler

Writing Venice:
Paradoxical Signification as Connotational Feature

> Ogni volta che descrivo una città dico qualcosa di Venezia.[1]
>
> Venedig aber ist die künstliche Stadt.[2]

1. Metaphors

I will begin with two fantasies.

When, twenty-five years after his first visit, the well-known English traveller and Catholic, Henry Vollam Morton, chose to stay a second time in Venice, he took a hotel quite near the San Zaccaria *vaporetto* stop on the Riva degli Schiavoni, in the so-called Calle delle Rasse.[3] Eager reader of sites that he was, he immediately wanted to find out what the name of the street in which he was to spend the next couple of weeks meant, and he came across two things typically Venetian. What he first learnt was that the *calle* took its name from the type of weather-resistant black cloth imported from the Serbian landscapes of Raska or Rassia and used for the covering of gondola roofs, a cloth which, at one time, had been the main trade of the row.[4] The *calle* thus proved to be a rightfully Venetian site, a place not merely situated in the city of gondolas but also metonymically designating it: not just a mere part of the city's syntax but also already part of its semantics. In addition to this, however, H.V. Morton also learnt that, in the eighteenth century, a *rasse*-like fabric formed the basis for the production of some kind of ribbon, a ribbon strong enough to hold together long thin slats of wood, which were then arranged in such a way as to produce a type of blind which, from that time on, became known all over Europe as 'Venetian'.

> While discovering the meaning of *rasse*, I solved a mystery which may perhaps have puzzled others: why window-blinds of a type never seen in Venice should be called 'Venetian'. The explanation is that during the eighteenth century, when this kind of blind was first made, the slats were bound with a strong canvas similar to *rasse* known as *Venetian*.[5]

The name of the *calle* thus also referred him to the central element in the construction of such a blind, i.e. to the instrument with which you can shut out, or let in, the view. Reading a city is to try and raise its blinds. Any travel writer's fantasy is to see himself

---

[1] Calvino 1972/1985, 94.
[2] Simmel 1907/1993, 259.
[3] See Morton 1964, 332 ff.
[4] Ibid., 333.
[5] Ibid., 333 f.

as 'master of the *rasse*', as the one manipulating the strings in order to make his readers see the, or at least his, view. Detecting, discovering, unveiling are his main activities. So are explaining, interpreting, attributing meaning. With the choice of his hotel, Morton had quite inadvertently hit the very centre of the semiotic mechanism governing travel writing: the more you manage to manipulate the strings, the more you will be able to let in new signifiers, which you will then combine with the signifieds already deciphered so as to complete the semantic profile of the place.

The best way for an observer to find out the true semantics of a place is to strip it down to its foundations. At least, this is the point the great nineteenth-century demystificator of life's profundities, Honoré de Balzac, tries to make right at the beginning of his novel *La Recherche de l'absolu*.

> Les événements de la vie humaine, soit publique, soit privée, sont si intimement liés à l'architecture, que la plupart des observateurs peuvent reconstruire les nations ou les individus dans toute la vérité de leurs habitudes, d'après les restes de leurs monuments publics ou par l'examen de leurs reliques domestiques. L'archéologie est à la nature sociale ce que l'anatomie comparée est à la nature organisée. Une mosaïque révèle toute une société, comme un squelette d'ichthyosaure sous-entend toute une création. De part et d'autre, tout se déduit, tout s'enchaîne.[6]

According to Balzac, finding the truth of a site means to deconstruct it to its founding principle, its last visible signifier, and then to reconstruct its meaning from that basis onwards. This 'archaeological' approach advocated by Balzac would, however, encounter severe difficulties when put into practice to find out the '*vérité*' of things Venetian. No matter how far you manage to open the blinds, the central signifier, the foundations of Venice, will always remain out of sight, submerged, perhaps blurred, but never in full view.

It is my argument that it is precisely this elusiveness which constitutes the main semiotic impact and scope of Venice as a semantic construct in texts from the early modern period up to our 'postmodern' times. The 'Venetian', I want to argue, is less readable in the concrete signifiers taken from, and referring to, the city of Venice than in the type of signification itself, less readable in the privileging of the view against the blind, or *vice versa*, than in the simultaneous allocation of a double meaning which ineluctably combines two signifieds - the aspect of the blind *and* the aspect of the view - without deciding which of the two is the right one. This doubleness is what I want to call the semiotics of the masquerade.

---

[6] Balzac 1834/1976, 21 f.

2. The principle

I will try and illustrate this with an emblem.

The motto of the first invitational letter to our conference on 'Venetian Views, Venetian Blinds' was a not totally unknown quote from *Othello*. In it, Iago is once more trying to explain to the 'ignorant' stranger Othello the specificities of Venetian 'nature', with particular reference to women.

> I know our country disposition well;
> In Venice they do let God see the pranks
> They dare not show their husbands: their best conscience
> Is not to leave undone, but keep unknown.
> (*Oth.*, III.3.205-8)[7]

The central signifier in Iago's quote, with which he endeavours to put to his own use the basic principle underlying a Venetian semiotic, is 'women', but it is a signifier which is, as I shall argue, arbitrary, and for that reason, exchangeable. For what is really important are the two meanings attributed to it: one, the aspect of the blind, which is the 'show' of the faithful wife, and two, the aspect of the view, the purported 'truth' of the immoral woman. Which of the two is the right one is not for man to see: whereas Othello finally seems to get the 'view', the spectator already knows this view to be nothing but another 'blind' strategically set up in front of him. The 'country disposition', which Iago under the guise of his personal interest, obliquely refers to thus lies not in the 'truth', whatever it is, revealed, but in the simultaneous attribution of two mutually exclusive meanings [± honour], and it is precisely this double semantics with its undecidability as to which is the blind, which is the view which makes the women described 'Venetian' women.

In drawing on Roland Barthes' theory of connotational meaning[8], I want to formalize this as follows. Whenever in a text set in Venice, a signifier x, no matter what it refers to, is invested with the paradoxical feature [± a], the connotational feature attributed to this sign is [+ Venetian].

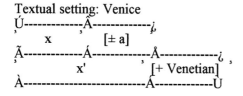

This is what I would like to call the signature of the Venetian.[9]

---

[7] Shakespeare 1604/1975.

[8] Cf. Barthes 1964 and Barthes 1957/1985, 195 ff., esp. 200; for a concise introduction see Hawkes 1977, 130 ff.

[9] Note that in my formalization I use the word 'whenever' and not 'if'. I would contend that what I say about Venice cannot be formulated in the same way for, say, Paris or London. Of course, there are a

The emblematic example taken from *Othello* demonstrates quite clearly the basic principle of a semiotics of the masquerade within the framework of which the signature of the Venetian can best be described as a reiterated connotational effect of such a semiotics. Italian society, and Venetian society in particular, has always been regarded as a *società spettacolo*, a society in which the concepts of face and façade, mask and masquerade play an important part.[10] The importance of the mask lies precisely in the fact that you can be yourself and not yourself at the same time.[11] The masquerade is a play which can only be stopped by the one who knows which is which: either the 'master of the *rasse*' (in H.V. Morton's case), or 'God' (in Iago's quote), or Balzac's observer-figure, or a detective, or the player himself, or the 'author'... In any case, the textual play based on a semiotics of the masquerade is kept going for as long as its ambiguities remain unresolved.

I will now attempt to show how texts organize their signs in such a way as to signalize themselves as specifically 'Venetian' texts, and the example I have chosen as a first specimen of demonstration is one of Donna Leon's currently highly popular detective novels, *Death at La Fenice*.

3. Metonymies

Basically, there are two major ways of constituting textual cities.

The first way is by reference to the city's prototypical elements: the Grand Canal, the Bridge of Sighs, the Doge's Palace; the second way is by calling up the city's pre-existent myths: city of lovers, of carnival, of whores, of transgression.[12] And a 'third' way, which in fact is a very special variety of the second, is that of taking the paradoxical attribution of denotational meanings as the basis of a connoted signature of Venice.

In *Death at La Fenice*, the textual Venice needed for the universe of discourse of Commissario Brunetti's cases is built up first and foremost by means of descriptive passages recurring on the prototypical. Take a look at the following example:

The boat moved out into the Grand Canal and turned left, toward San Marco, which they would have to pass in order to get to the cemetery. Brunetti went back to the cabin door and looked forward, taking his intrusive gaze away from the grief within. The campanile flowed by them, then the checkered rectangularity of the Ducal Palace, and then those happy carefree domes. When they were approaching the Arsenale canal, Brunetti went up on deck and asked the boatman if he could stop at the

---

great number of texts such as Sue's *Les mystères de Paris* or Dickens' *Our Mutual Friend*, and their successors, which also employ self-contradictory signification, but in all those texts, at least as far as I can see, this technique is never really exploited 'self-referentially', as it were, as a secondary signifier for the designation of place. This remains a specificity of Venice alone.

[10] I have tried to develop this in Mahler 1993a, esp. 53 ff.; for the term see Titone 1978, 116.

[11] See Mahler 1995, 117 ff.

[12] Again, in the Barthesian sense, myth here means a connotative meaning imposed on 'normal' denotational meanings (Barthes 1957/1985, 199 f.). For the distinction of the prototypical as opposed to the mythical in the constitution of textual cities see Weich 1998, 68 ff.

embarcadero of the Palasport. He went back into the cabin and heard the three people there conversing in low voices.[13]

The passage selects seven more or less prototypical elements of the city - the 'Grand Canal', 'San Marco', the 'campanile', the 'Ducal Palace', the 'domes', the 'Arsenale canal' and the 'Palasport' - to promote a textual Venice providing the backdrop for the detective story unfolded in the book. Such passages based on the prototypical, I want to argue, serve in the text as referential anchors or moorings to which the other type of description developing the stabilizing connotational feature [+ Venetian] can then be tied. The objects of that second type of description are no longer prototypical elements of the city of Venice but mere metonymies of an urban landscape - houses, characters, and sites.

In the course of his investigation, Commissario Brunetti is confronted with a number of interiors that seem puzzling at first sight. One of them is the apartment inhabited by the opera singer Flavia Petrelli and her American (girl-)friend Brett Lynch. Brunetti enters with a ritual *'Permesso'* and is then astonished by what he sees.

> He was surprised to find himself in a vast open space, easily ten meters by fifteen. The wooden floor was made of the thick oak beams used to support the oldest roofs of the city. The walls had been stripped of paint and plaster and taken down to the original brick. The most remarkable thing in the room was the tremendous brightness that glared from the uncovered skylights, six of them, set in triple pairs on either side of the peaked ceiling. Whoever had received permission to alter the external structure of a building this old, Brunetti reflected, either had powerful friends or had blackmailed both the mayor and the city planner. And it had all been done recently, the smell of fresh wood told him that.[14]

The object described is the interior of a *palazzo* (x). It follows the semiotics of the masquerade (± a) in the sense that it is old and new, closed and open, original and altered, 'permitted' and not 'permitted'. The façade of the building is just as it ought to be and, at the same time, it is not. The interior has been renovated in order to render it more authentic and, at the same time, one becomes aware of this authenticity mainly through the inauthentic skylights added in the renovation. In short, in its thorough-going doubleness, in its play on blindness and insight, the interior is signalized as typically 'Venetian'. This specification is, on the one hand, corroborated by the inhabitants of the *palazzo*, since (the androgynous) Brett Lynch, for example, is characterized as an American and, at the same time, as a speaker of Veneziano, "the local dialect, which she spoke fluently"[15]. On the other hand, the description of the *palazzo* takes up the description of Commissario Brunetti's own Venetian home, an apartment on the fourth floor of another *palazzo*.

> The previous owner had built the apartment illegally more than thirty years before, simply added another floor to the existing building without bothering with official permission of any sort. The situation had somehow been obscured when Brunetti bought the apartment ten years ago, and ever

---

[13] Leon 1992/1994, 106.
[14] Ibid., 66.
[15] Ibid., 26.

> since, he had lived in recurrent fear of being confronted with a summons to legalize the obvious. He trembled at the prospect of the Herculean task of getting the permits that would authenticate both that the apartment existed and that he had a right to live there. The mere fact that the walls were there and he lived within them would hardly be thought relevant.[16]

Again, the object described is simultaneously present and absent, obvious and inexistent, authentic but not authenticated.

This structure of the paradoxical pervades the whole text. It reappears, for example, in the portrait of the Count and Countess Falier, in the description of the feast held at their *palazzo*, in the visit Brunetti pays to Signora Santina on the Giudecca and at numerous other points in the text.[17] Its function is to call up time and again the signature of the Venetian as the decisive semantic element underpinning the novel. Donna Leon's *Death at La Fenice* thus turns out to be a truly 'Venetian' text in that it is not only set in Venice but also hinged on a Venetian semantics that takes its impact from a powerful structure apt to generate, and reaffirm, its proper connotation.[18]

4. Universes

The signature of the Venetian can be traced back from Winterson to Coryate, perhaps even as far back as Mandeville.[19] It subtends Coover's Pinocchio fantasy just as much as Shakespeare's *Merchant*; it informs Nicholas Roeg's *Don't look now* just as completely as it does Thomas Mann's *Der Tod in Venedig*.[20] I want to corroborate this by considering three more examples.

One of the most classical 'Venetian' texts is, of course, the long description of Venice in Marcel Proust's *A la recherche du temps perdu*. Take a look at a passage from near the beginning:

> Ma gondole suivait les petits canaux; comme la main mystérieuse d'un génie qui m'aurait conduit dans les détours de cette ville d'Orient, ils semblaient au fur et à mesure que j'avançais, me pratiquer un chemin, creusé en plein coeur d'un quartier qu'ils divisaient en écartant à peine, d'un mince sillon arbitrairement tracé, les hautes maisons aux petites fenêtres mauresques; et comme si le guide magique eût tenu une bougie entre ses doigts et m'eût éclairé au passage, ils faisaient briller devant eux un rayon de soleil à qui ils frayaient sa route. On sentait qu'entre les pauvres demeures que le petit canal venait de séparer, et qui eussent sans cela formé un tout compact, aucune place n'était réservée. De sorte que le campanile de l'église ou les treilles des jardins surplombaient à pic le rio,

---

[16] Ibid., 43.
[17] Cf. ibid., 89; 108 ff.; 141 ff.
[18] I would consider Donna Leon's novels in general fairly typical examples of texts playing on the signature of the Venetian. Of course, there may be mystery and masquerade in a text set in Bury St. Edmunds, too. But there are very few places in which tradition and intertextual play have crystallized into a specific semiotics that manages to reproduce the reference of the place without even mentioning its name.
[19] For a diachronic *tour de force* see Manfred Pfister's contribution to this volume; for a first anthology of British 'Venetian' texts cf. Pfister 1996, 337 ff., for Mandeville see Tanner 1992, 5.
[20] For different sections of a literary history of Venice see Mahler 1989, Tanner 1992, Corbineau-Hoffmann 1993 and Keller 1997.

Writing Venice: Paradoxical Sifnification as Connotational Feature

comme dans une ville inondée. Mais, pour les églises comme pour les jardins, grâce à la même transposition que dans le Grand Canal, la mer se prêtait si bien à faire fonction de voie de communication, de rue, grande ou petite, que, de chaque côté du canaletto, les églises montaient de l'eau devenue un vieux quartier populeux et pauvre, comme des paroisses humbles et fréquentées, portant sur elles le cachet de leur nécessité, de la fréquentation de nombreuses petites gens; que les jardins, traversés par la percée du canal, laissaient traîner jusque dans l'eau leurs feuilles ou leurs fruits étonnés, et que sur le rebord de la maison dont le grès grossièrement fendu était encore rugueux comme s'il venait d'être brusquement scié, des gamins surpris et gardant leur équilibre laissaient pendre à pic leurs jambes bien d'aplomb, à la façon de matelots assis sur un pont mobile dont les deux moitiés viennent de s'écarter et ont permis à la mer de passer entre elles.[21]

The main object of the description is an unspecified quarter of Venice (x); it is constituted metonymically by reference to its sites, the houses, churches and gardens to be seen from the boat, and is in itself - 'grâce à la même transposition que dans le Grand Canal' - a metonymy for Venice as a whole. The passage falls into two parts. The first part offers a view of the impossible: Venice as an oriental city, a place of the unreal, of isolation, and death; whereas the second part, beginning with '[m]ais', subverts this impression by adding elements of necessity, communication, and life. The quarter thus finds itself semanticized in a twofold way (± a): it is known to be part of a European city and at the same time seems to belong to an anonymous East ('ville d'Orient', 'fenêtres mauresques'); it looks inaccessible ('entre les [...] demeures [...] aucune place n'était réservée') and can at the same time be mysteriously traversed by boat ('génie', 'guide magique'); it is marginal ('détours') and at the same time leads the traveller right into the very centre of things ('en plein coeur'); the water seems to serve as a line of demarcation and death ('divisaient', 'écartant', 'séparer') and at the same time constitutes the very bridge of life transforming the lifeless 'ville inondée' into a busy hive of everyday activity ('communication', 'fréquentation') where the incompatible meets ('l'eau devenue un vieux quartier', 'laissaient traîner jusque dans l'eau'). Venice thus appears as a place of East and West, land and sea, life and death, reality and dream, a place of at once fulfilled and renewed desire, and, again, it is precisely through this type of paradoxical signification that it manages to connote itself.[22]

Similarly, in Jeanette Winterson's Venetian fantasy *The Passion*, the textual Venice deployed finds itself right from the start imbued with double meanings.[23] The second chapter, which is significantly titled "The Queen of Spades", begins like this:

---

[21] Proust 1926/1986, 283 f.; the entire description covers far more than thirty pages (ibid., 279-315).

[22] In my reading I largely follow Corbineau-Hoffmann 1980, 96 ff., who also points out that the usual technique of description employed by Proust, that of opposing primary ('referential') and secondary ('metaphorical') signification, finds itself neutralized when it comes to the descriptions of Venice, thus producing the deconstructive effect, "daß Venedig jene Grundoppositionen vermittelt, die als semantische Relationen von Referenz und Metaphorik die Beschreibungen der Recherche bestimmt hatten" (97). For a short characterization of Venice in Proust cf. Sprenger 1997, 213 ff., for a brilliant discussion in much more detail see Tanner 1992, 228 ff.

[23] For a general characterization of Jeanette Winterson's novels as "realistic stories about fantasies" and "fantastic stories about realities" see Quadflieg 1997, both quotes ibid., 97.

> There is a city surrounded by water with watery alleys that do for streets, and roads and silted up back ways that only rats can cross. Miss your way, which is easy to do, and you may find yourself staring at a hundred eyes guarding a filthy palace of sacks and bones. Find your way, which is easy to do, and you may meet an old woman in a doorway. She will tell your fortune, depending on your face.
>
> This is the city of mazes. You may set off from the same place to the same place every day and never go by the same route. If you do so, it will be by mistake. Your bloodhound nose will not serve you here. Your course in compass reading will fail you. Your confident instructions to passers-by will send them to squares they have never heard of, over canals not listed in the notes.
>
> Although wherever you are going is always in front of you, there is no such thing as straight ahead. No as the crow flies short cut will help you to reach the café just over the water. The short cuts are where the cats go, through the impossible gaps, round corners that seem to take you the opposite way. But here, in this mercurial city, it is required you do awake your faith.[24]

The description starts with the well-known 'mythical' element of Venice as a place situated between land and water and then takes as its main object the city's topography (x), which it qualifies as at once transparent and oblique (± a), as a site in which you can just as easily '[f]ind your way' as 'miss' it, have the same way but not 'the same route', or take as a 'short cut' the 'opposite' direction. All three paragraphs thus develop the paradoxical topographical feature [± orientation], which endows the city described with the semantic doubleness typically used for the characterization of Venice: the city appears as a 'city of mazes', as a place where 'in front' and 'ahead' do not tally. This doubleness is mirrored in the central character of Villanelle, who finds herself semanticized as a specifically 'Venetian' character in the sense that she is both amphibious and human, female and male, fantastical and real. As a girl born with webbed, i.e. "boatman's feet"[25], she at once bears the marks of the masculine and the feminine, belonging as much to the sea as to the land and fulfilling the rumour "that the inhabitants of this city walk on water"[26]. Accordingly, in the Casino where she works, she dresses "as a woman in the afternoon and a young man in the evenings"[27]; she is "pragmatic about love" taking her "pleasure with both men and women"[28]; and when she tries to find out whether she can walk on water, the following morning a beggar is said to be "running round the Rialto talking about a young man who'd walked across the canal like it was solid"[29]. The signature of the Venetian is thus extended from the mere setting to the characters in the setting. In placing Villanelle right in the centre of her textual Venice, Jeanette Winterson underlines the idea that the chosen locale is not a mere *lieu* but an *espace*, not just a place situating the fiction but a semantic universe filling it with life.[30] "*[L]'espace*", defines Michel de Certeau, "*est un*

---

[24] Winterson 1987/1996, 49.
[25] Ibid., 50.
[26] Ibid., 49.
[27] Ibid., 62.
[28] Ibid., 59 f.
[29] Ibid., 69.
[30] For the distinction between '*lieu*' and '*espace*', 'place' and 'space' see de Certeau 1980/1990, 172 ff.

Writing Venice: Paradoxical Sifnification as Connotational Feature

lieu pratiqué"[31]; it is a place which people take possession of, make use of, inscribe with meaning. The Venice of *The Passion* is a place where the paradoxical and the ambiguous are put into practice; as such, it is a 'space' in which the signature of the Venetian can be appropriated and explored.

The same type of world-making can be observed in my third example Ian McEwan's *The Comfort of Strangers*. It again addresses the *topos* of disorientation, discussing the various types of maps available at the newspaper kiosks in the 'city of mazes'.

> The kiosks were centres of neighbourhood intrigue and gossip; messages and parcels were left here. But tourists asking for directions were answered with a diffident gesture towards the display of maps, easily missed between the ranks of lurid magazine covers.
> A variety of maps was on sale. The least significant were produced by commercial interests and, besides showing the more obvious tourist attractions, they gave great prominence to certain shops or restaurants. These maps were marked with the principal streets only. Another map was in the form of a badly printed booklet and it was easy, Mary and Colin had found, to get lost as they walked from one page to another. Yet another was the expensive, officially sanctioned map which showed the whole city and named even the narrowest of passageways. Unfolded, it measured four feet by three and, printed on the flimsiest of papers, was impossible to manage outdoors without a suitable table and special clips. Finally there was a series of maps, noticeable by their blue-and-white striped covers, which divided the city into five manageable sections, none of them, unfortunately, overlapping. The hotel was in the top quarter of map two, an expensive, inefficient restaurant at the foot of map three. The bar towards which they were now walking was in the centre of map four, and it was only when they passed a kiosk, shuttered and battened for the night, that Colin remembered that they should have brought the maps.[32]

The passage begins with a description of newspaper stands (x) as specifically 'Venetian' places where information - 'gossip', 'messages', 'directions' - can just as 'easily' be obtained as 'missed' (± a) and then goes on to give a list of four different types of maps, all of them representing Venice but none quite serving the purpose of giving orientation, being either too exact ('named even the narrowest of passageways') or too imprecise ('marked with the principal streets only'), too unreliable ('it was easy [...] to get lost') or too difficult to handle ('impossible to manage outdoors'). With the city's syntax remaining thus unclear, it becomes all the more difficult for the tourist to get a pragmatic grip on the place: both *lieu* and *espace* alike remain in a blur. Accordingly, Colin and Mary live in constant fear of getting lost, and even when they come to the most prototypical of sites in Venice, their perception of it is curiously oblique:

> To reach the hotel, it was necessary to walk across one of the great tourist attractions of the world, an immense wedge-shaped expanse of paving, enclosed on three sides by dignified arcaded buildings and dominated at its open end by a redbrick clock tower, and beyond that a celebrated cathedral of white domes and glittering façade, a triumphant accretion, so it had often been described, of many centuries of civilization. Assembled on the two longer sides of the square, facing across the paving

---

[31] Ibid., 173 (italics his); in other words, whereas '*lieu*' designates the mere syntactic aspect of a place, '*espace*' rather refers to its pragmatic potential.
[32] McEwan 1981/1997, 19f.

stones like opposing armies, were the tightly packed ranks of chairs and round tables belonging to the long established cafés; adjacent orchestras, staffed and conducted by men in dinner jackets, oblivious to the morning heat, played simultaneously martial and romantic music, waltzes and extracts from popular operas with thundering climaxes. Everywhere pigeons banked, strutted and excreted, and each café orchestra paused uncertainly after the earnest, puny applause of its nearest customers.[33]

All three examples, different as they may be, show that Venetian world-making is closely bound up with the type of paradoxical signification that I have called the signature of the Venetian.[34] It creates universes that are intrinsically double. "A Western city saturated with the East; a city of land and stone everywhere penetrated by water; a city of great piety and ruthless mercantilism; a city where enlightenment and licentiousness, reason and desire, indeed art and nature flow and flower together - Venice is indeed", Tony Tanner concludes, quoting Georg Simmel and Schopenhauer, "the surpassing-all-other embodiment of that 'absolute ambiguity' which is radiant life containing certain death."[35] As such an *espace double*, representational Venice consequently appears to have strong affinities to what Michel Foucault has called "[d]es espaces autres" and, above all, to his idea of the heterotopia.

> Il y a également, et ceci probablement dans toute culture, dans toute civilisation, des lieux réels, des lieux effectifs, des lieux qui sont dessinés dans l'institution même de la société, et qui sont des sortes de contre-emplacements, sortes d'utopies effectivement réalisées dans lesquelles les emplacements réels, tous les autres emplacements réels que l'on peut trouver à l'intérieur de la culture sont à la fois représentés, contestés et inversés, des sortes de lieux qui sont hors de tous les lieux, bien que pourtant ils soient effectivement localisables. Ces lieux, parce qu'ils sont absolument autres que tous les emplacements qu'ils reflètent et dont ils parlent, je les appellerai, par opposition aux utopies, les hétérotopies [...].[36]

Foucault defines heterotopias as 'effectively realized utopias', places which are actually there and not there, part of a given culture and outside it, both representing that culture as well as contesting it. One of the main characteristics of heterotopias lies in the fact that they bring together the incompatible: "L'hétérotopie a le pouvoir de juxtaposer en un seul lieu réel plusieurs espaces, plusieurs emplacements qui sont en eux-mêmes

---

[33] Ibid., 48 f.; for a much more detailed interpretation of McEwan's novel see Virginia Richter's contribution to this volume.

[34] For the general notion of world-making see Goodman 1978; for a brief introduction to the idea of fictitious worlds as universes of discourse cf. Elam 1980, 99 ff.

[35] Tanner 1992, 368; see also Simmel 1907/1993, who, in his concise 'proto-deconstructive' essay laconically titled "Venedig", insists on the city's essential ambiguity ("Zweideutigkeit") in which each pole of an opposition such as e.g. 'land' vs. 'sea' appears like the protean garment of the other pole as a substantiality that can, however, nowhere to be substantiated ("jedes erscheint als das proteische Gewand, hinter dem jedesmal das andere als der eigentliche Körper lockt"; Simmel 1907/1993, 262).

[36] Foucault 1967/1984/1994, 755 f.

incompatibles."[37] Uniting the heterogeneous, heterotopias are thus marked by the same principle of paradoxical signification that I have called the semiotics of the masquerade. Significantly, Foucault cites among his examples the institution of the honeymoon, which has in Western civilizations traditionally been connected with the city of Venice.[38] In the following, final section of the paper, I want to explore to what extent Venice finds herself used as a heterotopic space in literary world-making; in doing so, I will refer to Henry James' *The Wings of the Dove* and Thomas Mann's *Der Tod in Venedig*.

5. Performances

Plot-making is based on oppositions.

According to the Baltic semiotician Yuri Lotman, plot finds itself structured topologically in the sense that it is based on two semantic fields following fundamental topological oppositions such as 'here' and 'there', 'up' and 'down', and is then dependent upon the violation, or the recognition, of the boundary between these fields, which negotiates either something like an 'event' or the stabilization of 'order'.[39] Plot-making is thus concerned with the potentiality of change. Going to Venice and coming back a 'woman' is a good example illustrating this. I now want to argue that 'Venetian' world-making selects the heterotopia of Venice as the one semantic field in its plot-making process while it chooses any other place as the opposite one, contrasting the ambiguity of the heterotopia (± a) with the unambiguousness of an ordinary *topos* (+ a).[40] The transfer of characters from the ordinary into the heterotopic place of Venice does not only change their semantic context, however; it also makes them act differently in the sense that the semiotics of the masquerade becomes part of their pragmatic behaviour. To the extent to which 'place' transforms itself into 'space', paradoxical signification

---

[37] Ibid., 758; Foucault makes a distinction between heterotopias of transition and those of deviation and names as examples rites of passage (e.g. adolescence, child-bearing, festivity) and sites of segregation (e.g. lunatic asylums, prisons, graveyards).

[38] "Pour les jeunes filles, il existait, jusqu'au milieu du XXe siècle, une tradition qui s'appelait le 'voyage de noces'; c'était un thème ancestral. La défloration de la jeune fille ne pouvait avoir lieu 'nulle part' et, à ce moment-là, le train, l'hôtel du voyage de noces, c'était bien ce lieu de nulle part, cette hétérotopie sans repères géographiques." (Ibid., 757)

[39] See Lotman 1970/1977, 209 ff., esp. 240: "It follows from the above that the mandatory elements of any plot will include: 1) some semantic field divided into two mutually complementary subsets; 2) the border between these subsets, which under normal circumstances is impenetrable, though in a given instance (a text with a plot always deals with a *given* instance) it proves to be penetrable for the hero-agent; 3) the hero-agent." (Lotman's italics) Cf. also, with particular reference to what he then calls the 'semiosphere', Lotman 1990, 121 ff.

[40] This is the plot pattern of carnival (see Mahler 1993b, 94 ff.). It is important to note that the opposition is not [+ a] vs. [- a] but [+ a] vs. [± a], in other words, the dominant relation is not that of an antonymy but rather of an inclusion. This is what Avraham Oz, in an otherwise very interesting article, seems to confuse when he speaks, with respect to the function of Italy - and Venice - in the canon, of an "ontology of negation" used for the "effective representation of the other" (Oz 1993, 187). What is important is not so much the negation but the suspension of identity.

changes into paradoxical behaviour and the signature of the Venetian shifts into a predicament of performativity. The Venetian chapters of *The Wings of the Dove* are a good case in point.

The plot-making of the Jamesian novel[41] relies on the transfer of the three main characters from the realm of the non-Venetian (New York, London) to the city of Venice. The non-Venetian is characterized by a strict separation of 'wealth' (and 'death') represented in Milly vs. 'love' (and 'life') represented by Kate. In Venice, this social reality of oppositions finds itself overlaid with a second 'reality' of illusions, in which Merton is used as a catalyst figure both for Milly's desire for love as well as for Kate's need for money. The game staged (by Kate) is a game of make-believe, and it holds for as long as the illusion is kept up. Significantly, it is Kate herself - the character who leaves Venice - who breaks the illusion; while Merton and Milly are still caught in the ambiguities of pretended and real love, ignored and real death, Kate sends in Lord Mark with the unambiguous truth that Merton belongs to her. This act of disillusionment is the beginning of Milly's death. The heterotopia of Venice, in which life and death, illusion and reality, love and wealth (± a) are juxtaposed, turns, for the disillusioned, into a *topos* of negativity (- a). The game is over; Milly dies. On the occasion of the last visit of Sir Luke Strett, her medical doctor, Merton Densher begins to reflect on this:

> It was strange enough, but he found himself as never yet, and as he couldn't have reckoned, in presence of the truth that was the truest about Milly. He couldn't have reckoned on the force of the difference instantly made [...] by the mere visibility, on the spot, of the personage summoned to her aid. He hadn't only never been near the facts of her condition - which counted so as a blessing for him; he hadn't only, with all the world, hovered outside an impenetrable ring fence, within which there reigned a kind of expensive vagueness made up of smiles and silences and beautiful fictions and priceless arrangements, all strained to breaking; but he had also, with every one else, as he now felt, actively fostered suppressions which were in the direct interest of every one's good manner, every one's pity, every one's really quite generous ideal. It was a conspiracy of silence, as the *cliché* went, to which no one had made an exception, the great smudge of mortality across the picture, the shadow of pain and horror, finding in no quarter a surface of spirit or of speech that consented to reflect it. 'The mere aesthetic instinct of mankind -!' our young man had more than once, in the connexion, said to himself; letting the rest of the proposition drop, but touching again thus sufficiently on the outrage even to taste involved in one's having to *see*. So then it had been - a general conscious fool's paradise, from which the specified had been chased like a dangerous animal. What therefore had at present befallen was that the specified, standing all the while at the gate, had now crossed the threshold as in Sir Luke Strett's person and quite on such a scale as to fill out the whole precinct. Densher's nerves, absolutely his heart-beats too, had measured the change before he on this occasion moved away.[42]

Death is near, and Sir Luke is its harbinger. With him comes 'truth', 'visibility', 'the facts' and the inadmissibility of 'having to *see*'. What goes are the 'fictions', the 'suppressions', the 'conspiracy' of make-believe. Almost retrospectively now, the

---

[41] For a detailed discussion of James' relation to Venice cf. Tanner 1992, 157 ff., for *The Wings of the Dove* in particular see ibid., 200 ff.
[42] James 1902/1986, 440 f.

heterotopia of Venice turns out to have been a 'general conscious fool's paradise', a place where everybody knowingly consents to engage in a game of mutual make-believe. And, what is more, the game would have worked, if Kate had not lost her nerve: If Milly had been allowed to die with the illusion of love, Merton and Kate would have found themselves in the position to accept the illusion - the 'reality' - of her money.[43] With the advent of the 'specified', however, the façade, the masquerade, the 'performance' is over; as a mere *topos*, Venice loses its magic, the magic of 'realizing' dreams.[44]

This same structure of mutual make-believe can also be observed in Thomas Mann's novella *Der Tod in Venedig*. I only select one passage, which describes how Gustav von Aschenbach and Tadzio, the boy he has fallen in love with, 'perform' Venice in the sense that they accept and deny, hide and show that some mutual interest has developed between them.

> Auf den Spuren des Schönen hatte Aschenbach sich eines Nachmittags in das innere Gewirr der kranken Stadt vertieft. Mit versagendem Ortssinn, da die Gäßchen, Gewässer, Brücken und Plätzchen des Labyrinthes zu sehr einander gleichen, auch der Himmelsgegenden nicht mehr sicher, war er durchaus darauf bedacht, das sehnlich verfolgte Bild nicht aus den Augen zu verlieren, und zu schmählicher Behutsamkeit genötigt, an Mauern gedrückt, hinter dem Rücken Vorangehender Schutz suchend, ward er sich lange nicht der Müdigkeit, der Erschöpfung bewußt, welche Gefühl und immerwährende Spannung seinem Körper, seinem Geiste zugefügt hatten. Tadzio ging hinter den Seinen, er ließ der Pflegerin und den nonnenähnlichen Schwestern in der Enge gewöhnlich den Vortritt, und einzeln schlendernd wandte er zuweilen das Haupt, um sich über die Schulter hinweg der Gefolgschaft seines Liebhabers mit einem Blick seiner eigentümlich dämmergrauen Augen zu versichern. Er sah ihn und verriet ihn nicht. Berauscht von dieser Erkenntnis, von diesen Augen vorwärts gelockt, am Narrenseil geleitet von der Passion, stahl der Verliebte sich seiner unziemlichen Hoffnung nach - und sah sich schließlich dennoch um ihren Anblick betrogen. Die Polen hatten eine kurz gewölbte Brücke überschritten, die Höhe des Bogens verbarg sie dem Nachfolgenden, und seinerseits hinaufgelangt, entdeckte er sie nicht mehr. Er forschte nach ihnen in drei Richtungen, geradeaus und nach beiden Seiten den schmalen und schmutzigen Quai entlang, vergebens. Entnervung, Hinfälligkeit nötigten ihn endlich, vom Suchen abzulassen.[45]

The signature of the Venetian is first called up by the image of the maze ('das innere Gewirr', 'des Labyrinthes'), in which he who gets lost ('[m]it versagendem Ortssinn', 'der Himmelsgegenden nicht mehr sicher'), begins to find and see; it is then taken up in the description of the protagonists' behaviour - of the lover following ('das sehnlich

---

[43] This would have completed the circle of mutual guardianship convincingly described by Winfried Fluck in his analysis of *The Wings of the Dove* as deconstruction of the *Bildungsroman*: "In *The Wings of the Dove*, [...] Kate Croy establishes herself as lover and guardian of Densher; she then pushes Densher, the potential seducer, into the role of an *ersatz*-guardian of Millie Theale, until the apparent victim Millie manages successfully to establish herself as guardian of both." (Fluck 1991, 26)

[44] For a highly suggestive reading of Venice in *The Wings of the Dove* as a site of the paradoxical and of mutual make-believe, with particular reference to the psychoanalytic idea of the 'protective fiction', see Elisabeth Bronfen's contribution to this volume.

[45] Mann 1912/1974, 64 f.

verfolgte Bild') and pretending not to follow ('hinter dem Rücken Vorangehender Schutz suchend') and of the boy seeing ('um sich [...] der Gefolgschaft seines Liebhabers mit einem Blick [...] zu versichern') and pretending not to see: 'Er sah ihn und verriet ihn nicht.' For a brief moment, Gustav von Aschenbach is allowed to live the illusion of being loved also. And it is right then, when he thinks that he has 'found' ('[b]erauscht von dieser Erkenntnis'), that he loses the boy out of his sight ('und sah sich [...] um ihren Anblick betrogen'). The Venice of the *novella* thus turns out to be precisely the same type of a 'conscious fool's paradise' as the Venice described in James, a place (space) whose dominant 'practice' lies in a complicitous exchange of avowed illusions, a heterotopia in which the imaginary can, for a time at least, pose as real.

6. Conclusions

Textual Venices are duplicitous. Deconstructing the (epistemological) metaphors of views and blinds, submersions and foundations, they are informed by a principle of paradoxical signification that is used to connote, self-reflexively, the city's own irreducible ambiguity. Accordingly, 'Venetian' texts are characterized, on the semantic level, by a syntagmatic deployment of metonymical descriptions continually reasserting this doubleness. This leads to the construction of semantic universes in which, on the pragmatic level, the characters are given one field of action where they are allowed to perform, for a given moment, both the real as well as the imaginary at the same time. In this lies the attraction, and perhaps the secret, of Venice as a literary (hetero)*topos*. If fictions are agencies for articulating the imaginary by means of signs 'normally' used for the representation of the real[46], Venice looks very much like fiction.[47] This homology makes it an ideal locale for the deconstruction of oppositions, norms, and hierarchies. Venice, for the traveller, writer, novelist, thus turns out to be not so much a place for the ethnography of the other but, rather, for an anthropology of the self. Venice is a place of fiction.

Bibiliography

Balzac, Honoré de: *La Recherche de l'absolu* (1834). Ed. S. de Sacy. Paris 1976.
Calvino, Italo: *Le città invisibili* (1972). Torino 1985.

---

[46] See Iser 1986, 5: "the act of fictionalizing is seen as a constant crossing of boundaries between the real and the imaginary", and ibid., 6: "Thus the fictionalizing act converts the reality reproduced into a sign which endows the imaginary with an articulate gestalt."

[47] For the idea of a structural affinity between Venice and fiction see Corbineau-Hoffmann 1993, passim, esp. 26, n. 45: "Die Zweideutigkeit der Stadt könnte wie ein Appell an die Literatur wirken, ihrerseits zwei- und mehrdeutig zu werden. Das Thema Venedig wäre dann nicht nur ein literarisches Sujet unter vielen anderen, sondern selbst strukturell der poetischen Sprachverwendung verwandt." Cf. also her summary ibid., 565 ff. - I would argue that the same affinity could also be traced between Venice and carnival; cf. Mahler 1993b.

Writing Venice: Paradoxical Sifnification as Connotational Feature

James, Henry: *The Wings of the Dove* (1902). Eds. John Bayley/Patricia Crick. London 1986 (Penguin Classics).
Leon, Donna: *Death at La Fenice* (1992). London/Basingstoke 1994.
Mann, Thomas: *Der Tod in Venedig* (1912). Frankfurt a.M. 1974.
McEwan, Ian: *The Comfort of Strangers* (1981). London 1997.
Proust, Marcel: *La Fugitive (Albertine disparue)* (1926). Ed. Jean Milly. Paris 1986.
Shakespeare, William: *Othello* (1604). Ed. M.R. Ridley. London 1975.
Winterson, Jeanette: *The Passion* (1987). London 1996.

Barthes, Roland: *Mythologies* (1957). Paris 1985.
Barthes, Roland: "Éléments de sémiologie". *Communications* 4 (1964), 91-135.
de Certeau, Michel: *L'invention du quotidien. 1. arts de faire* (1980). Ed. Luce Giard. Paris 1990.
Corbineau-Hoffmann, Angelika: *Beschreibung als Verfahren. Die Ästhetik des Objekts im Werk Marcel Prousts*. Stuttgart 1980.
Corbineau-Hoffmann, Angelika: *Paradoxie der Fiktion. Literarische Venedig-Bilder 1797-1984*. Berlin/New York 1993.
Elam, Keir: *The Semiotics of Theatre and Drama*. London 1980.
Fluck, Winfried: "Sentimentality and the Changing Functions of Fiction". In: Winfried Herget (ed.), *Sentimentality in Modern Literature and Popular Culture*. Tübingen 1991, 15-34.
Foucault, Michel: "Des espaces autres" (1967/1984). In: M.F.: *Dits et écrits 1954-1988*. Eds. Daniel Defert/François Ewald. 4 vols., vol. 4. Paris 1994, 752-762.
Goodman, Nelson: *Ways of Worldmaking*. Indianapolis 1978.
Hawkes, Terence: *Structuralism and Semiotics*. London 1977.
Iser, Wolfgang: "Fictionalizing Acts". *Amerikastudien/American Studies* 31 (1986), 5-15.
Keller, Luzius: "Postmoderne Venedig-Bilder". In: Schulz-Buschhaus, Ulrich/Stierle, Karlheinz (eds.), *Projekte des Romans nach der Moderne*. München 1997, 173-193.
Lotman, Yuri M.: *The Structure of the Artistic Text* (1970). Tr. Ronald Vroon. Ann Arbor 1977.
Lotman, Yuri M.: *Universe of the Mind. A Semiotic Theory of Culture*. Tr. Ann Shukman. Bloomington/Indianapolis 1990.
Mahler, Andreas: "Referenzpunkt oder semantischer Raum? Zur Funktion der italienischen Stadt im englischen Drama am Beispiel Venedigs". In: Dirscherl, Klaus (ed.): *Die italienische Stadt als Paradigma der Urbanität*. Passau 1989, 85-103.
Mahler, Andreas: "Italian vices. Cross-cultural constructions of temptation and desire in English Renaissance drama". In: Marrapodi, Michele et al. (eds.): *Shakespeare's Italy. Functions of Italian locations in Renaissance drama*. Manchester 1993, 49-68 [= 1993a].
Mahler, Andreas: "Komödie, Karneval, Gedächtnis. Zur frühneuzeitlichen Aufhebung des Karnevalesken in Ben Jonsons *Bartholmew Fair*". *Poetica* 25 (1993), 81-128 [= 1993b].
Mahler, Andreas: "Maske und Erkenntnis. Funktionen karnevalesker Identität bei Shakespeare". In: Bettinger, Elfi/Funk, Julika (eds.): *Maskeraden. Geschlechterdifferenz in der literarischen Inszenierung*. Berlin 1995, 117-134.
Morton, H.V.: *A Traveller in Italy*. London 1964.
Oz, Avraham: "Dobbin on the Rialto. Venice and the division of identity". In: Marrapodi, Michele et al. (eds.): *Shakespeare's Italy. Functions of Italian locations in Renaissance drama*. Manchester 1993, 185-209.
Pfister, Manfred (ed.): *The Fatal Gift of Beauty: The Italies of British Travellers. An Annotated Anthology*. Amsterdam/Atlanta, Ga. 1996.

Quadflieg, Helga: "Feminist Stories Told on Waste Waters. Jeanette Winterson's Novels". In: Maassen, Irmgard/Stuby, Anna Maria (eds.): *(Sub)Versions of Realism. Recent Women's Fiction in Britain*. Heidelberg 1997 (anglistik & englischunterricht 60), 97-111.

Simmel, Georg: "Venedig" (1907). In: G.S.: *Aufsätze und Abhandlungen 1901-1908*. vol. 2. Ed. Alessandro Cavalli/Volkhard Krech. Frankfurt a.M. 1993 (Gesamtausgabe, vol. 8), 258-263.

Sprenger, Ulrike: *Proust-ABC*. Leipzig 1997.

Tanner, Tony: *Venice Desired*. Cambridge, Mass. 1992.

Titone, Virgilio: *La società italiana sotto gli spagnuoli e le origini della questione meridionale*. Palermo 1978.

Weich, Horst: *Paris en vers. Aspekte der Beschreibung und semantischen Fixierung von Paris in der französischen Lyrik der Moderne*. Stuttgart 1998.

Tony Tanner

Which is the Merchant here? And which the Jew?*:
The Venice of Shakespeare's *Merchant of Venice*

> see how yond justice rails upon yond simple thief. Hark in thine ear: change places, and handy-dandy, which is the justice, which is the thief?
> (*King Lear* IV.vi.l51-4)

When Portia, disguised as Balthasar, "a young and learned doctor", enters the Court of Justice in *The Merchant of Venice*, her first, business-like, question is "Which is the merchant here? And which the Jew?" (IV.i.173) It is an astonishing question. We know that Shylock would have been dressed in a "gaberdine", because, we are told, Antonio habitually spits on it. This was a long garment of hard cloth habitually worn by Jews who, since 1412, had been obliged to wear a distinctive robe extending down to the feet. Shylock would have been, literally, a 'marked' man (in a previous century he would have had to wear a yellow hat). Antonio, a rich merchant who, we are again told, habitually comes "so smug upon the mart" (where 'smug' means sleek and well-groomed, as well as our sense of complacently self-satisifed), is more likely to have been dressed in some of the 'silk' in which he trades (look at the sumptuously dressed Venetian merchants in Carpaccio's paintings to get some idea). It would have been unmissably obvious which was the merchant and which was the Jew. So, is that opening question just disingenuousness on Portia/Balthasar's part - or what?

The first act is composed of three scenes set in the three (relatively) discrete places, or areas, each of which has its distinct voices, values, and concerns. Together, they make up the world of the play. I will call these - Rialto Venice; Belmont (Portia's house, some indeterminate distance from Venice; probably best thought of as being like one of those lovely Renaissance palaces still to be seen in the Veneto); and Ghetto Venice (Shylock's realm: the word 'ghetto' never appears in the play, and, as John Gross has pointed out, Shakespeare makes no mention of it. But the name *Ghetto Nuovo* (meaning New Foundry) was the name of the island in Venice on which the Jews were, effectively, sequestered (and from which the generic use of 'ghetto' derives); and, clearly, Shylock lives in a very different Venice from the Venice enjoyed by the confident Christian merchants. Hence my metaphoric use of the name for what, in Shakespeare, is simply designated as 'a public place'). The opening lines of the three scenes are, in sequence:

---

* The paper, printed with the author's permission here, is based on Tony Tanner's introduction to the play in his 8 vls. Everyman edition of Shakespeare's works (1998); all textual references are to this edition.

Tony Tanner

> In sooth I know not why I am so sad.
> It wearies me, you say it wearies you...

> By my troth, Nerissa, my little body is aweary of this great world.

> Three thousand ducats - well.

Sadness and weariness on the Rialto and in Belmont; money matters in the Ghetto. Is there any inter-connection? Can anything be done?

Antonio speaks first, which is quite appropriate since *he* is the 'Merchant' of the title - not, as some think, Shylock. Had Shakespeare wanted Shylock signalled in his title, he could well have called his play *The Jew of Venice*, in appropriate emulation of Marlowe's *The Jew of Malta* (1589), which was playing in London in 1596 when Shakespeare (almost certainly) started his own play, and which he (most certainly) knew and, indeed, deliberately echoed at certain key points (of which, more by and by). But Shylock is a very different figure from Barabas, who degenerates into a grotesque Machiavellian monster. In fact, Shylock only appears in five of the twenty scenes of the play; though he is, overwhelmingly, the figure who leaves the deepest mark - 'incision' perhaps (see later) - on the memory. He shuffles off, broken, beaten, and ill - sadder and wearier than anyone else in Venice or Belmont - at the end of Act Four, never to return. But, while the triumph and victory belong unequivocally to Portia, it is the Jew's play.

However, Antonio is our merchant, and very Hamlet-ish he is, too. He sounds an opening note of inexplicable melancholy:

> But how I caught it, found it, or came by it,
> What stuff 'tis made of, whereof it is born, I am to learn... (I,i,3-5)

We might later have a guess at at least some of the 'stuff' it is made of, but for now Salerio and Solanio (another of those effectively indistinguishable Rosencrantz-and-Guildenstern couples Shakespeare delights in - it offers another 'which-is-which?' puzzle in a lighter key), try to commiserate with him and cheer him up. And in their two speeches, Shakespeare - breathtakingly - manages to convey a whole sense of mercantile Renaissance Venice. Of course, they say, you are understandably worried - "your mind is tossing on the ocean" - about your "argosies" (a very recent English word for large merchant ships, coming from the Venetian Adriatic port of Ragusa - and also used in Marlowe's play). Salerio, packing all the pride and confident arrogance of imperial, incomparable Venice into his lines, imagines those ships as "rich burghers on the flood", or "pageants [magnificent floats in festival and carnival parades] of the sea", which

> Do overpeer the petty traffickers
> That cursy [curtsy] to them, do them reverence,
> As they fly by them with their woven wings. (I,i,12-14)

Which is the Merchant here? And which the Jew?

Other sea-faring traders are "petty traffickers": Venetian merchants, attracting and exacting world-wide admiration and deference, are something quite superbly else. Solanio chimes in, evoking a merchant's necessary anxieties about winds, maps, ports, piers, and everything that, he says, "might make me fear/Misfortune to my ventures" - 'ventures' is a word to watch. Salerio develops the theme, imagining how everything he saw on land would somehow remind him of shipwrecks:

> Should I go to church
> And see the holy edifice of stone
> And not bethink me straight of dangerous rocks,
> Which touching but my gentle vessel's side
> Would scatter all her spices on the stream,
> Enrobe the roaring waters with my silks -
> And in a word, but even now worth this,
> And now worth nothing? (I,i,29-36)

"But now a king, now thus", says Salisbury when he watches King John die, pondering the awesome mortality of kings (*King John* V,vii,60). In this Venice, there is much the same feeling about the loss of one of their argosies, monarchs (or burghers - it was a republic) of the sea as they were. And what a sense of riches is compacted into the lines imagining spices scattered on the stream, and waves robed in silk - an image of spilt magnificence if ever there was one.

It is important to note Salerio's reference to "church...the holy edifice of stone". In one of those contrasts dear to artists, the stillness and fixity of the holy edifice of stone is to be seen behind the flying ships on the tossing oceans and flowing streams - the eternal values of the church conjoined with, and in some way legitimating, the worldly wealth-gathering of the sea-venturing, transient merchants; the spiritual ideals sustaining the material practices. For Venice was a holy city (the Crusades left from there), as well as the centre of a glorious worldly empire. It was an object of awe and fascination to the Elizabethans. Indeed, as Philip Brockbank suggested, Venice was for Renaissance writers what Tyre was for the prophet Isaiah - "the crowning city, whose merchants are princes, whose traffickers are the honourable of the earth" (*Isaiah* 23:8). But Tyre was also a "harlot" who made "sweet music", and Isaiah prophesies that it "shall commit fornication with all the kingdoms of the world" (Venice was also famed, or notorious, for its alleged sensualities - in Elizabethan London there was a brothel simply named 'Venice'). But, also this about Tyre:

> And her merchandise and her hire shall be holiness to the Lord: for it shall not be treasured nor laid up; for her merchandise shall be for them that dwell before the Lord, to eat sufficiently, and for durable clothing. (23:18)

Traditionally, religion is ascetic and preaches a rejection of worldly goods. But here we see religion and the 'use of riches' creatively reconciled - and by spending, not hoarding. As Tyre, so Venice. But there is, in *Isaiah*, an apocalyptic warning - that God will turn the whole city "upside down" and "scatter" the inhabitants -

> And it shall be, as with the people, so with the priest...as with the buyer, so with the seller; as with the lender, so with the borrower; as with the taker of usury, so with the giver of usury to him.
> The land shall be utterly emptied, and utterly spoiled: for the Lord hath spoken this word. (24:2,3)

Ruskin would say that that that was effectively what *did* happen to Venice. But that is another story. The point for us here is that the Venetian setting of his play allowed Shakespeare to pursue his exploratory interest in (I quote Brockbank)

> the relationship between the values of empire and those of the aspiring affections, human and divine; those of the City of Man and those of the City of God...between the values we are encouraged to cultivate in a mercantile, moneyed and martial society, and those which are looked for in Christian community and fellowship; between those who believe in the gospel teachings of poverty, humility and passivity, and those who (as the creative hypocrisy requires) pretend to.

Returning to the play, Solanio says that if Antontio is not sad on account of his "merchandise", then he must be in love. Antonio turns away the suggestion with a "Fie, fie!". As it happens, I think this is close to the mark, but we will come to that. Here Solanio gives up on trying to find a reason for Antonio's gloom -

> Then let us say you are sad
> Because you are not merry; and 'twere as easy
> For you to laugh and leap, and say you are merry. (I,i,47-9)

And he leaves with Salerio, who says to Antonio - "I would have stayed till I had made you merry". 'Merry' is a lovely word from old English, suggesting pleasing, amusing, agreeable, full of lively enjoyment. "To be merry best becomes you," says Don Pedro to the vivacious Beatrice "for out o' question, you were born in a merry hour" (*Much Ado* II,i,313-4) - and we feel he has chosen just the right word. The princely merchants of Venice favour the word, for, in their aristocratic way, they believe in 'merriment'. It is an unequivocally positive word; it has no dark side, and carries no shadow. Yet in this play, Shakespeare makes it become ominous. When Shylock suggests to Antonio that he pledges a pound of his flesh as surety for the three thousand ducat loan, he refers to it as a "merry bond", signed in a spirit of "merry sport" (I,iii,170,142). The word has lost its innocence and is becoming sinister. The last time we hear it is from Shylock's daughter, Jessica in Belmont - "I am never merry when I hear sweet music" (V,i,69). After her private duet with Lorenzo, nobody speaks to Jessica in Belmont and these are, indeed, her last words in the play. It is hard to feel that she will be happily asssimilated into the Belmont world. Something has happened to 'merry-ness', and although Belmont is, distinctly, an abode of "sweet music", a note of un-merry sadness lingers in the air.

When Bassanio enters with Gratiano, he says to the departing Salerio and Solanio, as if reproachfully, "You grow exceeding strange; must it be so?" (I,i,67) It is a word which recurs in a variety of contexts, and it reminds us that there is 'strangeness' in

Which is the Merchant here? And which the Jew?

Venice, centring on Shylock, whose "strange apparent cruelty" (IV,i,21) is some sort of reflection of, response to, the fact that he is treated like "a stranger cur" (I,iii,115) in Venice. And he is, by law, an alien in the city - the stranger within. Gratiano then has a go at Antonio - "You look not well, Signior Antonio" ("I am not well", says Shylock, as he leaves the play - IV,i,395: now the merchant, now the Jew. Sickness circulates in Venice, along with all the other 'trafficking').

> You have too much respect upon the world;
> They lose it that do buy it with much care.
> Believe me, you are marvelously changed. (I,i,74-6)

His scripture is a little awry here: what people lose who gain the whole world is the *soul*, not the world. A *mondain* Venetian's slip, perhaps. But we are more likely to be alerted by the phrase 'marvelously changed'. Shakespearian comedy is full of marvellous changes, and we may be considering what transformations, marvellous or otherwise, occur in this play. In the event, the 'changes' turn out to be far from unambiguous 'conversions'. Somewhere behind all these conversions is the absolutely basic phenomenon whereby material is converted into 'merchandise' which is then converted into money - which, as Marx said, can then convert, or 'transform' just about anything into just about anything else. It is perhaps worth remembering that Marx praised Shakespeare, in particular, for showing that money had the power of a god, while it behaved like a whore.

Jessica willingly converts to Christianity, hoping for salvation, at least from her father's house, but it hardly seems to bring, or promise, any notable felicity or grace. Shylock is forced to convert to Christianity - which, however construed by the Christians (he would thereby be 'saved'), is registered as a final humiliation and the stripping away of the last shred of his identity. When Portia gives herself to Bassanio, she says:

> Myself, and what is mine, to you and yours
> Is now converted. (III,ii,166-7)

and this is to be felt as a willing conversion, a positive transformation - just as she will, like a number of other heroines, 'change' herself into a man to effect some genuine salvation. Sad Antonio, it has to be said, is not much changed at all at the end - though his life has been saved, and his ships have come sailing in. Venice itself, as represented, is hardly changed; not, that is, renewed or redeemed - though it is a good deal more at ease with itself for having got rid of Shylock. If that is what it *has* done. One hardly feels that, as it were, the realm has been purged, and that the malcontent threatening the joy of the festive conclusion has been happily exorcised. The play does not really end quite so 'well' as that. It is not a 'metamorphic' celebration.

It is Bassanio's plea for financial help from Antonio that concludes the first scene, and the way in which he does so is crucial to an appreciation of what follows. He admits that he has "disabled mine estate" by showing "a more swelling port" than he could afford. 'Swelling port' is 'impressively lavish life-style', but I think we will remember the 'portly sail' of the Venetian argosies just referred to, also, no doubt, 'swollen' by the winds (cf the 'big-bellied sails' in *A Midsummer Night's Dream*). The Venetian princely way of life is both pregnant and distended - fecund and excessive. As Bassanio is, however inadvertently, recognising by using a key word: he is worried about his 'great debts'

> Wherein my time, something too prodigal,
> Hath left me gaged. (I,ii,1490-50)

Shylock calls Antonio a "prodigal Christian", and it was always a fine point to decide to what extent 'prodigality' was compatible with Christianity (think of the parables of the Prodigal Son, and the Unjust Steward), and to what extent it contravened it. It is one of those words which look two ways, pointing in one direction to the magnanimous bounty of an Antony, and in the other to the ruinous squandering of a Timon. Clearly, the munificent prodigality of Antonio is in every way preferable to the obsessive meanness and parsimony of Shylock. But there is a crucial speech on this subject, tucked away, as was sometimes Shakespeare's wont, where you might least expect it. Salerio and Gratiano are whiling away the time in front of Shylock's house, waiting to help Lorenzo in the abduction of Jessica. Salerio is saying that lovers are much more eager to consummate the marriage than they are to remain faithful ('keep obliged faith') subsequently. "That ever holds" says Gratiano:

> All things that are
> Are with more spirit chased than enjoyed.
> How like a younger or a prodigal
> The scarfed bark puts from her native bay,
> Hugged and embraced by the strumpet wind!
> How like the prodigal doth she return,
> With over-weathered ribs and ragged sails,
> Lean, rent, and beggared by the strumpet wind. (II,vi,12-19)

An apt enough extended metaphor in a mercantile society, and the Venetians must have seen many ship sail out 'scarfed' (decorated with flags and streamers) and limp back 'rent'. It may be added that Gratiano is something of a cynical young blade. But the speech stands as a vivid reminder of one possible fate of 'prodigality', *and* of marriage. Ultimately of Venice too, perhaps.

Bassanio, whatever else he is (scholar, courtier) is a 'prodigal', and he wants to clear his 'debts'. Antonio immediately says that "my purse, my person" (a nice near pun, given the close inter-involvement of money and body in this play) "lie all unlocked to your occasions" (I,i,139). This open liberality might be remembered when we later hear the frantically retentive and self-protective Shylock (a name not found outside this play) repeatedly warning Jessica to "look to my house...lock up my doors...shut doors after you" (II,v,16,29,52). The difference is clear enough, and need not be laboured. Antonio also positively invites Bassanio to "make waste of all I have" (I,i,157) -

Which is the Merchant here? And which the Jew?

insouciantly negligent aristocrats like to practise what Yeats called 'the wasteful virtues'. The contrast with 'thrifty' Shylock, again, does not need underlining.

But Bassanio has another possible solution to his money problems; one which depends on 'adventuring' and 'hazard'.

> In Belmont is a lady richly left;
> And she is fair and, fairer than that word,
> Of wondrous virtues...
> Nor is the wide world ignorant of her worth,
> For the four winds blow in from every coast
> Renowned suitors, and her sunny locks
> Hang on her temples like a golden fleece,
> Which makes her seat of Belmont Colchos' strand,
> And many Jasons come in quest of her.
> O my Antonio, had I but the means
> To hold a rival place with one of them,
> I have a mind presages me such thrift
> That I should questionless be fortunate! (I,i,161-176)

Antonio, all his wealth at sea, at the moment has neither "money, nor commodity"; but he will use his "credit" to get "the means". He will borrow the *money* from Shylock to finance Bassanio's quest of a second *golden* fleece. So it is that the seemingly discrete worlds of the Ghetto, the Rialto, and Belmont are, from the beginning, indeed, inter-involved.

Venice, as we have seen it and will see it, is overwhelmingly a man's world of public life; it is conservative, dominated by law, bound together by contracts, underpinned by money - and closed. Belmont is run by women living the private life; it is liberal, animated by love, harmonised by music and poetry ('fancy'), sustained by gold - and open. However cynical one wants to be, it will not do to see Belmont as "only Venice come into a windfall" (Ruth Nevo). It is better to see it as in a line of civilised, gracious retreats, stretching from Horace's Sabine farm, through Sidney's Penshurst, Jane Austen's Mansfield Park, up to Yeats's Coole Park. As Brockbank said, such places ideally offered "the prospect of a protected life reconciling plenitude, exuberance, simplicity and order." It was Sidney who said that "our world is brazen, the poets only deliver a golden", and you might see Belmont as a kind of 'golden' world which has been 'delivered' from the 'brazen' world of trade and money. Yes, somewhere back along the line, it is all grounded in ducats; but you must think of the churches, palaces, art works and monuments of the Renaissance, made possible by varying forms of patronage, and appreciate that the "courtiers, merchants and bankers of the Renaissance found ways of transmuting worldly goods into spiritual treasure" (Brockbank). Belmont is a privileged retreat from Venice; but, as Portia will show, it can also fruitfully engage with it.

In scene two, we are in Belmont, and Portia is weary. Partly surely, because she must be bored stiff with the suitors who have come hopefully buzzing round the honey-pot - the silent Englishman, the mean Scotsman, the vain Frenchman, the drunken German, and so on, as she and Nerissa amuse themselves discussing their different intolerabilities. But, more importantly, because she is under the heavy restraint of a paternal interdiction (familiar enough in comedy, though this one comes from beyond the grave). She has been deprived of *choice* - and she wants a mate. Then we learn from Nerissa about the lottery of the casquets, which she thinks was the "good inspiration" of a "virtuous" and "holy" man. We shall see. But we note that, in this, Belmont (in the form of Portia) is as much under the rule of (male) law as Venice. There are "laws for the blood" in both places, and they may by no means be "leaped" or "skipped" over (I,ii,17ff.). In other comedies, we see inflexible, intractable, unmitigatable law magically, mysteriously melt away or be annulled. Not in this play. Here, the law is followed, or pushed, to the limit - and beyond. Indeed, you might say that Belmont has to come to Venice to help discover this 'beyond' of the law.

And now, in scene three, we are in Shylock's Venice; and we hear, for the first time, what will become an unmistakable voice - addressing, as it were, the bottom line in Venice: "three thousand ducats - well". Shylock speaks in - unforgettable - prose, and this marks something of a crucial departure for Shakespeare. Hitherto, he had reserved prose for, effectively, exclusively comic (usually 'low') characters. With Shylock, this all changes. For Shylock is *not* a comic character. He has a power, a pain, a passion, a dignity - and, yes, a savagery, and a suffering - which, whatever they are, are not comic.

On his first appearance, Shylock establishes his 'Jewishness' by, among other things, revealing his adherence to Jewish dietary rules - "I will not eat with you, drink with you, nor pray with you" (I,iii,34-5). But when Antonio appears, Shylock reveals a darker side of his nature in an 'aside':

> I hate him for he is a Christian;
> But more, for that in low simplicity
> He lends out money gratis, and brings down
> The rate of usance here with us in Venice.
> ...
> He hates our sacred nation, and he rails,
> Even there where merchants most do congregate,
> On me, my bargains, and my well-won thrift,
> Which he calls interest. Cursed be my tribe
> If I forgive him. (I,iii,39-49)

Shylock gives three good reasons for his hating of Antonio - insofar as one can have *good* reasons for hatred: personal, professional, tribal. This is interesting in view of his response during the trial scene, when he is asked why he would not prefer to have ducats rather than Antonio's flesh:

> So can I give no reason, nor I will not,
> More than a lodged hate and a certain loathing
> I bear Antonio... (IV,i,59-61)

Which is the Merchant here? And which the Jew?

His opening exchange with Antonio really defines the central concern of the play, and is crucial. He has already mentioned 'usance' ('a more cleanly name for usury'), 'thrift' (which means both prosperity and frugality - 'thrift, Horatio, thrift'), and 'interest'. And 'usury', of course, is the heart of the matter. Any edition of the play will tell you that the law against lending money at interest was lifted in 1571, and a rate of 10% was made legal. Queen Elizabeth depended on money borrowed at interest, so did most agriculture, industry, and foreign trade by the end of the sixteenth century (according to R H Tawney). So, indeed, did Shakespeare's own Globe Theatre. Plenty of Christians lent money at interest (including Shakespeare's own father); and Bacon, writing "Of Usury" in 1625, said "to speak of the abolishing of usury is idle". Antonio, scattering his interest-free loans around Venice, is certainly an 'idealised' picture of the merchant, just as Shylock sharpening his knife to claim his debt, is a 'demonised' one. But Aristotle and Christianity had spoken against usury, and there was undoubtedly a good deal of residual unease and ambivalence about it. Ruthless usurers were thus especially hated and abused, and since Jews were identified as quintessential usurious money-lenders, (and, of course, had killed Christ), they were available for instant and constant execration. This must certainly be viewed as a collective hypocrisy - one of those 'projections' by which society tries to deal with a bad conscience (not that Shakespeare would have seen many Jews in London; it is estimated that there were less than two hundred at the time). Shakespeare was not addressing a contemporary problem; rather, he was exploring some of the ambivalences and hypocrises, the value clashes and requisite doublenesses, which inhere in, and attend upon, all commerce.

The play is full of commercial and financial terms: 'moneys', 'usances', 'bargains', 'credit', 'excess' and 'advantage' (both used of usury and profit), 'trust', 'bond' (which occurs vastly more often than in any other play: curiously 'contract' is *not* used - Shakespeare wants us to focus on 'bond'), 'commodity' and 'thrift'. Launcelot Gobbo is "an unthrifty knave", while Jessica flees from her father's house with "an unthrift love". This last serves as a reminder that both here and elsewhere in Shakespeare the language of finance and usury could be used as a paradoxical image of love (happiness accrues and passion grows by a form of *natural* interest). You will hear it in Belmont as well as on the Rialto. When Portia gives herself to Bassanio, she, as it were, breaks the bank:

> I would he trebled twenty times myself,
> A thousand times more fair, ten thousand times more rich,
> That only to stand high in your account,
> I might in virtues, beauties, livings, friends,
> Exceed account. (III,ii, 153-7)

Rich place, Belmont; generous lover, Portia!

The absolutely central exchange occurs when Antonio and Shylock discuss 'interest', or 'borrowing upon advantage'. "I do never use it" declares Antonio (what is the relationship between 'use' and 'usury'? Another consideration.) Shylock replies, seemingly rather inconsequentially: "When Jacob grazed his uncle Laban's sheep...."

Antonio brings him to the point. "And what of him? Did he take interest?" Shylock seems to prevaricate: "No, not take interest - not as you would say /Directly int'rest" and then recounts the story from Genesis. This tells how Jacob tricked - but is that the right word? - his exploitative uncle, Laban: they agreed that, for his hire, Jacob should be entitled to any lambs, in the flocks he was tending, that were born "streaked and pied". Following the primitive belief that what a mother sees during conception has an effect on the offspring, Jacob stripped some "wands" (twigs or branches), so that some were light while others were dark, and "stuck them up before the fulsome ewes" as the rams were impregnating them. In the subsequent event, a large number of "parti-coloured lambs" were born, which of course went to Jacob. Nice work; but was it also sharp practice? Or was it both, and so much the better? Or, does it matter? Not as far as Shylock is concerned:

> This was a way to thrive, and he was blest;
> And thrift is blessing if men steal it not. (I,iii,86f.)

'Ewes' may be a pun on 'use'; and for Shylock, it is as legitimate to use ewes in the field as it is to use usury on the 'mart'. Not so for Antonio:

> This was a venture, sir, that Jacob served for,
> A thing not in his power to bring to pass,
> But swayed and fashioned by the hand of heaven.
> Was this inserted to make interest good?
> Or is your gold and silver ewes and lambs? (88-92)

And Shylock:

> I cannot tell; I make it breed as fast. (88-93)

Antonio's last line effectively poses *the* question of the play. It was a line often quoted, (or more often, slightly misquoted), by Ezra Pound in his increasingly unbalanced vituperations against usury and Jews. The root feeling behind it is that it is somehow *unnatural* for inorganic matter (gold, silver, money) to reproduce itself in a way at least analogous to the natural reproductions in the organic realm ("they say it is against nature for *Money* to beget *Money"*, says Bacon, quoting Aristotle). This enables Antonio to reject Shylock's self-justifying analogy: Jacob's story does *not* "make interest good", because he was having, or making, a "venture", and the result was, inevitably, "swayed and fashioned" by - heaven? nature? some power not his own. This, revealingly, was how Christian commentators of the time justified Jacob's slightly devious behaviour (as Frank Kermode pointed out) - he was making a *venture*. Antonio's ships are 'ventures', and Bassanio is on a venture when he 'adventures forth' to Belmont. It seems that the element of 'risk' (= to run into danger) and 'hazard' purifies or justifies the act. As 'hazard' was originally an Arabian word for a gaming die, this would seem to enable gambling to pass moral muster as well. Perhaps it does.

Which is the Merchant here? And which the Jew?

Whatever, there is seemingly *no* risk, as well as no nature, in usury. Shylock's answer, that he makes his money "breed as fast", is thought to tell totally against him; and Bassanio's subsequent remark, "for when did friendship take /A breed for barren metal of his friend?" (I,iii,130-1), is taken to orient our sympathies, and values, correctly. But this won't quite do.

Because, like it or not, money most certainly *does* 'breed'. It may not literally copulate, but there is no way round the metaphor. Sigurd Burckhardt is the only commentator I have read who has seen this clearly, and he wrote: "metal ['converted' into money] is not barren, it does breed, is pregnant with consequences, and capable of transformation into life and art". For a start, it gets Bassanio to Belmont, and the obtaining of Portia and the Golden Fleece (or Portia *as* a golden fleece). And, as if to signal his awareness of the proximity, even similitude, of the two types of 'breeding', with the lightest of touches: when Gratiano announces he is to marry Nerissa at the same time as Bassanio marries Portia, Shakespeare has him add - "We'll play with them the first boy for a thousand ducats" (III,ii,214). You 'play' for babies, and you 'play' for ducats. Which also means that when Shylock runs through the streets crying "O my ducats! O my daughter!", (echoing Marlowe's Barabas who cries out "oh, my girl, my gold", but when his daughter *restores* his wealth to him), we should not be quite so quick to mock him as the little Venetian urchins. He may not use his money to such life-enhancing and generous ends as some of the more princely Venetians; but he has been doubly bereaved (which literally means - robbed, *reaved,* on all sides, *be-).*

Having mentioned that robbery, I will just make one point about the Jessica and Lorenzo sub-plot. However sorry we may feel for Jessica, living in a 'hell' of a house with her father; the behaviour of the two lovers is only to be deprecated. Burckhardt is absolutely right again: "their love is lawless, financed by theft and engineered by a gross breach of trust". Jessica "gilds" herself with ducats, and throws a casket of her father's wealth down to Lorenzo ("Here, catch this casket; it is worth the pains" II,vi,33 - another echo-with-a-difference of Marlowe's play, in which Abigail throws down her father's wealth from a window, to her *father).* This is an anticipatory parody, travesty rather, of Portia, the Golden (not 'gilded') Fleece, waiting to see if Bassanio will pass the test of *her* father's caskets (containing wisdom, rather than simple ducats). He 'hazards' all; this couple risk nothing. They squander eighty ducats in a night - folly, not bounty. Jessica exchanges the ring her mother gave her father as a love-pledge, for - a monkey! They really do make a monkey out of marriage - I will come to their famous love duet in due course. Their's is the reverse, or inverse, of a true love match. It must be intended to contrast with the marriage made by Bassanio and Portia. This marriage also, admittedly, involves wealth - as it does paternal caskets; but, and the difference is vital, wealth *not gained or used in the same way.*

Those caskets! Shakespeare took nearly everything that he wanted for his plot (including settings, characters, even the ring businees in Act V) from a tale in *Il Pecorone* (The Dunce), a collection of stories assembled by Giovanni Fiorentino, published in Italy in 1558 - everything except the trial of the caskets. In the Italian story, to win the lady, the hero has to demonstrate to her certain powers of sexual performance and endurance. Clearly, this was not quite the thing for a Shakespearean heroine. So Shakespeare took the trial-by-caskets from a tale in the thirteenth-century *Gesta Romanorum,* which had been translated into English. Here, a young woman has to choose between three vessels - gold, silver, lead - to discover whether she is worthy to be the wife of the Emperor's son. All we need note about it is one significant change that Shakespeare made in the inscriptions on the vessels/caskets. Those on the gold and silver ones are effectively the same in each case - roughly, "Who chooseth me shall gain/get what he desires/deserves". But in the mediaeval tale, the lead casket bears the inscription *"Thei that chese me, shulle fynde [in] me that God hath disposid".* Now, since the young woman is a good Christian, she could hardly have been told more clearly that this was the one to go for. It is, we may say, no test at all. Shakespeare changes the inscription to "Who chooseth me must give and hazard all he hath" (II,vii,9). This is a very different matter. Instead of being promised a placid and predictable demonstration of piety rewarded, we are in that dangerous world of risk and hazard which, at various levels, constitutes the mercantile world of the play. And to the prevailing lexicon of 'get' and 'gain' has been added the even more important word - 'give'. One of the concerns of the play is the conjoining of *giving* and *gaining* in the most appropriate way, so that they may 'frutify' together (if I may borrow Launcelot Gobbo's inspired malapropism). "I come by note, *to give* and *to receive",* Bassanio announces to Portia (III,ii,140 - my italics). Which is no less than honesty.

While she is anxiously waiting as Bassanio inspects the caskets, Portia says:

Now he goes,
With no less presence, but with much more love,
Than young Alcides [Hercules], when he did redeem
The virgin tribute paid by howling Troy
To the sea monster. I stand for sacrifice;
The rest aloof are the Dardanian wives,
With bleared visages come forth to view
The issue of th' exploit. Go, Hercules! (III,ii,53-60)

The "virgin tribute" was Hesione, and her rescue by Hercules is described in Book XI of Ovid's *Metamorphoses* (where it is preceded by stories concerning Orpheus, who turned everything to music, and Midas, who turned everything to gold - they are both referred to in the play, and are hovering mythic presences behind it). Portia's arresting claim - "I stand for sacrifice" - resonates through the play; to be darkly echoed by Shylock in court - "I stand for judgment...I stand here for law" (IV,i,103,142). When she says "stand for", does she mean 'represent', or 'embody'; or does she imply that she is in danger of being 'sacrificed' to the law of her father, unless rescued by right-choosing Hercules-Bassanio? Or is it just that women are always, in effect, 'sacrificed' to men in marriage, hence the "bleared visages" of those "Dardanian wives"? Something of all of these, perhaps. In the event, it is Portia herself who, effectively rescues, or - her word - 'redeems', not Troy, but Venice. Bassanio (courtier, scholar, *and* fortune-seeker) is, as we have seen, if not more, then as much Jason as Hercules.

> Which is the Merchant here? And which the Jew?

The point is, I think, that he has to be *both* as cunning as the one *and* as bold as the other. The 'both-ness' is important.

This is how Bassanio thinks his way to the choice of the correct casket:

> So may the outward shows be least themselves;
> The world is still deceived with ornament.
> In law, what plea so tainted and corrupt,
> But being seasoned with a gracious voice,
> Obscures the show of evil? (III,ii,73-7)

This, *mutatis mutandis,* is a theme in Shakespeare from first to last - "all that glitters is not gold", and so on (II,vii,65). Bassanio is on very sure grounds in rejecting the gold and silver and opting for lead, *in the context of the test.* But - 'ornament': from *ornare* - to equip, to adorn. Now, if ever there was an equipped and adorned city, it was Venice. It is aware of dangerous seas and treacherous shores, of course; but it is *also* a city of beauteous scarves, and silks and spices - and what are they but 'ornaments' for the body and for food? Bassanio is an inhabitant and creation of an ornamented world, and is himself, as we say, an 'ornament' to it. So why does he win by *going through a show* of rejecting it? He wins, because he realises that he has to subscribe to the unadorned modesty of lead, *even while* going for the ravishing glory of gold. *That* was the sort of complex intelligence Portia's father had in mind for his daughter. Is it hypocrisy? Then we must follow Brockbank and call it "creative hypocrisy". It recognises the compromising, and willing-to-compromise, doubleness of values on which a worldly society (a society in the world) necessarily rests, and by which it is sustained. The leaden virtues, and the golden pleasures. Bothness.

Such is the reconciling potency of Belmont; and Portia seals the happy marriage with a ring. But, meanwhile, Shylock is waiting back in Venice for his pound of flesh, and he *must* be satisfied. Must - because he has the law on his side, and Venice lives by law; its wealth and reputation depend on honouring contracts and bonds - as Shylock is the first to point out: "If you deny [my bond], let danger light/Upon your charter and your city's freedom". Portia, as lawyer Balthasar, agrees: "There is no power in Venice /Can alter a decree established" (IV,i,38-9,220-1). "I stay here on my bond" (IV,i,241) - if he says the word 'bond' once, he says it a dozen times (it occurs over thirty times in this play - never more than six times in other plays). We are in a world of law where 'bonds' are absolutely binding. Portia's beautiful speech exhorting to 'mercy' is justly famous; but, as Burckhardt remarked, it is impotent and useless in this 'court of justice', a realm which is under the rule of the unalterable letter of the law. Her sweet and humane lyricism founders against harsh legal literalism. The tedious, tolling reiteration of the word 'bond' has an effect which musicians know as 'devaluation through repetition'. The word becomes emptier and emptier of meaning, though still having its deadening effect. It is as if they are all in the grip of a mindless meachanism, which brings them to a helpless, dumb, *impasse;* with Shylock's dagger quite legally poised to strike. Shylock, it is said, is adhering to the old Hebraic notion of the law - an eye for an eye. He has not been influenced by the Christian saying of St

Paul: "The letter killeth but the spirit giveth life." For Shylock, the spirit *is* the letter; and Antonio can only be saved *by* the letter. It is as though Portia will have to find resources in literalism which the law didn't know it had.

And so, the famous moment of reversal.

> Tarry a little; there is something else.
> The bond doth give thee here no jot of blood;
> The words *expressly* are "a pound of flesh."
> Take then thy bond...
> Shed thou no blood, nor cut thou less nor more
> But just a pound of flesh. (IV,i,304-7, 324-5; my italics)

Ex-press: to press out. Portia squeezes new life and salvation out of the dead and deadly law - and not by extenuation or circumvention or equivocation. "How every fool can play upon the word!", says Lorenzo, in response to Launcelot's quibbles. But you can't 'play' your way out of the Venetian law courts. Any solution must be found within the precincts of stern, rigorous law. "The Jew shall have all justice... He shall have merely justice and his bond". (IV,i,320,338) And, to Shylock: "Thou shalt have justice more than thou desir'st". (315) Portia makes literalism yield a life-saving further reach. Truly, the beyond of law.

Life-saving for Antonio - and for Venice itself, we may say. But not, of course, for Shylock. He simply crumples; broken by his own bond, destroyed by the law he "craved". But prior to this, his speeches have an undeniable power, and a strangely compelling sincerity. Necessarily un-aristocratic, and closer to the streets (and the ghetto life back there somewhere), his speech in general has a force, and at times a passionate directness, which makes the more 'ornamented' speech of some of the more genteel Christians sound positively effete. Though his defeat is both necessary and gratifying - the cruel hunter caught with his own device - there is something terrible in the spectacle of his breaking. "I pray you give me leave to go from hence. I am not well." (Iv,i,394-5) And Gratiano's cruel, jeering ridicule, with which he taunts and lacerates Shylock through the successive blows of his defeat, does Christianity, does humanity, no credit. Like the malcontent or kill-joy in any comedy, Shylock has to be extruded by the regrouping, revitalised community, and he is duly chastised, humiliated, stripped, and despatched - presumably back to the Ghetto. He is never seen again; but it is possible to feel him as a dark, suffering absence throughout the final Act in Belmont. And in fact, he does make one last, indirect 'appearance'. When Portia brings the news that Shylock has been forced to leave all his wealth to Jessica and Lorenzo, the response is - "Fair ladies, you drop manna in the way /Of starved people." (V,i,293-4) 'Manna' was, of course, what fell from heaven and fed the children of Israel in the wilderness. This is the only time Shakespeare uses the word; and, just for a second, its deployment here - at the height of the joy in Christian Belmont - reminds us of the long archaic biblical past stretching back behind Shylock - who also, just for a second, briefly figures, no matter how unwillingly, as a version of the Old Testament God, providing miraculous sustenance for *his* 'children' (a point made by John Gross).

Which is the Merchant here? And which the Jew?

But why did not Shakespeare end his play with the climactic defeat of Shylock - why a whole extra Act with that ring business? Had he done so, it would have left Venice unequivocally triumphant, which perhaps he didn't quite want. This is the last aspect of the play I wish to address, and I must do so somewhat circuitously. Perhaps Shylock's most memorable claim is:

> I am a Jew. Hath not a Jew eyes? Hath not a Jew hands, organs, dimensions, senses, affections, passion? - fed with the same food, hurt with the same weapons, subject to the same diseases, healed by the same means, warmed and cooled by the same winter and summer as a Christian is? If you prick us, do we not bleed? (III,i,55-61)

That last question, seemingly rhetorical (of course you do), but eventually crucial (Shylock seems to have overlooked the fact that if he pricks Antonio, *he* will bleed too), is prepared for, in an admittedly small way, by the first suitor to attempt the challenge of the caskets. The Prince of Morocco starts by defending the "shadowed livery" of his "complexion", as against "the fairest creature northward born":

> And let us make incision for your love
> To prove whose blood is reddest, his or mine. (II,i,6-7)

So, a black and a Jew claiming an equality with white Venetian gentle/gentiles (another word exposed to examination in the course of the play), which I have not the slightest doubt Shakespeare fully accorded them (the princely Morocco, in fact, comes off rather better than the silvery French aristocrat who follows him). And Morocco's hypothetical 'incision' anticipates the literal incision which Shylock seeks to make in Antonio. When Bassanio realises that Portia is going to ask to see her ring, which he has given away, he says in an aside:

> Why, I were best cut my left hand off
> And swear I lost the ring defending it. (V,i,177-8)

So, there may be 'incisions' made 'for love', from hate, and out of guilt. Portia describes the wedding ring as

> A thing stuck on with oaths upon your finger,
> And so riveted with faith unto your flesh. (V,i, 168-9)

'Rivetting on' is, I suppose, the opposite of Shylock's intended cutting out; but, taken together, there is a recurrent linking of law (oaths, bonds, rings) - and flesh. The play could be said to hinge on *two* contracts or bonds, in which, or by which, the law envisions, permits, requires, ordains, the exposing of a part of the body of one party to the legitimate penetration (incision) by the other party to the bond. If that party is Shylock, the penetration/incision would be done out of hate - and would prove fatal; if that other party is Bassanio it should be done out of love - and give new life. Shylock swears by his 'bond'; Portia works through her 'ring'.

It should be noted that, in the last Act, when Bassanio is caught out with having given Portia's ring away to Balthasar, he stands before Portia as guilty and helpless as Antonio stood before Shylock. And, like Shylock, she insists on the letter of the pledge, and will hear no excuses and is not interested in mercy. Like Shylock too, she promises her own form of 'fleshly' punishment (absence from Bassanio's bed, and promiscuous infidelity with others). As with the word 'bond' in the court scene, so with the word 'ring' in this last scene. It occurs twenty-one times, and at times is repeated so often that it risks suffering the semantic depletion which seemed to numb 'bond' into emptiness. *Both* the word 'bond' and the word 'ring' - and all they represent in terms of binding/bonding - are endangered in this play. But the law stands - and continues to stand; bonds must be honoured or society collapses: there is nothing Bassanio can do. Then, just as Portia-as-Balthasar found a way through the Venetian *impasse*, so Portia-as-Portia has the life-giving power to enable Bassanio to *renew* his bond - she gives him, mysteriously and to him inexplicably, the same ring, for a second time. (She has mysterious, inexplicable good news for Antonio, too, about the sudden safe arrival of his ships.) A touch of woman's magic. For Portia is one of what Brockbank called Shakespeare's "creative manipulators" (of whom Prospero is the last). Like Vincentio (in *Measure for Measure),* she uses "craft against vice". She can be a skilful man in Venice (a veritable Jacob), and a tricky, resourceful, ultimately loving and healing woman in Belmont (a good Medea with something of the art of Orpheus - both figures invoked in the scene). She can gracefully operate in, and move between, both worlds. Because she is, as it were, a man-woman, as good a lawyer as she is a wife - more 'both-ness'; she figures a way in which law and love, law and blood, need not be mutually exclusive and opposed forces. She shows how they, too, can 'frutify' together.

The person who both persuades Bassanio to give away his ring, and intercedes for him with Portia ("I dare be bound again") is Antonio. He is solitary and sad at the beginning, and is left alone at the end. He expresses his love for Bassanio in an extravagant, at times tearful way. It is a love which seems to be reciprocated. In the court scene, Bassanio protests to Antonio that

> life itself, my wife, and all the world
> Are not with me esteemed above thy life.
> I would lose all, ay sacrifice them all
> Here to this devil to deliver you.

Portia, (she certainly does "stand for sacrifice"!), permits herself an understandably dry comment:

> Your wife would give you little thanks for that
> If she were by to hear you make the offer. (IV,i,283-8)

Perhaps this is why she decides to put Bassanio to the test with the ring. I do, of course, recognise the honourable tradition of strong male friendship, operative at the time. I also know that 'homosexuality', as such, was not invented until the late

> Which is the Merchant here? And which the Jew?

nineteenth century. I am also totally disinclined to seek out imagined sexualities which are nothing to the point. But Antonio is so moistly, mooningly in love with Bassanio (and so conspicuously uninvolved with, and unattracted to, any woman), that I think that his nameless sadness, and seemingly foredoomed solitariness, may fairly be attributed to a homosexual passion, which must now be frustrated since Bassanio is set on marriage. (Antonio's message to Bassanio's wife is: "bid her be judge /Whether Bassanio had not once a love", which implies 'lover' as much as 'friend'; revealingly, Antonio's one remaining desire is that Bassanio should witness the fatal sacrifice he is to make for him.) Even then, we might say that that is neither here nor there. Except for one fact. Buggery and usury were *very* closely associated or connected in the contemporary mind as unnatural acts. Shylock is undoubtedly a usurer, who becomes unwell; but if Antonio is, not to put too fine a point on it, a buggerer, who is also unwell, well....

Perhaps some will find the suggestion offensively irrelevant; and perhaps it is. But the atmosphere in Venice-Belmont, is not unalloyedly pure. The famous love duet between Lorenzo and Jessica which starts Act Five, inaugurating the happy post-- Shylock era - "In such a night..." - is hardly an auspicious one, invoking as it does a faithless woman (Cressid), one who committed suicide (Thisbe), an abandoned woman (Dido), and a sorceress (Medea whose spells involved physical mutilation), before moving on to a contemporary female thief - Jessica herself. I hardly think that she and Lorenzo will bear any mythological 'ornamenting'. And that theft has become part of the texture of the Belmont world. It is a place of beautiful music and poetry - and love; but with perhaps just a residual something-not-quite-right lingering from the transactions and 'usages' of Ghetto-Rialto Venice. (The very last word of the play is a punningly obscene use of 'ring' by Gratiano, the most scarbous and cynical voice in Venice - again, a slightly off-key note.) There is moonlight and candle-light for the nocturnal conclusion of the play, but it doesn't 'glimmer' as beautifully as it did at the end of *A Midsummer Night's Dream*. Portia says:

> This night methinks is but the daylight sick;
> It looks a little paler. 'Tis a day
> Such as the day when the sun is hid. (V,i,124-6)

A little of the circulating sickness has reached Belmont. The play is a comedy; but Shakespeare has here touched on deeper and more potentially complex and troubling matters than he had hitherto explored, and the result is a comedy with a difference. And, of course, it is primarily Shylock who makes that difference.

Now, let's go back to the beginning. "Which is the merchant here? And which the Jew?" It turns out to be a good question.

Bibliography

Brockbank, Philip: "Shakespeare and the Fashion of These Times". *Shakespeare Survey* 16 (1963).

Burckhardt, Sigurd: "The Merchant of Venice: The Gentle Bond". *Journal of English Literary History* 29 (1962).

Gross, John: *Shylock. Four Hundred Years in the Life of a Legend.* London 1992.

Kermode, Frank: "The Mature Comedies". In: Brown, J. R./B. Harris (eds.): *Early Shakespeare*. Stratford-upon-Avons Studies, 3. London 1961.

Nevo, Ruth: Comic *Transformations in Shakespeare*. London 1980.

Tawney, R. H.: *Religion and the Rise of Capitalism*. London 1926.

Jürgen Schlaeger

Elective Affinities: Lady Mary Wortley Montagu in Venice

Out of altogether 25 years abroad, Lady Mary lived only six years in Venice and only one year of those six during that crucial period just after she had turned her back on England. Although it was the embassy letters from Constantinople where her husband was the British Ambassador 1717-18, that were to make her famous and although she spent four comfortable, even happy years in Avignon with her own bower of intellectual bliss high over the city walls and lived ten years in the hands of the shady Count Palazzi in and near Brescia, the evidence of her letters and of other personal material leave no doubt that Venice meant more to her than any of these other cities including London. In her life, in her imagination, and in her memories, Venice played a key role. It was obviously the place that suited her best, when she was looking for a refuge for herself and her lover, that most perfectly answered her intellectual needs and that most closely corresponded to her notion of the ideal combination of personal independence and social recognition, a combination which she had found difficult to achieve anywhere else.[1]

Why Venice? Why did she feel attracted to a place she had not seen before? We know that cities are imaginary topographies, that they are coded in specific ways and are often presented as quasi-anthropomorphic entities, as constructions which offer unique opportunities for personal identification. More than any other European city Venice had already developed such a character, when Lady Mary decided to go there. Yet her imaginary Venice was obviously not perfectly matched with the Venice most of her contemporaries knew from descriptions, reports and hearsay. It could not simply have been the lasciviousness of its lifestyle, the attractions of its location and architecture or the republican nature of its government which she found so enticing. Her own needs and desires and the stereotypical image of Venice others had constructed and transmitted over the centuries were not so completely in accord that they would provide a satisfactory explanation for the kind of special relationship, one is inclined to say "elective affinity" which she established to the Serenissima.

It is the purpose of this paper to investigate the reasons for and the character of this special attachment. By claiming that we are here confronted with a peculiar form of rapport between a city and an extraordinary individual, we will have to carry the argument way beyond the usual motivations that brought tens of thousands of visitors from all over Europe every year to Venice in the early 18th century. We will have to analyse the personality structure of our heroine and will have to establish plausible links between the character of Venice as an imaginary construction, as a location and as a lifestyle, and Lady Mary's perceptions of herself, of her needs and the realities of her life.

---

[1] Halsband 1956.

Jürgen Schlaeger

Who was Lady Mary Wortley Montagu? She was born in 1689 as the daughter of Evelyn Pierpont, 3rd son of the Earl of Kingston, and of Lady Mary Fielding, only daughter of the 3rd Earl of Denbigh. One year after her birth, her father succeeded to the Earldom of Kingston, which brought her the courtesy title of Lady for life. Her aristocratic background clearly shaped her views of society. Throughout her life she never lost the sense of her own elevated rank and she always enjoyed the special attention it brought her. She not only accepted this role and the social privileges it implied, but she was deeply convinced that aristocrats are special people with special rights and obligations, a conviction that grew even stronger as she grew older.[2]

But, she not only wanted to be an aristocrat, she also wanted to play a role in the republic of letters. She educated herself, taught herself Latin, French and Italian, read voraciously whatever she could lay her hands on - romances, the classical authors, criticism, philosophy, etc. In her family and among her friends she very early acquired a reputation as a woman with considerable intellectual ambitions and talents. Her biographer Halsband described this aspect of her character as "one of the strongest, most persistent impulses of her long erratic life: her desire to win fame as a woman of letters."[3]

Obviously, at the beginning of the 18th century and for a long time afterwards, the role society had assigned to female members of the upper classes and the social role of a member of the intelligentsia, clashed violently. The model of the meek, obedient, feminine mother of future generations of aristocrats to be given to the highest bidder on the marriage market, and the role of the witty, knowledgeable, sharp-tongued and aggressive person of letters could not easily be reconciled. Her determination to play both roles tells us not only a great deal about her convictions and her strength of will, but also about her lifelong predicament as a person trying to fulfill two incongruous aspirations at one and the same time. Indeed, "Mary can no longer be regarded as merely a member of an aristocratic family. This extraordinary woman had gone beyond the boundaries of her time and class."[4] But she had also stayed firmly within them, willing to live with the resultant tensions and face the consequences.

From early on in her life she developed sophisticated techniques to deal with these conflicting demands. One of these techniques consisted in adopting some literary role model; this practice even extended to the period later in her life when she had to come to terms with yet another role, that of the lover of an Italian more than 20 years her junior; a role that clashed even more violently with her rank and her moral convictions.

In her early autobiographical attempt, for instance, she presents herself like a heroine in a French romance.[5] On the one hand she appears there in the conventional role of a victim of paternal machinations. On the other, however, she insists on her intellectual accomplishments as the main reason for Wortley's, her later husband's, falling in love with her. The active role of the learned, intellectually astute authoress

---

[2] Halsband 1956, 255.
[3] Halsband 1956, 287.
[4] Halsband 1956, 292.
[5] Halsband/Grundy 1993, 77-81.

and the passive role of the romance heroine, co-exist side by side. Equally, in the many letters which she exchanged with her future husband, Edward Wortley Montagu, who was 11 years her senior, and then Speaker of the House of Commons, whereas she was barely 15, she reiterated traditional positions on the roles of wives at the same time leaving not the slightest trace of doubt that she is on an equal footing with him and has her own ideas about what marital relationships should be like: "Obedience is a doctrine should alwaies be receivd among wives and daughters", she writes in a letter to Wortley. But to forestall any misapprehensions on his part she adds: "That principle makes me cautious who I set for my Master."[6] "She had" she writes perceptively about herself, "a way of thinking very different from that of other Girls."[7] And, in a spectacular self-assertive declaration of faith she tells her future husband: "I had much rather be my own mistrisse as long as I live" and travel rather than be confined to 'the Country' as many married women of her class were.[8]

From the beginning she defines Wortley not as a man who is interested in her as a woman or an appropriate match for someone with her standing and expectations, but also as a hero in her own romance. So she constructs imaginary catastrophes, poses in front of him in the various roles of offended lover, dutiful future wife, neglected bride, meekly resigning any claims on him and so on. Yet underneath and behind these romanticising antics, she has already made up her mind about his part in her story. He is her man and she will not let him go. When he hesitates, she goads him on: „Make no answer to this. If you can like me on my own terms, 'tis not to me you must make your proposals."[9] And almost a year later: "My Schemes of Happiness are pritty near what I have sometimes heard you declare yours."[10] When he still procrastinates, she becomes even more urgent: „I know how to make a Man of sense happy, but then that man must resolve to contribute something towards it himself."[11]

When her father rejects Wortley's official suit because Wortley is unwilling to entail his estate on his first born son, Mary comes up with the idea of an elopement which is actually carried into execution when her father provides the last missing element of a romance-like plot: i.e., when he tries to force her to marry someone else. So her secret marriage to Wortley is clearly the fulfillment of the first act in a drama which she had set in motion with herself as the heroine.

"Before the elopement and the marriage she had envisioned 'romantic scenes' to herself of 'Love and Solitude'".[12] But, Wortley's insensitivity and his inability to play the important part in politics Lady Mary had envisaged for him (and herself), soon killed the romance. Wortley was obviously too much down to earth and too pragmatic to fancy figuring endlessly as a heroic character in her story. In the end, when he was

---

[6] Halsband 1965, I, 54.
[7] Halsband/Grundy 1993, 79.
[8] Halsband 1965, I, 53.
[9] Halsband 1965, 31.
[10] Halsband 1965, 73.
[11] Halsband 1965, 25.
[12] cf. Halsband 1956, 31.

called back from his post as ambassador to the Osman Empire and when, on his return, his political ambitions came to nothing, the relationship cooled off. These disappointing developments obviously failed to satisfy her social, as well as her intellectual and emotional expectations. So she withdrew whatever feelings and hopes she had invested in Wortley and concentrated her efforts on the second great ambition of her life: to make a reputation as a woman of letters. This ambition forced her again and again to struggle with social incompatibilities. As a woman among men she was an outsider. But she is determined to leave her mark on the intellectual scene, even if it meant to publish anonymously or to restrict herself to private circulations of her manuscripts. She continues to write poems, she mixes with the Steeles, with Addison and Pope, who is, for a time, deeply infatuated with her. She takes part in literary and political controversies; she even edits a periodical *The Nonsense of Common Sense* which runs through nine issues and which is designed to defend Walpole and his ministry from attacks of the opposition press.[13]

All this she does anonymously, because she believes that such activities would be considered a violation of her elevated status. Even when her relationship with Pope turns sour (either because of some linen returned dirty or because she refuses Pope's wish to become her lover) she hides behind others to attack him in satiric verse or to answer his attacks on her reputation. That there was a strong masculine streak in her personality, which, when prominent, completely erased her usual feminine sensibility and restraint, is shown by the following episode:

In 1757, that is to say, thirteen years after Pope's death, twelve years after Swift's and six after Bolingbroke's, she showed an English friend, who visited her in Venice, how her close-stool was painted like the backs of books by these three. "She had known them well", she said, "they were the greatest Rascals, but I have the satisfaction of shitting on them every day."[14]

Isobel Grundy has written perceptively on Lady Mary's ability to adapt to complex circumstances, to cross boundaries and play different roles:

> Her choice of a persona so unlike herself is typical as well as extraordinary. Though she also wrote self-revealingly in both poetry and prose, she is fond of masquerading as her Other, from the shepherd 'Strephon' to the professional widow, from the eclogue courtiers to male practitioners of the trade: Turkey merchant, Italian inventor, the poet Pope. She crosses and re-crosses gender boundaries at a bound; even whilst speaking in a female voice, as in most of her poems about sex and marriage, she draws on ideas and language generally classed as 'masculine'.[15]

So by the time a new hero appeared on the stage on which the drama of her life was being acted out, she had already earned a reputation for versatility and moral ambiguity. Her friends admired her learning and her sense as well as her feminine graces. Her enemies hated her intellectual sharpness, feared her tongue and doubted her morals.

---

[13] Halsband/Grundy 1993, 105-149.
[14] Mack 1985, 555.
[15] Halsband/Grundy 1993, XIV.

Elective Affinities: Lady Mary Wortley Montagu in Venice

In the spring of 1736, at the age of 47, Lady Mary met a young Italian on his first visit to England. This meeting turned out to be the most dramatic turning point in her life for she entered upon the most sensational friendship with this attractive young man. This deep involvement remained virtually unknown until the publication of Robert Halsband's biography in 1956.[16]

The remarkable young man was Francesco Algarotti, born in 1712; he was about half her age at the time of their first meeting. Born as the son of a Venetian merchant he had made a brilliant career in natural science, in French and English *belles-lettres* at the University of Bologna. He was obviously a very attractive man with androgynous tastes, capable of love-affairs with either sex and using his uncommon attraction to further his fortunes.

In less than two weeks he won Lady Mary's heart and that of Lord Harvey, who was Lady Mary's most intimate friend, too. She developed, she later confessed, "a frantic passion" for him. [17] "You, Lovely Youth", she rhymes, "shall my Apollo prove/Adorn my Verse, and tune my soul to love."[18]

Mary must have realized that this new story with a new hero could not be acted out on the London stage, but that she needed a new setting. She, therefore, suggested that she would move to Venice and that he should join her there later.

> I am leaving to seek you. One need not accompany such a proof of an eternal Attachment with an embroidery of words. I shall meet you in Venice.
>
> If I find you such as you have sworn to me, I find the Elysian Fields, and Happiness beyond imagining; ... If you want to repay me for all that I am sacrificing, hurry to me in Venice, where I shall hasten my arrival as much as possible.[19]

This plan she put into execution a year later. As far as her husband knew, she journeyed abroad for the purpose of improving her health, but in her own mind she travelled towards a new life, towards her Elysium, as she preferred to call it.

The letters she sent to Algarotti on her journey and the letters from Venice show a completely different and new Mary. As her biographer Halsband comments: "The reader rubs his eyes in disbelief. Can this be the 47 years old Lady Mary, the hard-mouthed social gossip and heartless versifyer?"[20] But here she is, in the role of a passionate lover who has found the long-wanted Swain, whose name she has engraved on her "marble breast", as one of her poems phrases it. What is at stake here can easily be gathered from the letters she started to write to Algarotti shortly after they met: "I no longer know how to write to you. My feelings are too ardent; I could not possibly explain them or hide them. ... The very Idea of seeing you again gave me a Shock

---

[16] cf. Halsband 1956, chap. X.
[17] Grundy 1997, 285, Letter to Francesco Algarotti.
[18] In a letter to Francesco Algarotti, 24 February 1737 in: Grundy 1997, 235.
[19] Grundy 1997, 245f., Letter to Francesco Algarotti.
[20] Halsband 1956, 157.

while I read your Letter, which almost made me swoon."[21] Or in September 1736: "All that is certain is that I shall love you all my life in spite of your whims and my reason."[22] Or a few days later (10 Sept. 1736):

> I am a thousand times more to be pitied than the sad Dido. ... I have thrown myself at the head of a foreigner just as she did. ... I have a devotion for you more zealous than any of the adorers of the Virgin has ever had for her ... I have no purpose except to satisfy myself by telling you that I love you ... You possess in me the most perfect friend and the most passionate lover.

The more evasive and elusive the opportunistic Algarotti becomes, the more fervent sound her declarations of love. Never a personality that could wait for things to happen, she eventually makes the decisive move to force him into compliance with her wishes.

So her desires and her passions, but also her good judgment carried her to Venice as the place where she hoped to be able to find surroundings that would allow her to reconcile the different roles she considered important in her life: her role as an aristocratic woman, as a woman of letters, and as an individual passionately in love.

Why Venice? Apart from the fact that Venice was Algarotti's home town, it is very difficult to discover any traces of how she formed an image of the place before she actually got there. Once she had suggested to Wortley that they should escape to Italy - so there must have been some romantic notions in her head about Italy. But no more than that.

Perhaps Algarotti had told her in the many intimate hours they must have spent together in England, that Venice, the city of lax morals and intellectual intensity, would be a place most suitable for their plans. Maybe it was something like this in conjunction with the idea of the city she had constructed from what she had heard or read about it.

What we do have are her descriptions of how she experienced Venice and her reasons for liking it there even when Algarrotti, who had preferred the young Prussian King Frederick II's advances to hers, failed to turn up. In these statements a picture of her imaginary Venice emerges, which explains the affinities she must have felt between her own situation and the lifestyle the city offered. "She was," as her biographer Halsband noted, "complex, versatile and changeable, responding with bewildering energy to the constantly shifting patterns of her life."[23] Or in the words of one of her later visitors: "Lady Mary is one of the most extraordinary shining characters in the world; but she shines like a comet; she's all irregular, and always wandering."[24]

Her habitual restlessness was clearly a result of her moving back and forth between different roles, of her continuous crossing of boundaries. So it is understandable that she felt attracted to a city that stood for shifting boundaries, social fluidity and

---

[21] Grundy 1997, 226.
[22] Halsband 1965 - 67, II, 501.
[23] Halsband 1956, VI; for Venice as an imaginary topography see also Tanner 1992, 3ff.
[24] Halsband 1956, 210.

Elective Affinities: Lady Mary Wortley Montagu in Venice

intellectual excitement. She also was in search of a suitable setting for acting out the romance with Algarotti, and here, too, Venice seemed to be the ideal location: Venice, the amphibious city, the hybrid construction shaped by water and land, the city in which East and West fused most luxuriously, the city that managed to combine elaborate ritual with social informalities, spectacular self-presentation with masked anonymity, and, above all, Venice the city that was quite literally conceived as a stage on which a large variety of players could act out their favourite phantasies.

In a letter to Henrietta, Countess of Pomfret, written shortly after she had arrived in Venice, she described her first impressions as follows:

> ...and here is a universal liberty that is certainly one of the greatest *agréments* in life. We have foreign ambassadors from all parts of the world, who have all visited me. I have received visits from many of the noble Venetian ladies; and upon the whole I am very much at ease here. If I was writing to Lady Sophia, I would tell her of the comedies and operas which are every night, at very low prices; but I believe even you will agree with me that they are ordered to be as convenient as possible, every mortal going in a mask, and consequently no trouble in dressing, or forms of any kind. ... I still hope you will come to Venice; where you will see a great town, very different from any other you ever saw, and a manner of living that will be quite new to you.[25]

If we take this together with passages from a letter, written to the same friend about a month later when the novelty of her acquaintance with Venice had somewhat worn off, we have assembled, I believe, the most essential ingredients of her affinity:

> Upon my word, I have spoke my real thoughts in relation to Venice; but I will be more particular in my description, ... It is impossible to give any rule for the agreeableness of conversation; but here is so great a variety, I think 'tis impossible not to find some to suit every taste. Here are foreign ministers from all parts of the world, who, as they have no court to employ their hours, are overjoyed to enter into commerce with any stranger of distinction. As I am the only lady here at present, I can assure you I am courted, as if I was the only one in the world. ... It is the fashion for the greatest ladies to walk the streets, which are admirably paved; and a mask, price sixpence, with a little cloak, and the head of a domino, the genteel dress to carry you everywhere. ... And it is so much the established fashion for everybody to live their own way, that nothing is more ridiculous than censuring the actions of another. This would be terrible in London, where we have little other diversion; ... but for me, who never found any pleasure in malice, I bless my destiny that has conducted me to a part where people are better employed than in talking of the affairs of their acquaintance.[26]

First of all, Venice's lifestyle and the social arrangements it consists of, relieve her of the troublesome tension between the two roles of female aristocrat and intellectual from the incongruity of which she had suffered greatly at home. In Venice the two roles coexisted happily. Secondly, in spite of the freedom and fluidity of the social arrangements she must not fear losing the benefits and recognition of her rank. She is treated like a queen and she enjoys it. In her letters to Wortley and others, she expresses repeatedly her particular delight about this state of affairs. Thirdly, the

---

[25] Halsband 1965 - 67, II, 154f.
[26] Halsband 1965 - 67, II 159.

wearing of masks allows her not only to protect her pock-marked face from close inspection, but also to move freely between her different social roles, even crossing effortlessly the boundaries that normally separate the male from the female world. Fourthly, Venice is a place of transit, of porous boundaries. Its amphibious location and its hybrid nature as stone and water, its Occidental and Oriental flair, its character as a Republic free of court etiquette and at the same time, as a place full of pageantry, give it a fluidity in which a versatile personality like Lady Mary could move as she pleased.

As we have seen, Lady Mary's life was dominated by two different role models: a traditional aristocratic one and a bourgeois one based on personal achievements. Aristocracy and meritocracy, the nobility of birth and the nobility of mind, her social obligation as a member of the aristocracy and her burning desire as an individual to experience personal fulfillment for her intellectual ambitions and her emotional needs - these were the conflicting forces that shaped her life; but these were also the forces that characterized the fundamental social changes in her own country during her lifetime. So, in a sense she impersonated both worlds - the old one and the new one - two worlds between which she was unable and unwilling to choose. From this constellation it is plausible why she was looking for a suitable space that would allow her to act out the two sides of her personality. Role-model-oriented self-fashioning and individual self-assertion needed special conditions and a place like a stage - and Venice provided it.[27]

Many visitors had commented on the theatrical character of this extraordinary city, particularly when the carnival season was gradually extended to last 6 months of the year.[28] In the process theatricality became a kind of second nature of the city. Its carnival was not, as in all other places, a short period of topsy-turvydom and misrule. In Venice, it did not lead to the spontaneous and orgiastic outbreaks which were typical of other places - and which can still be found today in cities such as Basle, Cologne and Nice. It retained an aristocratic air of elegance and discretion, even in its excesses, and filled one half of the year so pleasantly that the other half was defined by its absence. When it came around again, the city, as if touched by a magic wand, turned again into a kind of fairy world, where prosaic everyday life was forgotten, and everybody felt free to reinvent themselves at their own pleasure.

Goethe, who visited Venice in September 1786, described the theatrical character of Venetian life in the following words:

Throughout the day, on the Piazza and on the canals, in their Gondolas and palaces, the hawkers and shopkeepers, the beggars and the sailors, the neighbours, the advocate and his opponent, everybody lives and moves and is having a good time, talks and remonstrates, shouts and makes offers, sings and plays, swears and clamours. And in the evening they go to see a play in which they see and hear the life of their days, artfully rearranged.[29]

---

[27] For 'self-fashioning' see Greenblatt 1980.
[28] For the Venetian carnival see Morris 1993, 12; also Mar and Lohmann 1988; Castle 1986.
[29] *Goethes Werke* 1867, 19. Bd. 73 (my translation).

According to this, life in Venice provided the score for theatrical performances and theatrical performances set the pattern for everyday life. More than in any other city, this configuration tended to blur the boundaries between realities and fictions, hard facts and flights of the imagination.

To chose the role she thought attractive or convenient, to venture into the open in a mask during the carnival season and to be able to do that as an everyday practice gave the sharp-sighted Lady Mary also the opportunity to observe without being seen. The wearing of masks freed her not only from the obligations of her elevated status, but also from her role as a woman. In this way the Venetian way of life allowed its devotees to operate exactly as if they were behind Venetian blinds and it is this which, for reasons I have tried to show, contributed to make Venice so attractive to Lady Mary. Venice made it possible for her to move in a social atmosphere where the pressure to make choices between different roles was, at least temporarily, lifted. All this must have made Venice a congenial place to live in for her. Its theatricality, its metamorphotic character appealed to her desire for self-fashioning and her need for role shifting. It held her spellbound even after it became clear that Algarotti would not join her there, to fulfill her ultimate dream of a symbiosis between playing and being, between her different social roles, between her intellectual ambitions and her physical desires.

Bibliography

Castle, Terry: *Masquerade and Civilization*. Stanford/CA 1986.
Greenblatt, Stephen: *Renaissance Self-Fashioning*. Chicago/London 1980.
Grundy, Isobel (ed.): *Lady Mary Wortley Montagu. Selected Letters*. London 1997.
Halsband, Robert: *The Life of Lady Mary Wortley Montagu*. Oxford 1956.
Halsband, Robert (ed.): *The Complete Letters of Lady Mary Wortley Montagu*. Oxford 1965-67, 3 vols.
Halsband, Robert/Isobel Grundy (ed.): *Lady Mary Wortley Montagu. Essays and Poems and Simplicity, a Comedy*. Oxford 1993.
Mack, Maynard: *Alexander Pope. A Life*. New Haven/London 1985.
Mar, Pearl/ Rainer Lohmann: *Die Zeit der Masken*. München 1988.
Morris, Jan: *Venice*. London 1993.
Tanner, Tony: *Venice Desired*. Oxford 1992.

Elinor Shaffer

William Beckford in Venice, Liminal City:
The Pavilion and the Interminable Staircase

Venice was a centre of Beckford's imaginative life, second only to Fonthill itself. It was the site of personal passion, of a moral struggle between two aspects of passion, the occasion for some of his best writing in his minor masterpiece *Dreams, Waking Thoughts, and Incidents* – certainly one of the best works by any English writer on Italy –, the inspiration for some of his most spectacular effects even at Fonthill, and the source of his most serious and lasting contribution to aesthetics and art as well as literary history. It was the place where he seems decisively to have crossed over into a world of the illicit which he both feared and embraced. Its architecture melded with the fantasy architecture of his own experience.

Beckford's entry into the Venetian territories on his first Grand Tour has all the characteristics of crossing the border into a new land – a metaphorically new land as well as a new geographical region. His Grand Tour can be seen as a Black Mass – a reversal of the values normally attached to the Grand Tour as an educative experience preparing young gentlemen to take up their role in English society as landed proprietor, member of Parliament, pillar of the Anglican Church, and in due course *paterfamilias*.

William Beckford first travelled to Venice in 1780. He was just under twenty, and had been prepared for the Grand Tour in the prescribed manner. He had been sent abroad as the final phase of his education, first to Geneva for eight months, in the company of his tutor, in 1777. His father had died when he was ten, leaving him heir to a large fortune and master of Fonthill Splendens, a fine mansion in Wiltshire. He would shortly come of age, when he would be able to live in any manner that suited his wishes. A dutiful letter to his mother from Geneva harbours a declaration of independence: outlining Locke's views on the powers of mind, he distinguishes Imagination from Memory: memory is "a grave and respectable Matron" (like his mother), whereas imagination "delights to disjoin, or jumble them together with the wildest caprice, and cares not for method, arrangement, or anything else provided she holds up a pleasant Picture to the mind". Beckford declares, "I fear I shall stand self-convicted of having sacrificed a little too freely to Imagination."[1] His Grand Tour would extend his 'sacrifices to the imagination' well beyond what he could then have conceived.

He crossed into Italy in July 1780. He was already phenomenally well read, gifted in languages, with a visual sensibility carefully nurtured and trainedby his art master, Alexander Cozens, now accounted not only the founder of the English watercolour landscape but a gifted theorist and a persuasive teacher. His travel book, *Dreams*, was largely made up of long journal letters to Cozens, whose own letters Beckford kept all his life, dying with the box beside him; it is thought that they were destroyed by the

---

[1] William Beckford, Letter to his mother, Bodleian Library, University of Oxford, MS Beckford d. 9.

Hamilton family.² Or so legend has it. Beckford was one of the great letter writers of the eighteenth century – a century of brilliant letter-writers; yet there has never been an edition of them. On his second Italian journey, beginning in May 1782, he was accompanied by Cozens's son, John Robert, who became one of the finest painters of his generation, copied by Girtin and Turner; the sketchbooks from that journey, taken in part under Beckford's direction, and often representing his own visual experiences, are in themselves a major work, and many of them were afterwards worked up into large-scale paintings, again at Beckford's behest.³ His account of his Grand Tour, then, prepared for publication and printed in the months after his return to England from his second Italian journey in November 1783, and then suppressed by his family (only five copies survived), represented not one but two Grand Tours. Yet it is in the first Tour that Venice so largely figures, as his entry into Italy and a new world, which when he left it drew him back, almost against his will; he returned to the city only briefly on the second trip, in June 1782. Yet having once experienced the *rite de passage* there was no possible return to a previous state.

One of the prime sites of the Grand Tour was Venice. It summoned up an immense response in the young Beckford, setting him on his most characteristic path, in which rebellion against prescribed behaviour – which led to the suppression of the book of his Tour – conjured up a mental landscape which was to serve his 'oriental tale' of *Vathek* (1786) and the erotic *Episodes* (intended for inclusion within *Vathek* but not published in his lifetime). Both the mental landscape of the inversion of values and the form of the Oriental tale – as well as the circulation of the suppressed writings and the rumours of them afterwards – fed into the Romantic movement. Beckford's role as founder of a style is never clearer than here.

His description of his first approach to the Venetian lands – which was, significantly, also his first approach to Italy – captures precisely the sense of crossing a formidable and complex boundary:

> *July 31st [1780].* My heart beat quick, when I saw some hills not very distant, which I was told lay in the Venetian state; and I thought an age, at least, had elapsed before we were passing their base.⁴

The first phase of crossing was a "picturesque valley" full of unfamiliar life forms:

> Fratillarias, and the most gorgeous flies, many of which I here noticed for the first time, were fluttering about and expanding their wings to the sun. There is no describing the numbers I beheld, nor their gaily varied colouring. I could not find in my heart to destroy their felicity; to scatter such bright plumage, and snatch them for ever from the realms of light and flowers. Had I been less compassionate I should have gained credit with that respectable corps, the torturers of butterflies; and might, perhaps, have enriched their cabinets with some unknown captives.

This reference to the 'torturers of butterflies' might be taken as a light allusion to the many amateur naturalists of the day, did it not find an echo in one of Beckford's most powerful and moving stories, *The Tale of Darianoc*, in which a young man shows his

---

² Beckford's daughter Susan married the 10th Duke of Hamilton. His mother had been a Hamilton, the granddaughter of the sixth Earl of Abercorn.
³ For the tour with Cozens see Shaffer 1997, 226-232.
⁴ Beckford [1783] 1971, 106. For a wider context of Beckford's Italian journey, see Pfister 1996.

earliest proclivity towards evil by tearing off one wing of butterflies in order to prevent their flying away, and then presenting them as gifts to a young girl he wished to woo. Leaving the girl behind he then passes into a steep mountain range and finds the portal to hell.[5] This portal leads him into the grand and sombre architecture of hell. "The grandeur of the settings is matched by the growth of the propensity to evil in the boy Darianoc; as the settings gain a grip on him they are projected into external powers which reflect desires hitherto concealed even from himself and from which he cannot escape."[6]

Beckford approached Venice through a grim pass, "rocky and tremendous", guarded by a fortress belonging to the Empress of Austria:

> A black vapour...completed the terror of the prospect, which I shall never forget. For two or three leagues, it continued much in the same style; cliffs, nearly perpendicular, on both sides, and the Brenta foaming and thundering below.[7]

The unusual landscape, at once a prison and a battlefield, is reminiscent of Milton's hellish legions' terrain, and Beckford underscores the "terror of the prospect":

> There is no attaining this exalted hold[the fortress], but by the means of a cord let down many fathoms by the soldiers, who live in dens and caverns, which serve also as arsenals, and magazines for powder, whose mysteries I declined prying into, their approach being a little too aerial for my earthly frame.[8]

As at last he emerges from this pass, he passes into another land, apparently a land of pleasure and freedom, marked by an architectural limen:

> Passing under a Doric gateway we crossed the chief part of this town in the way to our locanda, pleasantly situated, and commanding a level green, where people walk and eat ices by moonlight.

He finds himself in a delicious twilight – always one of his favourite ambiences, 'between worlds', conducive to fantasy and erotic reverie:

> Twilight coming on, this beautiful spot swarmed with people, sitting in circles upon the grass, refreshing themselves with cooling liquors, or lounging upon the bank beneath the towers.

Arriving in this circle he craves and instantly finds a *cicerone*, a guide, and his life in Venice is begun:

> They looked so free and happy, that I longed to be acquainted with them; and, by the interposition of a polite Venetian (who, though a perfect stranger, shewed me the most engaging marks of attention)

---

[5] This tale, like *Vathek*, and a number of other tales, was written in French, and has been published in Beckford, ed. Girard 1992, but without all the sequels and fragments that belong to it. It is of unknown date, but has been associated with a date between *A Vision*, possibly as early as 1777, and the writing of *Vathek* (1786), by the foremost French authority on Beckford, Parreaux, 1960, 178. Crucial passages in French and in English translation may be found in Shaffer 1994, 65-83.
[6] Shaffer 1994, 70.
[7] Beckford 1971, 107.
[8] Ibid.

was introduced to a group of the principal inhabitants. Our conversation ended in a promise to meet the next evening at a country house about a league from Bassano, and then to return together, and sing to the praise of Pachierotti their idol as well as mine.[9]

Gasparo Pacchierotti was the leading singer among the much prized castrati of the time, of which Venice was a centre. Beckford was to make a friend of him, and invited him to perform at Fonthill at his 21st birthday party. He is an emblem of Venetian style.

It is evident that Beckford's account is not merely geographical. As Franco Moretti has pointed out, metaphors tend to cluster at borders. The border is less a geographical demarcation than a 'mental frontier'. He gives a number of examples, including the staircase:

> Although metaphors still increase near the border, the latter is only seldom a geographical entity: usually, it belongs to a scale of experience for which the term 'geography' is wholly inappropriate. The staircase of the Gothic, the window in *Wuthering Heights*, the threshold in Dostoevsky, the pit in *Germinal*: here are some 'frontiers' of great metaphorical intensity – none of which is however a geographical border.[10]

Metaphors may serve a cognitive purpose, especially where the material is difficult to access or to express openly. As Ricoeur put it, metaphors become indispensable when we must "explore a referential field that is not directly accessible":

> Unable to fall back upon the interplay between reference and predication, the semantic aim has recourse to a network of predicates that already function in a familiar field of reference. This already constituted meaning is raised from its anchorage in an initial field of reference and cast into the new referential field which it will then work to delineate.[11]

Beckford uses a variety of geographical and architectural features in this metaphorical way throughout his work. But Beckford's imagination responded with especial strength to actual architecture. Note that Moretti's examples are in fact nearly all architectural; their metaphorical power derives from their obviously 'liminal' nature – window, door/threshold, pit or underground hole (cellar). They are entry points to other territories, other worlds. Such features recur in Beckford's writings: the mountain in the *Histoire de Darianoc* that marks the divide between utopian Gou-Gou and hell; the bridge into hell (with its Miltonic allusion); the island in the later fragment of this tale ("L'Isle de Saîlah"), a natural geographical feature commonly used to signify isolation, but more importantly here an invented frontier between strongly contrasting societies and religions. In *Vathek*, a breathtaking example is the abyss (at the edge of a cliff) into which the Caliph Vathek, having made a pact with the demon, succeeds in luring 50 boys to their destruction – again a geographical feature yet an almost mystic limen between a human/moral state and a state of damnation and despair. The anthropologist Victor Turner has described the anthropology and the theatre of this rite of unholy

---

[9] Ibid., 109.
[10] Moretti 1998, 46.
[11] Ricoeur [1975] 1979, 298f.

passage across the uncrossable moral frontier.[12] (A fascination with this passage is a strong element in Byron too, much influenced by Beckford.) Beckford also uses processions and ceremonies moving between or negotiating between worlds, usually located in a meaningful space, a road, a grand architectural square or court. And as we shall see, he deliberately violates sacred spaces or uses them inappropriately, sometimes by personal invasion, sometimes by architectural or stylistic miscegenation.

Venice lends itself with special rightness to this language of geography, borders, frontiers, modes of transition and passage of the impossible – because of its very situation, an impossible city on the moving waters; the underwater piers that hold it up; the boats/gondolas that ply between the different entities/islands, the ubiquitous bridges –; and to its metaphorical extensions. Moreover, its landscape is inescapably and overwhelmingly that of fantastic architecture. The Doge's dungeon dug within the Palace itself seems transgressive; the passage through the Bridge of Sighs a special (internal, covered, secret) bridge from one world to another, from freedom to imprisonment, punishment.

In Venice Beckford led a fashionable life, in the society of Countess Justine Wynne d'Orsini-Rosenberg and her entourage. The Countess, although born in Italy, had spent much of her childhood in England, and her young womanhood in France; by a strange turn of events, when her father died, her two brothers were adopted in England, while she and her sisters were thought to require a Catholic environment, and found themselves in a heady social round in Paris. Beckford was in a cosmopolitan and worldly company far from his religious mother and accompanied only by his discreet tutor. This was the kind of amoral international society that Henry James was to work to such effect.

In that company Beckford met the sixteen-year-old Cornaro, of an aristocratic and illustrious Venetian family, and his sister Maria. Behind the cover of a flirtation with Cornaro's sister he contracted a 'most enthusiastic friendship' – a passion – for the young man. They went on splendid outings by water, along the Brenta Riviera, where the great Palladian houses such as the Villa Foscari and the Villa Pisani staged sumptuous entertainments. Night fêtes were held while orchestras played in hidden bowers. Mme Rosenberg herself in an extended, journal-letter to her brother described the visit of the Prince of Würtemburg to Venice only a little later, in January 1782, and the rich reception he received, with gala theatre parties, masked balls, and the firework displays of the famed Venetian regatta, culminating in a brilliant farewell party at the Villa Pisani as he took his departure from Venice.[13] She catches the grandeur, the excess and the sheer excitement of the spectacles, each outdoing the last. One wonders if her prose had not been ignited by Beckford's, as his by her company in that setting.

To describe their evening excursions Beckford went a step beyond the brilliant processions and staged festivities of the aristocracy. He fashioned an erotic language borrowed from Oriental travels he had already read and taken notes from before leaving home, in particular the Chinese travels of the French Jesuits. The exotic oriental allusion led over a further boundary within the already exotic Venetian landscape. Certain words convey a clue leading into another world. The word 'pavilion' here and elsewhere in *Dreams* occurs in proximity to an imaginary Chinese landscape,

---

[12] Turner 1987, 36-58.

[13] Biblioteca Marziana, Tursi Collection, Venice.

again in the context of illicit sexuality. While in Venice, he went on a boating excursion along the river Brenta with Madame de Rosenberg, her count, and his own Cornaro, for whom he felt "a most enthusiastic friendship":

> Our navigation, the tranquil streams and cultivated banks, in short the whole landscape, had a sort of Chinese cast, which led me into Quang-Si and Quang-Tong. The variety of canes, reeds, and blossoming rushes shooting from the slopes, confirmed my fancies; and when I beheld the yellow nenupha expanding its broad leaves to the current, I thought of the Tao-Sé, and venerated one of the chief ingredients in their beverage of immortality.[14]

Behind this apparently casual observation of the nenuphar or water lily in an Italian landscape, which 'led' him mentally to the Southern Provinces of China, with their canals and waterways, lay a wealth of reading of descriptions of China, from as early as 1777, and a mass of manuscript notes he kept on them, including a number of passages on that fascinating plant.[15]

He recorded the climactic moment of its blossoming, which the Chinese row out in boats at night to watch:

> Towards the end of May – the stalks shooting up from the waters – and in a few days are Mantled with Leaves of the brightest green interspersed with vivid buds like Tulips that in expanding assume the appearance of enormous Roses.[16]

He writes of expeditions like his own in the watery regions of the Southern Provinces:

> The Empress and her attendants often resort by moonlight to those rural spots – where the Lien-hoa floats on the surface of the water – for of an evening their fragrance is diffused in every gale – [A]t that still hour nothing can be more pleasing than to hear the rippling of the current round their leaves – to see them gently agitated by the wind-growing down the stream – to crop their luxuriant clusters – Many a Chinese Bard has sung the praises of Lakes ennamel'd with this florid vegetation, and envies not the Lords of Heaven when roving with his beloved on their shore.[17]

Its aesthetic, sensuous, almost synaesthetic effect (where sound, sight, perfume, and movement are interchangeably blended) is matched by the special powers attributed to the plant:

> It is no wonder this species of Nenupha meets with such universal admiration since the Tao-tsée – have number'd it amongst those divine plants – which compose the legion of immortality.[18]

---

[14] Beckford 1971, 133.

[15] The 'nenuphar' may be derived from an Arabic-Persian word for 'blue lotus', but in its usage in all Romance languages refers to the white or yellow water lily.

[16] Bodleian Library, MS Beckford c. 55. f.14, f.27. This passage is a composite of two different folio entries, in which he appears to have translated the same passage slightly differently.

[17] MS Beckford c.55. fols 1-27. Beckford drew on a number of sources for his notes on the nenuphar: Athanasius Kircher, *La Chine illustrée*; Louis Du Halde, *Descriptions de la Chine*; Le Conte, *Mémoires de la Chine*; *Voyages de Gemelli Careri*; *Dictionnaire de la Martinière*: Article 'Peking'. Beckford absorbed all the major sources of European knowledge about China available at the time, and had the books in his own library. - See also Shaffer 1993b.

[18] MS. Beckford c.55. fols 1-27.

He had also gathered notes about the Tao-Tse, the sect who grew the nenuphar in a remote mountain region in their quest for immortality.

That evening at Fiesso near Venice, the evening of the water party, Beckford's party walked under a 'pavilion', while singing of a 'celestial harmony' transported him, and he woke from his 'trance' only at dawn. Eroticism and immortality are linked through this Chinese subtext which surfaces through Beckford's translations, paraphrases and collages from the French of the seventeenth-century travellers. So vivid are the original notes that one can hardly believe he is not there, in China; and one only knows he is not there by his occasionally breaking into a lament that he is not. His mental travelling which antedated his real travels is incorporated and inlaid in this way throughout *Dreams* and expresses erotic feelings for which no words are permissible. The most striking set piece is his pitching his pavilions, for himself and his lover, in the huge free yet prohibited space of the cupola of St Peter's in Rome.[19]

As his description of his first welcome in Venice shows, his *cicerone* led him straight to the admirers of the noted castrato, Pachierotti. The musical life of Venice provided another set of stimuli – and Beckford was a connoisseur of music, indeed himself both a performer and a composer, and was especially captivated by the castrati. These were among the most famous and sought after singers of eighteenth-century Europe, and Venice was a centre of them. Beckford became friendly with Pachierotti, went on a walking tour with him to Lucca, described in *Dreams*, and later invited him to sing at his 21st birthday party at Fonthill.

Finally he tore himself away from Venice and continued on his tour, of which the southernmost destination was the villa of Sir William and Lady Hamilton near Naples. This was the endpoint of the Grand Tour for many English visitors, most of whom did not continue on to Sicily. Hamilton, plenipotentiary to the Court of Naples, was a convivial diplomat, a collector, and a serious scientific observer of volcanic phenomena whose communications about the eruptions of Vesuvius were invaluable to the Royal Society. Thanks to a large-scale exhibition and colloquium at the British Museum in 1996, accompanied by an excellent catalogue, he is better known now for himself, rather than simply as the complaisant husband of that later Lady Hamilton, Emma, his second wife, who carried on with Lord Nelson.[20] At the time of Beckford's visits he was befriended by the first Lady Hamilton, a sensitive woman and a gifted musician, who learning of his Venetian escapades tried to wean him from, in her words, his "criminal passion". They were genuinely attached to one another, and their correspondence is another of the exchanges that make Beckford's letters as moving as they are dramatic.

There can be little doubt that Venice represented a confirmation of his strong tendency to be drawn to boys, which had already manifested itself several times (to our knowledge), first in his sentiments for the young William Courtenay (whom he had met first in 1779 when the boy was eleven), then for a young man in Geneva, and now

---

[19] On the Chinese imagery of 'pavilion' and 'pagoda' in relation to St Peter's, see Shaffer 1997, 226-232.

[20] Jenkins/Sloan 1996. This combines the colloquium papers on Hamilton and a catalogue of the exhibition. See also the account by one of Beckford's biographers, Fothergill 1969. Susan Sontag's novel, *The Volcano Lover*, has a chapter depicting Beckford and the first Lady Hamilton, as well as a full-blown treatment of Emma Hamilton and Lord Nelson.

for Cornaro. The 'rite of passage' theme had been sounded before, in veiled terms, in "A Vision", written in Geneva. The discussion with Lady Hamilton, and his decision to return to Venice, are an acknowledgement of his erotic nature. At the same time, and Beckford was scarcely unaware of it, the shared concern for his moral salvation was a mode of increasing the intensity of the relationship between the young man and the older woman. When he returned to England in September 1781, on the death of Lady Hamilton, he saw Courtenay again, and entered into an affair with his cousin's wife Louisa, in which his passion for the boy became a game between them, but a deadly game, as Louisa grew more serious. The letters he wrote to her during the second journey in Italy are intimate, open and taunting about his attachment to 'Kitty' Courtenay. These letters lie behind the great set pieces to Cozens which form *Dreams*.

This drama is foreshadowed in the letters he wrote to Venice from Naples. Notwithstanding his regard for Lady Hamilton, he wrote to Count Benincasa, in Venice, in French, on 21 October 1780:

> Alas I can find no distractions. Fate gives me no peace. Landscapes and the splendours of the setting sun have lost their effect...One image alone possesses me and pursues me in a terrible way. In vain do I throw myself into Society – this image forever starts up before me. In vain do I try to come up to the great expectations formed of me – my words are cut short. I am halted in mid-career. This unique object is all I hope for – I am dead to everything else.[21]

Beckford writes to each correspondent in the tone – often in the language – most appropriate to him or her. He carried on extensive correspondence in French and Italian. He retained copies of some of his letters, and of those he received, some of which have accompanying drafts of his own replies, giving the gist with a brevity and metaphorical charge sometimes smoothed out in his final draft. He had fair copies made of some of the exchanges; he sometimes rewrote his earlier letters at a later date while having the fair copies made. A completer picture of his Grand Tour can be pieced together from the letters contemporary with his travels that he did not write for or include in *Dreams*.

It is typical of him that we find among his papers an extract from a French letter to the 'Duchesse de S.C.', 6th Jan 1781, on the reverse side of a draft to Lady Hamilton, 29 December 1780. Having returned to Venice in December 1780, despite Lady Hamilton's attempts to deflect him, his serious letter promising reform to Lady Hamilton is belied by the louche letter to the Duchess:

> I idle away my mornings in my gondola, wrapped up in furs, reading and making calls. My body is frozen [from the winter cold], but my ardent imagination wanders in the Indies and frolics in the rays of its own sun. The night is spent in cafés and at the opera, where Bertoni's voluptuous music, supported by the artistry of the world's finest singer, makes me more than ever effeminate.[22]

Again he calls on a still more exotic country – the Indies – to express the sensous wanderings of his imagination; both the North ('furs') and the South ('rays') are places

---

[21] Quoted in Alexander 1962, 75f. French originals in MS in Bodleian.
[22] Letter to the Duchess de S.C.

of his imagination discovered within Venice. The singer was again the most admired of the castrati, Pacchierotti; the opera was *Quinto Fabio* by F.B. Bertoni.[23]

He writes on 12 March 1781 to Mme Rosenberg of a strange dream:

> Yesterday in my troubled dreams, I thought I saw your Adriatic Sea under a blood-red moon. I saw the porticos of that dark palace which is only too well known to us, hung with mourning crêpe. The voice of Lamentation was heard. I was being called. I ran up. I was about to touch the blond head of – when a dagger pierced my heart. I awoke with a piercing cry, bathed in a mortal sweat.[24]

Despite the context of his passion here to one who knew of it and played hostess to it, we are reminded again of the architectural strand that twined itself into his descriptive style in Venice. The visual stimulus in this case is Piranesi.

Piranesi was of prime importance for Beckford's personal style and for his links with later Romanticism, especially Coleridge and DeQuincey, and their French counterparts.[25] The images with their associated feeling tones that Beckford developed from Piranesi continued to have a powerful presence in French poetry down through the surrealists.[26]

In *Dreams* he had already invoked Piranesi by name in describing the landscape of the Rhine:

> Our roadside was lined with beggarly children, high convent-walls, and scarecrow crucifixes; lubberly monks, dejected peasants, and all the delights of Catholicism. Such scenery not engaging a great share of my attention, I kept gazing at the azure, irregular mountains, which bounded our view; and, in thought, was already transported to their summits. Various are the prospects I surveyed from this imaginary exaltation, and innumerable the chimeras which trotted in my brain. Mounted on these fantastic quadrupeds, I shot swiftly from rock to rock, and built castles, in the style of Piranesi, upon most of their pinnacles. The magnificence and variety of my aerial towers, hindered my thinking the way long.[27]

Thus actual travel became the occasion for mental travel in which the well-stocked mind of the traveller constructed his own landscape, sometimes merely whimsically, but gradually refashioning the raw materials of familiar Grand-Tour topoi into new modes of visual encounter with inner landscapes. The playfulness of this passage, at the start of his journey, deepened into the shock of encounter with the images of inner compulsion.

Beckford's *Dreams* gives an account of his experience in Venice, Piranesi's birthplace, and on the site of the fearsome prisons inside the Doge's Palace, which he links explicitly to Piranesi's engravings:

---

[23] Heriot, *Castrati in Opera*, quoted in Alexander; F.G. Bertoni (1728-1813) was well-known at the time.

[24] Alexander 1962, 77.

[25] See Shaffer 1993a, 123ff.; for a discussion of Beckford's priority, and probable influence on, Coleridge's and De Quincey's interpretation of Piranesi's imaginary prisons as exemplified in *Carceri*, plate VII.

[26] See Keller 1966.

[27] Beckford 1971, 82f

...I left the courts; and stepping into my bark, was rowed down a canal, over which the lofty vaults of the palace cast a tremendous shade. Beneath these fatal waters, the dungeons I have been speaking of, are situated. There, the wretches lie marking the sound of the oars, and counting the free passage of every gondola. Above, a marble bridge, of bold majestic architecture, joins the highest part of the prisons to the secret galleries of the palace; from whence criminals are conducted over the arch, to a cruel and mysterious death. I shuddered whilst passing below; and believe it is not without cause, this structure is named PONTE DEI SOSPIRI. Horrors and dismal prospects haunted my fancy upon my return. I could not dine in peace, so strongly was my imagination affected; but, snatching my pencil, I drew chasms and subterraneous hollows, the domain of fear and torture, with chains, racks, wheels, and dreadful engines in the style of Piranesi.[28]

This passage of Beckford formulates in words the immediate effect of 'Gothic' terror that was ascribed to Piranesi's late reworking of his *Prisons* drawings and foreshadows the use of the imagery of the bridge and the stair by English and then French Romantic poets. As De Quincey wrote, in a much better-known passage, in the *Confessions of an English Opium Eater*:

Many years ago, when I was looking over Piranesi's *Antiquities of Rome*, Coleridge, then standing by, described to me a set of plates from that artist, called his *Dreams*, and which record the scenery of his own visions during the delirium of a fever. Some of these (I describe only from memory of Coleridge's account) represented vast Gothic halls; on the floor of which stood all sorts of engines and machinery, wheels, cables, catapults, &c. &c. expressive of enormous power put forth and resistance overcome. Creeping along the sides of the walls, you perceived a staircase; and upon this, groping his way upwards was Piranesi himself: follow the stairs a little further, and you perceive it come to an abrupt termination, without any balustrade, and allowing no step onwards to him who had reached the extremity, except into the depths below. Whatever is to become of poor Piranesi, you suppose, at least, that his labours must in some way terminate here. But raise your eyes, and behold a second flight of stairs still higher: on which again Piranesi is perceived, by this time standing on the very brink of the abyss. Again elevate your eye, and a still more aerial flight is beheld: and again is poor Piranesi, busy on his aspiring labours: and so on, until the unfinished stairs and Piranesi both are lost in the upper gloom of the hall. With the same power of endless growth and self-reproduction did my architecture proceed in dreams. In the early stage of the malady, the splendours of my dreams were indeed chiefly architectural; and I beheld such pomp of cities and palaces as never yet was beheld by the waking eye, unless in the clouds.[29]

The work by Piranesi that Coleridge and De Quincey were looking at was the *Antichità romane (Antiquities of Rome)*; but the work Coleridge launched into a description of was the *Carceri d'invenzione (Imaginary Prisons)*.[30] Both consist of a series of plates, but are otherwise quite different from one another. One of the *Antichità*, Plate LVI, the 'Interior of Burial Vault' (Ill. 1), conveys a similar feeling of monumental and profound imprisonment, though without the dizzying upward sweep of the *Carceri*, especially Plate VII (Ill. 2). It may have been precisely the difference between them that set

---

[28] Beckford 1938, I, 98.
[29] De Quincey 1971, 105-f. In De Quincey's 1856 revision the passage differs in a number of small particulars, mainly stylistic.
[30] Piranesi's *Carceri* consisted of 14 plates of 1745, *Invenzioni capricci di carceri*, reworked and reissued with two new plates in the mid-1760's. Retitled they became *Carceri d' invenzione (Imaginary Prisons)* and in this form enjoyed an immense vogue.

Coleridge off. The assimilation of this material to 'the Gothic' has long been recognized as an important step in the advance of the Gothic revival.[31] Beckford's own sense of personal shame and dread may have been behind this reading of the 'interminable staircase', as Coleridge's shame at his opium habit engendered a need for punishment. Beckford's creative vision of the Piranesian landscape paved the way for the Romantic's assurance of its 'Gothic' nature.

Whereas Coleridge and DeQuincey were looking at a book, Beckford was recording direct experience in Piranesi's native place – not the Rome with whose views he had become so identified, but the place of his origin. Piranesi had died in 1779, and the obituaries had begun to create a legend about him. The fact that Piranesi's birthplace was Venice was either unknown or was ignored; through his long residence in Rome, and the fame of his *Vedute* and *Antichità* of Rome he was assumed to be Roman. One early obituary, by an adherent of the 'Greek' school, recalled that he had been born in Venice but only to gibe at him as a provincial who had brought his strange ways to the centre of art, Rome.[32] The first accurate biography of him was by a German, Albert Giesecke (1911), in which his Venetian training in the *capricci* of the school of Tiepolo begins to be explored.[33] Thus Beckford's association of him with the terrifying prisons of the Doge's palace has been credited with great acumen, as is Théophile Gautier's Venetian setting for Piranesi visions.[34]

Although Piranesi's recent death may have sharpened Beckford's awareness of his origins in Venice, returning the dead man to his native place in order to fix the character of his formative style was a mode of characterisation already established in the Lives of Beckford's imaginary painters in his first published work, *Biographical Memoirs of Extraordinary Painters* (1780). Moreover, his experience of Piranesi went back to his childhood, when his father collected and befriended Piranesi, who gained a very considerable reputation and clientele in England. In 1757 he was elected Hon Fellow of the Society of Antiquaries of London after publishing the *Antichità Romane*. He was most admired in England for his interiors, with the Egyptian and Etruscan motifs he championed against the 'Greek' party of Winckelmann and Robert Adam, especially his magnificent chimney-pieces, attaining great success. He dedicated his book *Vasi, Candelabri* to forty English collectors, including Beckford's father.

---

[31] Only one of the *Carceri* actually shows a Gothic arch, plate XIV. (See A. Robison, *Piranesi: Early Architectural Fantasies*, pp. 194 -5 for reproductions of plate XIV and a related drawing.)

[32] G.L. Bianconi, 'Elogio storico del Cavaliere Giambattista Piranesi celebre antiquario ed incisore di Roma', *Antologia Romana*, nos. 34-6, Feb. - Mar. 1779.

[33] Giesecke 1911. See also Giesecke's briefer account in Thieme-Becker (1933).

[34] See Poulet on Gautier, quoted in Keller.

Illustration 1

Illustration 2

William Beckford's own experience was often couched in terms of Piranesi's visual idiom; indeed, Piranesi is perhaps the deepest influence on the architectural fantasy that lay behind Beckford's own most characteristic visual inventions.

Beckford's description, often quoted, of his notorious three-day twenty-first birthday party, in the Egyptian Hall of the house his father had built, Fonthill Splendens, contains architectural images clearly linked to Piranesi, in particular the 'interminable staircase' whose top and bottom are undiscoverable. It was this image that was so important in Coleridge and De Quincey's account of *Le Carceri* published in the *Confessions of an English Opium Eater* (1821), and that was passed on to the French Romantics through Musset's translation of the *Confessions* (1828):

> The solid Egyptian Hall looked as if hewn out of a living rock – the line of apartments and apparently endless passages extending from it on either side were all vaulted – an interminable stair case, which when you looked down it – appeared as deep as the well in the pyramid – and when you looked up – was lost in vapour, led to suites of stately apartments gleaming with marble pavements – as polished as glass – and gawdy ceilings....[35]

He had, moreover, already used Piranesi's idiom to describe a mental landscape directly. The context is in the first instance literary. In perhaps the most powerful of his early stories, the *Histoire de Darianoc*, whose description of the entry into hell we have already cited as offering a parallel to Beckford's description of his entry into Venice, the Piranesian idiom is mediated through a Miltonic landscape of hell.[36] The story shows how a rebel in the Golden Age broke away into a 'gothic', Miltonic landscape of inner torment. The young Darianoc takes his way out of his idyllic Golden Age society to a freedom in an elective hell whose torment proves at each step to have been beyond his capacity to imagine what he was so boldly choosing.[37] There can be little doubt that this is a 'rite de passage' reflecting Beckford's own early experience; perhaps only the first of the Episodes, "Prince Alasi", registers equal pain. In "Alasi" the conflict between sexual goads and the claims of justice mounts to an almost tragic intensity.[38] Darianoc's dark 'Tour' of Enlightenment is described in an arresting series of images of the bridge strung over the dark abyss, and the Temple of the Serpent (the equivalent of Milton's building, Pandemonium, where Satan rules over the fallen gods, and himself turns serpent on his return from the tempting of Eve).

This is an expression of the inner landscape of the Miltonic sublime that had already begun to transform the traditional classical topography of entrances to hell in the Italian landscapes painted by British painters in Italy; again, there is a mutually reinforcing movement between the visual and literary evocations. In a wide survey of the styles of European sensibility in the eighteenth century and Romanticism, Jean

---

[35] Quoted in Lonsdale 1983, 3. For Beckford's complete description of the birthday celebrations, see Oliver 1932, 89-91. Note also Beckford's comparison of the Hall to "a Demon Temple deep beneath the earth set aside for tremendous mysteries", and "the intricacy of this vaulted labyrinth..."

[36] Beckford 1992, "Histoire de Darianoc", 181-234.

[37] Shaffer 1994, 65-83.

[38] See 'The Tale of Prince Alasi' in *The Episodes of Vathek*, trans. Sir Frank Marzials [1912] (Dedalus 1994). The translation from French into English waited until 1912; no edition yet exists in English of *Vathek* together with the *Episodes* as Beckford intended, although there are four in French.

Hagstrum singles Beckford out: "Beckford's tortured and haunted imagination could...produce memorably rhythmic prose and plastically conceived scenes that embody as well as illustrate sensibility."[39] It is often forgotten that Beckford lived on until 1844, and rewrote his *Dreams* – which had already passed into the Romantic imagination – for a new generation. The revised (and bowdlerised) version of his travels, *Italy, with Sketches of Spain and Portugal*, enjoyed critical and public acclaim on its publication in 1834. In France, Mallarmé, in his Preface to *Vathek* of 1876, kept alive the subterranean Beckford whose delicate and sinuous prose touched a moral nerve.[40]

In *A la Recherche* Proust wrote of Venice that the name *Venice* gives access to that city:

> 'I did not then represent to myself cities, landscapes, historical monuments, as more or less attractive pictures, cut out here and there of a substance that was common to them all, but looked on each of them as on an unknown thing, different in essence from all the rest, a thing for which my soul thirsted and which it would profit from knowing. How much more individual still was the character they assumed from being designated by names, names that were for themselves alone, proper names such as people have.'[41]

Proust is ironising his aesthete and dilettante Swann, a faint echo of a Beckfordian reputation; but for Beckford the name of Venice was not mere *Schall und Rauch*, it was an intense and inward focal point of his innovative visions in literary and visual style which reached as far as Proust himself.

Bibliography

Alexander, Boyd: *England's Wealthiest Son*. London 1962.
Beckford, William: "Letter to his mother", Bodleian Library, University of Oxford, MS Beckford d. 9.
Beckford, William: *Dreams, Waking Thoughts, and Incidents* [1783], ed. Robert G. Gemmett. Rutherford 1971.
Beckford, William: *Suite de Contes arabes*, ed. Didier Girard. Paris 1992.
Beckford, William: *Travel-Diaries*, 2 vols., ed. Guy Chapman. Cambridge 1938.
De Quincey, Thomas: *Confessions of an English Opium Eater*, ed. Alethea Hayter. Harmondsworth, repr. 1971 (first publ. 1821 in two parts in the *London Magazine*, IV, nos. xxi and xxii).
Fothergill, Brian: *Sir William Hamilton, Envoy Extraordinary*. London 1969.
Giesecke, Albert: *G.B. Piranesi* (Meister der Graphik, Bd. VI). Leipzig o.J., 1911.
Hagstrum, Jean: *Eros and Vision. The Restoration to Romanticism*. Evanston/Il. 1989.
Hillis Miller, J.: *Topographies*. Stanford, Ca. 1995.
Jenkins, Ian/Kim Sloan (eds.): *Vases and Volcanoes. Sir William Hamilton and His Collection*. London 1996.

---

[39] Hagstrum 1989, 61.
[40] Mallarmé 1876, "Préface" to Beckford, *Vathek*.
[41] Quoted in Hillis Miller 1995, 2f.

Keller, Luzius: *Piranèse et les romantiques français : le mythe des escaliers en spirale*. Paris 1966.
Lonsdale, Roger (ed.): "Introduction" to Beckford, *Vathek*. Oxford/New York 1983, 3.
Mallarmé, Stéphane: "Préface" to Beckford, *Vathek*. Paris 1876.
Moretti, Franco: *Atlas of the European Novel 1800-1900*. London/New York 1998.
Oliver, J.W.: *The Life of William Beckford*. London 1932.
Parreaux, André: *William Beckford, auteur de Vathek (1760-1844)*. Paris 1960.
Pfister, Manfred (ed.): *The Fatal Gift of Beauty. The Italies of British Travellers. An Annotated Anthology*. Amsterdam 1996.
Ricoeur, Paul: *Rule of Metaphor* [1975]. Toronto 1979.
Shaffer, Elinor S.: "Coleridge and the Object of Art", *The Wordsworth Circle*, XXI, No. 1 (Winter 1993), 117-128. [=1993a]
Shaffer, Elinor S.: "William Beckford's Transformation of Chinese and Pseudo-Chinese Tales". In: Chang, Han-liang (ed.): *Concepts of Literary Theory East and West*, Taiwan 1993, 399-440. [=1993b]
Shaffer, Elinor S.: "Milton's Hell: William Beckford's place in the graphic and the literary tradition". In: Low, Lisa/Anthony John Harding (eds.): *Milton, the Metaphysicals and Romanticism*. Cambridge 1994, 65-83.
Shaffer, Elinor S.: "'To remind us of China' - William Beckford, Mental Traveller on the Grand Tour: The Construction of Significance in Landscape". In: Chard, C./H. Langdon (eds.): *Transports: Travel, Pleasure, and Imaginary Geography, 1600-1830*, New Haven 1997, 207-242.
Turner, Victor: "Are there Universals of Performance?". In: *Comparative Criticism* 9. Cambridge 1987, 36-58.

Barbara Schaff

Venetian Views and Voices in Radcliffe's *The Mysteries of Udolpho* and Braddon's *The Venetians*

When Ann Radcliffe used Venice as a setting for a relatively short episode in her gothic novel *The Mysteries of Udolpho* (1794), she created a myth of origin for the many later literary imaginings of Venice in the 19th century. Her image of Venice as an enchanted place, where fear and desire, love and death are closely bound together, was taken up and reproduced in infinite versions[1] until it had, by the time Mary Elizabeth Braddon wrote her sensational novel *The Venetians* (1892), coagulated into a worn-out cliché. Different as they are, Radcliffe's and Braddon's novels are linked by more than just the theatrical Venetian setting. Both the gothic and the sensational novel rework the conventions and the assumptions of the ideal of the proper feminine and both discuss issues of feminine confinement and fear. Apart from the obvious intertextual relations between the texts - Braddon uses the Radcliffean image of a nightly Venice for her initial setting - both novels link their negotiations of the question of female authorship and autonomy to singing Venetian women, presenting them as exemplary models of female self-assertiveness. Likewise both novels create a stage-like and ambiguous Venice which relates to patriarchal dominance as well as to fantasies of female liberty and subject position. The way in which Radcliffe and Braddon foreground views of Venice points to the relation between spectator and spectacle and finally refers to questions of gender and authorship.

1. Blurred visions: Venice in *The Mysteries of Udolpho*

The relatively short episode in Venice (it consists of approximately 50 pages of a novel which is 670 pages long) has not yet been studied very closely in secondary literature, although it already introduces many significant motives and features of the later Udolpho episode. The representation of Venice and Venetian places in the novel is marked by a very strong ambiguity. Houses and places in Radcliffe's novel *The Mysteries of Udolpho* are usually closely linked with notions of patriarchal power and female dependence. Whereas La Vallée, Emily de St.Aubert's childhood home, represents security, taste and comfort, the grim castle Udolpho, La Vallée's dark opposite, represents danger, confinement and male violence. Venice in a way anticipates the horrors of Udolpho, because it is related to images of confinement and imprisonment, but it is also a space which incites Emily to develop fantasies of female autonomy, power and creativity. The traditional gothic qualities, i.e. the claustrophobic and horrifying connotations of a setting, are in this Venetian sequence closely tied to Montoni's palace on the grand canal, a place which in a very similar way to the castle

---

[1] Tanner 1992, 19.

of Udolpho functions as a metonymy of its owner.[2] When Emily arrives at Montoni's palace on the grand canal, she is impressed by the magnificent style and noble appearance of the place, which seem to disarm Emily's fears that Montoni has married her aunt only because of his own financial needs. But it soon becomes clear that the splendour of the place is only a surface feature. On the way to her own apartment - which, according to gothic conventions means long passages and endlessly winding corridors - she observes that under the mask of the outward luxury there is dampness, disrepair and dilapidation. In this aspect the house bears witness not only to the taste and ambition of its owner, but also to his character and moral values. Hidden under the glittering outward appearance of this mini-Udolpho lurks the evil reality which is personified in the figure of Montoni's criminal friend Orsino who, as the reader will learn later in novel, has committed a murder and is therefore hidden and protected by Montoni in his house.

Likewise, Emily's own room, which is described as "spacious, desolate and lofty" (179)[3] conveys the spatial ambiguity which anticipates the description of Udolpho. On the one hand, it represents a place of refuge and security, whereto Emily withdraws from the threatening outside world. On the other hand, its dark and gloomy aspects enhance Emily's feeling of imprisonment. It is a strange room, whose boundaries seem to be obscured and whose seeming limitlessness is as threatening to Emily as its confining aspect. A room without clearly defined firm walls is a room which is out of control. Montoni's power and desire to marry her to the hateful count Morano, notwithstanding her steady refusal, seems to Emily as unlimited as her room. Montoni's House is a nightmarish trap from which she cannot escape: When he informs her that she will be married to her suitor the next morning, Emily is virtually paralysed in this patriarchal power centre. She is too frightened to move: "she trembled to look into the obscurity of her spacious chamber and feared not what; a state of mind, which continued so long, that she would have called Annette, her aunt's woman, had her fears permitted her to rise from her chair, and to cross the apartment" (221). The notion of paralysis is related to nearly all of Emily's movements in Venice that are connected with either Montoni or Morano. Emily does not seem to be able to walk on her own and she is continually being led from the house to the gondola and back - a metaphor for the men's control and power over her body. The gondola Emily sits in during her tours through the Venetian canals is a space which equally imprisons her and from which she cannot escape. In a most claustrophobic situation Emily sits alone in a boat together with Montoni and Morano and both men urge her to consent to Morano's wish for her to marry him. But these notions of threatening spatial confinement are nearly always counteracted by Emily's capability to let her gaze wander even if she herself cannot. For all Radcliffean heroines who suffer from imprisonment, windows, visions and views are extremely important as a counterbalancing feature. Emily's prison-like room at Montoni's Venetian palace, desolate as it is, is at least a room with a view over the wide, unconfined Adriatic and

---

[2] Berglund 1993, 32.
[3] Page numbers in brackets refer to Radcliffe, 1980.

it is Radcliffe's emphasis on Emily's different views of Venice, which subvert the notion of the heroine's helplessness and passive despondency.

Even though Montoni's Venetian palace is a symbol of male repressive power in its most sinister aspect, Venice itself is not. The city's links with the Adriatic as a wide and sublime space undermine the image of patriarchal power and control, which is represented through the figures of Montoni and count Morano and the symbol of Montoni's palace. Venice is not the first Italian city Emily sees, but it is the first which is described at length. Turin, Milan, Verona and Padua are only very briefly mentioned as having grand churches, palaces and views, but the narrator emphasizes the fact that neither Emily nor her aunt are allowed to enjoy the views but are hurried on by Montoni to Venice with the greatest rapidity. Thus, when the party finally arrives in Venice, Emily's expectations culminate: "Nothing", the narrator tells us, "could exceed Emily's admiration of her first view of Venice" (174). This view of Venice is marked with a strong unrealistic, fairy-tale-like tinge. Emily arrives in the evening, when the setting sun casts shadows and different colours on the architectural structures and the city and its reflection in the water are perceived as an apparition more than a material structure. Consequently, the imagined origin of the city is linked to supernatural forces – e.g. "the wand of an enchanter"(175) - and its description is rendered with the same "sublime" rhetoric as is the scenery of the Alps. Emily's view of Venice constantly relates to her emotions, thoughts and memories of her lover Valancourt and her dead father. The image of Venice is doubled by its reflection in the water and the city becomes a double space, a world above and a world below the water. Later in the Venetian episode Emily links gendered notions with both aspects of Venice - the architecture of Montoni's palace signifying a patriarchal space and the wide sea signifying a contrasting space of female autonomy. But these distinctions are never very strict and definite. In Emily's perspective both spaces sometimes seem to fuse and threaten each other. This merging of contrastive elements means that in this twilight zone there never is an absolute, self-contained power, hierarchy, system, relation, sex or gender. Everything in Venice is endangered by its mirror image, which dissolves all firm stabilities. In this "tremulous picture"(174) of a Venice reflected in the water all outlines are blurred, and beyond that the vision is dimmed by the shadows of the evening, which seem to enfold the city in a veil. The twilight makes it difficult to identify individual structures.

This setting of Emily's first encounter with Venice, the slow approach towards the city in a boat across the moon-lit sea, does not only distance the narrative from reality, it also relates to conventions of perception which are typical of the gothic novel. The view of Venice is only presented from Emily's perspective, and far more important than the romantic setting itself is Emily's perception of it. It is significant that almost all of the action in Venice takes place at night, and that all the nightly spectacles Emily sees - either from the balcony of Montoni's mansion or from the boat - are rendered as being either poetical visions or fanciful images of an unreal, dreamlike quality. Marilyn Butler has pointed out that this feeling of unreality makes it possible for Radcliffe to emphasize Emily's position of helplessness, loss of control and "gothic" nightmare.[4] But one could also argue that Radcliffe uses her heroine's way of seeing things unclearly in order to articulate her subject position as a female spectator.

As a metaphor, this blurred vision refers to the eighteenth-century discourse of gendered modes of perception, where the image of the veil is used to stigmatize the female view as unclear and non-rational.[5] But it is exactly this mode of perception, the curious gaze through the veil, which Radcliffe's narrator declares to be most fascinating and attractive, and it is a distinctly female gaze: Montoni, the narrator assures us, "cared little about views of any kind" (171). Venice is the more appealing to Emily, because its vision is blurred, because it can't be categorized in simple binary oppositions and because it is secretive and dreamlike: an imagined image more than a real one. Emily's view of Venice is an attempt to look through the veil and perceive realities that are different from the patriarchal realities linked with Montoni. Her view of Venice is distinctly marked as a different female view and is thus linked to cultural female otherness. This perception of Venice subverts the traditional gendered notion of a male spectator and female spectacle, the culturally assigned role of the woman as the object of a man's gaze.[6] Here Emily occupies the position of the gazing subject; she has the authorial perspective, and if Venice appears to her like a dream-like vision, one could just as well say that she dreams, imagines and creates her own Venice. Emily never sees anything at all in Venice without immediately constructing her own fantasies of Venice as a result, sometimes even in the form of a poem. For the reader Venice becomes legible only through Emily's perspective.

A crucial scene in the Venetian sequence is the moment when Emily, on her first night in Venice, steps onto a balcony from which she looks down on the Venetian carnival. The narrator makes it clear from the start who is looking and who is being looked at. Emily assumes the position of the spectator who sees but is not seen; her position is behind a lattice and she takes care to throw on a veil before she steps out. Thus she reverses the conventional gendered code of the male voyeur and the female looked-at object. Again, Emily watches something she is not sure about and for which she has no rational explanation, "something like a procession floating on the light surface of the water" (178). This fantastical apparition is a nuptial scene, an allegorical presentation of Neptune taking Venice as his bride and the erotic, sensuous quality of the scene has a deep impact on Emily. She is now confronted with the underwater-aspect of Venice, which she interprets as an opposite world to the male-dominated world above. The sea is everything which the oppressive and limiting confines of the city are not. It is spacious, endless and definitely a feminine space, with "secret caves" and "coral bowers" (179) inhabited by sea-nymphs. Emily fantasizes about a democratic sisterhood of sea-nymphs, which would enable her to have full control over her desires, movements and actions - a space where she would not be paralysed anymore, but would be free to "plunge into the green wave and throw off the habit of mortality" (178).

---

[4] Butler 1980, 131.
[5] Schabert 1994, 117.
[6] Wolstenholme 1993, 12.

Venetian Views and Voices in Radcliffe's *Udolpho* and Braddon's *The Venetians*

This vision and later, in her room, the view of the sea stimulate one of Emily's most powerful poems, which is a creative expression of Emily's desires and needs. In this poem she sketches a world where female bonding constitutes a powerful community and she herself identifies with the autonomous sea nymph, who has the power to guide men and their ships safely through the waves; thus subverting the traditional role concept of the male hero who saves the girl from danger. In an escapist fantasy Emily explores her own subconscious, for which the underwater world is a metaphor and contrasts her own dependency and helplessness with the maritime visions of a world where women are free to roam about. That even this underwater space is not paradise but is endangered by male violence, is mediated through the figure of Neptune, who, as a symbol of male authority, binds the nymph to rocks and punishes her for saving the seamen. Neptune and Montoni literally merge into one figure when only a few lines after the poem Montoni is described with the same imagery as Neptune - as somebody delighting in tempests "which wreck the happiness of others" (182). In a way these underwater visions anticipate the later events in Udolpho; like Udolpho the realm of the deep sea is a metaphor for Emily's subconscious and the threat of patriarchal power is inherent in both.

A main issue of this poem is the detailed description of the nymph's voice, to which her power is mainly attached. It is a sweet and magic voice, which charms as well as terrifies the sailors who listen to it and it is a potent voice which is obeyed by dolphins and the air spirits. This power of the female voice is a central issue in the Venetian sequence of *The Mysteries of Udolpho*. A voice can function as powerfully as a sublime view and Radcliffe introduces several female singers with conspicuously enchanting voices to emphasize its importance. The first voice Emily hears on her approach to Venice is a female voice and in contrast to the views of Venice, which are blurred and difficult to differentiate, the voices of Venice are clear and "flow", as the narrator assures us, "from no feigned sensibility" (175). As much as the view of Venice becomes Emily's construction, her own image, the voice of Venice does not. It is always considered to be the true expression of the singer's mind and emotions and the sounds are, declares Emily "strains from the heart" (175). There are three different female singers in the Venetian sequence: an anonymous singer at the beginning, a girl with a guitar who leads a group of dancers and musicians in front of Montoni's palazzo and a young lady called Signora Herminia, who, during a dinner party given by Montoni, entertains the guests with singing and lute playing. Signora Herminia represents a much admired model of ideal femininity for Emily. Her grace and beauty as well as her sincere emotions fulfil the standard of true womanliness. But her rich and powerful voice in a way does not. She starts to sing and does not care in the least who sits around and listens. Signora Herminia does not sing to please others but, unconscious of the power of her voice, she sings with "easy gaiety, as if she had been alone" (188) for herself alone. She is entirely independent of her audience and whereas Emily takes great care to throw a veil over herself whenever she goes out, Signora Herminia throws her veil back when she starts to sing, thus signifying that she is not afraid to show herself and her emotions. Emily however, when she and her party are rowed around in Montoni's gondola, fears to betray her own emotions by singing and carefully chooses a deceptively "gay" song to masquerade her feelings. Emily is far more in need of a protecting veil for herself than the Venetian women who are traditionally connected with masques and masquerades, but who in this text seem to be in no need of protecting veils for their emotions, desires and identities.

The singing Venetian women represent a self-contained, powerful femininity which is denied to Emily. They sing their songs fearlessly and passionately. Their voices are marked as full of true emotions and as sexually seductive voices, a quality which Emily can only claim for herself in her underwater fantasy in the guise of a sea nymph. Emily will be taken through many more dark passages and it will mean much more metaphorical veiling and unveiling of bodies in the novel, until near the end of the novel the possibilities of her own passionate femininity are revealed to her.

2. Venice on stage: Mary Elizabeth Braddon's novel *The Venetians*

Almost exactly hundred years after Radcliffe, Mary Elizabeth Braddon resumes the image of the Venetian singer and focuses upon it as the centre of her sensational novel *The Venetians*. I will very briefly summarize the story, because it is one of Braddon's lesser known novels and has not been republished for some years.
The story is situated in Braddon's contemporary Venice, that is in the years 1885-1892. John Vansittart, a young Englishman with money and leisure, is on the Grand Tour. In Venice he meets Fiordelisa, a young beautiful Venetian and former poor lace maker, who is now being trained as a singer. He entertains her during the carnival, but, as the narrator explicitly states, he is not in love with her. On their way home from the opera Vansittart buys her a couple of cheap bead necklaces and, without an obvious purpose, a dagger for himself. He then takes her to the Caffè Florian for a coffee where he is assaulted by another Englishman who claims Fiordelisa is his girl. They fight, Vansittart stabs the other with his dagger and escapes the crowd by jumping into the canal. He takes a ship home to England, meets a very young, poor, blonde and angelic woman whom he marries. After some time he visits the opera in London and sees Fiordelisa on the stage. He goes to see her after the performance and because Fiordelisa is the only witness to his crime and because he has a very bad conscience, he promises to provide her with money and a flat, if she promises never to tell anybody about his crime. Fiordelisa, who loves him from her heart, now stays in London with her aunt and her little son by the dead Englishman and becomes a much celebrated opera star. It is then revealed to Vansittart that the man he had murdered was in fact the beloved (albeit morally questionable) lost brother of his wife. Although he does all he can to keep this knowledge from her, she, whose name of course is Eve, in the end discovers the secret. Eve then rejects her husband, because she could not possibly live with the murderer of her brother, even though she loved him. Vansittart goes to Africa, and she herself becomes consumptive and travels to Venice to find the grave of her brother before her own death. Shortly before she dies she calls Vansittart to Venice and they are reconciled.

Venetian Views and Voices in Radcliffe's *Udolpho* and Braddon's *The Venetians*

Braddon starts her novel with the already well-established stereotype of a nightly Venetian setting. All the necessary ingredients are there, it is carnival time, the fronts of the palaces are illumined with a "rosy glow", "the gondolas are floating in a golden haze" (7) and, a little later, the moon and the stars change the city and the lagoon "into something supernal, unimaginable, dreamlike" (17).[7] But unlike Radcliffe, who used a historically distanced Venice, Braddon shows a contemporary Venice, which directly contrasts with contemporary England. The otherness of Venice and Venetian femininity is presented as a positive counter image to English decadence, whose representative is the central figure of the narrative, John Vansittart.

For the English tourist Vansittart Venice is a well-known place. He knows the literary Venice - "The sands over which Byron used to ride" (14) - and he knows the stones of Venice "almost as well as Ruskin" (16). And, young and unmarried as he is, he knows what he wants in Venice: "being free to wander" (16), and some "casual rambling" (16). Venice seems to be the right place for safe sexual encounters without any obligations: "He was rich idle, alone in Venice, and he thought it was his right to amuse himself to the uttermost at this Carnival season" (14). Therefore he invites Fiordelisa into his gondola, for dinner and further entertainments. Vansittart, as the narrative argues, uses the city and the woman in a perverse and exploitative way. Idle and without any employment or vocation he represents the improper masculine, the heartless, class-conscious young gentleman, the philandering grand tourist. And it seems that just at this point of the narrative, when the narrator has explicitly shown that Vansittart has no serious concern for the Venetian girl and that no romance is going to develop, Venice stops being readable to him. The city puts up more and more resistance to him, his romantic views are closed and Vansittart is lost. He plans to get rid of the girl after the opera, but as there is no coach, he has to escort her home. Vansittart is hardly able to follow Fiordelisa and he does not know "by which particular windings of the labyrinth" (20) they finally arrive at a shop which is described as having all the attributes of a really horrifying "gothic" place. Here Vansittart buys the necklace and the fatal dagger and, as this place marks the beginning of his doom, it is significantly described in gothic terms as a half Venetian, half Moorish place, whose owner - with a "Jewish nose" (21) - is compared to a spider, waiting in his web for flies. The maze of Venice and the web is the same: a trap were the male tourist is caught.[8] One nearly gets the feeling that here Braddon parodies the gothic Venetian setting. In this image the gothic discourse of female confinement and masculine power is reversed - it is the exploring and exploiting male tourist, who loses his sovereignty and unwillingly becomes involved in violence and murder. From the moment Vansittart enters the shop, he is no longer in control neither of his desires, nor of the place. Consequently, the purchase of the dagger is narrated as being merely

---

[7] All further page numbers in brackets refer to Braddon, 1892.
[8] For a detailed analysis of the tourist condition see Virginia Richter's contribution to this volume. Richter argues that tourism can be defined as a periodical crossing of a border to a realm with a different reality status, but that literature often transforms this crossing of boundaries into an irreversible process. In Braddon's novel it is Vansittart's exploiting behaviour towards Venice and Fiordelisa as an allegory of the city, which completely alters his life.

accidental. When after the murder Vansittart escapes onto a steamer sailing to Alexandria, he sadly reflects upon what he has lost and he personifies Venice as his beautiful lost love, "fading like a vision of the night". In his last view of Venice the city is staged as a feminine space, whose interiority Vansittart had tried to violate, but which has resisted, a feminine space which has expelled the intruder and successfully defended itself.

I have shown that Radcliffe used images of singing Venetian women as representatives of an alternative passionate, self-contained and independent femininity - an ideal, which is, however, not available for the English heroine. Whereas in Radcliffe's novel these alternatives are only carefully hinted at, Braddon focuses this role model centrally and uses it in the triangular pattern of the novel - one man between two women - to juxtapose the English woman with the Venetian singer. Much of the pleasure one gets from reading this novel results from Braddon's way of satirising and undermining the conventional national and gender stereotypes. The blonde English woman turns out not to be quite so angelic in the end - having had incestuous desires towards her brother - and the dark Venetian singer, whom London society unjustly labels as a prostitute, turns out to be more honest and compassionate than her English counterpart. In her representation Braddon combines moral and aesthetic categories to undermine the dominant ideas and images of Victorian femininity. Her heroine is an active, warm-hearted, self-assertive and, in the course of the novel, more and more independent woman, who earns her own living respectably and represents autonomous femininity as well as caring and feeling motherhood.

At the beginning of the novel Fiordelisa is represented in a very voyeuristic mode through different perspectives[9]. She is first shown through the eyes of the manager of the hotel Danieli, who, on seeing Vansittart and Fiordelisa, instantaneously denies her access to the hotel. His disdainful view stigmatizes Fiordelisa as a fallen woman. In this she can be read as an allegory of Venice, because since the fall of the Republic, Venice had been represented in literature in increasingly misogynistic shades as a prostitute.[10] Braddon marks this view of Venice as another typical male gaze which, just like Vansittart's view of Venice, characterizes the dominant discourse. Vansittart's perspective then depicts her – "this flower of a day, this beautiful stranger" (18) – as the object of his erotic desire, towards whom he feels neither love nor responsibility.

Against these uncaring and superficial male views Braddon sets the sympathetic gaze of the narrator. This perception, which opposes the men's outer perspective, is the narrator's inner perspective, who shows Fiordelisa as a young, naive, uneducated and emotionally honest woman, who comes from a very low social background and hopes to ameliorate her situation by making a successful career as an opera singer. The foregrounding of the gaze at the beginning of the novel hints at the inherent theatricality of Venice and these different ways of seeing Fiordelisa refer not only to

---

[9] For the importance of the gaze in Braddon's novels see Pykett 1992, 99f.
[10] Pemble 1995, 112ff.

Through these different gazes, Fiordelisa is introduced above all as a glittering spectacle and desired object of the male gaze, and Braddon in the further course of the novel very cleverly undermines this dominant discourse of feminine representation, when she lets her heroine self-assertively stage herself as a spectacle. In this, Fiordelisa recovers her subject position as a performing artist. When Fiordelisa becomes a celebrated opera singer in London, she fully understands the importance of the staging of femininity. In her own home she dresses almost always in black and in very simple clothes; but on the stage she wears the most glittering dresses and precious jewels. She had bought these jewels with her first earned money and they are not only ornaments but also a security investment for the future. They are the only luxury she allows herself. By everybody else in the novel these jewels are falsely interpreted as gifts from a lover and thus they brand her as a prostitute. Through these jewels, her body becomes a sign which is misread by the characters within the text. To them, her body is a fantasy for the projection of masculine erotic desires. In this, Braddon once more links her figure to stereotypical images of Venice as a fallen woman, as a rotting body under an alluring mask. But in looking, together with her readers, behind the facade and pretences of the opera singer, Braddon recovers for Fiordelisa and for Venice many positive attributes male writers of the late 19th century were unwilling to link with Venice, such as truthfulness and honesty, and thus makes her readers interpret Fiordelisa's jewels differently as a sign for female independence.

One aspect of Fiordelisa, however, which always remains resistant to speculations and misreadings, is her voice. Her voice is something which is her own capital, something which cannot be violated and slandered. Fiordelisa's voice is constructed as being always true and beautiful. It never signifies ambiguities and always expresses passion and vitality - something the nearly choked English women in the novel fail to do. Unlike a body, which can be represented and read or misread in the text, the voice cannot. It is beyond representation in a written text and thus it cannot deceive. The voice of the singer is the language of immediate presence only and its passion and truthfulness are never questioned. Fiordelisa's voice can evade the male gaze and possessiveness, and it is this voice which gives her independence and autonomy.

The significance of the female voice eventually links Braddon's novel with the Venetian episode in *The Mysteries of Udolpho*. In using the female Italian voice as a metaphor for female wholeness and self-assertiveness, both Radcliffe and Braddon integrate their constructions in a long female poetic tradition, which has represented Italy as a utopian, feminine, artistic, emotional and maternal country as opposed to patriarchal England.

The one novel, which epitomizes this view of Italy, and which Mary Elizabeth Braddon must certainly have known, is Mme de Staël's *Corinne*. Braddon, having been an actress herself, often devised the central female figure of a novel as an actress or singer[11]. Even if there are no direct references to *Corinne* in *The Venetians*, de Staël's heroine undeniably functions as a role model for the conception of Fiordelisa. Braddon uses a very similar configuration - Fiordelisa, like Corinne, is passionate and highly acclaimed as a performing artist and, like Corinne, she uncompromisingly loves an Englishman who then marries an English woman. But whereas Corinne represents complete female artistic autonomy up to the ultimate consequence of her death, the figure of Fiordelisa in the end has to submit to Victorian hierarchical notions of gender. Braddon sees no way to integrate de Staël's far-reaching scheme of feminine intellect, passion, moral superiority and artistic autonomy into her representation of the Venetian singer. Fiordelisa follows Corinne in so far as she remains true to her love and her art. But unlike Corinne, who acts as a female mentor for her lover and opens up for him a wide range of knowledge and experience, Fiordelisa, notwithstanding her final wealth and success, remains the uncultivated and unrefined child of nature who, in the eyes of Vansittart as well as in the eyes of the narrator, could never be an equal partner for an educated Englishman. In this, Vansittart's view and the narrator's view are not so different after all.

Bibliography

Berglund, Birgitta: *Woman's whole existence. The House as an Image in the novels of Ann Radcliffe, Mary Wollstonecraft and Jane Austen.* Lund 1993.

Braddon, Mary Elizabeth: *The Venetians.* London 1892.

Butler, Marilyn: "The Woman at the Window: Ann Radcliffe in the Novels of Mary Wollstonecraft and Jane Austen". In: *Gender and Literary Voice.* New York/London 1980, 128-148.

Ellis, Kate Ferguson: *The Contested Castle: Gothic Novels and the Subversion of domestic ideology.* Urbana 1989.

Pemble, John: *Venice Rediscovered.* Oxford 1995.

Pykett, Lynn: *The "Improper Feminine". The Women's Sensation Novel and the New Woman.* London 1992.

Pykett, Lynn: *The Sensation Novel. From the Woman in White to the Moonstone.* Plymouth 1994.

Radcliffe, Ann: *The Mysteries of Udolpho* (1794). Oxford 1980.

Ross, Michael: *Storied Cities: Literary imaginings of Florence, Venice and Rome.* Westport 1994.

Schabert, Ina: "Amazonen der Feder und verschleierte Ladies: Schreibende Frauen im England der Aufklärung und der nachaufklärerischen Zeit". In: Schabert, Ina und Schaff, Barbara (eds.): *Autorschaft. Genus und Genie in der Zeit um 1800.* Berlin 1994, 105-123

Tanner, Tony: *Venice Desired.* Oxford 1992.

Weissmann-Orlowski, E.: *Das Weibliche und die Unmöglichkeit seiner Integration.* Frankfurt a.M. 1997.

Wolstenholme, Susan: *Gothic (Re)visions. Writing Women as Reader.* New York 1993.

---

[11] Compare, for instance, her wider known novel *Aurora Floyd*.

Werner von Koppenfels

Sunset City - City of the Dead:
Venice and 19th Century Apocalyptic Imagination

1. Prelude / Postlude

The following is an attempt to take a fresh look at an (admittedly) well-worn subject: Venice as an icon of European romanticism and decadence. My literary frame of reference will be largely Anglo-French - naturally so for this particular topic, as I hope to demonstrate with the help of a generous sprinkling of quotations.

Let me start by taking the term 'decadence' literally, in order to extract some of its hidden apocalyptic meaning so dear to romantics and post-romantics. 'Decadence', in the etymological sense of the word, is the process of falling to a lower level, a vertical downward movement, gradual but irreversible. Falling cities, or as the *Waste Land* has it,

> Falling towers
> Jerusalem Athens Alexandria
> Vienna London (372ff.),

tend to be visions of doomed civilizations, since city and civilization share a common lexical root. The fall of historical pride and artistic splendour is a spectacle on the grand scale, a sublime fusion of beauty and terror. The *Revelation of St. John* presents us with its biblical prototype:

> Babylon the great is fallen, is fallen...alas, alas, that great city, that was clothed in fine linen, and purple, and scarlet, and decked with gold and precious stones, and pearls! ... Alas, alas, that great city, wherein were made rich all that had ships in the sea...
> And a mighty angel took up a stone like a great millstone, and cast it into the sea, saying: Thus with violence shall the great city Babylon be thrown down, and shall be found no more...
> (Rev. 18: 2; 16; 19; 21)

The fall of the "great whore that sitteth upon many waters" (*Rev.* 17: 1), queen, courtesan, and ruler of the sea, counterpart to that other golden city, the New Jerusalem, descending from heaven onto earth in John's vision, reads like a prophetic allegory of the doom of Venice, as it was envisaged or rather gloated over by Europe's romantic travellers in the 19th century.

2. A ruin amidst ruins: Venice as a Byronic state of mind

When the Serenissima, after a century of political sickliness, lost her ancient liberty, first to Napoleon in 1797, afterwards to Austria in 1815, there was heard quite a chorus of poetic lamentation and epitaphing. On the English side Wordsworth's compact and noble sonnet rhetoric of

> Men we are, and must grieve even when the shade
> Of that which once was great is passed away.[1]

contrasts with the more personal and passionate effusion of Byron in his "Ode on Venice":

> Oh Venice! Venice! when thy marble walls
>   Are level with the waters, there shall be
> A cry of nations o'er thy sunken halls,
>   A loud lament along the sweeping sea!
> If I, a northern wanderer, weep for thee,
> What should thy sons do?[2]

In Byron's poem of 1818, with its reflection on the ruinous state of the Venetian palaces and on the lethargy of its population under the „barbarian drum" of Austria, the present political fall of Venice is translated into its future material counterpart; a metaphorical descent, viewed not as a sudden cataclysm like that of the biblical millstone hurled into the sea, but as a slow submersion into stagnant water. Madame de Staël, in her influential *Corinne ou L'Italie* of 1807, had presented a rather subdued first view of Venice as *une ville submergée*.[3] Byron's present-day Venice is not the magically removed romantic City in the Sea but rather a moribund spot of civilization being sucked in by the surrounding marsh. The fourth Canto of *Childe Harold's Pilgrimage*, that grand and gloomy afterthought to a poetic bestseller, has Venice sinking "like a sea-weed, into whence she rose".[4] But for the Byron persona standing on the Bridge of Sighs - a purely metaphorical point of vantage - "To meditate amongst decay, and stand/ A ruin amidst ruins" (st.1), decay becomes the revelation of supreme beauty experienced in an epiphany of its transience. The romantic death-wish (Byron himself wanted to be buried on the Lido, as it were with a posthumous view of the dying city[5]) finds its aesthetic correlative in a matchless union of glory and decay. This is how Harold metonymically addresses the mirror-image of Venice, ruinous Italy:

> Even in thy desart, what is like to thee?
> Thy very weeds are beautiful, thy waste
> More rich than other climes' fertility;
> Thy wreck a glory, and thy ruin graced
> With an immaculate charm...   (st. 26)

---

[1] "On the Extinction of the Venetian Republic" (c. 1802), v. 13f; in Wordsworth 1950, 242.
[2] Byron 1980-1993, vol. 4, 201.
[3] De Staël 1886, 354 (Book XV, ch. 7).
[4] Byron 1980-1993, vol. 2, 128.
[5] Letter to John Murray of June 7, 1819: "I hope, whoever may survive me, and shall see me put in the foreigner's burying Ground at the Lido...will see those two words [*implora pace*], and no more, put over me...I am sure my Bones would not rest in an English grave...I would not even feed your worms - if I could help it." (Byron 1973-1983, vol. 6, 149.)

Sunset City - City of the Dead

The weeds of the lagoon are markedly less lovely in the ode. They represent the latter-day Venetians, who are made to reflect, again by way of metonymy, their city's rather unsavoury decay:

> as the slime,
> The dull green ooze of the receding deep,
> Is with the dashing of the spring-tide foam...
> Are they to those that were; and thus they creep,
> Crouching and crab-like, through their sapping streets... (8ff.)
>
> The weeds of nations in their last decay... (33)

Venice appears as a slowly-dying organism, an image of life bogged down - again a highly influential kind of imagery, with a few unmistakeably apocalyptic touches;[6] a scene of sluggish decay from which the observer recoils in horror - to search for what alternative? Heroic action, or a more active death:

> Better, though each man's life-blood were a river,
> That it should flow, and overflow, than creep
> Through thousand lazy channels in our veins,
> Damm'd like the dull canal...
>   better be
> Where the extinguish'd Spartans still are free,
> In their proud charnel of Thermopylae... (149-156)

The proud charnel is, somewhat rhetorically, exalted over the inglorious dead city or *ville cimetière*. (The dull canal and the slimy crawling creatures will turn up again in that mirror cabinet of decadent symbolism, *The Waste Land*.)

Byron places his view of decaying and fallen Venice within the traditions of a well-established European poetics of the ruin. There the elegiac observer moves from the ruin as an object under his eyes to the historical process whose results he is looking at, in order to meditate on the vanity of past greatness - as Byron does in both poems, though each time in a different mode. The rather grim turning away from Venice in the ode, which anticipates his departure from Italy for Greece, contrasts with a somewhat luxurious farewell to Venice in *Childe Harold*. Since romantic ruins need the cooperation of Nature (into whose realm they are about to return) to exert their full impact on the sensitive soul, the episode is rounded off with a glorious sunset and nightfall. The downward or 'decadent' movement of the city that had risen from the Adriatic in history, as well as in Byron's first stanza, back into the sea is symbolized by the sun; the lovely colours of the dying light serve to prefigure the final sunset of Venice:

---

[6] Cf. v. 54f. "And all is ice and blackness - and the earth/That which it was the moment ere our birth" with v. 4f. of Byron's "Darkness", a poem describing the death of the sun and earth: "the icy earth/Swung blind and blackening in the moonless air" (Byron 1980-1993, vol. 4, 40ff.).

>   parting day
>   Dies like the dolphin, whom each pang imbues
>   With a new colour as it gasps away,
> The last still loveliest, till - 'tis gone - and all is gray.   (IV, 29)

3. "Cette Palmyre de la mer"

The *fata morgana*-like quality of Venice rising like an exotic vision out of the sea has often been remarked on; memorably so in Harold/Byron's line "I saw from out the waves her structures rise/ As from the stroke of an enchanter's wand" (st.1). This image, which the poet borrowed from Mrs Radcliffe's famous Venetian sunset in *The Mysteries of Udolpho*[7], confers an oriental colouring, an insubstantial and phantasmagoric quality on the "dying glory" of the golden city.

"To meditate amongst decay" on the futility of human history, preferably at sunset or nightfall, in an exotic setting, overlooking the picturesque ruins of past magnificence in the pose of a solitary observer, who is at the same time depressed and elevated by the sublime spectacle - all this is, of course, part and parcel of the romantic iconography of pleasurable decay. Byron was far from being its inventor, though he did a great deal to propagate it. An extremely influential prototype can be found in the first chapters of François de Volney's *Les Ruines, ou méditations sur les révolutions des empires* of 1791.

Volney's elegiac observer contemplates, at sunset, and from a point of vantage, the ruins of the mighty city of Palmyra in the middle of the desert - a configuration to be remembered by Shelley for his "Ozymandias":

> je m'étais avancé jusqu' à la Vallée des Sépulcres; je montai sur les hauteurs qui la bordent,et d'où l'oeil domine à la fois l'ensemble des ruines et l'immensité du désert...l'éclat mourant du jour tempérait l'horreur des ténèbres...un vaste silence régnait sur le désert...L'ombre croissait, et déjà dans le crépuscule mes regards ne distinguaient plus que les fantômes blanchâtres des colonnes et des murs...Je m'assis sur le tronc d'une colonne; et là, le coude appuyé sur le genou, la tête soutenue sur la main, tantôt portant mes regards sur le désert, tantôt les fixant sur les ruines, je m'abandonnai à une rêverie profonde.[8]

This *rêverie*, inspired by the *squelette lugubre* of the ancient city turned city of the dead, is rather similar, in its generalizing drift, to Byron's musings on Venice: the places of one-time splendour have fallen into abandonment and solitude, temples and palaces have crumbled away, profound silence has replaced the noise of the city, and the ground is nothing but a vast cemetery. But the *genius loci*, who proves to be *le génie de la liberté*, appears helpfully on the scene in order to explain the ruinous characters inscribed by man onto the surface of the earth. Man is not the helpless plaything of some cruel godhead, but a reasonable creature fully responsible for his own history: he is, in other words, the architect of his own ruin. Volney's final vision of mankind delivered from greed and superstition, i.e. from the power of kings and priests, is clearly marked by the revolutionary spirit of its time. Byron, who had seen

---

[7] Radcliffe 1970, 175 (vol. 2, ch. 2).
[8] Volney 1821, 8f.

Bonaparte subduing Venice and turning into Napoleon, is less sanguine in this respect; the invocation of freedom at the end of his ode has a more private and desperate, even suicidal ring.

Although Byron's letters from Venice sound, on the whole, far from gloomy, his stylization of the city in the two poems seems to harp relentlessly on its ruinous character and doomed state. In a telling manner Childe Harold's Venetian meditation amongst decay leads the way to other cities of the dead like Arqua, with Petrarch's tomb, Ravenna, and above all Rome. There is a marked continuity and increasing intensity to these musings among ruins, from the sunset at Venice to the climactic midnight scene in the Coliseum, the final stage of Harold's Pilgrimage. Byron seems to me clearly indebted to the Volney tradition. His reminiscences of Shakespeare, Otway, Schiller and Mrs Radcliffe in Venice testify to the literariness of his Italian experience.

After Byron, the association of Venice with the ruins of Palmyra was to become something of a topos. In his much-read guide book *Voyages historiques et littéraires en Italie*, Antoine Valéry adds a framework of romantic meditations on the city's ruinous beauty to his listing of the sights of Venice in the Eighteen-twenties:

> Cet aspect de Venise [its ruinous state] a quelque chose de plus triste que celui des ruines ordinaires: la nature vit encore près de celles-là et quelquefois elle les décore...ici les ruines nouvelles périront rapidement, et cette Palmyre de la mer, reprise par l'élément vengeur sur qui elle était une conquête, ne doit point laisser de traces. Il faut donc se hâter de visiter Venise...

After describing its touristic attractions in detail, Valéry concludes his Venetian section on a note of romantic *rêverie*, conjuring up a moonlight scene which, as in Volney, casts an air of oriental enchantment over the ruinous beauty of the place:

> Le silence de Venise, l'aspect oriental de St.-Marc et du palais ducal, ont à cette heure quelque chose d'enchanté, de mystérieux...La lune, appelée par les artistes le soleil des ruines, convient particulièrement à la grande ruine de Venise.[9]

Even the silence of coachless Venice, comparable to the *vaste silence* of Volney's desert ruins, is felt to be a kind of graveyard silence.[10]

The Byronic image of Venice as Palmyra-of-the Sea, a dead city entombing its own glorious past, rapidly became an icon of decadent and moribund beauty, a melancholy and phantom-like vision of History's Nevermore - to be revived and elaborated on from Chateaubriand's *Mémoires d'Outre-Tombe* (1833/1848) to Barrès' *Mort de Venise* (1903). Even when the much-reviled Austrians linked Venice with the terra ferma, and things took a turn for the better economically, the change did not really affect the city's literary reputation for necropolic romance. This paradox was duly noted by the French traveller J. Leconte as early as 1844: "Ses palais sont loin d'être aussi croulants que le

---

[9] Valéry 1835, 114 and 150 (Book VI, ch. 1 and ch. 24). - Corbineau-Hoffmann 1993, 161-164, tentatively sketches a Volneyan context of "Ruinenpoesie" for the Venice of the Romantics without focussing on its central, i.e. Byronic, aspect.

[10] Cf. de Staël 1886, 354 (book XV, ch. 7): "Le silence est profond dans cette ville, dont les rues sont des canaux"; echoed by Shelley, 1964, vol. 2, 42: "The silent streets are paved with water."

disent ceux qui tentent de continuer Volney... Venise n'est ruine que dans la littérature."[11]

4. Lyrical Narrative: Venetian Sunset and the Journey to the End of Night

Let us now look at the way the Sunset City figures within various romantic narrative structures; for the Venetian sunset tends to be more than a mere episode in actual or fictional romantic travel writing. The fourth book of *Childe Harold's Pilgrimage* establishes a pattern in which the dusk over Venice serves as first stage for Harold's Journey to the end of Night; for a melancholic catabasis such as befits souls that love

> to dwell in darkness and dismay,
> Deeming themselves predestin'd to a doom
> Which is not of the pangs that pass away;
> Making the sun like blood, the earth a tomb,
> The tomb a hell, and hell itself a murkier gloom.   (st.34);

that is to say, souls, whose gloomy vision of the world anticipates the apocalypse. For Harold the whole of Italy turns into a field of tombs, a vast, if picturesque, charnel-house of history. The moment of midnight among the ruins of Rome, in which the blood-stained stones of the Coliseum become the symbol of futile historical greatness, constitutes the nadir of Harold's pilgrimage:

> What matters where we fall to fill the maws
> Of worms - on battle-plains or listed spot?
> Both are but theatres where the chief actors rot.   (st. 139)

After the final, nihilist lesson the pilgrim, shadowy like the phantoms of greatness around him, is allowed to breathe his last: "His shadow fades away into Destruction's mass" (st.164).

Clearly, the romantic sunset (and nightfall) in Venice reflects not only the observer's momentary state of mind; with respect to narrative structure it is of an ominous nature, foreshadowing worse things to come. This plot pattern emerges as early as *The Mysteries of Udolpho*, 1794. Emily St. Aubert, the heroine, enters Venice by boat at sunset in the company of the formidable Montoni, who has recently married her aunt, Madame Cheron.

Emily's sensitive soul is deeply moved by the magical first view of the city under the "melancholy purple of evening", and as she listens in rapture to a sad love song floating across the water from another gondola she sighs and thinks of her lover Valancourt, from whom she has been separated. Nor are her sad premonitions at all deceptive. Venice (where she is subjected to the hateful attentions of Count Morano) -

---

[11] L'Italie des gens du monde, Venice 1844, 647; quoted in Petriconi, 1958, 95. - The vogue of Venice as a decadent complex of eros and death at the fin de siècle provoked similar reactions; cf. Bac, The Mystère Vénitien, Paris 1909, 109: "Tout le romantisme de notre ville n'existe que dans vos imaginations! Vos perpetuelles extases devant notre 'agonie' nous horripilent...et nous exaspèrent." (quoted in Schenk 1987, 129).

with all its picturesque beauty so eloquently described by Mrs Radcliffe who had never set foot there - soon turns into a place of persecution. The ominous shades deepen in the course of a second sublime sunset, watched this time from a bark on the Brenta. Bathed in tears, Emily is haunted by the conviction that she will never see Valancourt again.[12] While looking at the snow-capped Apennines in the distance she thinks of Montoni's castle, where she is to spend her future days, and shudders in terror.

For the walls of a prison more terrible than that of a Venetian palazzo are soon to close round her. Udolpho will fulfil what the melancholy beauty of Venice had intimated, her ordeal of Gothic horror. Her entry into the grim, half-ruinous castle is heralded by - what else? - another ominous sunset:

> Emily gazed with melancholy awe upon the castle...; for though it was now lighted up by the setting sun, the gothic greatness of its features, and its mouldering walls of dark grey stone, rendered it a gloomy and sublime object. As she gazed, the light died away on its walls, leaving a melancholy purple tint...As the twilight deepened, its features became more awful in obscurity...[13]

This is gothic foreboding with a vengeance. The Venetian "melancholy purple" is getting more sombre, and the oriental palace scenery transforms into that of a medieval mountain castle, rugged and mouldering at the same time. Like Childe Harold, though in a different manner, Emily will die a symbolic death among the ruinous masonry of Italy, in a nocturnal vault-like world ushered in by the twilight of Venice.

Ann Radcliffe's Emily is not the only high-strung romantic heroine to be seized by dark premonitions, which turn out to be well-founded, on entering Venice. "D'où vient la mélancholie profonde dont je me sens saisie en entrant dans cette ville? n'est-ce pas une preuve qu'il m'y arrivera quelque grand malheur?" Madame de Staël's Corinne asks herself at that very moment.[14] The first impression is one of silence, darkness, and death:

> Le silence est profond dans cette ville...Ces gondoles noires qui glissent sur les canaux ressemblent à des cercueils ou à des berceaux [an obvious echo from Goethe's *Venezianische Epigramme*]... Le soir on ne voit passer que le reflet des lanternes qui éclairent les gondoles...On dirait que ce sont des ombres qui glissent sur l'eau...[15]

In three cannon-shots heard from the distance, which announce a young woman's entry into the cloister, and celebrate „l'obscur sacrifice d'une jeune fille", Corinne forsees her own fate; and in fact, Venice will become for her the sad scene of fatal separation from her lover Oswald. One day, later on, during a *rêverie* at San Marco, she overcomes the cruel emptiness of his absence by imagining the marriage ceremony that should have joined her to Oswald in that church, only to be shocked into the awareness of a coffin that is being carried in. "A cet aspect, elle chancela, ses yeux se troublèrent, et, depuis cet instant, elle fut convaincue par imagination que son sentiment pour Oswald serait

---

[12] Radcliffe 1970, 175 and 208f. (vol. 2, ch. 3).
[13] Radcliffe 1970, 226f. (vol. 2, ch. 5).
[14] De Staël 1886, 355 (book XV, ch. 7).
[15] De Staël 1886, 354.

la cause de sa mort."[16] And of course this Venetian foreboding of emotional decay and bodily death will come true later on, in her great dying scene at Rome, an orgy of high sentiment, and generous pardon granted to faithless Oswald (who had married her sister in the meantime).

A different Venetian descent into darkness is recorded in Shelley's conversation poem "Julian and Maddalo". It was (at least partly) written after the death in Venice of his daughter Clara and seems to reflect a subsequent emotional estrangement from his wife.[17] In a letter to Charles Ollier the author calls it, and the accompanying poems (probably "Lines Written Among the Euganean Hills" and "Stanzas Written in Dejection"), "my saddest verses raked up into one heap".[18] Venice had become a deeply ambivalent experience for him, as the place of artistic brilliance, symbolized by his renewed friendship with Byron, and of Clara's fatal illness and death, for which he might well feel some responsibility.

"Julian and Maddalo" - the names are thin disguises for Shelley and Byron: the Apostate and the mad one - starts off with a delightful mounted ramble on the Lido - then a perfect wilderness -, where Byron kept his horses (and where he wanted to be buried). Both friends are engrossed in philosophical debate - Julian the utopian and Maddalo the abysmal sceptic: "We descanted, and I.../ Argued against despondency, but pride/ Made my companion take the darker side" (46ff.).[19] A glorious Venetian sunset, watched first from horseback, then from a gondola, transfigures the "Paradise of exiles, Italy" (57).

> "Ere it fade",
> Said my companion, "I will show you soon
> A better station" - so, o'er the lagune
> We glided; and from that funereal bark
> I leaned and saw the city, and could mark
> How from their many isles, in evening's gleam,
> Its temples and its palaces did seem
> Like fabrics of enchantment...   (v. 85ff.)

The metamorphosis of the gondola into a funereal bark, conventional as it is, casts an ominous spell over the bright scene (with its obvious reminiscence of Mrs Radcliffe's Venice)[20]. The „better station", ironically announced by Maddalo, who seems to continue his pessimistic argument in an underhand manner, is an island symbolically situated in the West, whose uninviting aspect emerges starkly against the last rays of the setting sun[21]:

---

[16] De Staël 1886, 400 (book XVII, ch. 1).
[17] Cf. White 1947, vol. 2, 42-50.
[18] Letter of Nov. 10, 1820; in Shelley 1964, vol. 2, 246.
[19] Shelley 1961, 191.
[20] Cf. Radcliffe 1970, 175: "its terraces, crowned with airy yet majestic fabrics [*Childe Harold*, IV, st. 1, - another echo of this passage which Shelley may have had fresh in mind - has „structures"]...appeared as if they had been called up by the wand of an enchanter..."
[21] The companion piece to "Julian", „Lines Written Among the Euganean Hills", presents us with an (equally ambivalent) glamorous sunrise view of Venice; which leads on to a vision of the city's doom in future times: "A less drear ruin then than now.../Wilt thou be, when the sea-mew/Flies, as once

> I looked, and saw between us and the sun
> A building on an island; such a one
> As age to age might add, for uses vile,
> A windowless, deformed and dreary pile;
> And on the top an open tower, where hung
> A bell...
> The broad sun sunk behind it, and it tolled
> In strong and black relief. (98ff.)

This dreary pile, which recalls the appearance, at sunset, of the phantom ship in the "Ancient Mariner"[22], must be the first mention made in English Literature of the Venetian madhouse on San Servolo. The black asylum bell, tolling "in a heaven-illumined tower", and calling the madmen to vespers, is promptly declared by Maddalo to be an emblem of the soul as it assembles man's thoughts and desires "round the rent heart" to pray -

> For what? they know not, - till the night of death
> As sunset that strange vision, severeth
> Our memory from itself, and us from all
> We sought...   (126ff.)

Thus the Venetian sunset takes a sinister turn which leads to both friends visiting, on the next day, a benighted inmate of the asylum, whose fragmentary life-story of despair offers some support for Maddalo's dim view of human affairs. This tale, it is true, is a vicarious journey to the end of night, told by a third party, and used as an exemplum for Maddalo's argument; but then the maniac displays so many traits familiar from Shelleyan self-portrayals that we finally realize the poet's twofold presence in the poem, both as the relatively detached first-person narrator and as the desperately eloquent victim of the story, betrayed by life and love. Again the deceptive sunset splendour of Venice has lead us to a place of solitary confinement in the dark night of the soul.

For Chateaubriand the autobiographer, Venice, a late stage in his aptly termed *Mémoires d'Outre-Tombe*, seems the stylistically appropriate final destination of life, where he can turn his back upon a contemporary scene he hates, and identify, in the glow of the Venetian sunset, with the dying beauty and greatness of the past. "Vous aimez à vous sentir mourir avec tout ce qui meurt autour de vous" he says by way of introduction, transposing Byron's "ruin amidst ruins" into a prose-poem of his own.

---

before it flew,/O'er thine isles depopulate,/ And all is in its ancient state,/ Save where many a palace gate/With green seaflowers overgrown/Like a rock of Ocean's own,/Topples o'er the abandoned sea..."(v. 121-141; Shelley 1961, p.555). The ruinous city returns to Nature and becomes a sea-rock. The Shelleys were familiar with Volney's book: its presence is obvious in *Queen Mab*, and it is referred to in *Frankenstein*, ch. 13.

[22] Cf. "The Ancient Mariner", v. 171ff.: „The western wave was all aflame,/The day was well-nigh done!/Almost upon the western wave/Rested the broad bright Sun;/When that strange shape drove suddenly/Betwixt us and the Sun" (Coleridge 1969, 193).

> Que ne puis-je m'enfermer dans cette ville en harmonie avec ma destinée...! Que ne puis-je achever d'écrire mes Mémoires à la lueur du soleil qui tombe sur ces pages! L'astre brûle encore dans ce moment mes savanes Floridiennes et se couche ici à l'extremité du grand Canal...Les enclôtures des magasins de la *Giudecca* sont peintes d'une lumière titienne; les gondoles du Canal et du port nagent dans la même lumière. Venise est là, assise sur le rivage de la mer comme une belle femme qui va s'éteindre avec le jour: le vent du soir soulève ses cheveux embaumés; elle meurt saluée par toutes les grâces et tous les sourires de la nature.[23]

This is how Chateaubriand concludes his first chapter on Venice - quite a program. His Venetian rovings follow the traces of his poetic predecessors, above all, of Lord Byron (to be followed, in their turn, by later pilgrims like Maurice Barrès). In a letter to Madame Récamier of September 15, 1833, however, he stresses his disinclination to imitate Byron ("Je n'ai pas voulu passer pour la copie de l'homme dont je suis l'original") and the rest of the travellers:

> J'ai pris Venise autrement que mes devanciers; j'ai cherché des choses que les voyageurs qui se copient les uns les autres, ne cherchent pas. Personne, par exemple, ne parle du *cimetière* de Venise; personne n'a remarqué les tombes des Juifs au Lido...[24]

These cemetery excursions form the counterpoint to Chateaubriand's sociable and touristic activities in Venise. He contemplates lizards and butterflies playing among the skulls and bones at San Cristoforo, where he compares the gondolas that bear the coffins to Charon's bark; at San Michele he desires a cell in the Franciscan convent, close to the newly established cemetery: "Donnez-moi là, je vous prie, une cellule pour achever mes *Mémoires*"; his visit to the abandoned Jewish cemetery on the Lido - the very place where Byron used to start his riding excursions - forms a transition to the final chapter "Rêverie au Lido", which gathers up "à la lueur du crépuscule" the elegiac mood of the Venise section, and of the *Mémoires* as a whole, into a poignant final movement, a sort of swan song for the great work. It is a meditation among the tombstones of the wilderness, where the author envisions, as it were, his own tomb, within full view of the *Dying City*; and it is furthermore an Imitation of Byron. Unlike Byron, however, he writes a name - of sixteen letters - into the sand of the beach (Juliette Récamier?) and watches the waves effacing its traces: "je sentais qu'elles effaçaient ma vie".[25] The final apostrophe to Venice repeats and confirms the initial act of identification *sub specie mortis*:

> Venise! nos destins ont été pareils! mes songes s'évanouissent à mesure que vos palais s'écroulent: les heures de mon printemps se sont noircies, comme les arabesques dont le faîte de vos monuments est orné. Mais vous périssez à votre insu; moi, je sais mes ruines...[26]

Chateaubriand, self-dramatizing like Childe Harold and his creator, is speaking his own epitaph. Venice and the Lido are his islands of the dead.

---

[23] Chateaubriand 1984, vol.. 8, 20f. (Part IV, book vii, ch. 1).
[24] Chateaubriand 1984, vol. 8, 362.
[25] Chateaubriand 1984, vol. 8, 38 (ch. 6); 41 (ch. 7); 89f. (ch. 17).
[26] Chateaubriand 1984, vol. 8, 97 (ch. 8).

5. Venetian Cities of the Dead

Venice, phantom of past greatness, magic place of beauty and decay, where Time seems to have a stop and sunsets assume an ultimate character, sinking city of marble liquefied and water petrified, appealed - as we have seen - to the (predominantly northern) romantic imagination as a powerful elegiac symbol, part of its death-in-life mythology made up of beauty and terror. But the Dead City myth could be carried to further extremes.

This is shown for the first time in Mary Shelley's fantastic romance *The Last Man* (1826), an extraordinary narrative, part utopia and part apocalypse. This *roman à clef* of the Shelley-Byron circle is set in the 21st century; after transposing her dead husband's political dreams into the fiction of a flawlessly democratic Great Britain und Europe, the author sets out to depopulate her ideal world by means of a universal plague. A rapidly dwindling small community of survivors move south, as the Shelleys had done years ago, through France and Switzerland into Italy - all of them countries by now void of human life. When the last men, who have melted down in the meantime to a mere group of three, arrive in Italy, the melancholy pattern of ruin enjoyment traced by Childe Harold, whose itinerary they follow, assumes a macabre quality. Venice is again the first stage of the final movement; the episode opens with the authorial invocation of a rather specific Muse:

> Now - soft awhile - have I arrived so near the end? Yes! it is all over now - a step or two over those new made graves, and the weary way is done...Arise, black Melancholy! quit thy Cimmerian solitude! Bring with thee murky fogs from hell, which may drink up the day; bring blight and pestiferous exhalations, which, entering the hollow caverns and breathing places of earth, may fill her stony veins with corruption...[27]

This highly melodramatic apostrophe is addressed to the Muse of Black Romanticism, who gives the ultimate lie to that favourite romantic dream, the imaginative fusion of self and nature. As in the dejection poems of Coleridge and Shelley, only more so, human desolation and natural beauty prove bitterly irreconcilable:

> We rowed lightly over the Laguna, and entered Canale Grande. The tide ebbed sullenly from out the broken portals and violated halls of Venice: sea weed and sea monsters were left on the blackened marble, while the salt ooze defaced the matchless works of art that adorned their walls, and the sea gull flew out from the shattered window.[28] In the midst of this appalling ruin of the monuments of man's power, nature asserted her ascendancy, and shone more beauteous from the contrast. The radiant waters hardly trembled, while the rippling waves made many sided mirrors to the sun... (ibid.)

---

[27] Mary Shelley 1965, 318 (book III, ch. 9); Mary Shelley borrowed her title, the doomsday pattern, and the turn from utopia to apocalypse from Cousin de Grainville's latter day romance *Le Dernier Homme* of 1805, a text well-known to Byron and his friends. This narrative is related back to Volney's *Ruines* by the fact that the author pretends to have found the MS of his story in a cavern near Palmyra. For this context see von Hop - Penfels 1991, 245-290; for the theme of the 'Last Survivor' see Stafford 1994.

[28] An obvious recollection of Shelley's "Lines Written Among the Euganean Hills"; cf. n. 21 above.

Mary Shelley's fiction realizes a situation that had been hypothetically foreseen by Volney's melancholy observer looking at the ruins of Palmyra:

> Quit sait, me dis-je, si tel ne sera pas un jour l'abandon de nos propres contrées? Qui sait, si sur les rives de la *Seine*, de la *Tamise*... un voyageur comme moi ne s'assoiera pas un jour sur de muettes ruines, et ne pleurera pas, solitaire, sur la cendre des peuples et la mémoire de leur grandeur?[29]

The apocalyptic imagination of late romanticism and the *fin de siècle* will take up the motif, making the Thames and the Seine, like the lagoon of Venice in Byron's Ode, swamp and swallow up their respective cities. Gustave Doré's final plate of his drastic woodcut series *London, a Pilgrimage* (1872), which highlights the seedier side of the Empire's capital, is a case in point. Thousands of years hence, London has been purified both of its industrial blemishes and of its submerged crowds (the metaphor is doubly apt here) of wage-slaves. There are no Londoners left, and the city, a picturesque heap of ruins with a distinct Venetian touch, is reflected in its Canal Grande, the river Thames; some half-sunken columns suggest that it is being gradually engulfed. Seated on a huge square stone, on top of a broken arch of London Bridge, an exotically dressed person - Macaulay's New Zealander - is looking across the water and sketching the picturesque ruins of St. Paul's (pl.2).[30] The whole composition harks back to Volney's frontispiece (pl.1); as does an illustration to Camille Flammarion's *La Fin du Monde* (1894) that shows, in a sunset scene, the usual melancholy observer looking across a huge expanse of water at the ruined palaces and classical columns of a Venice-like Paris (pl.3).[31] In Flammarion's sensational fiction on the end of the world through entropy, erosion has flattened down the continental profile of Europe, large parts of which have been flooded by its rivers. The final spectacle of doomed nature wiping out the traces of civilization promises the *non plus ultra* of decadent sublimity: the whole of civilized world is being turned into one vast ruin. Here as elsewhere, romantic Venice looms large in the iconography of doom.

There is, of course, some hidden connection between these truly apocalyptic visions and the vogue of what has been called the "Symbolist Dead City" during the last decades, and the turn, of the 19th century.[32] For artists disgusted with their
middle-class industrial surroundings, haunted by world-weariness and an end-of-time feeling, fascinated by dream landscapes promising the suspension of time and nature, and an intoxicating fusion of eros and thanatos, the dead city became a powerful symbol of artistic entrancement and nihilist dismay.
The supreme artefact of the canal city, whose stagnant waters seem to arrest the flow of time, and turn mirror instead, is ubiquitous in these fantasies, in which the

---

[29] *Les Ruines*, ch. 2; Volney 1821, 15.

[30] Cf. Macaulay 1889, 548 (essay on "Von Ranke"). - In Richard Jefferies, *After London or Wild England* (1885), a catastrophic change of climate sends London to the bottom of a poisonous swamp - a metaphor for the city's civilized corruption - at the eastern extremity of a vast lake that has formed in the centre of England; the survivors face the Darwinian struggle for survival in a half-savage but rather healthy way. Felix, the story's hero, explores the fatal site of the sunken metropolis in the course of his adventures, and narrowly excapes death through ist miasmal exhalations.

[31] Flammarion 1894, 265. Like Grainville (whom he imitates) and Mary Shelley, Flammarion has a golden age of civilization precede the final cataclysm.

[32] Cf. Friedman 1990 and Hinterhäuser 1970, 321-344.

Sunset City - City of the Dead

Pl. 1: François de Volney, <u>Les Ruines, ou méditations sur les révolutions des empires</u> (Paris 1791)- frontispiece

Pl. 2: Gustave Doré / Blanchard Jerrold, <u>London: A Pilgrimage</u> (London 1872) – Final plate "A few thousand years hence"

Pl. 3: "Paris, le beau Paris...n'était qu'un amas de ruines..." Engraving by O. Saunier, in Camille Flammarion, <u>La Fin du monde</u> (Paris 1894)

apocalyptic tendency may be more or less explicit. At one point of Maurice Barrès' *Mort de Venise* (1903), an insatiable quest for *tristesse voluptueuse* and *paludisme romantique*, the link between the symbolic Venetian sunsets savoured by the author and the cosmic death of the sun through entropy is explicitly established:

> Le soleil aussi passera de la phase éclatante, de la phase jaune, à cette phase rouge que les astronomes appellent de décrépitude. Le centre secret des plaisirs, tous mêlés de romanesque, que nous trouvons sur les lagunes, c'est que tant de beautés qui s'en vont à la mort nous excitent à jouir de la vie.[33]

This use of the dead city as a stimulus for the *élan vital* is less in evidence in earlier symbolist versions of the canal city, whose archetype is decadent Venice, even though it may be called, as in Rodenbach's romance of 1892, *Bruges-la-Morte*. This famous prose-poem narrative explicitly identifies Bruges, the Venice of the North, with the protagonist's dead wife. The site of absence, silted life, suspended time, predominance of past over present, black water, pallor and claustral silence punctuated by the sound of the city's many chimes, mirrors an existence of inwardness and solitude, where love is a synonym for death:

> Dans l'atmosphère muette des eaux et des rues inanimées, Hugues avait moins senti la souffrance de son cœur...retrouvant au fil des canaux son visage d'Ophélie en allée...Bruges était sa morte. Et sa morte était Bruges. Tout s'unifiait en une destinée pareille. C'était Bruges-la-Morte, elle-même mise au tombeau de ses quais de pierre, avec les artères froidies de ses canaux, quand avait cessé d'y battre la grand pulsation de la mer.[34]

This phantom of a city, a Venice not dying but actually dead, is not only the mirror of Hugues's state of mind, but actually a female love object, an object of necrophilia, to be precise. Just as Bruges is the perfect negation of a city, the protagonist's cult of love and art has turned into a negation of life, and his religion into a ritual revoking transcendence.

The nihilist misgivings symbolized by the romantic interest in doomed cities from Byron to Barrès finds its most radical expression in James (B.V.) Thomson's notorious *City of Dreadful Night*. The long poem's narrator, a visionary of nothingness, wanders through a metropolis turned necropolis: London, the city of fogs, and scene of Thomson's depressing existence, is transformed into a *città dolente* haunted by shades, a "Venice of the Black Sea":

> A river girds the city west and south,
>   The main north channel of a broad lagoon,
> Regurging with the salt tides from the mouth;
>   Waste marshes shine and glister to the moon
> For leagues, then moorland black, then stony ridges;
> Great piers and causeways, many noble bridges
>   Connect the town and islet suburbs strewn. (i)[35]

---

[33] Barrès 1990, 38.
[34] Rodenbach 1986, 26 (ch. 2).
[35] Thomson, 1963, 177-205; here 178.

Sunset City - City of the Dead

Venice, the city of light, has finally sunk into eternal night - not underwater, but underground. Its silence, found ominous by many of its romantic visitors, is intensified into "the soundless solitude immense/ Of rangèd mansions dark and still as tombs"; the sun, in this subterranean world, is the black and burnt-out eye-socket of the universe (iv; an image borrowed from Jean Paul), the heaven a "blue vault obdurate as steel", the empyrean „a void abyss" (xvii). From time to time, the wanderer sits down in utmost solitude, like the observers of ruins from Volney onward, to watch the dismal scene: "I sat forlornly by the river-side" (vi), or "I sat me weary on a pillar's base" (xx). The traditional posture of the melancholy spectator is repeated on a different level at the end of the poem, when the narrator describes the huge statue of a winged woman towering over Black Venice:

> Low-seated she leans forward massively,
>   With cheek on clenched left hand, the forearm's might
> Erect, its elbow on her rounded knee...
>   she gazes
> With full set eyes, but wandering in thick mazes
>   Of sombre thought beholds no outward sight. (xxi)

The statue reproduces, in colossal dimension, Dürers "Melencolia", whose heraldic sign is the black sun, "le soleil noir de la Mélancholie"[36], emblem of the century's *ennui* or loss of both immanent and transcendent faith. Byron's sinking Venice, bathed in the last splendour of the setting sun, heralded a suspicion that Thomson's Venice, on which the sun has set for good, finally confirms: that there will be no New Jerusalem after the fall of The City, that the final Revelation will reveal a void, or, in Thomson's words:

> That none can pierce that vast black veil uncertain
> Because there is no light beyond the curtain;
>   That all is vanity and nothingness.

---

[36] "El Desdichado", in Nerval 1951, vol. 1, 33

Bibliography

Barrès, Maurice: *La Mort de Venise*, ed. M.O. Germain. Saint Cyr 1990.
Byron, George Gordon Lord: *Complete Poetical Works*, ed. J. McGann, 7 vols. Oxford 1980-1993.
Byron, George Gordon Lord: *Letters and Journals*, ed. L.A. Marchand, 12 vols. London 1973-1983.
De Chateaubriand, François-René: *Mémoires d'outre-tombe*, ed. M. Levaillant, 8 vols. Paris 1984.
De Staël, Germaine: *Corinne ou l'Italie*. Paris 1886.
Coleridge, Samuel Taylor: *Poetical Works*, ed. E.H. Coleridge. London 1969.
Corbineau-Hoffmann, Angelika: *Paradoxie der Fiktion. Literarische Venedig-Bilder 1797-1984*. Berlin 1993.
Doré, Gustave/Jerrold, Blanchard: *London. A Pilgrimage*. London 1872.
Flammarion, Camille: *La Fin du monde*. Paris 1894.
Friedmann, D.F.: *The Symbolist Dead City*. New York 1990.
Hinterhäuser, Hans: "Tote Städte in der Literatur des Fin de Siècle". *Archiv für das Studium der neueren Sprachen* 206 (1970), 321-344.
Jefferies, Richard: *After London or Wild England*. London 1885.
v. Koppenfels, Werner: "Le coucher du soleil romantique. Die Imagination des Weltendes aus dem Geist der visionären Romantik". In: v.K., *Bild und Metamorphose*. Darmstadt 1991, 245-290.
Macaulay, John B.: *Essays*. London 1889.
Nerval, Gérard de: *Oeuvres*, ed. A. Béguin, 2 vols. Paris 1951.
Petriconi, Helmut: *Das Reich des Untergangs*. Hamburg 1958.
Radcliffe, Ann: *The Mysteries of Udolpho*, ed. B. Dobrée. Oxford 1970.
Rodenbach, Georges: *Bruges-la-Morte*, ed. Ch.Berg. Brussels 1986.
Schenk, Christian: *Venedig im Spiegel der Décadence-Literatur*. Frankfurt/M. 1987.
Shelley, Mary: *The Last Man*, ed. H.J. Luke, Jr. Lincoln/Neb. 1965.
Shelley, Percy B.: *The Complete Poetical Works*, ed. Th. Hutchinson. Oxford 1961.
Shelley, Percy B.: *Letters*, ed. F.. Jones. 2 vols. Oxford 1964.
Stafford, Francis: *Last of the Race*. Oxford 1994.
Thomson, James (B.V.): *Poems*, ed. A. Ridler. London 1963.
Valéry, Antoine: *Voyages historiques et littéraires en Italie*. Brussels 1835.
Volney, François de: *Les Ruines*. Paris 1821.
White, Newman F.: *Shelley*. 2 vols. London 1947.
Wordsworth, William: *The Poetical Works*, ed. Th. Hutchinson/E. de Selincourt. London 1950.

Sergio Perosa

Literary Deaths in Venice

In the following paper I will pursue two points: (1) nineteenth-century literary deaths in Venice are prepared, set up, and fostered by earlier complaints on her (historical) Fall; (2) they find their motivation in analogous, or homologous, stratifications of history (and art), of the organic and the inorganic, in "emerging" islands.

> ...in the fall
> of Venice, think of thine

writes Byron in *Childe Harold's Pilgrimage* (1816; canto IV, xvii). He is addressing Albion, England, a maritime power that did nothing against the fall of Venice, her sister, a daughter of the Ocean like herself. But we may take it as a motto for all: "in the fall of Venice, think of yours, of ours". Quite a few writers follow in Byron's wake, finding in that fall a premonition of (or a condition for) a doom of death, which in the nineteenth century becomes indeed a suggestion or a seduction of death.

William Wordsworth set the tone in his well-known sonnet, "On The Extinction Of The Venetian Republic" (1802, published 1807):

> Once did She hold the gorgeous east in fee;
> And was the safeguard of the west: the worth
> Of Venice did not fall below her birth,
> Venice, the eldest Child of Liberty.
> She was a maiden City, bright and free;
> No guile seduced, no force could violate;
> And, when she took unto herself a Mate,
> She must espouse the everlasting Sea.
> And what if she had seen those glories fade,
> Those titles vanish, and that strength decay;
> Yet shall some tribute of regret be paid
> When her long life hath reached its final day:
> Men are we, and must grieve when even the Shade
> Of that which once was great is passed away.

"The Shade/Of that which once was great" haunts the century. Knowing, as we do, the ruthlessness of her autocratic and oligarchic government, we may be surprised by this identification of Venice with "the eldest Child of Liberty". Wordsworth and his contemporaries, however, living in a climate of absolute monarchies, in the aftermath of the Napoleonic and post-Napoleonic restauration, were attracted by the fact that Venice had been a *republic*, and in her fall they saw the loss of those hopes for liberty that had been fostered by the French Revolution. This feeling is expressed in the third stanza of Byron's "Ode to Venice" (1818-19), and is echoed in P. B. Shelley's "Lines

Written among the Euganean Hills" (1818). It was sharpened by the perception of the exceptional length of her republican independence - ten or twelve centuries (as the case might be) of unbroken freedom; in Byron's "Ode to Venice", that freedom is paired off with Glory and Empire ("Glory and Empire! once upon these towers/With Freedom-godlike Triad!").

In English views of Venice, moreover, Venice represented a heroic and successful opposition to the abhorred papal dominance, to the oppressive rule of the Church in Italy, indeed to the Anti-Christ, so that everything combined and conspired to make of her that cradle and that beacon of liberty, which had been so miserably extinguished in 1797. A vision of Venice as the paragon of a perfect state already obtained in Elizabethan times (when it was hoped she might become a bridgehead for Protestantism in the Catholic South of Europe). In 1570, Sir Roger Ascham had viewed Venice as the seat of just laws, wise rulers, and free citizens; in the only republican period of English history, Cromwell's parliament had looked to Venice as to a model of republican survival; in the eighteenth century, John Locke and Voltaire, among others, had seen her as a fundamentally just society.[1]

All this may account for the shock and the reverberations of her fall. No wonder, then, that writers dealing, however indirectly, with the topic, all the way down to John Ruskin, seem to linger almost obsessively on signs and symptoms of decay and death, on features of splendid but painful dissolution, that would open the way to the *concetto*, the literary conceit, of Death in Venice, which became so prominent in the nineteenth century.

I speak of a *concetto* because death is feared, pursued, cherished and enacted in the decay of splendour, in the excess and corruption of beauty, in the surplus and added value of crumbling art and compromised history - in the ambivalence, that is, of sensual, mental joy, and a lugubrious atmosphere of doom. Oxymoron prevails in the term itself - "Death in Venice" (isn't Venice often equated and homophonous with Venus?): its outcomes are surprising and contradictory.

* * *

In Wordsworth's sonnet, 'fade', 'decay', 'final day', 'Shade' and 'passed away' are key-words, at the end of lines, and linked by rhyme. For Byron, Venice was "the greenest island of my imagination", but also a "sea-Sodom" (*Marino Faliero, V, III, 99*), an earthly paradise which was also the epitome of corruption and decay. The exaltation that inspires canto IV of *Childe Harold's Pilgrimage* goes together with the

---

[1] Cosgrave 1987, 145-69. Of course, Elizabethan writers, including Marlowe and Shakespeare, had also a fantasy of Venice as a hedonistic and corrupt state, as a den of iniquity. In the early nineteenth century, James Fenimore Cooper had no "political" delusions about Venice: his novel *The Bravo* (1831), which is set in a stereotypical Venice, was intended to illustrate the moral that "any government in which the power resides in a minority conduces to oppression of the weak and perversion of the good" (Perosa 1969, 379-401).

enunciation of features of death. There Byron contemplates a "dying Glory"; on the Bridge of Sighs, in the famous beginning, one has "A Palace and a prison on each hand"; the sea-Cybele born of the Ocean seems to be mute, her palaces are crumbling:

> In Venice Tasso's echoes are no more,
> And silent rows the songless Gondolier;
> Her palaces are crumbling to the shore. (iii)

If "Beauty is still there", and nature does not die, although born by enchantment and spreading her charms, Venice is a city of shadows and dissolution: "Sinks, like a seaweed, unto whence she rose!/...whelmed beneath the waves,.../Even in Destruction's depth" (xiii). Like her Doges, she is "declined to dust" (xv), enveloped by a cloud of desolation; the "fairy city of the heart,/Rising like water columns from the sea" is (please note)

> Perchance even dearer in her days of woe,
> Than when she was a boast, a marvel, and a show. (xviii)

Only the echoes of those who immortalized her in literature - Otway, Tasso, Shakespeare - can revive her: Venice is already a literary conceit. In the "Ode to Venice", too, we find "sunken halls", centuries of wealth and glory turned to ashes and tears (while, according to another view of the period, which was shared by Goethe, republican freedom moved from Venice to America). An oscillation between exaltation and death, the co-existence of glory and decay, are recurrent themes: in the very letter in which he writes of Venice as the greenest island of his imagination, Byron explicitly admits he is attracted by desolation: "I have been familiar with ruins too long to dislike desolation".[2]

Desolation, indeed, attracts. For Shelley in "The Lines Written among the Euganean Hills", too, the daughter of the Ocean, seen from afar as a glitter of light, turns into a "masque of death"; one would not suspect that her luminous and golden towers are, in fact,

> Sepulchres, where human forms,
> Like pollution-nourished worms,
> To the corpse of greatness cling,
> Murdered, and now mouldering. (146-49)

For Shelley, too, dying Venice is to survive in the words of those writers who sung her, like Shakespeare: the city is again brought near to a literary conceit. Along these

---

[2] "Canto IV is centrally concerned with ruin and decay; or, rather, in the absence of a centre it hovers restlessly and obsessively around ruins and ruination", writes Tony Tanner - though he properly adds that Byron looks for forms of energy to counteract "this deathward", this tendency to death which pervades Canto IV, and which Hobhouse's notes had stressed (Tanner 1992, 27, 30).

lines, writers are taught to make of that desolation and subtle ruin the *locus classicus* of exquisite deaths.

* * *

Strangely enough, it is the great singer of Venice, the one who made a literary and visual myth of her - John Ruskin - who sowed the seeds and drew the outlines of what would quickly become the *topos* or conceit of "death in Venice". Ruskin introduced the eminently literary element of Decadence - with a capital D - into the picture, which was to leave ineffaceable traces in those who came after him.

In his chapter on Ruskin in *Venice Desired*, Tanner warns us that his love affair with Venice was soon splintered - that in his highest exaltation of the myth of Venice he strewed signs of decadence and death. In an early fragment he had already noted "the shade of melancholy upon its beauty which is rapidly increasing, and will increase, until the waves which have been the ministers of majesty become her sepulchre". In Tanner's icastic comment: "So, from the start, delight - certain; disappointment - possible; doom - inevitable".[3]

"I do not *feel* any romance in Venice. It is simply a heap of ruins", Ruskin had also written in a letter to his father. In spite of his claims, he worked a totally ahistorical and moralized myth about her; by rationalizing her decadence, however, he would portray it - the decadence - as a wood-worm worming its way into, and corroding, the beauty of a lost Eden. Venice was for him a ruin vanishing into oblivion; "this amphibious city - this Phocaea, or sea-dog of towns" (as he called it in *St. Mark's Rest*) was

> left for our beholding in the final period of her decline: a ghost upon the sands of the sea, so weak - so quiet, - so bereft of all but her loveliness, that we might well doubt, as we watched her faint reflection in the mirage of the lagoon, which was the City, and which was the Shadow.[4]

We know that for Ruskin Venetian history went from an early period of formation (to 1297) to a second period of Gothic maturity (to 1418), to a third (from 1423 onwards), in which all the symptoms and the manifestations of decadence prevailed. At the onset of the Renaissance, "Instant degradation followed in every direction"; rationalism and the loss of religious faith turned Venice into a "dying city, magnificent in her dissipation".

In tracing her dissolution ("a long time Falling and a long time Dying", as Tanner aptly notes), Ruskin deployed the lexicon, the very vocabulary, that would go into the making of so many literary deaths in Venice. Blight, stagnation, death, darkness, decline, and ruin, mark the end of volume I of *The Stones of Venice* ; in volume II, Time and Decay, which in the past were an adornment for the city, threaten her destruction, while images, situations, premonitions, even evocations, of her ultimate death are scattered in the narrative. Volume III - significantly titled "The Fall" -

---

[3] Ruskin 1903-12, I 544; Tanner 1992, 70.
[4] Ruskin 1903-12, IX 17.

registers a disintegration, whose features would reappear in quite a number of "deaths in Venice" to follow. The 'rot' and 'decay' of Venice show already those traits with which the *fin de siècle* Decadents will endow her: excessive luxury and excessive refinement, intemperance, physical feebleness and moral laxity, satiety, voluptuousness, morbid leanings, aesthetic superfetation. Here is a revealing passage:

> Venice had in her childhood sown, in tears, the harvest she was to reap in rejoicing. She now sowed in laughter the seeds of death. Thenceforward, year after year, the nation drank with deeper thirst from the fountains of forbidden pleasure, and dug springs, hitherto unknown, in the dark places of the earth. In the ingenuity of indulgence, in the variety of vanity, Venice surpassed the cities of Christendom as of old she had surpassed them in fortitude and devotion [...].
> That ancient curse was upon her, the curse of the Cities of the Plain, 'Pride, fulness of bread, and abundance of idleness'. By the inner burning of her own passions, as fatal as the fiery rain of Gomorrah, she was consumed from her place among the nations; and her ashes are choking the channels of the dead, salt sea.[5]

Ruskin could indeed be biblical and moral. In spite of his conception of Venice as "the Paradise of cities" (in a late note, referring to a 1841 diary entry, that echoes the overall effect of *The Stones of Venice*), he presented a twilight view of it in the present, where the excess of beauty becomes a disease, unreality dismays, the labyrinth drags into the abyss. Venice confronts her pilgrims with a Medusa-like face: "Désespoir d'une beauté qui s'en va vers la mort" (as Maurice Barrès was to write in 1902 in *Amori et Dolori sacrum,* "La Mort de Venise" chapter: "une ville où nulle beauté est sans tare").

As we read elsewhere, if Carthage exhibits the death following the vain pursuit of wealth, and Rome the death due to the vain pursuit of power, Venice exhibits "the death which attends the vain pursuit of beauty".[6] In Ruskin, too, only the great artists - Giorgione, Turner - immortalize her fascination: Venice is becoming the superfetation of an artistic concept: her splendor harbours the seeds, as well as the attributes, that would make a literary *topos* of the "death in Venice" (with a further element to be discussed later on).

* * *

These particular views of the historic, artistic, and moral Fall of Venice were to provide the seedbed of the many literary deaths in which the nineteenth century revelled, all the way down to Thomas Mann, *et al.*

I will proceed to a quick survey of the variegated diffusion of the *topos*. It touches Charles Dickens (who in *Pictures from Italy* wrote of Venice with an eye on her commercial nature): Little Em'ly, in *David Copperfield* (1849-50), views Venice as "a superior form of Marshalsea". It is found in Wilkie Collins, who in *The Haunted Hotel*

---

[5] Ruskin 1903-12, XI, 194-195, - On all this, Tanner 1992, 78ff. (124 for the quotation), and Clegg 1981.
[6] Ruskin, 1903-12, VII 439-40.

(1878) sets the crucial murder of Lord Montberry, and the ensuing ghostly or macabre apparitions, in an old Venetian palace turned into a hotel. It involves Hugo von Hofmannsthal and Arthur Schnitzler (*Casanovas Heimkehr*, 1918); it culminates in Thomas Mann. It shows even in Marcel Proust - who for *his* love-affair with Venice starts from Ruskin, and when he makes her the place in which to be free from love (*Albertine disparue*), in order to be reborn must rely on the disappearance of the city itself. (Or indeed, as Stefano Agosti convincingly argues, Marcel's final access to Venice is allowed and enacted only after the death of Albertine: the famous *dalle* of his revelation in Venice is the sepulchre of the two primary women of the *Recherche*, Albertine and Grand'mère, who are both - just like Venice - simultaneously endowed with life *and* death).[7]

In English, the best example of a novel in which a death in Venice is enacted is Henry James's *The Wings of the Dove* (1902). James, too, followed in the steps of Ruskin and was a "passionate pilgrim" in Venice, celebrating the spell and the beauty of the city in magnificent essays. Yet the city is for him, as Leon Edel has aptly remarked, both a phoenix and a sepulchre; she is gradually brought under the shadow of death, and becomes an appropriate setting for death.[8]

This is how she is significantly characterized in his essay "The Grand Canal" (1892), where the idea of Venice as sepulchre is overtly put forth:

> Venetian life, in the old large sense, has long since come to an end, and the essential present character of the most melancholy of cities resides simply in its being the most beautiful of tombs. Nowhere has the past been laid to rest with such tenderness, such a sadness of resignation and remembrance. Nowhere else is the present so alien, so discontinuous, so like a crowd in a cemetery without garlands for the graves.[9]

In the novella *The Aspern Papers* (1888), Venice is a city of darkness, mystery, and mystification - where the past of the Misses Bordereau is buried and the protagonist is lost in the maze of conscience. In the short story "The Pupil" (1891), we have a cold, wind-swept Venice, with the rain lashing the lagoon; though the literary conceit is barely present (the young protagonist dies elsewhere), the city acquires a livid, lurid air, and is shaken by "A blast of desolation, a prophesy of disaster and disgrace". This is already a prefiguration of the meteorological and symbolic climate - wind and rain - in which Milly Theale's emblematic death in Venice is enacted in *The Wings of the Dove* :

---

[7] Agosti 1997, 12, 20, 27.- In writing about their double "death in Venice", Agosti stresses the "overplus of life" with which both are endowed (28).

[8] On this, and related, aspects, Perosa 1987 (3-11 for Edel's essay "Phoenix and Sepluchre. Henry James in Venice"); Tuttleton (ed.) 1990 ; Battilana 1971.

[9] James n.d., 32. - Even on the biographical level, the suicide in Venice of James's friend, and possibly *innamorata*, Constance Fenimore Woolson, seems to foreshadow his leaning toward the death in Venice literary motif: see Alide Cagidemetrio's and Alberta Fabris Grube's essays in Perosa (ed.) 1987, 53-64, 189-202.

> It was a Venice all of evil that had broken out for them [...] a Venice of cold lashing rain from a low black sky, of wicked wind raging through the narrow passes, of general arrest and interruption [...] the rain was ugly, the wind wicked, the sea impossible. (Book IX, ch. 30)

It comes as no surprise that "the vice in the air, otherwise, was too much like the breath of fate". Death is almost courted, pursued, sought, in Venice by Milly, because there is the perfect coincidence of place and destiny; there, among the ghosts of vanishing life, can her fate of betrayal, dissolution, and death be best achieved. Death also involves the love of Kate and Merton, the betrayers, because deterioration, doom and perdition sit between them in an uncanny way: the city *is* for all of them a city of death,[10] as if an air of cold corruption and steady decline marked people and places alike. This death in Venice has a cutting edge, it has nothing in common with the enervating, sirocco atmosphere prevailing in Thomas Mann.

Even in that beautiful novel-confession, *The Desire and Pursuit of the Whole* (c.1908), by the self-stiled Fr. Rolfe, Baron Corvo, one can say that the protagonist's quest in Venice has all the traits of a prolonged, pre-Mannian courtship of death; but in this exasperated daydream in the midst of the miseries of Venice we are surprisingly given a happy ending and a final transfiguration, that deny and overturn that streak of dissolution that so strongly runs through most of the narration. Here what looms like an inescapable, final death in Venice, is miraculously negated at the end.

* * *

But I am not satisfied, of course, with a simple *recensio*, or survey, of Anglo-American variants of the motif. I must needs ask the reason *why*: what may motivate, account for, or justify at a deeper level the insurgence and the diffusion of the *topos*?

For Leon Edel (who asked the question about James), the smell of decay emanating from the city, and the urge to attain the impossible that pervades it, lead to a kind of symbiosis/dichotomy whereby the splendour of the past, when seen in connection with the decay of the present, provokes the coexistence of a "death-in-life" and a "life-in-death" - an oxymoron that invokes, induces, and involves destruction. For Tony Tanner (who faced the question implicitly), Venice is a city of extremes in which the beauty of life, the hope for art and passion, must coexist with a sense of loss and dissipation, restriction and waste; a city of transformations and regenerations, Venice is a city of gold *and* shadows, of transfigurations *and* deep-seated mortality.[11]

That the aesthetic and decadent imagination of the *fin de siècle* should see and envelop Venice with those symptoms of excess and superfetation, of satiety and dissolution, that are the signs, premonitions, and preconditions of literary death, is a

---

[10] Cf. Tanner 1992, 202: "In *The Wings of the Dove* Venice is indeed a place of death - actual physical deterioration, pain, decay and collapse; and also more subtle forms of spiritual death and decline (Merton Densher also announces his own death while he is there[...])"--though Venice is also a place of love and carnality: the inescapable oxymoron.

[11] Edel, in Perosa (ed.) 1987, 3-11; Tanner 1992, 203 and *passim*.

fact, rather than an explanation. Just as it is an established fact (or again, purely a starting point) that Venice lives with - or dies of - an inbuilt obsolescence.

I wish then to suggest or to submit another possible explanation, which is linked to, and stems from, my recent studies on the ambivalent, indeed equivocal, nature that islands developed and acquired in our literary and cultural imagination (especially in the nineteenth century).[12]

The idea that all happy isles, the Fortunate Isles of the Blessed, of happiness and love (Venice included), are also inescapably islands of death, or intrinsically leading to death, in which death is ingrained, rooted, and embedded, is only the beginning of the explanation. More to the point is the concept that islands are usually characterized by incrustation and stratification - the phenomenon whereby culture is incrusted over nature, and nature over culture, in an indissoluble way, or indeed cultural, historical, and artistic stratifications are ostensibly added onto geological stratifications.

This fact is more predominant and more visible in islands on account of their closed-in and isolated - insulated - nature: it can more easily be detected, felt, and observed, both in itself and in its consequences - which are of de-naturalization, de-familiarization, and in the long run, *ultimately* (I stress *ultimately*), of death.

I am led to suggest this proposal by the same issue emerging on "newer" islands (which however have something in common with Venice...): I refer to the Caribbean islands, involved as they also are in tangles of literary deaths.

Derek Walcott, in his Nobel Prize lecture *The Antilles. Fragments of Epic Memory* (1992), insists on the fact that those "natural" islands, where untouched nature is presumed to prevail, have layers, strata, and sedimentations of history inscribed and *embedded* (his own words) in nature itself, which results in an explosive incrustation and conglomeration of history and nature, a long past and a compressed (or compromised) present:

> It is not that History is obliterated by this sunrise. It is there in the Antillean geography, in the vegetation itself. The sea sighs with the drowned from the Middle Passage, the butchery of the aborigines, Carib and Aruac and Taino, bleeds in the scarlet of the immortelle, and even the actions of surf on sand cannot erase the African memory, or the lances of cane as a green prison where indentured Asians [...] are still serving time.[13]

To give another example: V.S. Naipaul, a descendant of those "indentured Asians" in Trinidad, devotes at least three books to his native island, notably, for my purposes, *The Loss of El Dorado* (1969, rev. 1973) and *A Way in the World* (1994), in order to show how in that tourists' paradise (or purgatory...) history has been forcefully removed by the newcomers, but is actually present there in a bloody sedimentation. Caribs and Aruacs, Spaniards and Englishmen fighting for the island since Columbus, Berrio and Sir Walter Raleigh, then the French, the Blacks brought in from Africa, the Dutch, the Indians, the English again, and finally the Americans - battles and

---

[12] Perosa 1996, ch. 1; "In Search of Islands" (forthcoming).
[13] Walcott 1992, no pagination.

invasions, massacres and murders, all leaving a heavy sedimentation and incrustation on and in nature, which end by compromising and de-naturalizing it.

In *A Way in the World*, which covers much of the same ground as the previous work, the concept is memorably reinforced: in those islands - in Naipaul's beautiful phrase - history "was set on its head"; but it is there all the same. The writer's task is precisely to reinstate the past which is embedded and inscribed in them.[14] The same can be said of the other islands of Central America. The revealing aspect, in Naipaul's as well as in Ondaatje's book, for instance, is that the writer's task can be accomplished only by having one's private self take an active and complementary part in the process of perception and rediscovery.

Going back to my central issue: in the island *par excellence* (I believe the title is appropriate), in Venice, one did witness for centuries an imposing series of historical, cultural and artistic incrustations, sedimentations, and superfetations over nature, over the lagoon which pre-existed the island: even as a conglomeration of islands Venice was *created* by man. The nature/ culture oxymoron is predominantly and obsessively at work there.

First, as many writers - from Herman Melville to Ezra Pound - have observed, in Venice we have a *naturalization* of architecture: her palaces appear as coral reefs and such-like natural concretions (hence the possibility of my previous connection with far-away islands in other continents). "Reefs of palaces", Herman Melville called them; R. W. Emerson was ill at ease in a "beavers' city"; J.A. Symonds wrote of the pathos of a marble city sinking into her sepulchre of mud and brine; Proust, too (echoing Ruskin), in *De coté de chez Swann* (III, Noms de pays: le nom) writes of "those rocks of amethyst, like a reef in the Indian ocean" [I, 426], and in *Albertine disparue* of the rows of palaces as "a chain of marble cliffs" [III, 644: "une chaîne de falaises de marbre"]. Nature is indeed for him a dream "in which nature has learned from art". Ezra Pound, throughout *The Cantos*, plays on the glimmering perception of palaces as forests of marble, or petrified forests.

Second (and conversely), in Venice nature has been subjected to a drastic form of *culturization*. It was built, starting from its very foundations, in the water; it is a water city - more than an oxymoron, a contradiction in terms - on which a massive stratification of history, art and culture was endlessly piled. These stratifications of history and art were made *one* with the island; they make a splendid conglomerate and incrustation of it - as well as a *deadly oxymoron*.

In the passage in which he equates the buildings of Venice to "a chain of marble cliffs", Proust goes on to specify that they "made one think of objects of nature, but of a nature which seemed to have created its works with a human imagination" [III, 644:

---

[14] Cf also,"We, who had come in a variety of ways from many continents, were made to stand in for the aborigines and were held responsible for the nullity which had been created long before we had been transported to it"; Naipaul 1995, 79; the past was cancelled on behalf of the tourists, after the island had become a "ghost province" and had been driven out of history. - The various layers of sedimentation and incrustation existing in the island of Sri Lanka are also beautifully emphasized by Michael Ondaatje in his "memoir" *Running in the Family* (1982): Ondaatje 1984, 64 and *passim*.

"une nature qui aurait créé ses œuvres avec une imagination humaine"]. In *Andreas, oder Die Vereinigten,* Hofmannsthal hints at an "impossibility" of Venice, owing to her fusion of antique and oriental elements.

The heaviest and most disturbing co-presence and stratification is in particular that between past and present, on which Proust and James have written beautiful, suspended pages: Proust, in *On Re-Reading Ruskin* (Proust 1987, 128f), has an intense page on the Piazzetta before its two columns of gray and pink granite:

> that impression of having before me, inserted in the present actual hour, a little of the past [...] All around, the actual days, the days we are living, circulate, rush buzzing around the columns, but suddenly stop there, flee like repelled bees; for those high and slender enclaves of the past are not in the present, but in another time where the present is forbidden to penetrate. Around the pink columns [...] the days of the present crowd and buzz. But, interposed between them, the columns push them aside, reserving with all their splendid impenetrability the Past; of the past familiarly risen in the midst of the present.

As well as magical, the effect is uncanny, disquieting, disturbing.

My key-words have not been used at random: they all express and entail an oxymoron.

Ruskin writes of Venice as of a *wilderness of brick* (in Italian, we would say a *giungla di mattoni*), and a petrified sea; her "whole architecture is architecture of incrustation" - this is the point I left for my conclusion:

> The whole architecture of Venice is architecture of incrustation [...] the Venetian habitually incrusted his work with nacre: he built his houses, even the meanest, as if it had been a shell-fish, - roughly inside, mother-of-pearl on the surface: he was content, perforce, to gather the clay of the Brenta banks, and bake it into brick for his substance of wall; but he overlaid it with the wealth of the ocean, with the most precious of foreign marbles. You might fancy early Venice as one wilderness of brick, which a petrifying sea had beaten upon till it coated it with marble: at first a dark city - washed white by the sea foam.[15]

Both Proust and Pound would use the same word - incrustation - to define the inner nature of Venice.[16] Elsewhere, John Ruskin likens Venice to an opal and a coral reef,

---

[15] Ruskin 1903-1912, IX, 323; also Tanner 1992, 77-78.

[16] It is significant, however, that the incrustation of art and architecture, of historical and personal vicissitudes on Venice has for Pound a totally positive value (the very principle of incrustation and sedimentation is literally at work in *The Cantos*). Some critics (Guy Davenport and Hugh Kenner, for instance) see in the "white forest of marble" of his Venetian buildings an image of de-naturalization, almost of death; others have noted that he was instead following the lead of his friend Adrian Stokes, who in his study *The Stones of Rimini* (1934) had viewed the superimposition of the inorganic on the organic in Venice as the perfect symbiosis of an organic whole. For Stokes, the Istrian stones were salt's crystals perfectly married to petrifying waves; marble came from limestone, which "for the most part formed of organic deposits, is the link between the organic and the inorganic worlds" and "suggests concreted time" - just like Venetian glass, made as it is of sand and water. Both were *living* things - just like the Tempio Malatestiano at Rimini, an apotheosis or "stone-blossom" of Venice in itself and in its reliefs, in its ideal combination of "sea collected into

and writes that the branches of forests have *physically* turned into marble. These images of the organic turning into the inorganic are in themelves a further threat - once more unsettling and disquieting.

In this architecture of incrustation and interpolation (another term used by Ruskin), where styles are endlessly superimposed one upon the other, one runs the risk of a loss of identity and historical memory. In fact, the Fall of Venice begins for Ruskin with her highest moment of incrustation and superfetation - the Renaissance, which threatens at every moment to bury her under its weight and burden.

"Burden" becomes another key-word: for Ruskin the incrustations of all the great civilizations in the past - Assyrian, Egyptian, Arabic, Persian, Greek, Gothic, etc. - create a kind of noble grotesque (which he distinguishes from Hindi, Indian, or Polynesian grotesque, as we do not), from which it is painful and difficult to extricate oneself. The burden of such a stratification may ultimately prove a deadly burden.

Tu sum up: Venice is a city where palaces are coral reefs or marble cliffs; her buildings, steeples, and spires resemble a petrified forest ("a stone fable", Rilke would call her; Chateaubriand had called her an unnatural city, *une cité contre nature*). The sea is her life, and yet her constant threat of dissolution.

History and art have inscribed not only a stamp, but an imposing, massive, beautiful *and* deadly construction on her, in which the crucial boundaries between nature and culture, individuality and history, domesticity and art, are blurred - and in an overwhelming, excessive, threatening way.

The city is basically an *arti-fact*, and an artifice; a hybrid. One is beyond all measure, in Venice, constantly on the brink of rupture and dissolution, on account of an excess of contrasts, tensions, oxymora. An extreme kind of what Freud called *das Unheimliche* is at work there. Why otherwise would Melville (and others with him) believe that in St. Mark's the Great Turk has pitched his tent for a summer day? Why did Sartre feel *vide*, empty, there?

The burden of excessive beauty led decadents and aesthetes to cherish and court thoughts and experiences of death in Venice. My next step is: the burden of those innumerable incrustations, layers, sedimentations and stratifications (of which I have spoken so far), so visible and so obsessively present, makes of Venice a dangling, suspended city - a city forever on the brink of dissolving, disappearing, in spite of all her stones; a city, one might say, more on the other side than on this side - be it Paradise or Hell.

Can one therefore think of a better place and a better cradle of death? - indeed, of a better place where literary deaths are bound, doomed to happen, haunting and hovering

---

solid stone" (Tanner 1992, 316-319). Precisely as an example of artistic and historical conglomeration that temple was for Pound the peak of Renaissance art and culture, and was given a central role and function in *The Cantos,* His Venice (see below, note 17) thrives on superfetations and conglomerations, as *living* forest and petrified sea, as a synthesis of the organic and the inorganic: "*La pietra stessa vuol vivere una vita umana*" he had written in a late unpublished fragment (now in Mamoli Zorzi 1985, 47). In its stratification Venice is a synthesis of the Mediterranean, born from the water as naturally as Aphrodite, glittering in air, light, sea - and stones.

over writers and artists, almost by definition? This is then my final contention: constituted as she is by and on oxymora, contradictions, historical and artistic incrustations, revelations and concealments, a splendid example at once of de-naturalization and culturization, Venice proves inescapably the perfect, compelling place for literary deaths.

I may add a final qualification: this is truer of outsiders than of insiders, of those who come from elsewhere than those living there, of sojourners than inhabitants. The Venetians may wearily become accustomed and adjusted to the lingering fall of the city; coming from outside, the force of the oxymoron is more forcefully felt. It is no coincidence that almost all singers (as well as victims) of literary deaths in Venice are foreigners, *foresti*, from Ruskin to James, from Hofmannsthal to Mann, from Lord Montberry to Milly Theale, to Aschenbach (with the only exception of Schnitzler's Casanova).

The "quest" for a Death in Venice is then a projection mostly from the outside: Venice acts as a disquieting mirror of conditions of displacement, dismay, uncertainly, between here and there, the natural and the unnatural, the organic and the inorganic, vegetation and history, past and present, one piled uncannily on top of the other. This is why it arouses the sense, the temptation, the lure, the need, indeed the urge, of an *easeful death.* In this way Venice becomes an alluring trap or gulf, but also a liberating experience of death (one more oxymoron, which seems to prove her DNA).

I am suggesting, in conclusion, that besides the Stendhal syndrome - dismay and unease felt in front of an excess of art for which we were not prepared - one may postulate a Ruskin or an Aschenbach syndrome: when facing or entering too much art and history, nature and culture, past and present, stratified and compressed in the short confines of an island, not only does the heart misgive and the mind feel at a loss, but the overwhelming force of the oxymoron arouses and compels yearnings for death. It is, as in Poe, an eddy or a whirlpool into which one may wish to descend, a vortex to which one may let oneself go, but also a way of escape from the oppression caused by the anomalous situation which obtains in Venice.

"Take me [us] away from this land of impossible beauty", Roderick Hudson had cried in Henry James's novel of that title; so many passionate pilgrims seem to echo inwardly that feeling of entrapment in the city in the sea and to invoke a similar escape, knowing full well that when they stay, they die. In "the most unbelievable [die *unwahrscheinlichste*] of cities", as Thomas Mann called her, dreaming of going or staying there involves a dark, unfathomable yearning and determination for death.

Der Tod in Venedig, too, is ostensibly played and enacted on an oxymoron: the Apollonian, ethereal, perfect beauty of Tadzio set against the perturbation of an ageing soul and the mephitic miasma of a diseased city. After the Fall, so many literary deaths in Venice seem forcibly to testify to the deadly force of the oxymoron. But let us be assured: it is a condition or a proneness in all sense literary, and of the foreigner.

These are *paper* deaths, fantasies of annihilation - just like so many transfigurations and resurrections in Venice are daydreams, mirages and wish-fulfilment.[17]

Bibliography

Agosti, Stefano: Realtà e metafora. Indagini sulla Recherche. Milano 1997.
Battilana, Marilla: Venezia fondo e simbolo nella narrativa di Henry James. Milano 1971 (rpt. 1987).
Clegg, Jeanne: Ruskin and Venice. London 1981.
Cosgrave, Denis: "The Myth and the Stones of Venice". Journal of Historical Geography VIII 2 (1987), 145-169.
Honour, Hugh and Fleming, John: The Venetian Hours of Henry James. Whistler and Sargent. London 1991.
James, Henry: Italian Hours. New York, Grove Press, n.d.
Mamoli Zorzi, Rosella (ed.): Ezra Pound a Venezia. Firenze 1985.
Naipaul, V.S.: A Way in the World. New York 1995.
Ondaatje, Michael: Running in the Family. Toronto 1984.
Perosa, Sergio: "Romanzieri americani a Venezia". In: Italia e Stati Uniti nell'età del Risorgimento e della Guerra Civile. Firenze 1969, 379-401.

---

[17] Against the deadly force of the oxymoron, writers in English who identify Venice as the place for transfigurations and resurrections are notably Robert Browning, Baron Corvo and Pound. Opening the way to Pound's *Cantos*, in *Sordello* (1840, Bk. III) Browning muses on the steps of a Venetian palace; in the dream-sequence or reverie of *Fifine at the Fair* (1872), the carnival in Venice viewed from the Campanile in St. Mark's proves a positive experience of humanity and fulness of life; in spite of the crumbling palaces (cvi) Venice is a *topos* of Life (cviii), against all stereotypes, she brings down to, not away from, reality: "from such pinnacled pre-eminence, I found/Somehow the proper goal for wisdom was the ground/And not the sky" (ciii). Mutability turns to permanence in Venice: "Mutation was at end" (cvii), "I perceived arrest/O' the change all round about/.../unity in the place/ Of temple, tower" (cxx), etc. (St. Mark's is the realm of unity and wholeness for Proust, too: *Albertine disparue*). For Baron Corvo, Venice is the place where, in true Platonic terms, a split self can be made whole, where wholeness can be achieved in spite of dire separations (*The Desire and Pursuit of the Whole*). Finally, Venice is dealt with and evoked as the ultimate place of life, as the image of light, rescue and salvation in Pound's poetry, and extensively in *The Cantos:* "Venice seems a type/Of Life,'twixt blue and blue extends/.../'Tis Venice, and 'tis Life" (Ur-Canto 1). Against Ruskin, Pound (together with Browning) views the Renaissance as the culmination of Venice (Cantos 25 and 26), whose epitomes are provided by the Tempio Malatestiano in Rimini and the church of Santa Maria de' Miracoli (Cantos 72-73). In the *Pisan Cantos* Venice acts as sentimental recollection and elegiac appearance, as an image of appeasement and consolation in the midst of ruins, especially through the evocation of places ("the Squero where Ogni Santi/meets San Trovaso", etc., Canto 76, "Will I ever see the Giudecca again?", etc., Canto 83); in *Section: Rock-Drill 85-95 de los cantares* Venice is projected in flashes of fragmentary but luminous heavenly presence, as a *terzo cielo*, while into the last *Drafts and Fragments* are woven references to her crystalline, almost miraculous essence ("granite next sea wave/is for clarity", Canto 106; "The marble form in the pine wood", Canto 110, "A nice quiet paradise", Canto 111, where Venice becomes an epitome of serenity, the conclusion of the world: "Soul melts into air/anima into aura,/Serenitas"). Elsewhere Venice is Demetra and Aphrodite, an image of light, rebirth and almost divine unity, leading to endless transfigurations (see Perosa 1991, *passim*, Mamoli Zorzi 1985, *passim*).

Perosa, Sergio (ed.): Henry James e Venezia. Firenze 1987.
Perosa Sergio (ed.): Hemingway e Venezia. Firenze 1988.
Perosa Sergio (ed.): Browning e Venezia. Firenze 1991.
Perosa, Sergio: L'isola la donna il ritratto. Quattro variazioni. Torino 1996.
Proust, Marcel: On Re-Reading Ruskin, trans. and ed. J. Autret, W. Burford and P. J. Wolfe. New Haven 1987.
Proust, Marcel: Remembrance of Things Past, trans. C. K. S. Moncrieff and T. Kilmartin. Harmondsworth 1984, 3 vols.
Ruskin, John: Complete Works, ed. Edward T. Cook/Wedderburn, London 1903-12.
Tanner, Tony: Venice Desired. Oxford 1992.
Tuttleton, James W./ Agostino Lombardo (eds.): The Sweetest Impression of Life. The James Family and Italy. New York 1990.
Venezia da stato a mito (Catalogue of the Exhibition). Venezia 1987.
Walcott, Derek: The Antilles. Fragments of Epic Memory. New York 1992.

Elisabeth Bronfen

Venice - Site of Mutability, Transgression and Imagination

1. Shared secrets and cryptic lies

Describing how the sanctified and sanctifying bond of affection between a son and his mother is based upon a shared secret, whose content is never explicitly named, the narrator in Melville's *Pierre* suggests the following, "For, whatever some lovers may sometimes say, love does not always abhor a secret, as nature is said to abhor a vacuum. Love is built upon secrets, as lovely Venice upon invisible and incorruptible piles in the sea." Indeed, he continues, this mutually yet tacitly shared clandestine knowledge is comparable to airy bridges, "by which our further shadows pass over into the regions of the golden mists and exhalations; whence all poetical, lovely thoughts are engendered, and drop into us, as though pearls should drop from rainbows"[1]. I want to use the analogy between the way love is sustained by something known but not directly uttered and the city of Venice, sustained by edifices that are invisible to the eye, yet whose endurance is the very condition of its survival, to frame my discussion of *The Wings of the Dove*. My wager is that Henry James deconstructs the notion of romantic love by pitting his cruelly sober protagonists, who know that it is the rottenness in the law which preserves the very symbolic network it inhabits, against his self-deluded romantic protagonists, who are sustained by a fascination for fatal jouissance. As part of this narratorial game, Venice is chosen by James as the site where this battle of imaginations finds its apotheosis precisely because it so readily serves as the scene where both sides can protect their interests by celebrating a precarious preciousness of art.[2]

The intertextual reference to *Pierre* has not, however, been chosen at random. For it allows me to illuminate both the resilient power as well as the fatal consequences which love bonds infused with clandestine knowledge play through. The protagonist of Herman Melville's novel is, after all, haunted by the notion that he has inherited from his father a family secret. This conviction is sustained on the one hand by his recollection that, while on his deathbed, his father had murmured something about a lost daughter. On the other hand it is also nourished by the stories his aunt told him about how his father was in love with a French woman before his marriage and how this clandestine relation came to be recorded in a portrait made of him at the time. In other words, Pierre's sense of identity is intimately connected to his phantasy of paternal transgression, namely that his father had an illegitimate daughter he never

---

[1] Hermann Melville 1984, 99.
[2] As Tony Tanner 1992, 169 notes, what the dying heiress Milly Theale most desires is to emulate "one of those first ladies in glorious garments in a recreated Veronese painting." But what she ultimately has to experience and live with, "and from which there is finally no escape into art - is, indeed, 'conscious, reluctant mortality'." See also Hubert Teyssandier 1985, 69-82.

openly acknowledged. When in the strange and mysterious Isabel Pierre believes to have found the sister whose existence has haunted him as an inherited family secret, he comes to pit what could be termed an obscene, incestuous law against his mother's symbolic family codes. He breaks his engagement with Lucy, who has been preordained to be his wife, and, disinherited, moves to New York to set up a family, jettisoned from his father's official symbolic inheritance. However, at least by conviction, he is in fact living through his father's inofficial inheritance, namely the consequences of his alleged transgressions.[3]

If, then, the analogy between love's secrets and Venice's construction is introduced to describe how the mother, though cognizant of the existence of the paternal portrait, never speaks to her son about its import, while he doesn't ask her about it either, the second part of Melville's tale works with a similar exchange of implicitly shared clandestine knowledge, whose power resides precisely in the fact that it is never directly named. For like Pierre, Isabel is a cryptophore - a lover and bearer of secrets - telling him tales of how in her early years she was vagabonding, homeless, her origins obscure and in so doing, staging for his benefit a lack in knowledge, whose gaps she invites him to fill even while preserving the secret. She possesses him because of these obscurities, just as his conviction of his father's transgression had possessed him. Indeed she is the objectification of this inherited gap in knowledge. As she explains, in a quote which resonates with the way James' heroine, Milly Theale, fashions herself:

> Pierre, I am a poor girl, born in the midst of a mystery, bred in mystery, and still surviving to mystery. So mysterious myself, the air and the earth are unutterable to me; no word have I to express them. But these are the circumambient mysteries; thy words, thy thoughts, open other wonder-worlds to me, whither by myself I might fear to go [...] I am a nothing. (319)

Their bond is as sanctified by a sustained secret as the one to his mother had been, only now the secret has a different and ultimately fatal twist. While nominally the shared secret is that, because they know they are siblings, the marriage they have proclaimed to the world is a fiction, this story hides a second level of clandestine knowledge they both possess, yet have not actually shared with each other, namely that while Isabel believes Mrs. Glendenning to be her parent, Pierre is convinced she is the illegitimate daughter of his father. The anagnorisis of the narrative occurs when Pierre and Isabel see a portrait in a gallery bearing the title, 'A stranger's head, by an unknown hand.' While Isabel recognizes in this painting the man who used to visit her when she was a child and whom she imagined was her father, but who has nothing to do with the Glendenning estate, to Pierre this image recalls the paternal portrait he burnt the night before he left for New York, a portrait of which Isabel has no knowledge. Thus, rather than confirming their secret, the portrait introduces doubt into his aunt's nebulous legend, Isabel's still more nebulous story, his own dim reminiscences of his father's mental wandering at his death-bed. All Pierre had had to

---

[3] For a discussion of the law into two figurations - one normative and the other transgressive, see Slavoj Žižek, 1991 and Eric Santner, 1996.

sustain his conviction was a portrait, whose semiotic power consisted in the fact that, although the actual link between the meaning he attributed to the painted image was invisible - the love to a woman never admitted and its offspring never acknowledged - he believed this reference to be incorruptible. Yet with the emergence of a second portrait, just like the first - only now of a complete stranger, and a European to boot, with the painting imported to America, indeed perhaps purely imaginary, with no model at all as its real reference - Pierre's fantasmatic universe collapses. As the corruptibility, which is to say the fragility of a love based on shared secrets becomes visible, so, too, does the fact that it was never anything other than a protective fiction. In the logic of Melville's narrative, once the players are faced with the traumatic truth of the abyss subtending their romantic game they can do nothing but perform its logical fatality. The obscene, illegitimate family unit - Pierre, living with Isabel and Lucy - transforms into a triple corpse.

I invoke this literary predecessor to *Wings of the Dove* in order, before turning to a reading of James' text itself, to raise some theoretical implications inherent to two conceptions raised by Melville: on the one hand the notion that love is founded on secrets everyone is in on, while no one will name them directly, and on the other hand the proposed analogy between such cryptophoric love bondage and the special imaginary quality of Venice. I take the term 'cryptophore' from Nicolas Abraham and Maria Torok, who, in their work on fantasy, define reality as a secret:

> Just as desire is born along with prohibition, Reality too, at least in the metapsychological sense, is born of the necessity of remaining concealed, unspoken. This means that, at the moment of its birth, Reality is comparable to an offense, a crime. The crime's name is not identical with prohibition [...] Its name is genuinely affirmative, therefore unutterable [...] All secrets are shared at the start. Hence the 'crime' under consideration cannot be a solitary one, since it was turned into a secret. The 'crime' points to an accomplice, the locus of undue enjoyment, as well as to others who are excluded and, by dint of this same enjoyment, eliminated.[4]

Precisely because cryptophores cannot put the unnamable into words, given that - as Melville's narrative illustrates - this would cause their psychic reality to implode, they engage their peers as accomplices, so as to relive with them, in an intricate game of oblique utterances, that which has no place in words. The critical wager I want to propose is that *The Wings of the Dove* traces a communicative situation in which the psychic reality shared by the various characters is held together by the shared bond of a committed crime, though I am interested in this transgressive bond not as a pathological but rather as an existential issue. This inaugurating crime - which in James' narrative could be designated as the courtship plot involving a dying American heiress - must be covered up, even while it functions as a secret everyone is in on. In language that plays with the analogy of cryptophoric love and Venice as site of romantic performance, Abraham and Torok uncannily argue that in such an exchange of tacitly accepted secrets an already fulfilled desire lies buried, which is both incapable of rising to the foreground as it is also incapable of disintegrating. In other

---

[4] Nicolas Abraham and Maria Torok 1994, 158.

words, it is invisible to any direct viewing but also incorruptible. Indeed, the resilience of such a tacitly constructed bond consists in the fact that it haunts those in on the secret as clandestine knowledge, as unspeakable words buried alive, held fast, with everyone cognizant that they are implicated in the exchange that prohibits direct utterance so as to sustain the fulfillment of a cryptophoric desire.

Dissecting *The Wings of the Dove* in a somewhat structuralist manner one could say, in the first phase of the novel a crime is committed, and the shared secret at stake is both the marriage plot concocted by Aunt Maud, involving the rich heiress and Merton Densher, as well as Milly's own secret, the silence about her physical condition. In the second phase, Venice turns into the scene where this shared clandestine knowledge can fantasmatically be staged. Its cryptophoric topology functions as an actual embodiment of what up to that point had been a metapsychological reality. What is born in Venice -the crime (be this Mark's betrayal, Merton's lie or Milly's unexplained dying) - then comes to play itself out in the final phase of the novel, so as to cement the cryptophoric bond between the living and the death. As Abraham and Torok describe it, "[t]he objective and active existence of a secret can be posited as the very criterion of Reality, with reality a conscious and shared denial of some knowledge."[5] But - and therein lies James' ironic comment on this infection of romance not just by materialism but by cryptomania - a progression has taken place. What was initially unutterable has now changed its sign. Once Kate throws Milly's letter into the fire, she signals that the shared secret revolving around the value of the American girl's death is an actively and dynamically repressed desire not to tell, with the deceased transformed into a veritable phantom, which Abraham and Torok speak of as "an invention of the living [...] in the sense that the phantom is meant to objectify [...] the gap produced in us by the concealment of some part of a love object's life."[6] Indeed the dead Milly comes to haunt the living precisely by virtue of the gaps left within them by the secrets that have circulated around her illness and finally her death. Yet what is so compelling in James' narrative is that this gap is consciously produced. As Kate, perhaps, best knows, all of Milly's alleged friends are cryptophores; they all need the secret.[7] That is the perversion of their desire. And Venice is the site where this desire can be played through par excellence because, given that it is grounded on invisible piles, our belief in its survival welds together the knowledge that its foundations are precarious with the conviction that they are incorruptible. In analogy, the bond between the survivors is that it, too, is grounded on something invisible - what Milly did for her friends - even while this silence is performative. The illegibility of her act, consciously procured, is the precondition for the stability of their affective bond after her demise.

---

[5] Abraham and Torok, 160.
[6] Abraham and Torok, 171.
[7] As Tony Tanner 1992, 200 remarks, the knowledge Milly and her friends share can be compared to fog: "It is a knowledge which is not a knowledge. It is unnamed, unnameable, and no one wishes to know or name it. It is surrounded by a silence, a tacit conspiracy of not-asking."

Yet the question of scene in *The Wings of the Dove* is more complex. Venice is not just significant as a cryptophoric site, but also as an extraordinary site, the arsenal of inherited fictions and the scene where these come to be realized. For this reason I want to add Michel Foucault's notion of the heterotopia to Torok and Abraham's discussion of cryptophores. Though linked to normal sites, heterotopias are radically other sites, real places that do exist but as counter-sites, "a kind of effectively enacted utopia [...] Outside of all places, even though it may be possible to indicate their location in reality".[8] Though Foucault offers various criteria, the following are particularly relevant to *The Wings of the Dove*. Heterotopias are the "privileged places, reserved for individuals who are in a state of crisis," and since this often involves questions of death, they are also those privileged places that juxtapose not only several spaces in a single real place but also harbor slices in time, opening up onto "what might be termed, for the sake of symmetry, heterochronies". Venice, and particularly Milly's Palazzo, splice together two such heterotopic moments - the museum, marking an infinite accumulation of time, and the festival, where "time in its most fleeting, transitory, precarious aspect" comes to be performed.[9] For owing to its rich display of cultural artifices of the past, Venice accumulates historical time, making what is temporally lost and foregrounding decay, even while the Italian city also marks the precariousness of Milly's time, which is to say the fact that her time is running out. Furthermore, Venice, and again the Palazzo Leporelli in particular, like Foucault's heterotopias, presupposes a system of opening and closing that both isolates these sites and makes them penetrable. Though a site of freedom from everyday reality, Venice is not freely accessible. One must be invited to come, and, particularly seminal to James' narrative, the opening also hides curious exclusions. Though in Venice, Milly's friends partake only of those public places made available to them, not the Venice of the indigenous population, they may enter Milly's palazzo, but not her private chamber. But above all Venice - built on an invisible but incorruptible pile in the sea - is such a compelling heterotopia because it functions as a site of illusion and compensation, as what Foucault calls the "reserve of the imagination";[10] the harbor and progenitor of fantasy, of sexual transgression, of adventures in betrayal and immolation.

2. To think tremendously of money

Turning to the semantic encoding of Venice in James' *The Wings of the Dove*, one could ask what, in this narrative about love's secrets and the love of secrets, is it the scene for? If for all the other characters Venice is a transitory site - the setting designated to play through a profitable intrigue - for the protagonist it is the spatial materialization of her psychic topology. It is her site of crisis. She comes here, after all, to die. This double function of Venice - namely as the scene for the unfolding of narratives and as an analogy to the psyche of the endangered, mysterious heroine - as

---

[8] Michel Foucault 1986, 24.
[9] Foucault, 25-26.
[10] Foucault, 27.

well as the incommensurability between these two functions, is addressed in a rather striking passage placed fairly late in the text. As he is speaking to Dr. Luke Strett about Milly's declining health Merton Densher suddenly realizes:

> He had not only never been near the facts of her condition - which had been such a blessing for him; he had not only, with all the world, hovered outside an impenetrable ring fence, within which there reigned a kind of expensive vagueness, made up of smiles and silences and beautiful fictions and priceless arrangements, all strained to breaking; but he had also, with everyone else, as he now felt, actively fostered suppressions which were in the direct interest of everyone's good manner, everyone's pity, everyone's really quite generous ideal. It was a conspiracy of silence, as the cliché went, to which no one had made an exception, the great smudge of mortality across the picture, the shadow of pain and horror, finding in no quarter a surface of spirit or of speech that consented to reflect it. 'The mere aesthetic instinct of mankind -!' our young man had more than once, in the connexion, said to himself. (388).[11]

What I am interested in is the way Venice invites overlooking the particularity of death in favor of an aestheticization, even while it also points to the fact that it invites such an oversight. The contingency of human existence those in Venice choose not to see refers not only to the fact that the unafflicted can never share in the dying of another, but rather that this dying - and thus any plot contrived to protect oneself and profit from it - is incalculable. In other words, at issue is not just the inaugural crime Abraham and Torok speak about, the knowledge that something one has no control over has happened before any plotting can begin, but also that at any point chance can intercede. Or put another way, the analogy between the fated orphan, Milly Theale, and Venice consists in the fact that both the heiress and the place she has chosen as her crisis heterotopia, can't be calculated, even while both the woman and the city ask those speculating on their value to indulge in, indeed, to celebrate their calculations.

The manner in which Venice will come to correspond so perfectly to the way Milly chooses to stage her dying is foreshadowed by two earlier scenes, the first occurring on an Alpine mountain, where Milly's companion Susan Stringham finds her seated on the dizzy edge of a slab of rock, "thrown forward and vertiginous," to enjoy a "view of greater extent and beauty" (84). In this liminal site - combining risk and chance - Milly seems to enjoy the experience of hovering between fatal accident and, as Susan sees it, "the state of uplifted and unlimited possession," she will come to fully realize in her palazzo. As Milly explains to Susan, who wishes to designate a clear location for the woman she treats as her trophy:

> Since I've lived all these years as if I were dead, I shall die, no doubt, as if I were alive - which will happen to be as you want me. So, you see...you'll never really know where I am. Except indeed when I'm gone; and then you'll only know where I'm not. (132)

Her sense of being nowhere consists in the preservation of a shared secret that will never be solved - "I don't know where I am, and you never will, and it doesn't matter"

---

[11] Henry James 1965. All page references are from this edition and will be marked with page numbers in the text of my essay.

(132). This is characteristic of her desire to live on the psychic limen between life and death, where slices of time come to be juxtaposed, with the past and its deceased made present, even while those partaking in her dying will only be able to locate her in the traces she will have left once she is gone. This cultivation of what Barthes calls the uncanny presence of the dead in photographic representation[12] - namely when we know in one and the same gesture that someone is dead and that she is going to die - is made most manifest in the scene when Lord Mark shows Milly the Bronzino portrait that resembles her. To her, the face of the young woman signifies above all mortality - "she was dead, dead, dead. Milly recognized her exactly in words that had nothing to do with her. 'I shall never be better than this'" (144). She notes later that this was the first moment she was able to acknowledge her fate by putting it into words and tears, thus quitting "ignorance and reaching her view of the troubled sea" (290). As in *Pierre*, the viewed resemblance allows her to turn the contingency of her illness into a coherent narrative sentence, namely one which explains to her that another, who resembles her visually, also resembles her in her mortality. But she undertakes this narrative transformation based on a purely accidental viewing of a portrait that someone happened to show to her. Nevertheless, this is also the narrative Dr. Luke Strett supports, when he suggests she has the power to choose between living and dying, refusing to pronounce her anything in particular. Like the city she chooses to go to, Milly is distinguished precisely because her illness is certain but also indeterminate. She embodies the state of endangered and thus precious uncertainty culturally connected with Venice, which, like her, exists over and against the threat of decay, thriving on this distinction, and corrupting those partaking of the spectacle with fantasies. Thus, if from the start, Milly is presented as a cryptomaniac, who infects her willing accomplices, engaging them in a plot where secrets engender more secrets, these plots are contrived to cover over a lack inherent to human existence, namely the larceny with which psychic reality begins; our vexed knowledge that we are always already robbed of some plenitude; that we are always already marked by some inherited stain. The transformation undertaken by her accomplices in crime works by turning contingency into an issue of fate and of manipulation; into a battle between sacrifice and self-interested intent. Each of her friends writes a narrative about her - Susan casting her in the guise of a rarified property, Merton Densher in that of the American girl he invented during his trip to New York, Kate as the dove who will protect her and her illicit lover. Milly is such a powerful catalyst for fictions, however, because her accomplices cannot determine whether she is "as ill as she looks" (227), extraordinary because she "has so much to lose" (228), because she appears to possess "something that's past patching" (229), but also affecting them as a "creature saved from a shipwreck" who, having "met her adventure" will now face future contingencies with confidence. Even while she explains to her friends that she lacks the "power to resist the bliss of what I have" (89), the nature of this possession remains undefined, referring either to wealth and/or fatal illness. As they tell each other "[s]he'll really live or she'll really not. She'll have it all or she'll miss is all," (230) what is clear is that,

---

[12] Roland Barthes 1980.

even before she arrives in Venice, Milly embodies one of the traits I have isolated for the crisis heterotopia. She is both the object of speculation, inviting those around her to enter into her drama, and she performs a scene with clearly defined boundaries. She will allow them to enter into her secret scenario only so far. Precisely because she, like Isabel in Melville's text, cultivates secrecy, she encourages the strange plot where making up to a sick girl comes to be coterminous with pretending that she doesn't affect them as sick.

Thus if, again in a structuralist mode, one were to label the progression of this *enchainement* of shared secrets, one would need to begin with, on the one hand, Kate and Merton's marked concealment of their clandestine engagement and on the other, Milly's marked display of her clandestine possession. Onto this is added Maud's nebulous plan to do something with Milly's prosperity for Kate. As these shared secrets merge and engender more secrets, Kate's clandestine engagement transforms into a game with Milly's infatuation for Merton labeled as 'she'll help us to go on', where, although they do so for different reasons, all women involved - Kate, Maud and Susan - offer Milly to Merton in marriage, clearly with her consent, while Dr. Strett gives a new turn to the screw by informing them that, although hers is not the case she thinks, there is something else. While Kate sees herself as being tainted by the stain of her father's dishonor, although the exact disgrace is never directly named, and Merton is marked by his want of means, Milly counters this with her knowledge of being the fated "survivor of a general wreck" (158). In this plot of secrets everyone appears to think tremendously of money, as though to cover over a traumatic knowledge that the bank is always already empty with any attempt at existence within a symbolic realm marked by this inaugural theft. In a strange aside, Maud, seeking to allay Susan's doubt about Kate's dissimulation regarding her romantic feelings for Merton, confesses "Kate thinks she cares. But she's mistaken. And no one knows it" (271).

3. Caged Freedom

The first, and perhaps most significant Venetian scene, is the Palazzo Leporelli, where "the servants, frescoes, tapestries, antiquities" embody a "thorough make-believe of a settlement", even while it holds "its history still in its great lap" (284) - a site where time is juxtaposed even as the expected crisis, "the avalanche Milly lived so in watch for" (288) is held at bay. It is a synthesis of the earlier liminal sites characterizing Milly; the seat on the edge of the Alpine mountain and the painting gallery in Matcham. For seated in the midst of remnants of the past, "as in the ark of her deluge" (289) she finds herself encased here, floating slightly above the city, cognizant of the summer sea, breathing into this veiled space. As she explains to Lord Mark, she never goes out, but rather stays up, because

> the romance for her [...] would be to sit there for ever, through all her time, as in a fortress; and the idea became an image of never going down, of remaining aloft in the divine, dustless air, where she would hear but the plash of the water against stone. (292)

Venice - Site of Mutability, Transgression and Imagination

Crucial about this palazzo is, moreover, the fact that it is both the site for utter honesty and for utter fiction. In the interview during which she rejects Mark's proposal of marriage she both admits 'I'm very badly ill' (297) and insists on entertaining a willful blindness towards the possibility that Kate might be hiding her true relation with Merton. In this caged freedom she externalizes the arrestation between life and death performed by her infected body; floating above the world yet also hooked into its ploys; offering her friends a setting and a display for the realization of fictions revolving around her illness and fulfilling the act of dying, as this marks the ground and vanishing point of the resilient and ultimately undecidable *chatoyement* of contingency and destiny. As Milly insists,

> her palace - with all its romance and art and history - had set up round her a whirlwind of suggestion that never dropped for an hour. It wasn't, therefore, within such walls, confinement, it was the freedom of all the centuries. (309)

As the party she stages to cement her unspoken engagement to Merton illustrates, the palazzo and its tenant seem to animate each other. By using it as the scene for her self-display, Milly appears to bring out, as Susan puts it, "all the glory of the place" (329), transforming it into a living Veronese painting, even while this staged scene allows her to enclose all her friends into a *tableau vivant*, depicting "one of the courts of heaven, the court of an angel," in which she figures as "the great and only princess" (333). In this other space - "the golden grace of the high rooms, chambers of art in themselves" - the individual figures merge into one big scenic display, because Milly, "let loose among them in a wonderful white dress, brought them somehow into relation with something that made them more finely genial" (334). During this moment, staged so explicitly as an arsenal of imagination, the Palazzo calls forth two turning points in the mutually shared narrative of secrets. Merton, recognizing that all the figures in the scene "came together round him," finally names, and thereby accepts, their desire to court a dying woman, while cultivating a willful blindness towards her illness, even while Milly, posing as the living embodiment of an ancient Venetian portrait, gives the final legitimation to this plot:

> her smile, the lustre of her pearls, the value of her life, the essence of her wealth. It brought them, with faces made fairly grave by the reality she put into their plan, together again. (345)

At the same time, it is in this heterotopic site that he is able to procure from Kate, in exchange, her promise to visit him in his rooms.

Pitted against the Palazzo we find on the one hand the open spaces of Venice, site for tourists, and the rooms Merton has decided to rent so as to get away from the foreigners indulging in their stay abroad. These rooms also function like a heterotopic site, positioned between the familiarity of home and the lack of intimacy of a hotel, and in the course of the narrative they come not only to serve as a site of sexual transgression but more importantly as a crypt, preserving his memory of this event. In contrast to the Piazza San Marco, presented as a site of perpetual feasting, of visiting, of possible acquaintance - "a great social saloon, a smooth-floored, blue roofed chamber of amenity, favourable to talk" (319) - but also, precisely because here everyone is fully visible, a site where Merton and Kate can say to each other what they like, the charm of his private rooms consists in the fact that they are utterly unexposed. In contrast to the harsh openness of the square, encouraging unprotected speech, these rooms reintroduce the issue of secrecy, even while they are the site where Merton's sexual desire for Kate comes to be consumed, a desire he was initially able to articulate in the uninhibited site of the Piazza but insist upon only in the festively decorated Palazzo. Indeed, these rooms are the scene of his inner theatre, offering a counter-point to Milly's cryptophoric desire in the sense that they preserve Merton's and Kate's shared secret. Serving as a monument to the fact that he had made her accept his proposition, they also commemorate the perverse enjoyment subtending symbolic bonds, the many lies that have been told to sustain the *tableau vivant* of the dying Milly surrounded by her caring friends. At the same time they also function as the uncanny harbinger of love's spectrality, for here Merton enjoys Kate's presence long after she has departed from Venice in much the same manner he will desire Milly after her demise. Here he is able to reiterate his clandestine enjoyment of Kate as

> a treasure kept, at home, in safety and sanctity, something he was sure of finding in its place when, with each return, he worked his heavy old key in the lock. The door had but to open for him to be with it again and for it to be all there; so intensely that, as we say, no other act was possible to him than the renewed act, almost the hallucination, of intimacy. (348)

This cryptophoric treasure is what allows him to court Milly, and significantly the turn of phrase James chooses is one that articulates the fault line between inclusion and exclusion - "when he closed the door behind him for an absence he always shut her in. Shut her out" (349). Pitted against the rooms in London that Kate refuses to go to in the first part of the novel, but which she so readily comes to at the end, so as to show Merton the will Milly left behind, these Venetian rooms signify his possession of her as a cryptophoric wealth: "As Kate was all in his poor rooms (...) it was only on reflection that the falseness came out." (349)

Venice, one can say, is thus heterotopically constructed in *Wings of the Dove* because it is a site of crisis and chance. Anything might happen. It is the scene where plots concocted in London can be played through, where phantoms can be cultivated; in Merton's rooms the hallucination of forbidden intimacy with Kate, in Milly's palazzo the fiction of a viable marriage between Merton and the dying heiress as this is interlaced with the fiction that she isn't as though dying. Henry James stages these heterotopic sights to reveal the cryptomania subtending his protagonists' rhetoric of love, namely the fact that Merton desires Kate as a secret, enjoys the traces she leaves in his imagination, as he will desire the image of Milly he produces in his imagination, his fantasy of her dying silently in her palazzo.[13] The juxtaposition of slices of time so characteristic of heterotopias translates into an exchangeability of the two love objects

---

[13] For a discussion of the final meeting between Merton and Milly see Quentin G. Kraft 1965, 217-223.

in Merton's psychic reality. When with Milly, Kate is spectrally present to him, and later, when with Kate, the impact Milly has made on him can not be effaced. At the same time, Venice is the site for a battle of diverse, though interfaced fictions; notably Maud's fantasy that with Kate's fortune made she and Kate could govern the word together; Susan's fantasy that while Milly looks death in the face she could live if she wanted to; Merton's ambivalent fantasy that, on the one hand, he would be happy with Kate, because he is innocent of the plot revolving around a dying heiress, given that he is nothing other than the instrument of his mistress, passively following her orders. On the other hand he also recognizes his own agency and feels responsible for his actions, since he has convinced himself that Milly's life depends on him: "It was on the cards for him that he might kill her". (358)

Finally there is the open Piazza, to which Merton flees once he discovers that Milly will not receive him. In the conventional correspondence between topology and psychic state, Venice - functioning up to that point as the site for abundant imagination - suddenly transforms into the place where James' protagonist discovers the limit of these fictions. Echoing Milly's change of heart, the weather turns, to illustrate that things happen to thwart even the most contrived plot. As he watches the storm gusts, Merton has "a sudden sharp sense that everything had turned to the dismal. Something had happened" (362). Venice suddenly becomes a city

> all of evil [...] a Venice of cold, lashing rain from a low black sky, of wicked wind raging through narrow passes, of general arrest and interruption, with the people engaged in all the water-life huddled, stranded and wageless, bored and cynical, under archways and bridges. (363)

It induces in Merton a sense of general suspicion but also a sense of a spell having broken:

> the wet and the cold were now to reckon with, and it was precisely, to Densher, as if he had seen the obliteration, at a stroke, of the margin on a faith in which they were all living [...] The shock, in some form had come. (364)

As he now wanders through the streets of Venice, he not only notices the grease, the rubbish in the shops, the way Venice in all its elegance and grand conception also signifies some "profaned and bewildered reverse of fortune" (364). It is above all in this melancholic mood that he sees Lord Mark in the Caffé Florians, and the silent recognition that passes between them does not signify the disclosure of a repressed secret (for their cryptomanic game thrives ever more resiliently), but rather the discovery of what the work of fiction represses, namely contingency. Something unexpected and not calculated has interrupted the courtship plot, even while Merton seeks to recuperate this accident into a narrative of calculated betrayal;

> The vice in the air, otherwise, was too much like the breath of fate. The weather had changed, the rain was ugly, the wind wicked, the seam impossible, because of Lord Mark. It was because of him a fortiori, that the palace was closed. (366)

Indeed, by declaring Mark to be the brute, responsible for Milly's demise, he is able to exonerate himself - "a sense of relief, and that, in turn, a sense of escape" (367). The narrative he constructs for himself, as the wind and weather continue to break the charm of Venice, is that he is a victim in a double sense; the medium of Kate's intrigue and the object of Mark's villainy.

Venice thus emerges as a fundamentally duplicitous site, on the one hand the place where one can produce and play through fictions to protect oneself from the traumatic knowledge of implenitude and vulnerability, and, on the other hand, the place where trauma catches up with you; the place where shock occurs. Venice both invites the visitor to be cognizant only of the aesthetic aspect of life and then suddenly allows all the decay and ephemerality subtending beauty to come to the fore. It functions as a privileged site, where self-aesthetization can be celebrated, as during Milly's party or during the meeting with Mark, when she is so honest about her desire to be deceived. Equally it serves as the site for erotic transgressions, notably the clandestine meeting between Merton and Kate as well as his cryptomanic preservation of this exchange in the form of reiterable hallucinations. Furthermore, it is the scene where fantasies of rivalry can be cultivated, where Mark can be transformed into the universal scapegoat, exonerating them all. However, Venice is above all the site for contingency. This question of chance, breaking in accidentally, and thus producing a shock to all efforts at writing and at living plots, involves, on the one hand, the question of death. The fatality it invokes applies to the various stagings of Milly's death, as well as to death as a shared secret, whose reality they know but choose not to see. It points to mortality as a piece of traumatic knowledge, which broadcasts the fact that one is haunted by the losses of the past, as these losses arrest one, envelope one; to mortality as a knowledge outside the category of representations yet calling forth protective narratives. On the other hand, the contingency I am concerned with also involves the fundamental antagonism at the heart of fantasy work. As Slavoj Žižek argues, in the debate over the incommensurability between traumatic knowledge, such as dying, and its narrative representation, at stake is not only the fact that narratives in some sense are always false, because based upon the exclusion of traumatic events and the patching up of the gaps left by these exclusions. Rather, in answer to the question 'Why do we tell stories?' he suggests "that narrative as such emerges in order to resolve some fundamental antagonism by rearranging its terms into a temporal succession. It is thus the very form of narrative which bears witness to some repressed antagonism. The price one pays for the narrative resolution is the petitio principii of the temporal loop - the narrative silently presupposes as already given what it purports to reproduce."[14]

What James so cannily plays through in *The Wings of the Dove* is that its narrative intrige does not only involve the incommensurability between random events and the stories we tell to make sense of these, and in so doing transforming an accident into a question of destiny or fate. Rather at stake also is the fact that things just happen to go in certain ways once an intrigue has begun, in a manner those involved have no control over. The accomplices in the crime called reality want to assign the question of agency

---

[14] Slavoj Žižek 1998, 10.

to someone, if only, as in the case of Mark, to declare someone to be a villain. But something always eludes narrative. Along these lines, Venice is a site for indeterminacy not just in the sense that we can never decide whether Milly dies because of the intrigue, with Mark or Merton responsible, or whether her dying is to a degree independent of all these plottings; a state they are not only willfully blind to, but something they, as non-afflicted actually can't know. Rather, equally indeterminate is the question whether all this talk about money and death might not itself be a protective fiction hiding a different traumatic knowledge, namely that of human fallibility.[15] This hidden knowledge involves the fact that all the characters are marked by psychic larceny and vulnerable before the onslaught of chance. This shock subtending and calling forth narratives, this impasse marring all explanations as it encourages them, can be named and worked through in a satisfying and protecting manner, once it is given a body (Milly) and a scene (Venice). I have invoked Foucault's notion of heterotopia so as to offer a speculation why Venice is not only configured as the topographical equivalent of the dying heroine but also as the site performing the fault line between beauty and decay. In Venice, an enigma can be performed, preserved and obliquely answered, namely the fact that although it is a concrete place it is also, for those coming to visit it from London or New York, outside reality. It is clearly a scene, not home, a theatrical materialization of projections. Yet it is also fluid, showing traces of precarious foundations that are hidden, because it is a city which appears to be floating on the water, while it is also clearly anchored. It is a city clearly marked by history yet also by the decay, which is written into the very walls of Milly's palazzo. Finally, it is the city of pure survival, embodied by the servant Eugenio, who, as a profane counter-figure to all the sophisticated talk about money, proves to be someone who performs his mistress' wishes but who will also cheat her whenever he can.

Like Venice, Milly signifies this draw between contingency and fiction, for her charm resides in the fact that, though fated, she also has chance. Things may turn for the better but they could also turn for the worse. Her beauty is so resilient because it precariously hovers between life and death. Her liminality calls forth fantasies about supreme loss and gain, because though something fatal is intimated, it is not clearly seen. She seems to make herself fully available to the speculations of her friends while also excluding them from her dying. Lord Mark's return to Venice also marks the return of the antagonistic impasse inherent to the schemes so brilliantly played through in Milly's palazzo. It directly names the fact that at the onset of their exchange of shared secrets lies a crime and, once more obliquely citing Melville's narrative, James suggests that by putting the unnamable into words, he provokes a collapse at least of the Venetian fiction. In narrative terms, putting closure on the sequence that began when Milly rejected his marriage proposal, Mark now pays back the utter honesty she had shown him then in a similar coin. He pits against the ploys and delusions

---

[15] For a discussion of how within Freudian psychoanalytic discourse inaugural traumatic knowledge finds an oblique representation in belated narratives one could call protective fictions because they seal off and cover over this distressing psychic material, see Elisabeth Bronfen 1998.

cultivated around her the shocking voice of revelation. We can, of course, only surmise what he said, but it would have run along the lines of a counternarrative - 'Yes, you are fated to die. Yes, you are being had. Yes, we are all in on it.'

But if Mark's return signals that, though for different reasons, all - including the dying woman herself - were implicated, one must, in Jamesian fashion ask, implicated in what? The wager I am proposing is that what *The Wings of the Dove* plays through, using Venice as its chosen scene, is the way fiction turns trauma into narratives, so that the ethics of this tale of morals and manners resides precisely in the way it dismantles any assurance we might have in being able to judge actions.[16] Given the way we are so clearly asked to recognize that the vilification of Lord Mark is part of Merton's strategy of self-exoneration, but also given the fact that, since everyone wants the same thing, including the alleged victim, the opposition between evil and good seems to collapse, James asks us to recognize that at issue is not how to label actions in a moral sense. Rather, at stake is the aporia that while any story we tell is always incommensurable with the traumatic knowledge of our own implenitude, it serve as a necessary, indeed unavoidable protective fiction. Did Merton, and with him, the entire band of friends, do harm to Milly, or is this a story they tell themselves to explain why, despite their concern for her she, nevertheless, died? Do the stories they circulate about what each has done for the other merely hide another, more distressing secret about their fundamental fallibility, namely that death can not be averted, much as neither romantic desire nor social ambition can ever be fulfilled? Is designating Milly as victim and Mark as villain a way to be blind to the fact that they not only never saw her death but that, even if they had, they could have effected nothing? In other words, is it easier to construct stories where guilt and responsibility can clearly be distributed among the players of a game, opening up the path to fantasies of regret, atonement, mourning as well as idealization of the deceased, rather than accepting that in questions of life and death one has no agency and no control other than accepting one's disempowerment before the accidents of mortal existence? James' ethical gesture, I want to argue, lies precisely in the suspension of moral values in favor of an acknowledgment that any story rearranges the antagonism between the shock of contingency and the events that respond to this into a temporal sequence. Venice so compellingly corresponds to this representational impasse, because, as a scene for the battle of imaginations, it is erected upon invisible and incorruptible piles in the sea.

---

[16] In a similar fashion Tony Tanner 1992, 203 surmises that the reason James chose Venice as the scene for this tale has to do with the fact that it is the city of two extremes: "of all the hope and beauty of life, the possibilities of art and passion; and all the sense of loss and despair, waste and belatedness." The ambigous transformations Venice can perform for its inhabitants ultimately come down to a question of ethics, "of mortality - and mercy".

4. Ah, there you are!

Back in London, a different battle is waged, not for the truth of what happened but for the power of fantasy work, for within the logic of James' universe, agency is ultimately in the hands of the one who recognizes that we need protective fictions. As Kate, proving herself to be the more viable player, explains to Merton, "[Milly] never wanted the truth. She wanted you" (405). While he insists on trying to disclose the secret - persistently asking how in the world Mark could have known about their engagement - Kate seeks to preserve their cryptophoric game. In contrast to Venice, London is the site of belated recognition rather than anticipation - they all realized that "something has happened" (421) to them. It is at the same time, however, the site of waiting rather than acting, with Kate adamantly cautioning against precipitous actions. Indeed, if in Venice shared secrets could be played through, with the effect of this clandestine game leaving its traces in London, it is here that things are precisely not performed but hidden; that secrets are not shared but destroyed, notably the letter Milly intended as Merton's Christmas gift. Yet the cruel turn James introduces into Kate's speculations, illustrating once again that the obscene underside of the law can never be effaced, is that, by virtue of her destructive gesture, they have now irrevocably lost

> the turn [Milly] would have given her act. That turn had possibilities that, somehow, by wondering about them, his imagination had extraordinarily filled out and refined. It had made of them a revelation the loss of which was like the sight of a priceless pearl cast before his eyes - his pledge given not to save it - into the fathomless sea. (451)

Yet it is precisely this loss Merton now enjoys, putting closure on the hallucinations cultivated in his rooms in Venice yet opening up a far more viable prospect of unlimited cryptophoric nostalgia. Milly's foreclosed voice

> was like the sacrifice of something sentient and throbbing, something that, for the spiritual ear, might have been audible as a faint, far wail. This was the sound that he cherished, when alone, in the stillness of his rooms. (451)

The difference resides in the fact that while in Venice he had encrypted a recollection of sexual knowledge shared with his beloved, in his rooms in London he encrypts an irretrievable lack in knowledge; which is to say precisely what Milly wanted to share with him, but which Kate destroyed.

Henry James's deconstructive turn consists in the fact that the phantom Merton erects in fantasy is the more powerful, prevailing against the voice of Milly which Kate, having opened the second letter containing her will, not only does not foreclose, but rather also insists that Merton hear, namely that the deceased has bequeathed her fortune to him. Against the more conventional reading, which suggests that Henry James conceived of Kate as an embodiment of materialism, and concomitantly as the force of evil, thwarting what is aesthetically precious in a harshly capitalist world, I want to suggest that Kate's double gesture is an ethical one. For its aim is the dismantling of romantic illusions in favor of a different narrative, namely one that addresses our emplacement within a symbolic world, which is to say within an economic and legal network of codes. Though the laws that govern this world are as much protective fictions as the network of romantic texts, they are at least more honest, given that they foreground how human existence consists in subjecting oneself to cultural constraints. While she wont break the seal of Milly's love letter, eclipsing her voice, and thus finally bringing Merton's cryptomania to full bloom, Kate will break the bank's seal, as though to signify that the symbolic exchange of money is the only fiction that really matters. Merton punishes her by not looking at the contents, preferring to preserve his own ignorance in the hope of getting back his innocence in return. He seeks to cultivate the fiction that he is untainted by what happened, by the shock of accident that thwarted all their plans, even while this event has left an undeniable stain on him as well. Kate not only astutely notes, "Your desire is to escape everything" (455), but, confronting him with his necrophilia, "Her memory's your love. You want no other" (456). She knows that they have no choice but to accept the double trace Milly's dying has left upon their own relation. In so doing she insists that they are all as irrevocably marked by what happened as by their respective family legacies; namely the crime of reality which served as the catalyst for the entire *enchainement* of secrets and lies. Avoiding the either/or proposition he makes to her, as though she knew that either decision - to relinquish their marriage or to relinquish Milly's inheritance - were nothing other than a protective fiction, covering over the fact that such an impasse can not be resolved, Kate's voice resonates at the end of the novel, with what is perhaps the most sober love declaration of British fiction - "We shall never be again as we were!" (457)

> But where does this leave us? As Mladen Dolar notes, Psychoanalysis doesn't provide a new and better interpretation of the uncanny; it maintains it as a limit to interpretation. Its interpretation tries to circumscribe the point where interpretation fails, where no 'more faithful' translation can be made. It tries to pinpoint the dimension of the object in that tiny crack before different meanings get hold of it and saturate it with sense, the point that can never be successfully recuperated by the signifying chain. [17]

This crack affords an insight into the contradiction which fictions seek to resolve, between the traumatic knowledge of contingency, of the fact that things happen accidentally on the one hand, and, on the other hand, our conviction that we are empowered, that we have agency. Staging the fluidity of undecidability to irritating perfection, Henry James' *Wings of the Dove* both supports and undercuts its own narrative desire, performing how traumatic reality as a crime, whose knowledge we share, is always already there, where we are, an invisible but also incorruptible pile, upon which the most exquisite fantasies come to be erected.

---

[17] Mladen Dolar 1991, 20.

Bibliography

Abraham, Nicolas and Torok, Maria: *The Shell and the Kernel. Vol 1*. Chicago 1994.

Barthes, Roland: *Camera Lucida. Reflections on Photography*. New York 1981.

Bronfen, Elisabeth: *The Knotted Subject. Hysteria and its Discontents*. Princeton 1998.

Dolar, Mladen: "'I Shall Be with you on Your Wedding-Night': Lacan and the Uncanny". *October 58* (Fall 1991), 5-23.

Foucault, Michel: "Of Other Spaces". *Diacritics 16.1* (1986), 22-27.

Kraft, Quentin G.: "Life Against Death in Venice". *Criticism 8.1* (Winter 1965), 217-223.

James, Henry: *The Wings of the Dove*. Harmondsworth 1965.

Melville, Herman: *Pierre, or The Ambiguities. Israel Potter. The Piazza Tales. The Confidance-Man. Uncollected Prose. Billy Bud. Sailor*. New York 1984.

Santner, Eric L.: *My Own Private Germany. Daniel Paul Schreber's Secret History of Modernity*. Princeton 1996.

Tanner, Tony: *Venice Desired*. Oxford 1992.

Teyssandier, Hubert: "L'image de Venise dans *The Wings of the Dove*". In: Hamard, Marie-Claire (ed.): *Home Sweet Home or Bleak House*. Paris 1985, 69-82.

Žižek, Slavoj: *Looking Awry*. Cambridge, Ma. 1991.

Žižek, Slavoj: *The Plague of Fantasies*. London: 1998.

Michael Gorra

The Venetian Hours of Henry James

Henry James and Venice - Henry James *in* Venice. It is a great pleasure to speak these words; but I am not sure there is not a certain impudence in pretending to add anything to them, at least in speaking before an audience that includes Tony Tanner. *Venice Desired* was sitting in the Harvard Square bookstores on the day I got back from my first trip to this city; until now I would have had to say my only trip. And since then that book has figured for me as an object of desire in itself, a model for the criticism that one might hope someday to write oneself.

In their call for papers Manfred Pfister and Barbara Schaff noted that in literature Venice has often figured as the site for the portrayal of "pathologies of vice and intrigues, revenge and jealousy, the dramatic use of masks and disguises ... the city of bridges ... transgression ... masquerades ... mazes", a city in which all that is solid seems to melt into water. Certainly that's true of its portrayal in the detective fiction that Indira Ghose describes elsewhere in this volume. I think here of Michael Dibdin's description, in *Dead Lagoon*, of how in Venice

> the hazy light and the pervasive instability of water defeated every attempt at clarity or precision ... here everything was a trick of the light, an endlessly shifting play of appearances without form or substance.[1]

And it is true as well of the major fiction that Henry James set here, stories of treachery in which the city's twists and turns and cul-de-sacs - in which the very ease with which one can get lost - serve as an objectification of their emotional landscape. The narrator of the *The Aspern Papers* does not even tell us his *assumed* name, let alone his real one, and the predations described in *The Wings of the Dove*, the intrigue and deception that James' characters work not only upon each other but upon themselves, need today no further comment.

Yet the ease with which Venice can be made to serve as the appropriate place to stage a sexual masquerade is not, of course, the only reason James chose to locate so much of the *Dove* along its canals. Because Venice also figures for him as the site of splendor, of splendor and of loss: the perfect many-pronged setting for the gem of a character he called Milly Theale. A city somewhat faded but still rich with the old gold spoils of many centuries - one whose ancient buildings do indeed transform Milly into a fairy-tale princess, but against which her ingenuous American freshness can also sparkle and shine. A fairy-tale princess for whom there is, in the end, no prince or rescue.

I am going to concentrate on James' travel essays about Venice, and it is with that sense of splendor that I want to begin. It is something that's far more marked and

---
[1] Dibdin 1994, 41, 254.

insisted upon in those essays than it is in the fiction he set here; so marked, in fact, that the idea of Venice as a setting for treachery and masquerade hardly figures in them at all. The first of those essays, the "Venice" of 1882, grows out of an extended visit James had paid to the city in the spring of the previous year. He found a flat on the "Riva Schiavoni, at the top of a house near the passage leading off to San Zaccaria"[2] - in other words just a few steps from where we can take what he called the "awful *vaporetto*"[3] for San Servolo. And there he worked on *The Portrait of a Lady*, which was already halfway through its serial publication.

When I started this paper, in fact, I thought it rather curious that the major novel on which James actually worked in this city is also one that says nothing about it - the *Portrait* has no Venetian sequence. And I tried to make that omission say something about either the novel, or Venice, or preferably both. But alas! my speculations were themselves but a trick of the light, a mark of the spell that even the thought of this city cast over me. In fact the novel's plot and settings were long-established and much of it already written by the time James got here. Venice's absence may simply point to the fact that he didn't yet really know the city; certainly not so well as he did Florence and Rome.

And yet I would still say that Venice would not have fit that novel even if James had known it well enough to use it. It would not have fit because his emphasis on the sensory impression that the city makes, the way it feeds what he calls "the lust ... of the eyes"[4] - that makes the value with which he invests this city differ from that he assigns to other Italian places, and in particular from that which he gives to Rome. Rome is for him not beauty so much as the echoing and endless corridors of the past - the place in which his sense of human history is most quickened. It offers him the note of immensity - St. Peter's is "the hugest thing conceivable"[5] and the Campagna is an "illimitable experience"[6], a realm of extinguished life in which the ruins seem conscious of their own desolation. It is a landscape in which one always knows - as indeed Isabel Archer knows - that here people have suffered. Not splendor, not even the treacherous maze of human motivation, but suffering, a suffering that seems not only ancient but endless - that is the emotion for which Rome best provides an objectification. And Isabel must be made to suffer the endlessness of her own marriage.

Of course people and even characters do suffer in Venice, characters like Milly Theale and the Misses Bordereau. They suffer in ways that James came to know intimately after the 1894 death of his friend Constance Fenimore Woolson. But that was not the value that the city had for him in the early 1880s. Though James was fully aware of the city's poverty and decay, the past was not to be made here into the site of suffering. Instead he treated it as a theme park of the picturesque, a splendid gaudy

---

[2] James 1908, 41.
[3] James 1909, 47.
[4] Ibid., 236.
[5] Ibid., 134.
[6] Ibid., 140.

show. And that splendor was not limited to the stone and water of the world outside, it extended as well to the colored panels of the world within. A painted glory, as in this account, in James' 1882 "Venice", of Giovanni Bellini's *Madonna Enthroned* at the Frari:

> Nothing in Venice is more perfect than this ... it is impossible to imagine anything more finished or more ripe ... .It seems painted with molten gems, which have only been clarified by time, and it is as solemn as it is gorgeous and as simple as it is deep.[7]

It is a description that makes me think of a very old great wine, its tannins softened by age, its structure unveiled by the passage of time. A description that suggests the painting is now somehow greater than it was when its colors were freshly ground - that time has here distilled a meaning and a beauty that no new work could possibly have.

Yet James' treatment of Venice as a kind of permanent celebration of the senses does nevertheless depend on his belief that its glory belongs to the past and not the present. It has so "consecrated" the union of "style" and "decrepitude"[8] as to make them indivisible, and if Venice seems "the most melancholy of cities" precisely because it is also "the most beautiful of tombs"[9] - well, somehow the American tourist contrives not to mind, and indeed makes that decrepitude into a positive attraction. His whole account of Venice reminds me of what that other New World émigré, V.S. Naipaul, says of an overgrown English garden in *The Enigma of Arrival*: that it is for him at its peak when it is past its peak.

Well - how should we understand the value that James assigns to Venice, and more generally to Italy itself? And what can that tell us about the nature of travel and tourism - even about our own visits to other lands? Today I can only sketch a set of answers, but in doing so I will suggest that James' attitude toward these questions is a good bit more complicated and also much more problematic than I have so far implied. I want to begin, however, with an anecdote about someone else, a story with which I am sure everyone of my readers is familiar, a paradigmatic account of the moment when one realizes that one is indeed in a different place, in the presence of an entirely other culture. A great writer notes in his journal that "Here I am really in a new country, a totally unfamiliar environment." The trees are different, the doors have no locks, and the windows are of oil paper, not glass. And above all his inn seems to lack what he calls a "highly necessary convenience."[10] When he asks for it, the hotel's servant gestures to the courtyard. But where? Comes the answer: wherever you like.

But this is not Naipaul in twentieth century India, outraged at the omnipresent squatting masses. No - it is of course Goethe in Italy. Yet for Northern Europeans of the eighteenth and nineteenth centuries, Italy was India, insofar as the rhetoric of the cisalpine journeys so often matches that of our own subcontinental ones. Beggars, dirt,

---

[7] Ibid., 26-27.
[8] Ibid., 61.
[9] Ibid., 33.
[10] Goethe 1816-17, 42.

smells, the people in rags. But happy. For James, Venice was the City of Joy. Its misery, he wrote, "stands there for all the world to see; it is part of the spectacle." Though it is not misery but rather the way the people elude it that pleases what he calls "the sentimental tourist." For the Venetians seem to him to "have at once the good fortune to be conscious of few wants," and so they contentedly allow "sunshine and leisure and conversation" to provide the greater part of their diet.[11] The children are especially beautiful, "the handsomest little brats in the world [with] ... their little bellies protrud[ing] like those of infant cannibals in the illustrations of books of travel."[12] And their parents? The price a gondolier "sets on his services is touchingly small," and while your Venetian hasn't "a genius for stiff morality and scruples but scantly to represent the false as the true," you nevertheless grow fond of him. His manners are so good "One feels the race is old."[13]

But then for James good manners are "perhaps what the races politically feeble" have most to offer the rest of us; though that is not, he admits, such a happy prospect" for those races themselves.[14] In *A Passage to India* Forster writes that his character Fielding tended to "regard an Indian as if he were an Italian." It is not "a common error, nor perhaps a fatal one," and it is in fact a point in Fielding's favor.[15] It separates him from the rest of the Raj, for whom it was indeed an error, and of a cruder kind than it would be for us. Or was it? For to treat an Indian as if he were an Italian was still to treat him as if he were a distinctly subordinate type of person. Look at Italy before what James calls "the great breach with the past" that occurred in September 1870, when Garibaldi's soldiers entered Rome and brought an end to papal rule[16]. It was not formally colonized, but French troops controlled Rome, as British forces did Delhi; the Austrians held the Veneto until 1866, the King of Naples was a Spanish Bourbon. Even English liberalism's support of Garibaldi finds a twentieth-century echo in that extended to Gandhi and Nehru. And James himself drew the Indian parallel, describing the Pope as "sitting dim within the shadows of his coach with two uplifted benedictory fingers - like some dusky Hindoo idol in the depths of its shrine."[17]

Perhaps all travel writing is shaped by what David Spurr calls "the rhetoric of empire." Perhaps the tropes through which we attempt to know and describe our experience of another country, another culture, are always marked by the distortions of metaphor, by what Spurr describes as "the violence of the letter and thus the imposition of power."[18] Yet in James' essays about France or England those tropes don't help to define a political hierarchy. In the pieces he collected in *Italian Hours* they do. *Aestheticization. Surveillance*: the panoramic view, perhaps from a cathedral dome, that allows for the *Appropriation* of the surrounding landscape, of the wealth of

---

[11] James 1909, 9.
[12] Ibid., 53.
[13] Ibid., 19.
[14] Ibid., 313.
[15] Forster 1924, 64.
[16] James 1909, 123.
[17] Edel 1974, 160.
[18] Spurr 1993, 12.

the past, a past that in James' time had made Italy so desirable as to ensure its weakness. *Debasement*, or "filth and defilement,"[19] like the "robust odour"[20] James picks up from a crowd gathered for a religious procession in Anacapri. The point, Spurr notes, is not to question the "factual validity" of such language, but to see both how it is "metaphorically loaded" and the way those metaphors persist over time.[21] *Negation*, the denial or disparagement of change - about Venice: "It would be a sad day indeed when there should be something new to say."[22] *Eroticization*. European politics traditionally weighed in favour of a feminized Italy. So the Master describes Venice as "a creature [that] varies like a nervous woman ... she is easy to admire, she is not so easy to live with," a land to be wooed and indulged but also to be kept in her place.[23] *Insubstantialization*, or "seeing in a dream," so that, as on the Campagna, "exotic geographical space is understood as an inner exploration of the boundaries of consciousnes."[24] *Idealization* - of Italy's very difference from America.

James writes that in Italy the "streets and inns are the vehicles of half one's knowledge."[25] And yet he had remarkably little to say about them. To read *Italian Hours* is to wonder at all that has been left out; the list "might indeed", as he wrote of Hawthorne's America, "be made almost ludicrous."[26] No agriculture, no ancient universities, no markets. No artichokes or oranges, no fish, no cheese, little coffee and less wine. No pasta. No cafes, except Florian's. No arguments in the street; no streets, except to get to churches. No lacemakers or leatherworkers or glassblowers - no artisans. No nuns. No opera; no books, by Italians. Almost, one might say, no Italians.

In the New York chapters of *The American Scene* James wonders what the "omnipresent ... appeal of the confectioner and the pastry-cook says about the relation of manners and wages."[27] And he lingers, oddly thrilled, over the fact that "everyone, without exception, no matter how 'low' in the social scale, wear[s] the the best and the newest, the neatest and the smartest boots."[28] But those are precisely the sorts of things he does not note in his European journeys. On his first visit to Italy he complained of not having "exchanged five minutes talk with any one but the servants in the hotels,"[29] and though he did learn the language he never quite lost the feeling that his own "inexorable Yankeehood"[30] doomed him to look at the country "from without." So in an 1873 essay on Siena he describes his wish that after

---

[19] Ibid. The italicized words in this paragraph are taken from Spurr's table of contents; each identifies a trope in what he calls "the rhetoric of empire,î and serves as the title for one of his chapters.
[20] James 1909, 308.
[21] Spurr 1993, 91.
[22] James 1909, 7.
[23] Ibid., 11, 10.
[24] Spurr 1993, 146.
[25] James 1909, 222.
[26] James 1879, 351.
[27] James 1907, 517.
[28] Ibid., 504.
[29] Edel 1974, 151.
[30] Ibid., 137.

peeping up stately staircases ... Murray in hand, one might walk up to the great drawing room, make one's bow to the master and mistress ... and invite them to favour one with ... a few first-hand family anecdotes.[31]

But his later visits were spent mostly with English and American expatriates, and his essays are virtually all scenery, without other people except as what James himself would have described as an element in a composed scene.

At Torcello he notes that "the poor lad who brought us the key of the cathedral was shaking with an ague." But would the lust of his eye have had it otherwise? - for the boy's "melancholy presence seemed" so perfectly "to point the moral of forsaken nave and choir."[32] In Venice itself James suggests that while it's "not easy to say one would have [the people] other than they are," it would nevertheless "make an immense difference should they be better fed."[33] But what *kind* of difference remains unsaid. For the altar of the picturesque at which he so devoutly worshipped carried with it a politics: the "perfectly honourable ... love of the status quo."[34] The tourist wants to see the real Italy. Yet at the moment that stately staircase becomes a picture, all hope of climbing it must vanish.

But James knew that; had always a teasing and ironic awareness of the limitations of his own point of view. What I would like to do in the space remaining is to show how in Venice - in Venice far more than in Florence or Rome - James tried to have it both ways: to preserve the picture and yet also to pursue what in *A Little Tour in France* he calls "the inner springs of the subject."[35] His earliest essays on the city suggests that the place lies now entirely open to view. In 1882, for example, he writes that

> There is as little mystery about the grand Canal as about our local thoroughfare ... The Venice of today is a vast museum where the little wicket that admits you is perpetually turning and creaking, and you march through the institution with a herd of fellow-gazers. There is nothing left to discover or describe and originality of attitude is completely impossible. This is often very annoying.[36]

Venice may have once had its secrets, but it is now a booth at the fair of modern tourism, deeply familiar and fully known. It has utterly lost its sense of the alien and the mysterious, a place that has now been subdued to - or by - description.

Or has it? Some of the great Venetian painters, he writes, can best be seen elsewhere - you can look at Titian and Veronese in Paris or Dresden or London. "But you must go to Venice in very fact to see the other masters"[37] and above all to see the figure he calls always "the Tintoret." Except, he adds, that "It may be said as a general

---

[31] James 1909, 226.
[32] Ibid., 54.
[33] Ibid., 9.
[34] James, quoted in Buzard 1993, 213. My argument throughout this section is indebted to Buzard's essential analysis of the role of the picturesque in nineteenth century travel writing.
[35] James 1900, 3.
[36] James 1909, 7, 10.
[37] Ibid., 21.

thing that you never see the Tintoret. You admire him, you adore him ... but ... your eyes fail to deal with him."[38] The canvases suffer from an "incurable blackness"[39] of soot and age; you know they are there, but you can't see them, read them, can't penetrate their secrets. And that will become the key signature of James' Venetian tone poems - an evocation of that which one sees and yet somehow does not; and even, finally, of that which James himself has experienced and with which he will tease us, but which he will not allow us to share, an evocation of places into which he won't let us follow him. So in his essay on "The Grand Canal" he speaks of enjoying "the hospitality of an old Venetian home," and suggests that "If it didn't savour of treachery to private kindness" he would twitch back its heavy curtains and offer an account of what life is now like "in the painted chambers that still echo with one of the historic names."[40] He could do that - but he won't.

In fact, of course, the old Venetian homes that James knew were tenanted by other Americans - with one crucial exception. This is the second of the houses that he describes in the curious 1899 essay he calls "Two Old Houses and Three Young Women." He begins his account by noting that there are today "few brown depths ... into which the light of the hotels does not shine, and few hidden treasures about which pages enough ... haven't already been written."[41] Here, however, he will show us one of those depths - show it to us without naming it, without telling us to whom it belongs, or what, precisely, it evokes. While looking for a church James' party meets three sisters - they have been identified as members of the Mocenigo family - and are invited to see their old *palazzo*. And once there in "the big, vague *sala*," a spectator to the sisters' "simplified state and their beautiful blighted rooms," James finds himself lost in a fiction-making reverie. "If I wanted a first chapter it was here made to my hand," a novel made up out of the sisters' "great name and fallen fortunes ... the absence of books, the presence of ennui,"[42] and indeed he goes on to imagine a scene in which the sisters' parents might have one day "looked at each other with the pale hush of the irreparable."[43]

"It is behind the walls of the houses that old, old history is thick and that the multiplied stars of Baedeker might often best find their application."[44] So James concludes, and one might in concluding simply agree with him. Yet I have first to note that James has told us almost nothing about this penetrated interior. He has climbed the staircase, entered the great drawing room, but the only family anecdote he has brought away - or at any rate the only one he will tell us - is one that he has himself made up. Nor has he told us what he has seen - what pictures on the walls, what cracked leather on the chairs. The only painting he mentions is one that he *has not* seen, at least not

---

[38] Ibid., 23.
[39] Ibid., 57.
[40] Ibid., 38.
[41] Ibid., 65-6.
[42] Ibid., 68.
[43] Ibid., 69.
[44] Ibid.

here; a painting that used to be in Venice but can now instead be found in London. In fact his description of this private space, this space that few have seen, is far less detailed, far less precise, than his accounts of those public places that everyone can see. He has here found a mystery - only he won't tell us what it is, and I suspect that it is such a passage that Tony Tanner has had in mind in writing that what James does is to give us the *sense* of the sense of a place.[45]

Tanner notes as well that in his later travel writing James cultivates "a preference for vagueness,"[46] that he tries increasingly to do without what he himself called the "solidity of specification."[47] I would add to that only that as James' awareness increases, his willingness to say of just what it consists diminishes. That the more intimately he knows a place, the less he is willing - or perhaps able? - to say about it, that his vagueness varies directly with the growth of his knowledge. These remarks are not of course limited to his travel writing; but in reading *Italian Hours'* evocation of an unspecifiable experience I sometimes feel as if we are about to enter the Marabar Caves.

Bibliography

Buzard, James: The Beaten Track: European Tourism, Literature, and the Ways to 'Culture' 1800, 1918. Oxford 1993.
Dibdin, Michael: Dead Lagoon. New York 1996.
Edel, Leon: Henry James Letters, vol I. Cambridge, MA 1974.
Forster, E.M.: A Passage to India. London 1924.
Goethe, J.W.: Italian Journey, trans. W.H. Auden and Elizabeth Mayer. Harmondsworth 1970.
James, Henry: A Little Tour in France (1900) in Collected Travel Writings (2 vols.). New York 1993.
James, Henry: The American Scene (1907) in Collected Travel Writings.
James, Henry: Hawthorne (1979) in Criticism, vol I. New York 1984.
James, Henry: Italian Hours (1909) in Collected Travel Writings.
James, Henry: "Prefaceî to The Portrait of a Lady (1908). In: *Criticism*, vol II. New York 1984.
Spurr, David: The Rhetoric of Empire: Colonial Discourse in Journalism, Travel Writing, and Imperial Administration. Durham, NC 1993.
Tanner, Tony: Henry James and the Art of Non-fiction. Athens, GA 1995.
Tanner, Tony: Venice Desired. Cambridge, MA 1992.

---

[45] Tanner 1995, 17.
[46] Ibid., 14.
[47] Quoted in Tanner 1992, 194.

Ina Schabert

An Amazon in Venice: Vernon Lee's "Lady Tal"

Feminist writers of the *fin de siècle* period found themselves caught in a trap not unlike that which hampers today's feminists who work in literary theory. Their feminism demanded the assumption of a unified female subject, a fully responsible woman who acts according to firm moral and political convictions. Yet in late nineteenth-century avant-garde novels this kind of character had become obsolete. In works by George Meredith, Henry James and Thomas Hardy the person turns out to be an enigmatic, changeable, elusive being, unfathomable both to him- or herself and to others. Characters in novels and stories by feminist authors of the so-called New Woman movement are marked and not seldom marred by the clash of feminist and early modern aesthetic ideals. In a detailed examination of the works written by Sarah Grand, John Kucich discloses "a crippling incoherence" in her narratives.[1]

Vernon Lee's stories document the conflict. In her first novel, *Miss Brown* (1884), she tries to cope with the problem by shifting the burden of justification toward avant-garde aestheticism. By representing and criticising the new concept of the person from the point of view of an upright, high-principled female character, she creates the illusion that it can be contained within the old Victorian frame. In Lee's narrative, the heroine is drawn into an artistic circle where self-fashioning according to the new aesthetic ideal has become the vogue. For a time Anne Brown is taken in by her friend Walter Hamlin who is a master of this kind of performative self-stylization:

> It did not occur to Anne, whose character was so completely of a piece, that there was any untruthfulness in this mode [...]. The sort of shimmer, as of the two tints in a shot stuff, of reality and unreality, of genuine and affected feeling, of moods which came spontaneously and of other moods, noticed, treasured up and reproduced in himself, – which existed in Hamlin, would be perfectly unintelligible to Anne.[2]

The morally negative overtones of the portrait, of which Anne seems unaware, are brought home even more clearly to the reader when later on the artist is contrasted with the woman, with Anne's mode of being, her

> unmistakable desire to know what was going on in the striving and suffering world outside the strongholds of aestheticism, to help in it to her utmost; to be, what the people believing only in beauty and passion could not conceive, responsible –[3]

---

[1] "Feminism's Ethical Contradictions. Sarah Grand and New Woman Writing", in: Kucich 1994, 239-279.
[2] Lee 1884, II, 57.
[3] Lee 1884 II, 136.

Aesthetic subjectivity is shown to be charming and seducing, yet under close scrutiny it turns out to be a set of pretences that serve the old cult of the masculine ego. The new mode of conceiving the person, so we are given to understand, has no liberating but, on the contrary, a narrowing effect. It does not come as a surprise that Henry James, to whom *Miss Brown* was dedicated, did not really like it.

The story "Lady Tal" (1892) is again preoccupied with the moral and the aesthetic problem of character. Now it appears as a double problem - the problem of the artist who, in his life as in his art, thinks of human beings in terms of transitory moods and changing masks, and the problem of the woman who, caught up in the fashionable manners of her time, might forget about her duties as a responsible human being. The story is about Jervase Marion, a novelist introduced as "an inmate of the world of Henry James and a kind of Henry James, of a lesser magnitude" (194),[4] a formula which can be read as a self-assessment on the part of Vernon Lee.[5] In contradistinction to *Miss Brown*, the narrative foregrounds not the perspective of the woman but that of the artist who projects his aesthetic assumptions upon the world. His art is put in question by the appearance of the title figure: Lady Tal eludes his novelistic imagination. His plan of a novel collapses under the pressure of the woman's impact upon him. Simultaneously the reader participates, although mainly through the uncomprehending eyes of Jervase Marion, in Lady Tal's quest for a meaningful life, for a self-definition which would enable her to become a positive influence in the social world. In the course of the narrative, Marion's aestheticism is clearly defeated, through the evidence of Lady Tal, in favour of a broader view of human possibilities. The lady, on the other hand, seems to have made some progress toward the vision of a fuller, more satisfactory life for herself.

"Lady Tal" forms part of a collection of stories entitled *Vanitas*. In an introduction added to the Tauchnitz edition of 1911, Lee explains that the title refers to the "sketches of frivolous women" in the stories. Through their careers, the protagonists are meant to document "the great waste of precious things". Their life is without purpose, because nobody has given them "the sense of brotherhood and duty, which changes one, from a blind dweller in caves, to an inmate of the real world of storms and sunshine and serene night and exhilarating morning." Yet, she adds, with reference to Lady Tal, "of my three frivolous women, [one] abandoned freely the service of the

---

[4] Page numbers in brackets refer to Lee, 1993.
[5] Henry James and Jamesian scholarship tend to stress, and complain of, the fact that some of James's traits and personal eccentricities have been projected onto Vernon Lee's portrait of Marion (cf. Henry James's letters of Jan 16, 1893 to Morton Fullerton, and to William James four days later [*Letters*, ed. Leon Edel. vol.III:1883-1895, London 1981, 399 and 402], Carl J. Weber, "Henry James and his Tiger-Cat," *PMLA* 68 [1953] 672-687, Leon Edel, *Henry James: The Middle Years*, London 1963, p.272-273). Biographical studies of Vernon Lee on the other hand have shown that other aspects of the person are taken from Lee's own life and that as a whole, the figure resembles literary self-portraits of Lee as an artist (Burdett Gardner, "An Apology for Henry James's Tiger-Cat", *PMLA* 68 [1953], 688-695, with a reply by Leon Edel in *PMLA* 69 [1954] 677-678; Gardner 1987, 472; and Gunn, 1964, 136-137).

Goddess Vanitas".[6] More exactly, "Lady Tal" combines two cases of *vanitas*, the vanity of the society woman and the vanity of the artist lionized by the aesthetic community. As the site for the display of this double vanity Lee chooses Venice.

Vernon Lee lived in Italy most of her life. She became famous for her historical studies and travel books on the country. Among them, *Genius Loci* (1899) gives the most impressive evidence of her sensibility to the special moods, the aesthetic and moral atmospheres of individual geographical places. She was severely critical of Venice. In her *Studies of the Eighteenth Century in Italy* (1880), Venice is characterized as a "crumbling city", an "effeminate, corrupt" city, a "prophane farce".[7] In *Genius Loci* it is considered a dead place. The late nineteenth-century Venice evoked at the beginning of "Lady Tal" is a site of decadence and artifice. However, human impulses reinstate themselves even here, taking the forms of social responsibility and personal attachment. The Venetian experience in "Lady Tal" turns out to be not unlike that in Lee's other Venetian story *The Wicked Voice* (1890) where the protagonist, again an avant-garde artist, has come to the place in order to compose a pure, superhuman work of instrumental music, yet becomes haunted instead by the sound of a human voice.

1. Literary Venice

In her critical writings Vernon Lee comments upon a type of artist whom she calls the "*Constructive* novelist", a writer who "thinks of the universe only as brick and mortar, or lath and plaster, for his august temple or pleasing gazebo".[8] Venice, as she represents it at the beginning of "Lady Tal", is exactly the right place for this kind of artist. It confirms his attitude, offering, instead of the "unsifted experience" which would disturb the constructive activity, only elements already processed through the medium of art.[9] Marion, the author within the story, offers to himself a season in Venice as an advance even upon his habitual ivory tower existence in a top flat at Westminster:

> being a methodical man, and much concerned for his bodily and intellectual health, he occasionally thought fit to suspend even this contact with mankind, and to spend six weeks at Venice, in the contemplation of only bricks and mortar. (221)

In Venice, no human interest whatsoever would upset his relaxed aesthetic sensibility.

---

[6] Lee 1911, Dedicatory Letter to the Baronessa E. French-Cini.
[7] Lee 1907, 55, 401, 384.
[8] Lee 1969, 279.
[9] In her late essay "Imagination Penetrative" Vernon Lee, under the influence of Percy Lubbock's view of James in *The Craft of Fiction,* takes Henry James as the prototype of the *Constructive* novelist (Lee 1969, 280). Her own literary program at the time of writing "Lady Tal" however, was also very close to the ideal of *Constructive* art, as her essay "On Literary Construction" testifies.

The first view fully answers his expectations. Nothing has changed since his last visit twelve years ago. The scene into which he enters is, of course, an old palazzo near the Piazza S. Marco, with the classical view of the Canale Grande and the cupolas and volutes of the church of S. Maria della Salute, with the tower and cupola of S. Giorgio Maggiore in the background. The scene is suffused with the light of the moon, which unites the luminous stonework of the churches and a shimmering strip of lagoon with the interior of the palazzo where Marion visits old friends. The moonlight is "spread in a soft, shining carpet to their feet". Eventually, the carpet displays a pattern, the moonbeams "weaving a strange intricate pattern, like some old Persian tissue, in the dark water". The plash of oar, the gondolier's cry, the sounds of a guitar, the murmur of voices and women's laughter, the heavy scent of some white flower and the cigarette smoke rising from the gothic balconies of the palazzo, balconies reminiscent of *Romeo and Juliet* – all combine to produce the perfect experience of Venice. The whiteness of the moonlit scene indicates the beauty of an art that has transcended human life. 'Whiteness', observes Burdett Gardner with regard to Vernon Lee's writings, is the common denominator of all her symbols of purity. In *Renaissance Fancies and Studies* (1896) she tells the fantastic story of a Renaissance artist who painted everything in white in order to attain to the highest degree of perfection.[10] However, when in the opening scene of "Lady Tal" the spectral white light of the moon comes down to the dark water and touches the "black gondolas, each with its crimson, unsteady prow-light," it seems to touch death. Perfection is as intimately connected with stagnation and death in this initial image of Venice as it is in Lee's theory of art. Venice's whiteness is like the marble whiteness of Keats's Grecian urn. The perfect quality of the Venetian experience is underlined by the circular movement of the descriptive passage, where the final sentences echo the beginning (192-195). It is confirmed by the satisfaction of Marion for whom everything in the scene is as it should be.

The conversation among Miss Vanderwerf's guests in the Palazzo Bragadin tunes in with the moonlit scene. It is pure ritual:

> Jervase Marion knew it all so well, so well, this half-fashionable, half-artistic Anglo-American idleness of Venice, with its poetic setting and its prosaic reality. He would have known it, he felt, intimately, even if he had never seen it before; known it so as to be able to make each of these people say in print what they did really say. (194)

Even the one disturbing element, the appearance of the enigmatic Lady Tal, confirms the aesthetic pattern. Woman as mystery symbolically mirrors the image of Venice, mysterious in the moonlight. And Marion, the psychological novelist, is confident that he possesses the key to the mystery of Lady Tal:

> This great strength, size, cleanness of outline and complexion, this look of masterfully selected breed, of carefully fostered health, was to him the perfect flower of the aristocratic civilisation of

---

[10] Gardner 1987, 384, 405.

An Amazon in Venice: Vernon Lee's "Lady Tal"

England. [...] there was no type more well-defined and striking, in his eyes. This woman did not seem an individual at all. (198)

Yet the utterly satisfactory first impression proves to be deceptive.

Marion, in order to be sure of a quiet residence, has chosen a hotel on a side canal off the Riva. His darkened room is invaded by all kinds of noises testifying to everyday Venetian life, on the canal and within the houses, in kitchens, in barracks and churches - "everything in short which could madden a poor nervous novelist" (208). At the same time, the relation to Lady Tal becomes complicated. Marion has gathered a few biographical items: the young woman, whose full name is Lady Atalanta Walkenshaw, had married a very rich old man. At his death he left her his immense fortune on condition that she did not remarry. As a widow she lived together with an invalid brother up to his recent death. Her tall Amazonian figure attracts all the young men of the Anglo-American set, yet she does not seem to care. The suggestion of a "dreadful strength" and an "appearance of never having felt anything" justify for Marion the conclusion that she has no soul (210). He sums her up in terms of a highly accomplished, routine performance.

By means of her "dreadful strength", Lady Tal has brought the novelist to help her revise her first attempt at a novel, entitled *Christina*. The study of the manuscript partly unsettles his theory. He gets the impression that he might have to change his diagnosis, after all: "he had found the indications of a soul, a very decided and unmistakable soul" (213). He tries to uphold his position by explaining the evidence of the manuscript as deceptive: Lady Tal's writing would have been pure imitation of other texts; like her face, it would serve her as a mask that "concealed the mere absence of everything" (215). It would be just another item in her performance.

The lady, however, involves him in serious conversations about the projects of her writing and her life, thus counteracting his negative move. Although, on his part, the novelist clings to the Palazzo Bragadin view of women and Venice:

[..] she swept back into the hum of voices and shimmer of white dresses of Miss Vanderwerf's big drawing room. Jervase Marion remained leaning on the balcony, listening to the plash of oars and the burst of hoarse voice and shrill fiddles from the distant music boats (218) –

he cannot prevent a perplexing change. Instead of mirroring the moon, and thus symbolizing the solipsistic imagination, the interconnected canals begin to serve as traffic routes, favouring an exchange of ideas between Marion and Lady Tal: "porters and gondoliers for ever running to and fro between 'that usual tall young lady at San Vio' and 'that usual short, bald gentleman on the Riva'" (219). The manuscript of *Christina* is being transported to Marion, back to Lady Tal and back again to Marion, with criticisms from him and with corrections made by her. However, Marion gets in control of all this movement. He takes in hand Lady Tal's literary self-portrait. In the course of some weeks, the work, which is written in a bold style, with a pen of brass, as Virginia Woolf would say, is gradually brought up to his aesthetic standards, suggesting "a personality contradictory, enigmatical, not sure of itself, groping, as it were, to the light" (251).

At the same time, he collects the materials for a novel of his own on Lady Tal. He does this in his usual oblique way. The narrator sums up his artistic creed for him:

> you must merely look attentively at the moving ocean of human faces, watching for the one face more particularly interesting than the rest, and catching glimpses of its fleeting expression, and of the impression of its neighbours as it appears and reappears (222).

This formulation of an aesthetic program which traces the person as a sequence of fleeting moments of appearance is followed by another remark. Marion, the narrator adds, would never be willing to take more than "a merely abstract, artistic interest" in other persons. He would "not give his heart, perhaps because he had none to give to anybody". (222 f.) His novelistic art is thus being characterized by a shallowness that results from the reluctance to become involved.

By means of the twofold literary project, Marion is able to recuperate the threatening possibility of a human intercourse that might subvert his principles as a psychological novelist. Both the woman's literary interpretation of herself, and the impression of her person upon him are being placed under the rule of his art. Movement in Venice serves the perfection of literary texts.

2. Literal Venice

"One morning Marion, by way of exception, saw and studied Lady Tal without the usual medium of the famous novel" (223). With the absence of the literary medium, Venice has changed as well. The mysterious moonlight has been replaced by the fresh light of the early morning sun; the city of shimmering canals has become the scene for the Rialto market, a place of ordinary every-day activities, and in Lee's writings generally the symbol of the realities of human life.[11] Instead of being carried along by gondolas, people walk, along the market stalls and through the little narrow streets in the vicinity of the Church of the Miracoli.

Marion likes the place because it functions as a contrast in his imaginative economy. It plays the other to his aesthetic self:

> pleasing him with a sense (although he knew it to be all false) that here *was* a place where people could eat and drink and laugh and live without any psychological troubles (224).

Surprisingly, he meets Lady Tal who visits the market for a different reason. Twice a week she goes there to buy fruit, fresh rolls, and tobacco for the patients of the near-by city hospital. This part of Venice is congenial to her because she can reach it by walking, which is her preferred manner of movement, and because it gives her the opportunity to be useful. Immediately she involves Marion in her humanitarian

---

[11] Gardner 1987, 417.

program, ignoring his obvious reluctance. Her question how to find out whether the eggs she is going to buy would be fresh is as alien to his epistemology as her task of distinguishing between different kinds of snuff desirable for individual old men. Together they walk with the goods to the *ospedale*. Lady Tal distributes them to the sick who are very grateful for the gifts and even more so for her kind and lively presence. The novelist is shocked; both the nightmarish hospital and the undaunted cheerfulness of Lady Tal jar terribly on his imagination. "All this was not at all what he had imagined when he had occasionally written about young ladies consoling the sick". (229 f.) In this place, their joint literary project of revising *Christina* is nothing more than a curiosity, serving for a few minutes' entertainment to a dying girl who used to be fond of reading. When they leave, Lady Tal tells him that, rather than participate in the life of fashionable society, she would want to do charitable work in the East End of London. Yet she is afraid this would alienate her completely from the class to which, in loyalty to her dead husband and her dead brother, she feels obliged to conform.

In spite of the evidence the novelist manages to save his aesthetic interpretation of Lady Tal. He takes the new side of her which is thus revealed to him as just another gesture of her performative self:

> Marion looked at her, standing there on the little wharf, [...]; her magnificent rather wooden figure more impeccably magnificent, uninteresting in her mannish flannel garments, her handsome pink and white face, as she smiled that inexpressive smile with all the pearl-like teeth, more than ever like a big mask -
> 'No soul, decidedly no soul,' said the novelist to himself. (231)

The market scene alludes to the myth referred to in Lady Tal's name. The mythical Atalanta is a virgin huntress. She refuses to accept any man who cannot defeat her in a foot-race. She vanquishes many suitors, they are all put to death. Finally Hippomenes, or Melanion, succeeds by means of a trick. He brings with him three of the precious apples of the Hesperides which he drops at intervals during the course. Atalanta cannot resist the temptation to stop and pick them up. Melanion thus wins the race and her person. In Lee's story, it is Lady Tal who gives the golden fruit, in this case bags of oranges, to Marion. Yet he carries them in such an awkward way that most of them would have tumbled down the stone steps of a bridge and into a canal, if Lady Tal had not rescued them. Marion misses the chance which offers itself to him on this clear early autumn morning outside of literary Venice of coming to know Lady Tal.

He is given another. This time the scene is a garden. In Vernon Lee's symbolic topography, gardens constitute the green contrast to the white perfection of art, signifying life, fertility, sexuality, growth and decay.[12] The garden in question is attached to Lady Tal's modern house on the Zattere. She cherishes the spot: "small indeed, but round which, as she remarked, one solitary female could walk" (234). Both

---

[12] Gardner 1987, 405.

her taste for modern, practical things and her need of a garden distinguish her from her friends.

When one night Lady Tal and Marion have a stroll in the garden, the conversation takes a personal turn. The novelist reproaches her for her lack of passion – an item which he would like to add to his literary portrait of her. Lady Tal insists that the right to abstain from romantic love should be granted to female as to male human beings, and she explains her uncommitted, mask-like manner by her attachment to her deceased brother. It is her general policy to conform to what he would have wished and expected of her. The confession leads up to some tears on Lady Tal's part and a moment of epiphany for the novelist:

> A sudden light illuminated Marion's mind: a light, and with it something else, he knew not what, something akin to music, to perfume, beautiful, delightful, but solemn. He was aware of being moved, horribly grieved, but at the same moment intensely glad". (238)

However, he shrinks away from the contact that has been established. Instead, he speechifies on the unreliability of one's self-assessment. "He had reacted against that first overwhelming sense of pleasure at the discovery of the lady's much-questioned soul. Now he was prepared to tell her she had none", the narrator tersely remarks. Lady Tal covers up her gesture of unseemly sincerity by joining in Marion's game. She has only tried to make Marion believe that she had a soul, she says; "I haven't got one. I'm a great deal too well-bred" (240). The conversation turns back to *Christina*; the scene changes back to the white moonlit view of literary Venice.

3. The yellow straw blinds

The next morning, the memory of the revelation of Lady Tal's inner self has dissolved into one of those fleeting impressions gathered by the novelist in the service of his art.

> Of course Marion, in his capacity of modern analytical novelist, was perfectly well aware that feelings are mere momentary matters; and that the feeling which had possessed him the previous evening, and still possessed him at the present moment, would not last. The feeling, he admitted to himself (...),[13] the feeling in question was vaguely admiring and pathetic, as regarded Lady Tal. He even confessed to himself that there entered into it a slight dose of poetry. (241)

Afloat in his gondola, and thus sheltered from real life, he sets his imagination to work on the germ of "poetry". The first scheme he develops is Shakespearian. The lady's love for her dead brother allows him to see her as a modern Countess Olivia, without the romantic prospect of a Viola/Sebastian entering into her life. The project is rejected as old-fashioned, the dead brother figure changed into a female friend who is mortally

---

[13] In brackets the narrator inserts the insinuation that for Marion there exists one permanent self as the exception to the rule of transient states of consciousness, namely that of the God-like author: "(it is much easier to admit such things to one's self, when one makes the proviso that it's all a passing phase, one's eternal and immutable self, looking on placidly at one's changing self)".

ill, which produces something like the story of Emma and Tony in *Diana of the Crossways*. Meredith's gloriously happy ending would not do, of course; it would have to be toned down at least to a muted, modest happiness. Or, better still, to the utterly negative ending preferred by decadent art. He gloats over the prospect:

> Yes – the sort of thing she would live for, a round of monotonous dissipation, which couldn't amuse her; of expenditure merely for the sake of expenditure, of conventionality merely for the sake of conventionality; – and the sham, clever, demoralised women, with their various semi-imaginary grievances against the world, their husbands and children, their feeble self-conscious hankering after mesmerism, spiritualism, Buddhism, and the other forms of intellectual adulteration – he saw it all [...] It would make a capital novel. (243)

Marion thus constructs Lady Tal along the *vanitas* scheme, to which, as Vernon Lee tells us in the Tauchnitz introduction, and as a sensitive reader would know anyhow, the heroine is not going to conform. The novelist can be so sure of himself, because the person who could correct his imaginative vision is absent. As he ascertains from his gondola, the yellow straw blinds of Lady Tal's house are let down. His is the case of the author diagnosed by Vernon Lee in her later essay entitled "Can Writing be Taught?" (1926). The literary gift, she observes, "hoodwinks" the writer. He disregards those aspects of experience which do not fall into the patterns established by his art, "creating and obeying a scale of 'values' purely literary and often oddly at variance with the values of real life".[14]

However, why not see oneself and the world completely in terms of art? Why not set one's life in order by adjusting it to a literary pattern? The novelist who brings *Christina* into shape for her and who is planning a novel about her might, Lady Tal comes to think, also find a solution for the dilemma in which she is placed through the extravagant conditions of her late husband's testament. Thus to his surprise Marion is confronted with her question: "Now, suppose I were the heroine of your novel, [...] what would you advise me?"(247 f.) This happens during an excursion to the island of Torcello, a place which, in Lee's story, is even less real than literary Venice. The city in the water is replaced by a marsh island disintegrating into the lagoon. An orchard marks it as a paradise, yet a thoroughly artificial one. The island's vegetation is transformed into feathery and fantastic shapes, like those of Japanese and Chinese art, fruits are rarefied to enamel colour spots, leaves withered to luminous transparency, branches twisted into grotesque forms. Nature withered to parchment-like thinness, especially in the state of sun-dried, fragrant herbs, has always been, together with the colour white, Lee's symbol for the purity of art.[15] Of course the novelist does not commit himself to any words of positive advice in matters of real life. He lets Lady Tal run into the fantasy, induced by his earlier flattering words, of becoming a famous writer. Yet the utterly artificial situation makes him think of his literary project in human terms: "He seemed suddenly to be in this young woman's place, to feel the

---

[14] Lee 1969, 293.

[15] Cf. especially Lee's essay "Among the Marble Mountains" in *Enchanted Woods* (quoted in Gardner 1987, 405 f.).

already begun, and rapidly increasing withering-up of this woman's soul, the dropping away from it of all real, honest, vital interests". (249) The concept of empathy, which in Lee's later aesthetic writings, such as *The Beautiful* (1913), will become important as a means of escape from egotism, is here anticipated: empathy enables Marion to guess the truth. However, he does not maintain the empathic effort for long. The only remedy he can think of is certainly inadequate for a person like Lady Tal, namely marriage to a nice young man in love with her. The artist figure in another of Lee's *Vanitas* stories is much happier in his conjecture about a heroine of the type of Lady Tal, summing her up as "a sort of female Hippolytus, but without a male Diana".[16]

Back in Venice, the novelist continues his revision of *Christina*, until this comes to an abrupt end with the revolt of Lady Tal. She feels she is not able and in any case no longer willing to carry out his literary directions. The two separate. At this point, with the crisis of his own project for what he thought of as a "capital novel" on Lady Tal, and the failure of changing her novel into something he was convinced would be "infinitely finer than herself" (256), Marion for the first time would prefer – to the view of the blinds which shut her out – the view of the person who has been the object of his literary imagination: "he caught himself, in the garden, looking up at her windows, half expecting to see her" (255).

4. Un-Venetian Venice

On the evening of the same day, Venice seems to have totally changed: "It struck him suddenly that something was over" (256). When he perceives Lady Tal among the strollers on the Piazza San Marco, she appears to him as a member of the British aristocracy who cuts an American author: their relationship has been replaced by social clichés. He ventures forth on the Riva, toward the Arsenal, and finds himself abruptly in a wintry world: a rough rainy wind, creaking masts and sails, darkness, scarcely any gondola lights. This time there is no carpet of moonlight with a pattern of shadows, instead there are unseen puddles on the pavement into which one stumbles in the dark. This is no condition for art. Marion "shut his window with a bang, receiving a spout of rain in his face" (258).

The story ends with a last encounter of Marion and Lady Tal in the un-Venetian Venice of darkness and bad weather. "A beastly place", the lady calls it. Both are leaving, he for the writing table in his fifth-floor flat in London, she for the social season in Rome. They talk, as always, about literary things, about her having finished *Christina* and dispatched it to a publisher without further ado, and about the novel he is going to write. The story will be, as he tells her not without some confusion, about an elderly artist who took an interest in a rich young girl, a beginner in his art, and who imagined that it was only an artistic interest. This was how he made a fool of himself. Lady Tal finds the *dénouement* a rather lame and unsatisfactory one. She feels sure that the young lady would propose marriage to the artist. She offers Marion to

---

[16] *A Worldly Woman*, in Lee 1911, 212.

cooperate with him in writing the new book, since she has already given him the ending.

> As Lady Atalanta spoke these words, a sudden downpour of rain drove her and Marion back into the drawing room. (261)

The conclusion is by no means conclusive. Is the gust of rain the prosaic negation of Lady Tal's generous suggestion? Or does it serve to demonstrate that the two are arriving at an in-doors understanding independent of poetic atmosphere? That Marion has, after all, got hold of Atalanta's fruit of life? In case a happy ending is meant, it can hardly be that of conventional romantic love. Considering the strength and independence of Lady Tal, it might be one of those generous, unselfish acts characteristic of Lee's Amazonian heroines. Love to these women, the narrator says in *Miss Brown*, is "the mere momentary diversion into a personal and individual channel of a force which constitutes the whole moral and intellectual existence, whose object is an unattainable ideal of excellence, and whose field is the whole of the world in which there is injustice and callousness and evil."[17]

5. Venice and the Amazon

The story about Lady Tal and Jervase Marion, and about the novels which, between themselves, they plan, revise, reject, is obviously a metaliterary narrative. By means of a sequence of well-selected and carefully moulded episodes, the literary question at stake is being discussed in a complex and undogmatic manner, from differing angles and in various stages of development. The reader's participation, always an important consideration to Lee,[18] is ensured through the tension that is created by the discovery scheme of the narrative.

Lee has adroitly managed the dilemma resulting from the contradictory norms of moral involvement and early modern aesthetics. The dilemma must have been her own. In a later book on ethics and epistemology, *Les Mensonges Vitaux* (1921), she comes to make the distinction between truth, which is in inaccessible to human beings, and 'vital lies', which have to be accepted for the survival of humanism. In "Lady Tal" the relativistic and impressionistic stance is represented by the professional writer. His contempt for Victorian realism and its moral conception of character answers early modern expectations. Exactly his avant-garde art, however, is made to appear, in the course of the narrative, as an already worn out literary habit, causing ennui and isolation from other human beings. His concept of the person obviously leaves out an important aspect of personality. The writer's general indeterminacy turns out to be the most determined thing, his openness another kind of limitation. The person whom he selects for his novel is doomed in advance. Whatever she might say or do, all will be interpreted in terms of posing and masquerade, whereas he, the author, is going to

---

[17] Lee 1884 II,307-308.
[18] Cf. especially the essay "On Literary Construction", Lee 1969, 1-33.

manage the performance, the play of evasion and displacement which he takes to constitute her self.

The older notion of the person as a morally responsible agent that was held up by the Victorians and, for obvious reasons, was adopted by the feminist movement and by the New Woman literature – more exactly by the so-called "purity school" within the movement – is introduced, or rather gradually revealed through the heroine. As the descendant of an aristocratic Scottish family she maintains a kind of Puritan stiffness and pride which contrasts strangely with the life-style of the Anglo-American aesthetes in Venice. Her personality works as a challenge on the artist, whose ambition it becomes to subdue her to his conception of the self. He works at her on two levels, rewriting the manuscript of her attempt of a novelistic self-portrait and rewriting the script of her life in a novel of his own. Yet Lady Tal resists being revised by Marion. There is considerable irony in the fact that the elements of moral sturdiness and responsibility undermine the artist's sophisticated psychology and poetics. What distinguishes the best kind of novelist, the one who is able to explore *"Character"* – in contradistinction to the *"Constructive"* author – is, according to Vernon Lee, that he

> intuitively, i.e. from a feeling left by repeated but unsifted experience, makes allowance for the potential and changing, for what the novelist is not clear about, the unknown of which he only knows that it exists. While the other [the *Constructive*] School of novelist is interested only in such qualities and probabilities as is needed for his little – or perhaps his magnificent! – scheme.[19]

In Marion's case, exactly the most commonplace character traits of conventional writing enter as the unexpected and bring about the fate that Lee prognosticates to the *Constructive* writer: "this constructive novelist is occasionally overtaken by the Nemesis of the thus discarded and disdained elements of human reality".[20] The otherwise rather trite ending of Lee's story is, at least partially, redeemed by this touch of metaliterary dramatic irony.

From the beginning, the tall and strong figure of Lady Tal is set against aesthetic Venice. Impenetrable to the charm of its canals, she prefers to walk. Instead of giving way to moonlight fantasies, she goes to bed and rises early for her charitable morning work. Whereas the feminine quality of the place is congenial to Marion (Tal's cousin likes to call him 'Mary Anne'), Lady Tal's angular masculinity resists its influence. Views of Venice serve as a running commentary to the story of the changing relations between the two. As a place infinitely pliable to the imagination, "to be populated at will according to the exigencies and caprices of fancy,"[21] it adopts itself to the different meanings of the encounters between the lady and the novelist. It serves as the symbol of pure art in its ideality, its constructiveness, its indeterminacy, its inhuman stasis and its late nineteenth-century bric-à-brac degeneracy. Its becomes, in the market and hospital episode, its own contradiction; it even complies, in the final scene, with its own negation.

---

[19] Lee 1969, 279.
[20] ibid.
[21] Bursani, Giorgio: *Le parole preparate*. Torino 1966. Quoted in Ross 1994, 113.

Throughout the nineteenth century Venice has been closely connected with the development of Romantic and post-Romantic subjectivity.[22] To the city of dreams, madness and masques, the early modern artist's program of the decentralized self, made up by transitory, insubstantial states of being, comes natural. It is in this context that Lady Tal's obsolete honesty can be made to appear refreshingly exotic. In a place where everybody is afloat in a gondola, the pedestrian movement regains the charm of novelty.

Bibliography

Dieterle, Bernard: *Die versunkene Stadt. Sechs Kapitel zum literarischen Venedig-Mythos.* Frankfurt a.M. 1995.

Gardner, Burdett: *The Lesbian Imagination (Victorian Style). A Psychological and Critical Study of 'Vernon Lee'.* New York 1987.

Gunn, Peter: *Vernon Lee. Violet Paget 1856-1937.* London 1964.

Jeffares, Bo: *The Artist in Nineteenth-Century English Fiction.* Gerrards Cross 1979.

Kucich, John: *The Power of Lies. Transgression in Victorian Fiction.* Ithaca 1994.

Lee, Vernon [Violet Paget]: *Miss Brown.* 3 vols. London 1884.

Lee, Vernon: *Vanitas. Polite Stories.* Leipzig 1911.

Lee, Vernon: *Studies of the Eighteenth Century in Italy.* 2nd ed. London 1907.

Lee, Vernon: *Les Mensonges Vitaux. Études sur quelques variétés de l'obscurantisme contemporain.* Transl. by Eugène-Bernard Leroy. Paris 1921.

Lee, Vernon: *The Handling of Words, and Other Studies in Literary Psychology*, ed. Royal A. Gettmann. Lincoln, Nebraska 1969.

Lee, Vernon: *Amour dure. Unheimliche Erzählungen*, ed. Frank Rainer Scheck. Köln 1990.

Lee, Vernon: "Lady Tal". In: *Daughters of Decadence*, ed. Elaine Showalter. London 1993, 192-261.

Ross, Michael L.: *Storied Cities. Literary Imaginings of Florence, Venice, and Rome.* London 1994.

---

[22] Dieterle 1995.

Erika Fischer-Lichte

Theatre as Festive Play:
Max Reinhardt's Production of *The Merchant of Venice*

At the beginning of the century, a new concept of theatre was propagated in Germany and in other Western cultures - the idea of theatre as a festival. By redefining theatre as festival, theatre reformers such as Peter Behrens, Georg Fuchs, Max Reinhardt, Adolphe Appia, Emile Jaques-Dalcroze and others wanted to bring about what they called a retheatricalization of theatre - a shift in focus from the referential function of theatre to a performative one and the unification of actors and spectators into a festive community: In 1899, Georg Fuchs published the manifesto *Die Schaubühne - ein Fest des Lebens* (*Wiener Rundschau*, III. Jg.); Peter Behrens followed a year later with *Feste des Lebens und der Kunst* (Leipzig 1900).

In 1902, an extraordinary meeting of young theatre artists took place at the Café Monopol in Berlin which included Max Reinhardt and his friend, and later dramatic adviser (literary director), Arthur Kahane. In the course of this meeting, Reinhardt developed his ideas and agenda for a future theatre which he summarized as follows: "The theatre will turn back into festive play, which was its original meaning."[1] He was convinced that the production of classical plays would fulfil a major function in realizing this vision: "New life will emerge on the stage out of the classics: colour and music and greatness and splendour and merry-making."[2]

Shortly after this, Reinhardt began work on achieving his goal. He produced Lessing's comedy *Minna von Barnhelm* and Schiller's domestic tragedy *Love and Intrigue* (both 1904, at the Neues Theater, Berlin). Still at the Neues Theater in 1905, he staged Shakespeare's *A Midsummer Night's Dream* - a legendary production. The following season, he became director of the Deutsches Theater where - despite interruptions in the twenties - he would work until 1933 when the Nazis forced him to leave Germany.

One of the first classics Reinhardt produced was Shakespeare's *Merchant of Venice*, an extraordinary choice. Why did he turn to a play whose performance traditions in Germany were as far removed as possible from the idea of theatre as a festive play? The theatre critic Siegfried Jacobson describes the situation as follows:

---

[1] "Das Theater wird wieder zum festlichen Spiel werden, das seine eigentliche Bestimmung ist." Kahane 1928, 119.

[2] "Von den Klassikern her wird ein neues Leben über die Bühne kommen: Farbe und Musik und Größe und Pracht und Heiterkeit." Ibid. p. 119.

> From the age of the Shakespeare-revival in Germany until today, most producers have transformed the comedy of the proud Venetian merchant into the tragedy of Shylock who, like all his race, was hounded to death.³

Nonetheless, it seems as if Reinhardt did regard this play as particularly suitable for his purpose. He produced it several times: first in 1905 at the Deutsches Theater in Berlin (with Rudolf Schildkraut as Shylock); then in 1909 at the Münchner Künstlertheater (again with Rudolf Schildkraut as Shylock); in 1913 at the Deutsches Theater as part of a Shakespeare Festival (with Albert Bassermann as Shylock); in 1915 at the Berlin Volksbühne (again with Rudolf Schildkraut as Shylock); in 1918 at the Deutsches Theater (with Alexander Moissi as Shylock); in 1921 at the Großes Schauspielhaus in Berlin which the architect Hans Poelzig rebuilt from the Schumann Circus (with Werner Krauss as Shylock); in 1924 at the Theater an der Josefstadt in Vienna (with Fritz Kortner as Shylock) and, finally, in 1934 in Venice (with Memo Benassi as Shylock). It seems that Reinhardt's approach to *The Merchant of Venice* was, like his work on *A Midsummer Night's Dream* though to a lesser extent - a work in progress. As in his first production of *A Midsummer Night's Dream*, Reinhardt did not bother much about performance traditions or theatrical conventions valid at the time in his first production of *The Merchant of Venice*; he radically did away with all of them.

What, then, might have been the reasons behind his choice? It seems that the location of the play, Venice, was a major factor. This small fact can be gleaned from Arthur Kahane's characterization of Reinhardt's production:

> The hero, focal point, heart and essence of this performance is Venice. Not Shylock, but Venice. The ever-singing, ever-humming Venice. A city which boisterously rejoices in the joys of life, its pleasures and delights. A city which believes it is the capital and centre of the world. The home of culture and intellectuals, university of *savoir vivre* and elegance, immersed in splendour and sun, flooded with music. And, of course, flooded with sadness and melancholy, since they are inseparably connected with joy; flooded with seriousness and sin, which, alas, though so beautiful, are so impregnated with inevitable fate. Venice, with its hidden corners, bridges, squares and narrow alleyways, where cheerful calls echo across the water, is a loud, merry, humorous, wonderful being.⁴

---

³ "Die Aufführungen seit der Zeit der deutschen Shakespeare-Renaissance bis heute hatten fast alle aus dem Lustspiel des königlichen Kaufmanns von Venedig ein Trauerspiel des zu Tode gehetzten Shylock und damit seines ganzen Volkes gemacht." Jacobsohn 1911, 1-5, 1.

⁴ "Held, Mittelpunkt, Herz und Wesen dieser Aufführung ist Venedig. Nicht Shylock, sondern Venedig. Das ewig singende, ewig summende Venedig. Eine Stadt, die von Lebenslust, Genuß, Freude und Ausgelassenheit jauchzt. Die sich als Hauptstadt und Mittelpunkt der Welt fühlt. Sitz der Kultur und feinen Geistigkeit, hohe Schule aller Lebenskunst und Eleganz, getaucht in Glanz und Sonne, durchflutet von Musik. Freilich auch von Schwermut und Melancholie, weil sie untrennbar zur Freude gehören, von Lebenssinn und Sünde, die ach! so schön sind, und von unheilschwangerem Schicksal. Venedig mit Winkeln, Brücken und Plätzen, mit den engen Gassen, in denen fröhliche Rufe über das Wasser hin hallen und ein lautes, heiteres, witziges, verliebtes Wesen treibt." Kahane 1914, 107-119, 116.

Theatre As Festive Play: Max Reinhardt's production of *The Merchant of Venice*

What was it that Reinhardt achieved by transforming Venice into the hero and centre of the performance, by putting Renaissance Venice on stage? Did he offer a new reading of the play? And, moreover, was it just such a new interpretation that so electrified and enthused critics and spectators alike that the production was shown to full houses 150 times during the 1905/6 season?

There is not much evidence to support this view. For, the critics who favoured the production seem to have avoided an open discussion of the question of a particular reading nor did they discuss the relationship between text and performance - in general the theatre critics' favourite subject. Rather, by re-telling the story of the play according to the performance, they seem to suggest that the performance was "truthful" to the text because it presented an interpretation in line with the poet's intentions. Only when describing and evaluating Schildkraut's performance of Shylock, do they deal with the question explicitly and take a clear stance. The liberal journals praised his acting for abandoning all the stereotypes and clichés of the Jewish merchant and presenting "not a trouble-maker, not a roaring predator, but instead, a human individual against the background of an entire national history"[5] so that the play revealed and underlined the "sermon for tolerance and humanity hidden in 'The Merchant of Venice'".[6] Even the conservative critics judged Schildkraut's performance as "unobtrusive" in "presenting the race and character of the Jew"[7]. The nationalist critics, however, who, in general did not approve of the production, attacked Schildkraut for "branding this malicious, insidious, vindictive haggling Jew as a martyr, as a prosaic defender of trampled human rights"[8]: "[...] this interpretation pursues no other aim than the political one to use Shakespeare as champion for philo-Semitism; there is no aesthetic purpose in it."[9]

These were the same critics who, in articulating their deepest disapproval, not only of Schildkraut's performance but also of the whole production, explicitly referred to the play's "truthfulness" to the text and, thus, the relationship between text and performance, as the climax to their criticism. Full of scorn and reproof, they state that during the entire performance, everything which delighted the audience - such as the set, the atmosphere, the music, the acting - "happens at the expense of the poet"[10].

---

[5] "Kein Schreier, kein brüllendes Raubtier, nur ein Einzelmensch auf dem Hintergrund einer ganzen Volksgeschichte". Engel, Fritz: *Berliner Tageblatt*, Nr. 575, 13. November 1905, In: Fetting 1987, 311-315, 313.

[6] p. 8 "(Es steckt) im 'Kaufmann von Venedig' eine heimliche Predigt für Toleranz und Humanität". Hart 1905, In: op. cit., 307-311, 310.

[7] "[I]n der Betonung der Rasse und des jüdischen Charakters zurückhaltend angelegt", Heinrich Stümcke, quoted from Jaron et al., 589.

[8] "[D]iesen boshaften, tückischen und rachsüchtigen Schacherjuden zum Märtyrer, zum deklamatorischen Verteidiger zertretener Menschenrechte zu stempeln". Diesel 1905.

[9] "(Aber) diese Interpretation hat doch nur den politischen Zweck, Shakespeare für den Philosemitismus zu retten; ästhetischen Sinn hat sie nicht." Müller-Füner, Theodor: *Neue Preussische Zeitung*. 10. November 1905, In: Jaron, 1986, 592f., 592.

[10] "Das alles geschieht auf Kosten des Dichters", Müller-Füner: op. cit. 592.

"And yet how nice it would have been, if only one could bring oneself to forget about the play and the poet altogether...".[11]

Naturally such phrases were meant to be devastating criticism - death sentences. For, at the beginning of the century, it was still common belief that the function and purpose of theatre was to convey works of literature. However, it seems that even Reinhardt's enemies grasped intuitively that his *Merchant of Venice* had another agenda than merely conveying a literary text. Instead of presenting a reading of the play - whether old or new - so I shall argue, Reinhardt presented and realized a new concept of theatre. As long as the audience and most of the critics felt enthused and charmed by the production, they did not so much respond to its referentiality, to the meanings it might have brought forth, to any kind of interpretation of the text (as did the disapproving nationalistic critics), but to its festive and playful spirit, to its particular performativity. And Reinhardt's method of casting Venice as the protagonist and centre of the performance worked as a most effective means of reducing and subduing its referentiality and, instead, foregrounding and strengthening its performativity.

There were mainly two devices by which Reinhardt achieved this goal: 1) by creating atmosphere, and 2) by exposing the performance's theatricality.

There is not one critic who did not mention the particular mood of the production. One calls it a "a touch of Venetian atmosphere"[12], another talks about "the magic of the atmosphere"[13]. Detailed descriptions are used to convey this particular atmosphere. Alfred Klaar writes: "Very characteristic were the narrow Venetian alleys with their atmospheric vistas, the mosaics and statues of saints at the front of gloomy palaces, the tight-packed architecture and the small, daringly curved bridges"[14]. The Danish critic, Georg Brandes, reports: "The scenes of Italian life not only made you realize the quick pulse of these people, but also the impetuous festive spirit of the early Renaissance. The stage pictures were reminders of paintings by Carpaccio, Giovanni Bellini, Paris Bordone or Paolo Veronese."[15] And in the *Berliner Volks-Zeitung* one reads:

> The Renaissance - it glowed everywhere in rich colours, in the fullness of life and happiness: Renaissance in the magnificent, cheery halls of Belmont Castle, where the rich, graceful, brilliant Portia holds court surrounded by pleasure and games, and is hotly pursued by princes from all the nations in the world! Renaissance in the secluded corners of the lagoon city. Richly dressed Venetian youths warm themselves on sun-drenched piazzas; [...] the night throbs to the tempting sounds of the guitar, serenades sing out, carnevalesque and masked figures flit over jetties and bridges to the

---

[11] "Und doch wärs herrlich schön gewesen, wenn mans bloß über sich gewinnen könnte, das Stück und den Dichter zu vergessen ...", Leosker, H.: *National-Zeitung*. 10. November 1905, in: Jaron et al., 1986, 591f., 591.

[12] "Hauch venezianischer Stimmung" Klaar, Alfred: *Vossische Zeitung*, Nr. 529, 10. November 1905 in: Fetting 1987, 302-307, 304.

[13] "Stimmungszauber", Hart: op. cit., 309.

[14] "Charakteristisch waren auch die venezianischen Gäßchen mit ihren stimmungsvollen Durchblicken, den Mosaikbildern und Heiligenstatuen an düstern Palästen, der gedrängten Architektur und der kleinen kühn geschwungenen Brücken." Klaar 1905 op. cit., 303 f.

[15] Styan 1982, 61.

Theatre As Festive Play: Max Reinhardt's production of *The Merchant of Venice*

flickering light of torches ... Then another moonlit night full of celestial poetry, full of love and music; a tender, warm haze in the air; a few stars looking down furtively from the dusky violet sky; the all-pervading scent of blossoms and the soft tones of a flute from behind the greenery ..."[16]

From such descriptions and reports we can guess that the atmosphere which the spectators could obviously sense physically came into being as a result of a particular interaction between stage architecture, colours, light, music, sounds and movement. Reinhardt's stage designer Emil Orlik built the streets of Venice (including Shylock's house), the hall in Portia's palace, the courtroom and Belmont park on a revolving stage. The city first came into life by way of sounds. A prelude of sounds opened the performance. First, distant animals' voices were heard, then rattling, clattering and clinking sounds, followed by single shouts of the gondolieri; ever more voices joined until, finally, there was an upsurge of crowd noise - the city was awake. Singing and distant violins were heard blending ominously with an almost imperceptible march. Humperdinck composed the music in such a way that at first, "the listener does not become aware of the march, still it is the march that heightens the more delightful, more tense atmosphere of this very moment, without, however, trespassing the limits of the listener's consciousness".[17] It is details like this that reveal how carefully and skilfully Reinhardt staged and fabricated the dominating atmosphere in each scene, as well as the moment of change of atmosphere.

Movement also contributed to the fabrication of the atmosphere - movement of the set as well as that of the actors. The revolving stage allowed for a quick change of scenes, thus heightening the quick pace and rhythm of the performance. On the other hand - and to a greater extent - it was the acting that gave rise to the impression of high spirits, of the joys of life, of pleasures, delights and exuberance. All the critics mention the frequency, rapidity and intensity of the actors' movements, whether or not they approve of it. Siegfried Jacobsohn states: "The Venetian joy of life is the dominant note of the performance ... whoever enters jumps for joy; whoever exits, does so trilling away to himself."[18] And Heinrich Hart writes: "I never before came across a

---

[16] "Renaissance - überall leuchtete sie in satten Farben, in Lebensfülle und Heiterkeit: Renaissance in den prunkvoll-lustigen Sälen des Schlosses Belmonte, wo die reiche, die anmutige, die geistvolle Portia inmitten von Lust und Spiel Hof hält, heiß umworben von Freiern aus allen Ländern der Welt! Renaissance in den lauschigen Winkeln der Lagunenstadt! Reich gekleidete Venetianerjünglinge wärmen sich an sonnigen Plätzen; [...]; die Nacht wird durchschwirrt vom lockenden Klange der Gitarren, Serenaden ertönen, Mummenschanz und Maskeraden huschen beim flackernden Fackellichte über Stege und Brücken, [...]. Dann wieder eine Mondesnacht voll himmlischer Poesie, voll Liebesschwärmerei und Musik; ein zartes, warmes Zittern in der Luft: aus dem violett-dunstigen Himmel blicken verstohlen ein paar Sterne; Blütenduft allerwärts und sanftes Flötenspiel hinter den Büschen [...]" *Berliner Volks-Zeitung* 10. November 1905, in Jaron et al. 1986 589-591, 589 f.

[17] "Ein straffes Marschmotiv, das dem Hörer gar nicht bewußt wird und doch die freudigere, angespanntere Stimmung der Stelle - eben unbewußt - erhöht". "Gespräch über Reinhardt mit Hugo von Hofmannsthal, Alfred Roller und Bruno Walter, 1910". In: Fetting 1974, 380-389, 383.

[18] "Venetianische Lebenslust ist die Dominante der Aufführung ... Wer auftritt, hüpft vor Freude, wer abgeht, trällert vor sich hin." Siegfried Jacobsohn, "Shakespeare: Der Kaufmann von Venedig", in: S.J. 1914, 1-5, 1 f.

more turbulent performance. It was a racing, romping, wriggling, storming from beginning to end. Movement in which all took part, even Shylock, Portia and the Duke of Venice. Großmann, playing Lancelot, was pure acrobat."[19]

This new style of acting, based on a fast rhythm, was noted by all critics - and presumably also by all spectators. First, it offended against the principles of realism. Thus, Hart complains "that the old Duke is permanently running around is as unroyal as it can get; he should be sitting on his throne, awe-inspiringly, and only in a moment of greatest excitement might he once get to his feet".[20] Second, it violated the rules of psychology. Alfred Klaar criticizes the difference between the Portia of the first and last acts and, in particular, that the actress - Agnes Sorma - did not show the development that resulted in the change: "But if this was the Portia of the first acts, did one see the path that led to these heights?"[21] And Fritz Engel laments the exaggerations that carried the actors away from any kind of psychology and realism. "The servants who have to announce a guest, bound into the room ... like madmen. And even if one is inclined to allow the grotesque figures of the Princes of Morocco and of Arragon [Albert Steinrück and Hans Waßmann] all the privileges of a burlesque comedy, certain moderation would have become them very well as it would Lancelot Gobbo [Richard Großmann]."[22]

Even if we concede that the actors were not all able to perform perfectly, it becomes quite clear from the criticism that they were not meant to follow the rules of psychology and realism all the time. This new kind of acting, as imperfectly as it might have been realized, brought about several changes. First, it focused on the situation, instead of delineating a development of a character or a story. In this way, it became capable of a second change: relating the actor's body to other elements - architecture, light, colours, sounds, music - within the situation and thereby to contribute to its particular atmosphere.

Third, this kind of acting realized a new body concept. The actor's body was not used as the source of verbal utterances, of lines to be spoken as effectively as possible, as was the case at the Court Theatre, nor as signs of the psychology of a dramatic figure - as in Otto Brahm's naturalistic performances. Rather, the actor's body was used as a means of movement to radiate sensuousness and a source of vitality which is

---

[19] "Eine bewegtere Darstellung ist mir noch nicht vorgekommen. Das war ein Rennen, Tollen, Zappeln, Stürmen von Anfang bis zum Ende. Eine Beweglichkeit, bei der alle mittaten, selbst Shylock, Portia und der Doge. Großmann als Lanzelot machte geradezu den Akrobaten". Hart 1905, *Der Tag*, op. cit., 310.

[20] "Daß der greise Doge fortwährend herumläuft, das ist so unköniglich wie möglich; er hat ehrfurchtgebietend auf dem Thronsessel zu sitzen und nur in höchster Erregung mag er einmal aufspringen". Hart, op. cit. 310.

[21] "Aber war das noch die Portia der ersten Akte, sah man den Weg, der zu dieser Höhe führt?", Klaar, op. cit. 306.

[22] "Die Diener, die einen Gast zu melden haben, springen [...] wie Besessene ins Zimmer. Und so sehr man geneigt sein kann, den grotesken Figuren der Prinzen von Marokko und von Aragon alle Privilegien der Possenkomödie zu gönnen, so können auch diese, ebenso wie Lancelot Gobbo gewisse Milderungen vertragen." Engel 1905, 315.

Theatre As Festive Play: Max Reinhardt's production of *The Merchant of Venice*

transmitted directly to the spectators by the actors when they move through the space. And this new concept of the actor's body enabled the actor to expose acting as something that is playing the part of a dramatic figure, instead of realizing and presenting it as the imitation of a "real" person's behaviour in everyday life, and as something that has presence on stage. The acting style, thus, can be understood as the most important means used to expose the performance's theatricality.

Another means, of course, was the revolving stage. While the first view of Venetian alleys, canals, bridges and palaces might confirm the spectators' expectation that the illusion of real Venice is accomplished on stage, the first movement of the revolving stage reminds the spectators that they are seated in a theatre responding to a theatrical performance - not observing and sympathizing with a scene from 'real' life.

By creating atmosphere and by exposing the performance's particular theatricality, Reinhardt demanded new ways of perception and reception from the spectators (as he had already done in his production of *A Midsummer Night's Dream*). In performances by the Meininger Company or their disciples, the spectators were used to a historically correct set which either confirmed or enlarged their historical knowledge. Thus, as a spectator, it was most important to grasp the meaning of all spaces shown and all objects used on stage. Similarly, it was essential to listen to the words which the actors uttered and to watch their gestures in order to follow the action and to understand the characters. That is to say, listening and watching were used as channels or tools that enabled the spectator to constitute certain meanings concerning the story and the psychology of the characters.

In Reinhardt's production of *The Merchant of Venice*, this was obviously not the case. Rather, everything that was shown and happened on stage had an immediate and strong appeal to the spectators' senses. By looking at the set, its forms and colours, by perceiving the light, by listening to the various sounds and to the music, by following the actors moving over the stage with their eyes, by listening to their voices, the spectators sensed the atmosphere of the scene physically, they were drawn into it, became immersed in it. That is not to say that they ceased to constitute meanings. Of course they continued to do so. But whereas in the historistic theatre of the time, the performative function of theatre served the only or at least, the main purpose, of supporting its referential function, of helping to carry the message, here, the performative function claimed at least equal rights to the referential one. The foregrounding of the performative function turned the performance into an "event" as one of the critics, strongly opposed to the production, sarcastically wrote.[23]

In and through his production of *The Merchant of Venice*, Reinhardt formulated and realized a new concept of theatre. For here, as one critic states, "everything is imagination, everything is play, everything is theatre"[24]. In this way, Reinhardt redefined theatre as a game whose rules are set up by the stage director and the actors but which can be renegotiated by the spectators. It is a play in which all take part - the spectators as well as the actors. What is shown and performed on stage is material for

---

[23] H. Leosker in the *National-Zeitung*, op. cit., 591.

[24] "Alles Phantasie, alles Spiel, alles Theater", Hart, op. cit., 308.

the play, material with which the actors as well as the spectators can play. The performance is a game that involves the senses as much as the imagination. And as a game, its performativity equals or possibly even outweighs its referentiality. Playing the game, taking part in the event, is more important than formulating an interpretation of the text or deciphering it.

As previously in his production of *A Midsummer Night's Dream*, in *The Merchant of Venice* Reinhardt renounced the idea of theatre as an illusion of reality, based on and controlled by a dramatic text and, instead, revived the idea of theatre as play, as a game which in many cases does proceed from a dramatic text, which nonetheless serves as nothing more than a kind of trigger that sets the theatrical imagination of the stage director and the actors in motion without guiding, let alone controlling them in the ways they choose. As the stage designer Alfred Roller stated: "Reinhardt plays comedy - others hand down literature"[25] Thus, it is small wonder that, with the course of time, his new concept of theatre led him to pantomime, dance, and *commedia dell'arte*, i.e. to theatre forms that privilege performativity instead of referentiality.

In the case of *The Merchant of Venice* it was Reinhardt's ingenious idea of "starring" Venice which contributed enormously to the realization of the new concept of theatre. For there seems to be a deep affinity between "festive play" and Venice - not only in the sense that Venice is the city of masquerades and carnival which blur the limits between actors and spectators, the city of the *commedia dell'arte* and the opera; a theatrical city *par excellence* that prides in exhibiting its theatricality to its own inhabitants as well as to outsiders but also Venice as a stage for the display of all kinds of theatrical architecture and behaviour. Such an affinity exists - possibly even more so - in the concept of Venice as a myth[26]. The myth of Venice interprets the city as a heterotopia in the Foucaultian sense[27]. It is a place "betwixt and between" (Victor Turner), a place of passage, of transformation as is theatre as festive play. That is to say that "Venice" appears almost synonymously with "festive play". Performing the poetic *topos* and the myth Venice on stage, thus, meant realizing the idea of theatre as festive play.

Since this is so, it seems all the more remarkable that Reinhardt's last production of *The Merchant of Venice* not only put Venice on stage, but also took Venice itself *as* a stage. In 1934, Reinhardt was invited to produce *The Merchant of Venice* as part of the first "Festival internazionale del Teatro di Prosa" in Venice with Italian actors. As stage and place of performance he chose the Campo San Trovaso, a quiet square marked off on one side by the Church of San Trovaso and on the opposite side by the Rio degli Ognisanti. A typical small Venetian bridge led to the other side of the narrow canal, where majestic doors formed the counter-point to Shylock's house. "Now it actually takes place amongst palaces from the age of the Venetian Dukes, on night-

---

[25] "Reinhardt spielt Komödie - die anderen tradieren Literatur", Gespräch über Reinhardt, op. cit., 382.
[26] Cf. the contribution by Manfred Pfister in this volume.
[27] Cf. the contribution by Elizabeth Bronfen in this volume.

black canals, slender, graceful bridges"[28], wrote the dramatic advisor Heinz Herald. The music, this time, was composed by Victor Sabata. Memo Benassi played Shylock, Marta Abba the part of Portia.

Reinhardt exploited to the full all the possibilities which this space, this very unique environment had to offer. He redesigned the pantomimic scenes that open and close each act or sequence of the production in order to allow the whole environment come into play. Before the first intermission (after II, 8; in Reinhardt's version II, 5) he inserted a pantomimic scene in which Shylock discovers Jessica's escape. Shylock enters from behind left and slowly moves towards the bridge. He climbs some steps, calling for Jessica, continues and crosses the bridge. He makes a halt before his house, looking up to the windows, calling Jessica's name again. Then he goes to the door, knocks several times and calls again and again. Suddenly he realizes that the door is open. He steps back, full of horror. Then he enters the house. The spectators hear how he climbs the stairs, calling for Jessica, murmuring. The spectators assume that he has reached the room with the balcony, for it lights up and a fearful shout is heard: "Jessi ...". After a silence Shylock could be seen stumbling out onto the balcony with a lantern in his trembling hand, looking down in all directions and calling: "Jessica!!!". He listens, murmurs some incomprehensible sentences; his knees buckle, forcing him to reach out to the balustrade for support. Suddenly he jumps up and goes back into the room. The spectators hear him stumbling down the staircase, chairs fall down, doors slam. The room on the first floor is lit up; tables are moved and drawers opened. Suddenly there is an alarming scream. The spectators see Shylock throw open the window tearing at his clothes. He rushes back into the room and the spectators hear him moaning, wailing and uttering inarticulate sounds. Then Shylock rushes out through the door, looks around and calls for Jessica, obviously out of his senses with rage and despair. He stumbles up the steps to the bridge, takes the cloth that he wears around his shoulders and rips it.[29] Then he is overcome by wild sobbing and he breaks down on the bridge.[30]

This scene provided the opportunity of making use of a large part of the environment - the bridge, the space in front of the house, the interior of house, the window, the balcony. After the intermission, some other parts of the environment came into play. First, trumpets were heard, announcing both the arrival of the Prince of

---

[28] "Nun findet es wirklich zwischen Palästen aus der venezianischen Dogenzeit, auf nachtdunklen Kanälen, schlanken, graziösen Brücken statt". Herald 1953, 65.

[29] This gesture is a traditional Jewish wailing gesture. It is the only allusion to real Jewish life in the production. This might seem surprising. Reinhardt left Germany a few days after his last Berlin production, Hugo von Hofmannsthal's *Salzburger Großes Welttheater*. The première was March 1, 1933 at the Deutsches Theater. The actor Werner Krauss was sent after Reinhardt in order to offer him "honorary Aryanship". After Reinhardt had declined the offer, he was dispossessed of his Berlin theatres. One could have expected him to use the opportunity of staging *The Merchant of Venice* outside Germany to point to or at least to hint or allude to the situation in Germany. But this was not the case. Instead he seized the opportunity of formulating and realizing his concept of theatre once more.

[30] Cf. the description of this scene in Braulich 1960, 85-86.

Arragon and the end of the intermission to the call the audience back to the play. High up on the tower someone called out: "Il Principe di Aragona." Music was heard. While Nerissa and the servants hurried to set up the table with the caskets, and Portia and her ladies solemnly walked down the steps in order to meet the Prince, torchbearers took their positions along the canal and a huge sailing barque with a Spanish coat of arms glided down the canal and docked at the jetty.

This use of the environment offered the spectators much more to hear and see than the previous productions and invited them to let their eyes wander over, through and in the environment as would never have been possible in a box set stage. The spectators were right in the middle of the environment. This greatly contributed to the creation of atmosphere in which players and co-players (spectators) were immersed. And it emphasized and magnified the theatricality of the performance as well as of the city. The theatricality of the one doubled the theatricality of the other; turning the city into a stage for this theatrical performance meant bringing to the fore the city's own theatricality displayed both in its architecture as well as in the behaviour of its inhabitants. Performing Venice, here, meant to let the city take part in the performance, to let it - so to speak - act itself.

This was even underlined by a small but telling accident. The beginning of the first night performance had to be delayed because the Crown Prince was late. He landed his *motoscafo* at the shore of the Rio degli Ognisanti which formed part of the environment and which was almost exactly the same spot where the Prince of Arragon's barque would later land. The Crown Prince disembarked, was applauded by the Italian audience and mounted the steps up to the centre of the performance site. Naturally, this was also part of the performance like everything else that happened during this "special event".

Here, theatre operated as a festive play that confronted the community taking part with an image of itself as the epitome and incarnation of a festive and theatrical spirit. Obviously, the audience greatly enjoyed the performance as a performance of the myth Venice. This is how one of the critics summarizes her review:

> And now, finally, God help your poor servant to find the words, I offer up a heart bursting with reverence while on bended knee to pay homage to the greatest actress of the evening: Thou - Venezia! You are the cause of all the beauty, greatness and nobility that today's splendour has awakened in the soul - and, triumphant, you shine over the whole - as if in a painting by Paolo Veronese.[31]

The production of *The Merchant of Venice* at the opening of the first "Festival internazionale del Teatro di Prosa" enacted the myth of Venice in and through Venice

---

[31] "Und nun zum Schlusse - Gottvater - hilf deinem armen Diener Worte finden, um sein von Andacht erfülltes Herz darzubieten und mit gebeugten Knien der größten Darstellerin dieses Abends zu huldigen: Dir - Venezia! Du bist die Ursache all des Schönen, Grossen und Edlen, das die heutige Pracht in der Seele erweckte - und triumphierend strahlst du über dem Ganzen - wie auf den Bildern Paolo Veroneses." Cerruti, 1934. The author was the wife of the Italian ambassador to Berlin.

Theatre As Festive Play: Max Reinhardt's production of *The Merchant of Venice*

and in this sense, can be understood as the epitome and incarnation of Reinhardt's of theatre.

Scene with Memo Benassi as Shylock (Österreichisches Theatermuseum Wien)

Bibliography

Braulich, Heinrich: Max Reinhardt - Theater zwischen Traum und Wirklichkeit. Berlin 1960.
Cerruti, Elisabeth: "Der 'Kaufmann' in Venedig. Shakespeare auf der Freilichtbühne". In: Berliner Tageblatt No. 351, July 27, 1934.
Diesel, Friedrich: Review of Reinhardt's Merchant of Venice. In: Deutsche Zeitung. November 11, 1905.
Fetting, Hugo (ed.): Max Reinhardt. Schriften, Briefe, Reden, Aufsätze, Interviews, Gespräche, Auszüge aus Regiebüchern. Berlin 1974, 380-89.
Fetting, Hugo (ed.): Von der Freien Bühne zum Politischen Theater. Drama und Theater im Spiegel der Kritik. Vol. 1: 1889-1918. Leipzig 1987.
Hart, Heinrich: Review of Reinhardt's Merchant of Venice. In: Der Tag (II. T.), N. 562, November 11, 1905, 307-11.
Herald, Heinz: Max Reinhardt. Bildnis eines Theatermannes. Hamburg 1953.
Jacobsohn, Siegfried: Max Reinhardt. Berlin 1911.
Jahrbuch der deutschen Shakespeare-Gesellschaft, 50. Jg. 1914.
Jaron, Norbert/Renate Möhrmann/ Hedwig Müller (eds.): Berlin - Theater der Jahrhundertwende. Bühnengeschichte der Reichshauptstadt im Spiegel der Kritik (1889-1914). Tübingen 1986.
Kahane, Arthur: Tagebuch des Dramaturgen. Berlin 1928.
Styan, J.L.: Max Reinhardt. Cambridge 1982.

Virginia Richter

Tourists Lost in Venice: Daphne du Maurier's *Don't Look Now* and Ian McEwan's *The Comfort of Strangers*

> Cities, like dreams, are made of desires and fears, even if the thread of their discourse is secret, their rules absurd, their perspectives deceitful, and everything conceals something else.
> Italo Calvino, *Invisible Cities*[1]

Joseph Brodsky's romance with Venice originated a long time before there existed the remotest possibility that he would ever be able to travel to that city, long before his emigration from the Soviet Union. His vision is prefigured by various artefacts which seem to symbolise, in their very material decay, the remote object of his longing: some novels by Henri de Régnier in moribund paperbacks, "published in the late thirties, with no bindings to speak of, disintegrating in your palm" (Brodsky 1992, 36f.), a coloured photograph of San Marco covered with snow, "an accordion set of sepia postcards" that his girlfriend's grandmother had "brought home from a pre-revolutionary honeymoon in Venice" (Brodsky 1992, 39), a piece of cheap tapestry depicting the Palazzo Ducale, a little copper gondola. Together with Visconti's film *Death in Venice*, seen in a "smuggled, and for that reason black-and-white, copy" (Brodsky 1992, 39), these items forge Brodsky's imaginary Venice. So, interestingly, even in the Soviet Union of the 1960s the image of Venice was reproduced and transmitted not only in literary representations and on the screen, but also on postcards, souvenirs, and bric-a-brac. These battered objects, having crossed the border from a hermetically sealed-off world, seem to carry with them, both metaphorically and metonymically, the fantasmatic kernel of Venetian associations: decay, desire, death. But the main point of Brodsky's retrospective account is not so much its imaginative content, but the evocation of Venice as a space of fantasy, a 'not-real', unattainable city.

"Venice is always the already written as well as the already seen, the already read." (Tanner 1992, 17). But it is, equally, always already framed by the tourist gaze, already reproduced by the tourist industry. The fictions on Venice after Henry James and Thomas Mann have to take into account the city's symbiotic and at the same time destructive relationship with mass travelling, as well as its status as an infinitely reproduced object of the literary text, the camera and the traveller's gaze. The mythic, poetic quality of Venice is thus undercut by the banality of mass travelling; in consequence, the tale of an individual's existential encounter with an erotic, faintly oriental Other, epitomised in Thomas Mann's *Death in Venice*, can only be retold with an ironic edge.

---

[1] Calvino 1979, 36.

In her study on Venice in literature Angelika Corbineau-Hoffmann has observed that the lagoon city was in Fin-de-siècle writing a privileged site of "Kunstrealität", a highly aestheticized counter-space opposed to the 'hard' reality of a utilitarian, industrialised society - and as such, the 'ideal vanishing-point of tourism' (Corbineau-Hoffmann 1993, 293). While the association with tourism makes Venice economically viable, the city is at the same time becoming progressively uninhabitable for her native citizens. The effect for literary treatment is equally ambiguous: the 'polyphony of discourses' (Corbineau-Hoffmann 1993, 3) generated by this favourite counter-space threatens to smother Venice as a poetic and poetically productive locality.

Corbineau-Hoffmann postulates two modes in which recent literature tries to reconstitute that lost alterity, to transform Venice back from banal tourist haunt to a literary generative location: on the one hand, a heightened reflexivity about the intertextuality of any Venetian text, on the other hand a conscious distancing from referentiality. In the latter mode, Venice and well-known Venetian landmarks are not named; in this way, the textual geography is marked as imaginary.[2] In addition, the topic of tourism itself is put to productive use in many recent texts, as in the two narratives at which I will take a closer look, Daphne du Maurier's *Don't Look Now* and Ian McEwan's *The Comfort of Strangers*. The protagonists' specific situation as tourists is functionalized in the retelling of that old story, the visitor's encounter with an indecipherable, unnavigable, potentially lethal Venice. My aim now is to show that there is a strong connection between the characters' transitional status, the ambiguity of the city as it is perceived by them, and the male travellers' final death.

Two questions are pertinent to my analysis. Firstly, what is the specific function of the Venetian setting - why Venice, and not, say, Florence?[3] Secondly, what is the meaning of 'transgression' in the texts? How is the notion of transgression linked to a discussion of the semantics of space, on one hand, and the question of gender difference, on the other?

Venice, according to Tony Tanner, is the embodiment of both polis and labyrinth: the consummation of reason and desire. Venice thus comprises the constructive and the subversive relationship between the city and desire (Tanner 1992, 2). In her physical shape, as labyrinth and as synthesis of stone and water, Venice is "the surpassing-all-

---

[2] This "Poetik des Verschweigens" (Corbineau-Hoffmann 1993, 543) is the strategy employed in McEwan's *The Comfort of Strangers*. Another recent text which deals with the anxieties of travelling to Venice is E.Y. Meyer's *Venezianisches Zwischenspiel* (1997). Meyer equally treats Venice as a place of ambiguity, evil and despair where hungry tourists get lost. But his effort to reinterpret Venice turns out to be rather disappointing, precisely because his very concrete citations of place names - Harry's Bar etc. - fall into the trap of simply reiterating clichés. His topographic precision has the effect of a rather pretentious namedropping, instead of evoking the desired threatening atmosphere.

[3] Indeed, J.R. Banks asks 'why not Broadstairs?'. He maintains that McEwan's achievement would have been even greater, if he could have made his story work in a place devoid of the Venetian literary associations (Banks 1982, 27). Perhaps so; but, as I will argue, McEwan's choice of setting is not at all arbitrary; it is a necessary part of his text.

other embodiment of that 'absolute ambiguity' which is radiant life containing death" (Tanner 1992, 368).

This paradoxical union grafted on the tangible location endows Venice with an "overpowering aura of unreality" (Ross 1994, 116). Michael Ross sees Venice as a city of desire, but, unlike Tanner, not of reason. In his view, Florence is the Italian city that welds vision and intellection, whereas perception in Venice remains on a purely sensual level. In Ross's study an Apollinian Florence is opposed to a dreamlike, erotically charged Venice, a stage-setting where fantasy displaces reality: "In narrative, Venice's dreamlike implausibility often endows it with an occult power to unhinge a character's sense of 'normal' reality." (Ross 1994, 116)

This 'unreality effect' can be linked to the workings of fantasy in the psychoanalytic sense. Jean Laplanche and Jean-Bertrand Pontalis locate fantasy "within the domain of opposition between subjective and objective, between an inner world, where satisfaction is obtained through illusion, and an external world, which gradually, through the medium of perception, asserts the supremacy of the reality principle" (Laplanche/Pontalis 1986, 6). In addition, they define fantasy not as the object, but as the setting of desire (Laplanche/Pontalis 1986, 26). In this sense Venice works, in literary texts, as a space of fantasy: a liminal realm where desire can be enacted. Ultimately, the power at work in this fantasmatic structure turns out to be a desire for death.[4]

Another crucial dimension of fantasy consists in its dynamic creativity: to fantasise is not a process passively undergone by the subject, but a productive act. This observation is not only valid in reference to fantasy as wish-fulfilment, but as a way of dealing with negative emotions or memories, such as fear, loss and horror. According to Slavoj Žižek, fantasy *creates* the horror it purports to conceal, as its 'repressed' point of reference. Fantasy in Žižek 's definition "mediates between the formal symbolic structure and the positivity of the objects we encounter in reality - that is to say, it provides a 'schema' according to which certain positive objects in reality can function as objects of desire, filling in the empty places opened up by the formal symbolic structure" (Žižek 1997, 7). As will be shown, this corresponds closely to the way in which the tourists in both texts select elements from the actual environment and work them into the fabric of their, mostly unconscious, desire.

This cursory glance at the psychoanalytic concept of fantasy allows us to reveal a structural analogy between fantasy and tourism, based on two crucial features: a liminal status - the incessant negotiation between two different levels of reality - and a creative potential, the ability to generate, transform and incorporate 'real' elements into a larger imaginary syntax. The cluster of connotations worked out by Tanner, Ross and Corbineau-Hoffmann permits us to describe Venice as a privileged site for the literary representation of the interaction between tourism and fantasy. To further clarify the

---

[4] At least in Thomas Mann's seminal story. In a further turning of the screw, the protagonists of du Maurier's and McEwan's texts actively seek out the place of their killing and the person of the killer, as if they secretly desired to meet their end.

indwelling relationship between these domains, it is pertinent to take a look at some theories of tourism as a last step prior to my textual analysis.

Venice is the city of paradox, Venice is the city of tourism. But then, according to German sociologist Christoph Hennig, tourism itself has to be seen as a fairly paradoxical enterprise. Hennig defines tourism as the sensual experience of imaginary worlds. We physically travel in immaterial countries. Travelling takes place in a liminal realm between reality and phantasy, i.e. there is a continuous slipping between an imaginary frame - the 'pictures in our minds' - and real acts (driving, shopping) or the real environment (bad weather, the topography of the foreign place).

Our expectations and hence our experiences are prefigured by literature and film, by our culturally encoded imagination, our individual wishes and dreams, as the above mentioned example of Brodsky's recollection clearly shows. But tourists do not only - as it were passively - reproduce certain gestures: taking pictures, gazing at monuments, endlessly repeating a stale, second-hand experience. As Hennig maintains, travelling is a creative act; indeed, he compares the tourist to an author who selects bits and pieces from the real world and incorporates them into his fiction. Of course, Hennig does not claim a complete equivalence between art and travelling. But he does contend that the construction of the tourist experience is comparable to other forms of symbolic production. Now, the travellers in *Don't Look Now* and *The Comfort of Strangers* also take part in the constructivist activity of tourism, but it is my purpose to show that they or, in fact, the male partners, fail to complete their task in some crucial way. Their failure to project themselves as proper tourists is an important factor in their trajectory towards death.

What is the ultimate gain of travelling? Hennig conceives of travelling as the periodical crossing of a border to a realm with a different reality status. The tourist leaves behind the strictures of his everyday life, the well-regulated relations to his social environment, the limits of his social identity. The traveller's anonymity allows a certain amount of socially transgressive behaviour and of experimentation with one's identity. Hennig compares these possibilities of travelling to those of carnival which can equally be defined as a limited period when rules are revoked. So, in a nutshell, the psychic value of tourism consists in the possibility of transgressing without running into danger. The return to your home country is, or seems, guaranteed. But literature almost by definition explores the irreversible crossing of a boundary: the protagonist is so transformed by his encounter with the Other that he will not be able to return as the same person, or not at all - that he will die. The stories by du Maurier and McEwan explore these very questions of boundary crossing and of the suspension of clear-cut dichotomies.

Whereas Christoph Hennig emphasises the fictional element of the tourist experience, John Urry stresses its oppositional structure. He sees tourism as a 'deviant' practice, counteracting but dependent on the structures of everyday life. The tourist gaze, which is socially and historically variable, "is constructed in relationship to its opposite" (Urry 1990, 2). It is further constructed through anticipatory activities such as daydreaming, fantasy and the consumption of films, tv programs, books, magazines etc. It is directed to such features of the landscape which separate them off from everyday experience. Finally, the tourist gaze is characterised by its reduplication: the view of a site is captured by photographs or videofilms and can be then reproduced infinitely.

An important feature of tourism is, as both Urry and Jonathan Culler point out, the search for the authentic. But the authentic is a problematical category:

> The paradox, the dilemma of authenticity, is that to be experienced as authentic it must be marked as authentic, but when it is marked as authentic it is mediated, a sign of itself, and hence lacks the authenticity of what is truly unspoiled, untouched by mediating cultural codes. [...] The authentic sight requires markers, but our notion of the authentic is the unmarked. (Culler 1988, 164)

Venice is a perfect trope for this dilemma: it is so abundantly marked and overdetermined, that the very stones of Venice seem to be quotations. It works as a tourist attraction precisely through its loss of authenticity, through its acquired quality as a many-layered palimpsest. This makes Venice the ideal site for 'post-tourism', a term coined by Maxine Feifer.

> 'Post-tourists' find pleasure in the multiplicity of tourist games. They know that there is *no* authentic tourist experience, that there are merely a series of games or texts that can be played. (Urry 1990, 11)

The couples in *Don't Look Now* and *The Comfort of Strangers* construct their holiday experience through games and rituals, and they use touristic props - guide-books, maps - with a certain amount of self-consciousness and even irony. However, they don't take photographs - a crucial break of tourist etiquette, indicative of their problematic status, their sliding from subject to object of the gaze. The visitors' detachment towards the artificial environment of 'Venice World' breaks down as the stories progress. Their constructivist activity collides with a reality that offers resistance to their selective gaze and their manipulative readings.

Evidently, there are important differences between both texts. Du Maurier's tourists are, in spite of a certain amount of playfulness, more serious about their 'duties' as tourists. Particularly Laura is an impeccable tourist who conscientiously takes on the position prescribed by the guidebook. She is more successful in her negotiations with the city than the sceptical John; he tries to maintain his individualistic stance in opposition to the crowd's perspective. In a way, *Don't Look Now* is an affirmation of the credulous and passive attitude of the package tourist. Those who are able to believe - in the guidebook or in a parapsychological message - will survive, the sceptics will be killed. By contrast, *The Comfort of Strangers* offers a complete deconstruction of the traditional tourist experience, and even of 'post-tourism'. Colin and Mary are, from their own point of view, indeed post-tourists who play at 'being on holiday'. But this rather lofty stance is subverted when it becomes clear that they, the subjects of the tourist gaze, have in reality been the objects of a secret gaze directed at them from the city.

On the level of plot, there are some striking parallels between both narratives; indeed, *The Comfort of Strangers* is a strong but unmarked intertext of *Don't Look Now*. In each of the texts, a couple travels together to Venice after several years of marriage or of a shared life. Both couples, and especially the male partners, prove to be particularly inadequate tourists. They get lost geographically and cognitively,[5] with fatal consequences: their disorientation and misinterpretation are directly contributive factors to the final catastrophe.

Don't Look Now sets in with an exchange of glances between Laura and John and the unnamed twin sisters who will later relay a spiritist message from the couple's dead daughter Christine. Having lunch at a restaurant in Torcello, John notices "a couple of old girls two tables away who are trying to hypnotise me" (du Maurier 1972, 9). Immediately, husband and wife begin to play a game about the sisters' identity, a game centered on the gender ambiguity of the twins' appearance: the "old girls" turn in Laura's playful invention into male twins in drags, "criminals doing the sights of Europe, changing sex at each stop", possibly "[j]ewel thieves or murderers" (9). The final version of their identity constructed by John and Laura is a most commonplace one: "a couple of pathetic old retired schoolmistresses on holiday, who've saved up all their lives to visit Venice" (10). But John retains a feeling of unease which is generated by the empty gaze of one of the women who, as it later turns out, is blind. Her unseeing eyes are perceived by John as disagreeably intent and penetrating:

> Two can play at the game. He blew a cloud of cigarette smoke into the air and smiled at her, he hoped offensively. She did not register. The blue eyes continued to hold his, so that finally he was obliged to look away himself, extinguish his cigarette, glance over his shoulder for the waiter and call for the bill. (13)

John can't read the sister's gaze as blindness, and he perceives the twins as uncanny because of their doubleness and gender ambiguity. The exchange of glances shows the vulnerability of his 'maleness' and also his own 'blindness', his deficiency in decoding the semiotic system of the foreign locality.

The confrontation with the blind woman's unseeing but penetrating eyes results in a distortion of John's clear and single vision. For the rest of the story, the sisters keep obtruding on his real or mental line of sight, further disturbing his cognitive power. By contrast, Laura, who accepts the guidance of the blind - i.e. she believes in Christine's message of warning 'transmitted' by the blind sister - is enabled to perform the quintessential task of the tourist: she goes sightseeing. She follows the fixed perspective of the guidebook; if her field of vision is not free and original, yet an aesthetic experience of art is accessible to her - but not to John:

---

[5] This intellectual disorientation ties in with Michael Ross's analysis of Venice as a domain of sensuality, not rationality.

> Laura, undaunted, asked her husband for the guidebook, and, as had always been her custom in happier days, started to walk slowly through the cathedral, studying mosaics, columns, panels from left to right, while John, less interested, because of his concern at what had just happened, followed close behind, keeping a weather eye alert for the twin sisters. [...] But the anonymous, shuffling tourists, intent upon culture, could not harm her, although from his own point of view they made artistic appreciation impossible. He could not concentrate, the cold clear beauty of what he saw left him untouched, and when Laura touched his sleeve, pointing to the mosaic of the Virgin and Child standing above the frieze of the Apostles, he nodded in sympathy yet saw nothing [...].(16f.)

John's intuition is right when he feels a sense of doom after the sisters' warning. He is too much caught up in his role as rational male to be able to follow his feelings, but at the same time he fails to deal analytically with the palpable evidence of danger that is successively presented to him. His cognitive blindness is connected with the topographical disorientation of the tourist. At first, the liminal position between familiarity and strangeness creates an exhilarating feeling of liberation and importance; the travellers appear to create the world they visit:

> The bedroom was familiar, like home, with Laura's things arranged neatly on the dressing table, but with it the little festive atmosphere of strangeness, of excitement, that only a holiday bedroom brings. This is ours for the moment, but no more. While we are in it we bring it life. When we have gone it no longer exists, it fades into anonymity. (20)

The tourist's gaze defines and transforms the place which exists, as it seems, only for him. At the same time, the oscillation between familiarity and strangeness allows the tourist to ease temporarily the burden of his identity. In the hotel room which is like home and yet different, festive, anonymous, it becomes possible for John and Laura to hold in abeyance the pain about Christine's death and, for the first time after their loss, to make love. Especially John interprets this act as a new beginning, a reinvention of their marriage, and a laying of ghosts. But the exhilarating moment when reality and memory are suspended passes quickly. The tourist's freedom to reinvent himself is superseded almost immediately by a deep-felt sense of displacement. The following passage, the couple's search for a restaurant, is overlaid with images of death, pointing back to Christine's decease and forward to John's murder. In this long sequence, the importance of the Venetian setting becomes clear: the narration is able to exploit the rich symbolism of the place to evoke the imagery, not only of death, but of perverse sexuality and violent death. The canals, so picturesque in daytime, are now dark and dank, the gondolas - not exactly an original trope - look like coffins (21f.). John now experiences the breakdown of the tourist's constructivist activity: he is no longer able to sustain the received image of a bright, glittering city. His romantic construction collides with a different 'reality', a reality, however, that is no more 'authentic' than the Venice of honeymoons. The lost tourists now enter the Venice of the Gothic tradition.

Adrift in an unknown quarter, John has the crucial encounter on his voyage towards death, without however recognising its importance or, rather, completely misreading its significance. After the visit to Torcello, John had imagined Christine running alongside the canal. Now he sees a scene that seems to mirror his fantasy of the lost daughter: a 'child' in a pixie hood, fleeing across a canal. In reality, this is an adult woman dwarf responsible for several murders. John explicitly connects this scene with Christine's death. He mistakes the running figure for a little girl in danger and fantasises about protecting her. Again it is Laura, the less imaginative, 'blind' average tourist, who comes closer to the truth. While missing the sight of the 'child', she yet seizes upon the one crucial sign of violence, the strangled cry of the murder victim heard just an instant before the fleeing figure's emergence. Laura understands that Venice is not just an artificial paradise but exists on the same reality level as any English town - including real crime and a working city administration. But her sensible proposal to call the police is rejected: "'Oh, for heaven's sake,' said John. Where did she think she was - Piccadilly?" (22)

John and Laura perceive Venice in an entirely different way. Laura's approach is straightforward, commonsensical and unoriginal; she represents the stance of the package tourist, happy to be shepherded to the obvious sites. And she is the survivor.[6] By contrast, John's attitude is much more complicated. One the one hand, he is - or poses as - the individualistic traveller who wants to lead the way, to make discoveries by himself.[7] He is imaginative and emotional - he constantly worries about the state of Laura's nerves, but it is he who is on the verge of hysteria throughout the story. On the other hand, John is a stickler for propriety. He wants to avoid any confusion of categories - hence his fear of the twins - especially of the categories that are at stake here: gender difference and the distinction between life and death. This is precisely why he so adamantly refuses to accept the sisters' assertion that he is 'psychic' - "You are somehow *en rapport* with the unknown, and I'm not." (28), as Laura tells him -, that he of all people should be able to cross the most decisive of borders and commune with his dead daughter.

Why is John killed? Is he 'punished' for being a potentially transgressive figure or precisely for his refusal to transgress? At any rate, it is this conflict that leads to John's fatal cognitive failure. Venice becomes a space where he can act out his fantasy about the returned daughter. In accordance with Žižek 's concept of fantasy as a creative negotiation with horror, John seizes upon a positively given object - the hooded girl - in order to restructure the trauma of his daughter's death. To protect this fantasy, even from Laura, he has to stave off the intruding reality. He ignores both Christine's 'message' - ironically, in du Maurier's story the supernatural sides with the banal - and

---

[6] Actually, Laura is a more interesting character in Nicholas Roeg's film based on du Maurier's story, mainly thanks to Julie Christie's performance. For a comparison between film and story see Schröder 1987; see also Sabine Schülting's essay in this volume.

[7] John's search for the authentic ends in minor disasters, signalling the greater resilience of Laura's attitude. For instance at the restaurant - "Mostly Italians - that meant the food would be good." (du Maurier 1972, 24), John thinks - which they finally reach, Laura orders scampi without even consulting the menu; John chooses a 'genuinely Italian' dish of boiled pork which proves perfectly inedible.

rational indicators of danger: police reports about the murders, his wife's cautions, the victim's cry he heard with his own ears.

When he encounters the running figure for the second time, his longing to protect and save a child, his child, hinders him from following his intuitive urge to run away. He correctly connects the appearance of the child with the murders, but he misreads the clues: the supposed victim is the killer, the would-be protector is the dupe of his own blindness. Only in the very last moment of his life does his vision come into focus:

> The child struggled to her feet and stood before him, the pixie hood falling from her head onto the floor. He stared at her, incredulity turning to horror, to fear. It was not a child at all but a little thickset woman dwarf, about three feet high, with a great square adult head too big for her body, grey locks hanging shoulder length, and she wasn't sobbing anymore, she was grinning at him, nodding her head up and down. (60f.)

Again, as in the beginning, John is paralysed by an old woman's gaze. But this time the danger is real: Little Red Riding Hood has turned into Medusa. John's belated clear-sightedness is no longer important. The subject of the gaze is now the other; John can only look at the murderer looking at him, the victim.

In *The Comfort of Strangers*, tourism is treated as a slightly unpleasant duty, taking place in a state of waiting. The transitional tourist status is experienced by Colin and Mary as a progressive detachment from reality and a loss of agency. They become increasingly unfit to communicate - with each other and the outside world - or to take care of themselves: they live in a state of child-like dependence from the hotel maid and other providers for their comforts. Although they "dutifully fulfilled the many tasks of tourism the ancient city imposed" (McEwan 1982, 14), yet, encumbered by their identity as a long-established couple, they fail as existential travellers, as explorers of the unknown:

> Alone, perhaps, they each could have explored the city with pleasure, followed whims, dispensed with destinations and so enjoyed or ignored being lost. There was much to wonder at here, one needed only to be alert and to attend. But they knew one another much as they knew themselves, and their intimacy, rather like too many suitcases, was a matter of perpetual concern; [...] and they would continue to explore the twisting alleyways and sudden squares in silence, and with each step the city would recede as they locked tighter into each other's presence. (14f.)

In contrast to du Maurier's story which works with binary oppositions and comes down on the side of conventional Laura, *The Comfort of Strangers* neither endorses the mass tourist perspective nor that of the individual traveller: Colin and Mary are 'blind' when they follow the guide book, but they get lost when they leave the hotel without their maps. Being a tourist in Venice is described here as a dreamlike state where action seems to be impossible:

> Since their arrival, they had established a well-ordered ritual of sleep, preceded on only one occasion by sex, and now the calm, self-obsessed interlude during which they carefully groomed themselves

before their dinner-time stroll through the city. In this time of preparation, they moved slowly and rarely spoke. They used expensive, duty-free colognes and powders on their bodies, they chose their clothes meticulously and without consulting the other, as though somewhere among the thousands they were soon to join, there waited someone who cared deeply how they appeared. (13)

This entropic state is energised only by the entrance of Robert, the third party to a game they don't know they are playing. Robert is the person for whom they were unconsciously preparing, the one who cared about their appearance. The friendly stranger had been stalking the beautiful Colin from the beginning of their stay. Robert has chosen him as the ideal victim in a sadomasochistic ritual which he carries out together with his crippled wife Caroline. Colin and Mary will find out that they have been framed, literally caught in the frame of Robert's camera and in the frame of his plot. But Robert can entice them into his game only because he has got something to offer that reaches out to their desire and opens Venice, hitherto retreating from their grasp, as a space of fantasy. Whereas John in *Don't Look Now* was ready to enter the fantasmatic structure of Venice because his desire was already 'activated' by his daughter's loss, Colin and Mary, the saturated post-tourists, have to be pricked into desire, pleasure and pain through an exterior agent. What Robert has to offer is, firstly, a narrative structure and, secondly, an affirmation of identity - that is, a return to a state before post-modernism.

McEwan's novel can legitimately be considered as a post-modern text in the sense of John Barth's 'literature of exhaustion'.[8] Indeed, the most consequent stylistic proceeding in *The Comfort of Strangers* is a radical depletion, a *désubstantialisation* at work on all levels of the narrative - the use of the Venetian setting, the *dramatis personae* and the plot. As a result, the text is marked by a reluctance to formulate a transcendent meaning, by an "ontologie faible": "Là réside la véritable altérité du texte, paradoxale, fondée sur l'absence du dépassement métaphysique, sur la fin du tragique et l'antimythe." (Duperray 1989, 300). In an interesting move, however, McEwan incorporates the orthodox metaphysical plot into the structure of his text, by embodying it in the figure of Robert. Before their encounter with Robert, Colin and Mary find themselves in a state defined by stasis and lack of differentiation. Robert's world is, on the contrary, both dynamic and reactionary - and strangely alluring, at the same time as it is revolting.[9]

---

[8] Barth's essay - first published in 1966, the year McEwan began writing fiction (cf. Slay 1996, 1) - diagnoses a "used-upness of certain forms or exhaustion of certain possibilities" (Barth 1982, 1) in contemporary literature; the traditional - pre-Joycean - form of the novel is no longer a valid model. The novelist's response advocated by Barth is not decadent languor, but rather a kind of concentration which "reflects and deals with ultimacy, both technically and thematically" (Barth 1982, 5), as in the work of Beckett and Borges. McEwan can be seen as belonging to this tradition, since he parts way with the humanist ballast of classical novels, nonetheless retaining a subtle insight into the human condition.

[9] A strong criticism of McEwan from a feminist perspective can be found in Roger 1996. She claims that *Comfort* does not challenge Caroline's masochistic submission and Robert's patriarchal domination; she accuses McEwan of being "complicit in subscribing the patriarchal power structures which the novel seeks to criticize" (Roger 1996, 18). In opposition, Christina Byrnes observes, with

The narrative frame which finally encloses the tourists is Robert's dualistic concept of gender, performed in his marriage to Caroline. In contrast to Colin and Mary's emancipated partnership and politically advanced notions of gender, Robert and Caroline enact the traditional gender roles up to the point of caricature. The British visitors experience an uneasy mixture of fascination and repulsion at the spectacle of sado-masochistic pleasure that is flaunted before them. Their visit to Robert's Venetian palace, a shrine to patriarchal values, triggers off a series of transgressive erotic fantasies; their love-making reaches a long-lost intensity. At last, Venice begins to fulfil the promise of the city of lust and desire, instead of being the disappointing, crowded venue of mass tourism.

Robert equally provides them with a precarious possibility of identification. Paradoxically, it is the appellation as tourists that puts them under his spell: "'Are you tourists?' he asked in self-consciously precise English and, beaming, answered himself. 'Yes, of course you are.'" (26) Although the role of a tourist is by definition an unstable, transitional condition, Colin and Mary are posited by this invocation within a fixed frame of reference. Initially Robert, appearing as an "authentic citizen" (30), satisfies their craving for recognition. As he takes them to his bar, frequented exclusively by Italian men, he allows Colin and Mary to see themselves for the first time as tourists "making a discovery" (29).[10] Thus in their first encounter, Robert offers them a possibility of self-definition and self-recognition. However, the binary opposition of tourist and native is, like all other dichotomies built up in this text, swiftly undercut: Robert is not an 'authentic' Venetian; raised abroad and married to a Canadian, he is partly alienated from his native city, a stranger himself. This precarious construction of a signifying network, based on multiple shifts of meaning rather than stable binarisms, marks an important difference to *Don't Look Now*.

Being a tourist entails, according to the sociological approach of Hennig and others, a transitory status, a constructivist activity, and transgression without danger. In *The Comfort of Strangers*, we rather find danger without transgression. When Colin and Mary come into contact with Venice, the city of desire, through Robert's mediation, they are enabled to articulate their fantasies, but not to act them out. The perverse wishes they whisper into each other's ears never cross the border from imagination to real acts. Unlike the visitors, Robert and Caroline really stage their desire: they want to join passion and death by murdering Colin as part of their sexual consummation, thus achieving a perfect pitch of *jouissance*. So from one perspective, Robert and Caroline appear as transgressive figures; Colin and Mary remain within the boundaries of 'decent' behaviour. Like John in du Maurier's story, they don't dare to transgress. But on the other hand, the English visitors do participate to some extent in Robert's game, and they are the representatives of a category crisis - a dissolution of gender distinctions - that is transgressive on a different level.

---

some justification, that the text's close observation of these attitudes, which may appear as a lack of critical distance, serves to heighten its disturbing effect (Byrnes 1995, 321).

[10] This discovery of an 'authentic' place unknown to other tourists echoes John and Laura's visit to the restaurant frequented by 'real Italians', where they, however, meet the spiritist sisters.

Both couples apparently engage themselves in a scopophilic partnership, the exhibitionistic desire of Colin and Mary finding a willing eye in Robert's teleobjective. By entering into this unspoken contract, the visitors unwittingly accept the notions of gender voiced earlier by Robert and Caroline, which come down in the final consequence to the simplistic binarism that men kill and women submit to being killed. So within this frame of reference set up by Robert, the English couple as a whole takes on the female part. But then, another shift disturbs the binary structure of the couples when Mary is cast in the role of the spectator, and Colin is singled out as the surrogate victim - for Caroline - in the sadomasochistic game; Caroline[11] shifts her position from the passive to the active side of the sexual scheme.

From Robert's point of view, Colin is the representative figure of gender-crossing. He is both a man and a feminized object of desire. By killing him with the most patriarchal of weapons, his grandfather's and father's razor, Robert punishes him for that transgression and reaffirms his own notions of gender. He punishes Mary for appropriating the male gaze by forcing her to watch the killing of her lover. He ascribes to her the voyeuristic position and thus separates her from Colin whom he has pinned down - both metaphorically and literally - on the opposite side of the scopophilic equation. The strange encounter seems to end, on a symbolic level, with the victory of a 'strong' over a 'weak ontology'. But in fact, this ending - "la banalisation de cette aventure sanglante" (Duperray 1989, 297) - is 'exhausted': McEwan's text has divested itself of that metaphysical fullness that saturates du Maurier's narration.

Don't Look Now and *The Comfort of Strangers* refer to Venice as a paradigmatic location where literature, fantasy and tourism interlock. In both texts, Venice is presented as an almost unreal, deceptive, highly ambiguous city. Nevertheless, the strategic use of the setting is entirely distinctive. Du Maurier's Venice is a place sated with stereotype, employed to heighten the atmosphere of horror in an, ultimately, fairly conventional Gothic story. McEwan's use of the location couldn't be more different: his Venice is radically emptied of referentiality, at least in so far as a conventional 'Venicity' is concerned. The concrete references to 'reality' serve to dislocate the myth of Venice, be it the glittering tourist haunt or the Gothic city of dark narrow canals. This most mythically charged place is used in the service of anti-myth. By adopting this strategy, McEwan deconstructs the received touristic stance - which is upheld in *Don't Look Now* - and regains Venice as an alienating counter-space.

Given this divergent function of the setting, it is evident that fantasy and transgression, too, work on different levels. *Don't Look Now* endorses a humanistic psychology; John's hovering on a mental borderline is fully explained in terms of his character and individual history. Transgression here means the crossing of a border, but the border itself remains firmly established. *The Comfort of Strangers* equally presents us with an aetiological explanation of Robert's sadistic drive; but the memory

---

[11] Caroline exchanges with Colin her position as victim; this congruence of functions is indicated by the similarity of their names.

of his childhood rather operates as a 'screen-explanation' - analogous to Freud's concept of 'screen-memory' - that not only fails to give a satisfactory answer to the enigma of his personality, but rather covers up the lack of such an enigma. Significantly, the main protagonists Colin and Mary are not fitted out with a similar psychological background. The figures in *Comfort* are defined by their positionality, not by inherent qualities. They are 'depleted' in a way that is collateral to the text's treatment of Venice.

Consequently, the question of transgression is subsumed under a different heading. The focus lies not on individual acts; rather, the text deals with the process of constructing opposite fields of signification. The gesture that draws a line across a field and thus produces difference is put *en abîme* in the narrative, which juxtaposes two competing orders: Robert is the representative of a dualistic scheme, expressed in his theory of a hierarchical gender distinction. Because he believes in this order, he is able to realise his transgressive desire. Robert is contrasted to Mary and Colin, who do not wish to cross a border - at the same time affirming it - but to dissolve and disappear. They yearn for reaching the vanishing point of the tourist's transitionality:

> To step down there now as if completely free, to be released from the arduous states of play of psychological condition, to have leisure to be open and attentive to perception, to the world whose breathtaking, incessant cascade against the senses was so easily and habitually ignored, dinned out, in the interests of unexamined ideals of personal responsibility, efficiency, citizenship, to step down there now, just walk away, melt into the shadow, would be so very easy. (McEwan 1982, 104f.)

But they even lack the limited power of agency required for this dream of self-effacement. Instead of turning away into the empty street, Colin, trapped, follows Robert.

The geometrical configuration of McEwan's novel could suggest that it fails to transcend the dichotomy personified by Robert - that Robert 'wins'. I want to propose, on the contrary, that *The Comfort of Strangers* does not end with a 'solution', a taking of sides, as does *Don't Look Now*. Robert's success is possible only within his binary frame of reference that conveys depth, ontology and 'master narrative'. But this frame does not usurp the entire text. When Mary, in the novel's final scene, sits by Colin's side in the mortuary, she indeed seems to be sucked in by the world of Robert and Caroline. She struggles for an explanation that echoes their pronouncements on gender: "her theory [...] which explained how the imagination, the sexual imagination, men's ancient dream of hurting, and women's of being hurt, embodied and declared a powerful single organising principle" (125). But the order of depth and single organising principles is displaced by the competing order associated with surface, positionality and silence: "But she explained nothing, for a stranger had arranged Colin's hair the wrong way. She combed it with her fingers and said nothing at all." (125). The novel ends with Mary's silence. The reader can now choose between the gross banality of Robert's exegetical efforts and the opacity of Mary's final attitude, a still, minute registering of external details. The tension between the two modes of signification is sustained in the text. The fact that it is feminist Mary who tries to collapse of binary structures, of the text's resistance to closure. But despite this persisting openness, surely the more intelligent and aesthetically pleasing response offered in the novel is that quiet attention to details with which it ends.

Bibliography

Banks, J.R.: "A Gondola named Desire". *Critical Quarterly* 24 (1982), 27-31.
Barth, John: "The Literature of Exhaustion". In: Barth, John: *The Literature of Exhaustion and the Literature of Replenishment*. Northridge, Cal. 1982, 1-17.
Brodsky, Joseph: *Watermark*. Harmondsworth 1992.
Byrnes, Christina: "Ian McEwan - Pornographer or Prophet?". *Contemporary Review* 266 (1995), 320-323.
Calvino, Italo: *Invisible Cities*. London 1979.
Corbineau-Hoffmann, Angelika: *Paradoxie der Fiktion. Literarische Venedigbilder 1797-1984*. Berlin/New York 1993.
Culler, Jonathan: "The Semiotics of Tourism". In: Culler, Jonathan: *Framing the Sign. Criticism and Its Institutions*. Norman, Okl./London 1988.
du Maurier, Daphne: *Don't Look Now*. New York 1972.
Duperray, Max: "L'étranger dans le contexte post-moderniste: *The Comfort of Strangers* d'Ian McEwan". In: Rigaud, N.J. (ed.): *L'étranger dans la littérature et la pensée anglaise*. Aix-en-Provence 1989, 291-306.
Hennig, Christoph: *Reiselust. Touristen, Tourismus und Reisekultur*. Frankfurt a.M./Leipzig 1997.
McEwan, Ian: *The Comfort of Strangers*. London/Basingstoke 1982.
Meyer, E.Y., *Venezianisches Zwischenspiel. Eine Novelle*. Zürich 1997.
Roger, Angela: "Ian McEwan's Portrayal of Women". *Forum for Modern Language Studies* 23 (1996), 9-26.
Ross, Michael L.: *Storied Cities. Literary Imaginings of Florence, Venice and Rome*. Westport, Conn./London 1994.
Schröder, Gottfried: "'Don't Look Now': Daphne du Maurier's Story and Nicolas Roeg's Film". *Literatur in Wissenschaft und Unterricht* 20 (1987), 232-245.
Slay, Jack Jr.: *Ian McEwan*. New York 1996.
Tanner, Tony: *Venice Desired*. Oxford 1992.
Urry, John: *The Tourist Gaze. Leisure and Travel in Contemporary Societies*. London 1990.

Sabine Schülting

'Dream Factories':

Hollywood and Venice in Nicolas Roeg's *Don't Look Now*

In August 1998, a short article in the German daily *Süddeutsche Zeitung* commented on the news that Felice Laudadio, manager of the 55th Venetian film festival, had addressed the public with the desperate plea to help him find appropriate hotel suites for the stars. Unexpectedly, Robert de Niro, Warren Beatty and Steven Spielberg had decided to come to Venice, each accompanied by a crew of several dozens. "No room for the grooms?" - Not without irony, the journalist pondered about the reasons for this logistic disaster, and wondered whether instead of holding Venice responsible, one should not rather seek the reasons for this awkward situation in Hollywood: "Verführt von den Bildern der eigenen Traumfabrik: seit Jahrzehnten kommt kein Kinojahr ohne Filme in und um Venedig aus [...]."[1] The filmstars, the author argued, were attracted by cinema itself, which, since its beginnings, had stylised Venice as the dream-city *par excellence*. Actually, only recently Venice appeared in Paul Schrader's *The Comfort of Strangers*, in Oliver Parker's adaptation of *Othello*, in Iain Softley's *The Wings of the Dove* and in Woody Allen's *Everyone Says I Love You*. Venice may not be the appropriate city for real-life actors, but it certainly is one of the most important settings for movies.

The representation of Venice in Nicolas Roeg's 1973 film adaptation of Daphne du Maurier's novella, *Don't Look Now*, can thus hardly be regarded to be original. Roeg - like other directors - shows the beautiful lagoon, the maze of canals and narrow alleys as well as Venice's decay. I would maintain, though, that Roeg's *Don't Look Now* is not just another example of Hollywood's fascination with Venice, which, in turn, has been fed by innumerable pictorial and textual representations of Venice since the early modern age. In his seminal book, *Venice Desired*, Tony Tanner writes that

> *as* spectacle - the beautiful city *par excellence*, the city of art, the city *as* art - and as a spectacular example [...], Venice became an important, I would say central, site (a topos, a topic) for the European imagination.[2]

Although Tanner does not analyse cinematic representations of Venice, his description applies equally well to the movies. Since the beginning of the twentieth century, Hollywood has appropriated the topoi and has thus continued the seemingly endless production of fantasies around Venice. Very often, films on Venice have adapted literary representations of Venice: *Morte a Venezia*, *The Comfort of Strangers* or *The Wings of the Dove* are obvious examples. Yet Venice in Roeg's film is more than

---

[1] *Süddeutsche Zeitung*, 26 August 1998, 13.
[2] Tanner 1992, 4.

merely a picturesque and yet slightly uncanny setting of a horror movie which evokes associations of Venice with ominous mysteries, an unresolved past and death. Even though Roeg still draws upon these traditional tropes and motifs, he does this in a very conscious way and employs them to a specific purpose. In an interview, Roeg has said,

> I am concerned with breaking barriers, challenging assumptions, and moving the possibilities of film for a bit. Part of my job is to show that the cinema is the art of our time and can break through previous terms of reference.[3]

For him, Venice's almost proverbial dissolution of differences and identities provides the very means of inserting meta-cinematic elements into the film and breaking with the tradition of classical Hollywood cinema.

Nicolas Roeg's *Don't Look Now* opens with the death of Christine, Laura and John Baxter's daughter, who drowns in a pond near the Baxter's home instead of dying of meningitis as in Daphne du Maurier's story. In the film, the accident is shown in a haunting sequence, which introduces the recurrent motifs of the film:[4] the figure in red, water, blood, broken glass, and John's second sight. While looking at slides of Venetian churches, John Baxter detects the red hood of a mysterious figure resembling the reflection of Christine's red mac in the water. When John knocks over a glass of wine, the liquid spreads across the slide, forming a semicircular or gondola-like shape. As he obviously foresees the tragedy, he stops in his work and goes to the door. Outside he sees his son running towards the house, which confirms his fears: having played near the pond, Christine has fallen into the water. During the sequence which shows Baxter's futile attempt to resuscitate his daughter Roeg repeatedly cuts to the 'bleeding' slide. When John carries the corpse back to the house, his wife Laura eventually realises what has happened, but her piercing cry soon fades into the noise of a pneumatic drill: the setting has changed. The Baxters are in Venice, probably some weeks after the accident. Whereas in du Maurier's story they have come to Venice as tourists, John Baxter in the film is in charge of the restoration of a church. The city is deserted, the tourists have left, and the hotels are closing down for the winter. In a restaurant, John and Laura meet Heather and Wendy, a pair of English sisters, one of whom, Heather, though blind has second sight. She claims to have seen Christine and be able to establish contact with her. Laura believes her, in contrast to her husband, who is annoyed by the sisters and their "mumbo-jumbo". He does not only refuse to participate in a seance, but also turns a deaf ear to Heather's warnings. She urges him to leave Venice maintaining that his life will be in danger if he remains there. Heather's premonitions seem to come true when the Baxters receive a telephone call from England, informing them that their son has had an accident. Laura returns to England, while John stays behind and, confronted with disturbing occurrences, gradually loses his self-assurance. Repeatedly he catches glimpses of a figure whose red coat reminds him of his dead daughter. John is nearly killed when a beam breaks loose in the church

---

[3] *Vogue*, August 1985, p. 333; quoted in Salwolke 1993, ix.
[4] Cf. Salwolke 1993, 39.

and crashes onto the scaffolding he is standing on. Outside the church, he joins a large crowd watching the police pull the body of a woman out of the water - presumably the victim of a serial killer haunting Venice. Later, while riding on a *vaporetto*, John Baxter sees his wife with the two sisters on another boat passing by. He can neither explain why she has remained in Venice nor why she has not tried to contact him. The murders have made him anxious, so that he informs the police when he cannot find her. When, however, he calls his son's school in England and Laura answers him on the phone to tell him that everything is alright, he realises he has made a mistake. In the meantime, Heather has been arrested, since John, suspecting her to be responsible for Laura's disappearance, had reported her to the police. He clears up the misunderstanding and brings her back to her hotel. When she seems to be having a fit, he leaves the hotel but, actually, she is foreseeing his death. Walking through the streets, he notices the figure in red again. Having been at a a loss to make sense of it before, he now assumes he has seen a child in trouble. He follows it through the streets and into a derelict building. While trying to soothe the 'child', he suddenly remembers the image on the slide. When the figure turns round, John faces a dwarf in a red cloak, who strikes him with a huge knife. He bleeds to death, and the film ends with his wife and the sisters riding on a boat, following another boat which carries his casket - the image John Baxter has seen before.

Hollywood Narratives

In a way, this summary does not do justice to the film because it turns it back into that kind of classical narrative which, as I will argue in my essay, the film tries to overcome. This contention might be surprising considering the fact that with *Don't Look Now* Roeg adapts a novella by a writer who could hardly be classified as postmodern. So *Don't Look Now*, which has been more successful as a film than as a literary text, only seems to be just another example of the innumerable cinematic adaptations of traditional narratives. It apparently corroborates the fact that film has become the most popular narrative genre, replacing narrative literature to a large extent. "Its *embourgeoisement*", Brian McFarlane writes,"inevitably led it away from trick shows, the recording of music halls acts and the like, towards the narrative representationalism which had reached a peak in the classic nineteenth-century novel."[5]

The outcome of this development has been termed by many as 'the classical Hollywood film', and most emphatically so by David Bordwell, Janet Staiger and Kristin Thompson in their important study *The Classical Hollywood Cinema* (1985). They argue that after 1917 a certain style of filmmaking became dominant whose aesthetic norms were drawn from traditional models of literary narrative:

---

[5] McFarlane 1996, 12.

> Here in brief is the premise of Hollywood story construction: causality, consequence, psychological motivation, the drive towards overcoming obstacles and achieving goals. Character-centered - i.e., personal or psychological - causality is the armature of the classical story.[6]

Bordwell et al. maintain that this fabula construction implies linear chronology and 'realist' spatiality. Dramaturgy and technique, usually induce and support, rather than prevent, the spectator's construction of the story. In his subsequent book *Narration in the Fiction Film* (1985) Bordwell emphasises the importance of this activity, and insists that it is the viewer who constructs the story in the first place. Comprehending a film means that the spectator "seeks to grasp the filmic continuum as a set of events occurring in defined settings and unified by principles of temporality and causation."[7] The analysis of *The Classical Hollywood Cinema* ends in 1960, but its authors maintain that in spite of fundamental modifications in the US film industry and decisive aesthetic innovations since the late 1960s and 1970s, "the classical premises of time and space remain powerfully in force, with only minor instrumental changes [...]."[8] This rather ahistorical notion of a continuity of film aesthetics since the early decades of the twentieth century has been widely questioned. Critics have pointed to the disruptions of classical narrative in genres such as the musical and the melodrama or suggested the development of a 'New Hollywood', which no longer adheres to the principles of classical filmmaking.[9] Others, however, like Murray Smith for example, argue that "the new technologies and new markets have encouraged certain kinds of narrative, traceable to serials, B-adventures and episodic melodramas", but that "even here, classical narrative is still omnipresent."[10] My point here is not to take a personal stance in this debate. Instead, I would rather describe 'the classical Hollywood cinema' as a highly influential cinematic style which may not have been as normative and totalising as Bordwell et al. have argued, but which certainly has set up the conventions for narrative genres such as the detective film, the gangster film, and the horror film.[11] My analysis of Nicolas Roeg's *Don't Look Now*, then, assumes the existence of intertextual references to these generic conventions in Roeg's film, which was released at a time when classical Hollywood style was being questioned, innovated and/or changed.

In spite of the obvious parallels between the classical Hollywood cinema and classical narrative, film and literature differ in one crucial aspect: the cinematic narration "resists traditional language-centered notions of the narrator."[12] Film theorists have drawn divergent conclusions from this fact. Whereas David Bordwell strictly negates the existence of a narrator in the film, others have criticised this

---

[6] Bordwell/Staiger/Thompson 1985, 13.
[7] Bordwell 1985, 34.
[8] Bordwell/Staiger/Thompson 1985, 375.
[9] Cf. the essays in Neale/Smith 1998.
[10] Smith 1998, 13.
[11] Cf. Cowie 1998, 184.
[12] Chatman 1990, 124.

anthropomorphic bias, analysing the "organizational and sending agency"[13] of a film or focusing on its 'impersonal enunciation'[14]. Most critics agree, though, that non-reliable narration is not the rule in traditional narrative cinema. Bordwell's notion that "classical narration tends to be omniscient"[15] is however rather too simplistic. Christian Metz maintains that, like the novel, the film, too, can 'tell' what a character knows, but additionally it can also communicate what the character sees or hears. In order to identify an image (or a sound) as subjective, the spectator either needs a clear marker (e.g. through the dialogue) or has to see the character shortly before and/or after this image.[16] An example from *Don't Look Now* may illustrate this technique: John Baxter walks over a bridge, stops, bends over the railing, and stares into the water. The next take shows a reflection of Christine in the water. The camera then slowly turns upwards, as if duplicating his gaze, and in a long shot we see the red-coated figure partly hidden in the entrance of a building. The spectator will definitely identify this image as subjective. Whereas he or she will probably regard the figure in red as the 'real' object of Baxter's perception, he or she will interpret Christine's reflection as a flashback or a product of Baxter's fantasy.

Venetian Narratives

However, it is not always as easy to distinguish between Baxter's perspective and that of the camera and between his own subjective perspective as opposed to an 'objective' point of view. The obvious similarity between the image of the girl and the figure in Venice implies an uncanny link between Christine and the dwarf, and thus between the present, the past and the future - a link which has already been established at the beginning of the film. "Nothing is what it seems", John Baxter says to his wife in the first sequence, and this sentence could serve as a motto for the whole film, whose title already implies a similar warning against the dangers of vision. Nothing, in Roeg's film, is in fact what it seems. The film juxtaposes not only present, past and future, but also reality and fantasy as well as subjective and objective images. It does not possess a reliable narrational agency, which would help the spectator order these images into a 'chrono-logical' story. Deviating from Hollywood conventions, Roeg leaves out "crucial narrative markers" to indicate breaks in the linear presentation of events (ellipses, parallel actions, flashbacks etc.) and thus "gives form to the larger, non-rational connections across time which the psychic sees and Baxter denies."[17] This is certainly the case when Baxter sees his wife and the sisters on the boat (plate 1). There is no reason to doubt the objectivity of the camera's eye, since for a moment, the camera shows not only what Baxter sees, but also part of his left shoulder and his coat as he stands at the rail. The camera is behind him and its focus is not exactly congruent

---

[13] Chatman 1990, 127.
[14] Cf. Metz 1991.
[15] Bordwell 1985, 160.
[16] Metz 1991, 114-116.
[17] Dick 1997, 13.

Plate 1

'Dream Factories': Hollywood and Venice in Nicolas Roeg's *Don't Look Now*

with his own gaze, so that the image is objective according to classical film language. In the original text, on the other hand, Baxter's vision is embedded in a longer passage presenting his thoughts, and the free indirect speech clearly marks the passage as more subjective than the film sequence:

> The water glittered in the sunshine, buildings shone [...]. So many impressions to seize and hold, familiar loved façades, balconies, windows, water lapping the cellar steps of decaying palaces [...]. Another ferry was heading downstream to pass them, filled with passengers, and for a brief foolish moment he wished he could change places, be amongst the happy tourists bound for Venice and all he had left behind him. Then he saw her. Laura, in her scarlet coat, the twin sisters by her side, the active sister with her hand on Laura's arm, talking earnestly, and Laura herself, her hair blowing in the wind, gesticulating, on her face a look of distress. He stared, astounded, too astonished to shout, to wave, and anyway they would never have heard or seen him, for his own ferry had already passed and was heading in the opposite direction.
> What the hell had happened? There must have been a hold-up with the charter flight and it had never taken off, but in that case why had Laura not telephoned him at the hotel? And what were those damned sisters doing?[18]

The greater impact of the images is also due to the fact that traditionally "the visual representation is the acceptable one, on the convention that seeing is believing."[19] However, John Baxter's vision in the film is an impossible picture: neither a subjective picture nor an objective flashforward, since both alternatives would necessarily exclude the presence of Baxter himself in the image. The sequence in the film is a "contamination"[20] of objective and subjective images, i.e. the camera's and the character's point of view. It can thus be defined as free indirect discourse, too.

In the end Baxter recognises his mistake, just as the spectator of Roeg's film only retrospectively realises that the sequence was a flashforward. Because of its "highly self-conscious and ambiguously communicative" nature, the flashforward is very rare in traditional cinema, as Bordwell explains, explicitly referring to *Don't Look Now*:

> One might argue that a film could plausibly motivate a flashforward as subjectivity by making the character prophetic, as in *Don't Look Now*. But this is still not parallel to the psychological flashback, since we can never be as sure of a character's premonitions as we can be of a character's power of memory. The forward movement of the syuzhet will inevitably involve the question "Will X be right about the future?" (indeed the case in *Don't Look Now*), whereas the psychologically motivated flashback does not necessarily raise the question "Was X right about the past?"[21]

Roeg's film is still more complicated. Whereas Heather's premonitions, which are clearly identified as those of a psychic, may raise Bordwell's first question, John Baxter's visions do not. At least, his premonition of his funeral does not raise this question, since it is not identified as a premonition at all. In contrast, Heather's second

---

[18] du Maurier 1973, 32.
[19] Chatman 1990, 136.
[20] Deleuze 1989, 148.
[21] Bordwell 1985, 79.

sight as well as the first evidence of John's paranormal abilities are clearly marked through their facial expression (Heather's blind eyes), their behaviour (Baxter's uneasiness, Heather's trances) or their speech (Heather's warnings, her incoherent speech during the trance). Additionally, Heather's prophecies are never visualised, so that her visions appear as less 'real' than his and - thus by implication - more subjective.

Through this subversion of traditional dramaturgy, the spectator becomes John Baxter's double, believing in what he sees and trying - to no avail however - to reconstruct the images in a chronological and causal order. Thus the spectator in a way shares John Baxter's fate by his or her inability to rationally organise the transitory impressions and to discriminate reality from fantasy as well as the present from the past and the future. In contrast to the other characters, Baxter stubbornly refuses to believe either in the prophecies or in his own psychic powers. When Laura tells him that in the seance Christine has warned them, he shouts, "She does not come peeping from the fucking grave. Christine is dead, dead, dead." Being led by reason alone," [h]e draws the audience to himself by embodying its skepticism."[22] Almost compulsively, both assume a causal interconnection between the enigmatic visions and try to (re-)organise them, without recognising that the images are only linked through the contingency of optical similarities.

In his review of *Don't Look Now*, Michael Dempsey describes the effect of Roeg's montage on the spectator by comparing it to Eisenstein's:

> Roeg joins Eisenstein, Resnais, and Lester in leaning heavily on editing for his effects, but his montage is not quite like anybody else's. [...] Eisenstein's montage creates or demonstrates connections between shots. We can be sure that these connections exist, at least in his mind, and we can almost always grasp them immediately [...]. But Roeg's montage does not say that two shots are connected; it says that they *might* be. Eisenstein's editing aims for certainty; Roeg's, for uncertainty. [...] When his rapid juxtapositions outrun our ability to sort them out, we tumble into an uncertainty that [...] becomes genuinely metaphysical. He uses them to undercut our total allegiance to reason, our dogged confidence that we are standing on solid ground.[23]

According to accustomed ways of seeing (at least in Western cultures), both the spectator and Baxter presuppose a pre-existent reality, and the validity of the laws of Euclidian space and chronological time. Yet in *Don't Look* Now, as in other films by Roeg, different time strands are juxtaposed and produce spaces in which geometrical relations have been suspended and actions based on Euclidian assumptions are necessarily wrong. When Baxter sees his wife and the sisters, he rushes from the boat, but, of course, he cannot find them. The title of the film is therefore an ironic reminder of the phantasmatic nature of both vision and its relationship to time. With regard to *Bad Timing*, another film by Roeg, Teresa de Lauretis has identified this concern as typical of Roeg's films. She maintains that Roeg's films hinder spectator pleasure "by undercutting spectator identification in terms of both vision (literally, a difficulty in

---

[22] Dempsey 1974, 42.
[23] Dempsey 1974, 40-41.

seeing) and narrative (a difficulty in understanding events in their succession, their timing)"[24]. The entry on *Don't Look Now* in *The Motion Picture Guide*, which praises Roeg's camera work but admits to be disappointed by the story, corroborates this verdict for this film as well:

> Visually, the picture is a treat. [...] But [...] he [i.e. Roeg] is not a master of story and often sacrifices communicating ideas for his incomparable camera style. [...] Enigmas are well and good, but one wants answers in the end and *Don't Look Now* proved unsatisfying in that department.[25]

The end of *Don't Look Now* provides at least some answers, but obviously, these explanations also cannot restore spectator pleasure. On the contrary, the murder ultimately denies any causality between the fate of the Baxter family and the occurences in Venice. Baxter's death differs from the protagonist's defeat in the classical fiction film, who has been overcome by his adversaries. In *Don't Look Now*, there are no adversaries, so that Baxter's struggle turns out to have been not only ineffective, but also entirely senseless. The reassuring teleology of Hollywood cinema has been replaced by a disturbing contingency.

"A Cinema of the Seer"

Nicolas Roeg's film, though adapting a more or less traditional narrative for the cinema, clearly breaks with the conventions of the classical Hollywood film and the corresponding customs of seeing. *Don't Look Now*, I would suggest, comes very close to a certain kind of cinematic style which Gilles Deleuze has called the "crystalline regime"[26]. The 'crystalline' in Deleuze's cinema book is opposed to the 'organic' and marks the break with traditional cinematic aesthetics in avantgarde cinema. Specific forms of narration are typical of the two systems:

> Organic narration consists of the development of sensory-motor schemata as a result of which the characters react to situations or act in such a way as to disclose the situation. This is a truthful narration in the sense that it claims to be true, even if in fiction.[27]

The narrative develops 'organically' under the laws of Euclidian space and chronological time, the latter of which is represented indirectly through the composition of "movement-images". In contrast to this regime, which resembles Bordwell's definition of the classical Hollywood cinema, Deleuze identifies a second regime, the 'crystalline', which he regards typical of the cinema since the 1960s and which constitutes "a cinema of the seer and no longer of the agent"[28]. Deleuze maintains that in Western cultures in the second half of the twentieth century, the

---

[24] Lauretis 1983, 24.
[25] Nash/Ross 1985, 693-694.
[26] Deleuze 1989, 126.
[27] Deleuze 1989, 127.
[28] Deleuze 1989, 126.

interrelation of space, time and action has been disrupted: "the post-war period has greatly increased the situations which we no longer know how to react to, in spaces which we no longer know how to describe."[29] In contrast to the 'organic narration', the 'crystalline' does not produce Euclidian spaces, but rather spaces in which relations are not merely spatial, but also temporal - as in the scene when Baxter sees Laura and the sisters on the other boat. For Deleuze, these images are "direct representations of time", and time, in turn, is "a chronic non-chronological time which produces movements necessarily 'abnormal', essentially 'false'."[30] In contrast to 'truthful narration', based on the characters' action, "[s]ensory-motor situations have given way to pure optical and sound situations to which characters, who have become seers, cannot or will not react [...]."[31] They resemble spectators who - like John Baxter in Roeg's film - are helplessly subjected to their visions, being only able to observe whilst remaining powerless to intervene. Actually, all the characters in *Don't Look Now* are not only doomed to passivity, but through the merging of actual and virtual images, their unique identity is also disintegrated: "the power of the false cannot be separated from an irreducible multiplicity. 'I is another' ['*Je est un autre*'] has replaced Ego = Ego."[32] The crystalline thus deconstructs the belief in a coherent subjectivity as the source of action and narration. Deleuze argues that this 'crystalline regime' functions not merely as a metacinematic device, but also as a Nietzschean critique of 'the True', identifying it as a fiction (re-)producing power and authority. In Deleuze's examples of the 'crystalline' style, the 'powers of the false', on the other hand, are very often a "source of inspiration"[33] and a rediscovery of "the pure and simple *story-telling function*".[34]

In *Don't Look Now* the dissolution of the subject's identity is realised on several levels. This becomes particularly evident when John and Laura meet the sisters for the first time. They are in a restaurant in Venice, and when John closes a window, a speck of dust blows into Wendy's eye. Laura accompanies them to the bathroom in order to help them. The women, who are observed by a cleaning woman in the background, are multiplied in the mirrors on the wall. When Wendy tells Laura, "My sister is blind, you see", Heather's face is shown for the first time - in a triple reflection in the mirrors and then in a close-up (plate 2). Surprised, Laura says, "Oh, I see." The silent observer, the mirrors, Wendy's momentary and Heather's constant blindness, their eyes, and the minimal dialogue centring around the verb 'to see', all contribute to making this scene into a - perhaps rather too - obvious exposition on the theme of vision. Since the early years of the cinema, mirrors have, of course, been a very popular device, serving a

---

[29] Deleuze 1989, xi.
[30] Deleuze 1989, 129.
[31] Deleuze 1989, 128.
[32] Deleuze 1989: 133.
[33] Deleuze 1989, 131.
[34] Deleuze 1989, 150.

'Dream Factories': Hollywood and Venice in Nicolas Roeg's *Don't Look Now*

Plate 2

great variety of functions.[35] Many films show the characters looking at themselves in a mirror, which usually induces the spectator to identify with the character. The mirrors in *Don't Look Now*, however, serve a different purpose: they are a means of questioning seemingly clear-cut identities. Although the takes show the women in front of the mirror, they do not represent subjective images, i.e. the women looking at themselves. On the contrary, the camera is always elsewhere - behind the women, below or above them. The only shot which comes closest - but thwarts any attempt at identification in the first place - is a medium shot of Heather's reflections in the mirrors. After a cut, a close-up of her face is seen, as if indicating that she has actually looked at herself. Because of her blindness, the psychoanalytic notion of a constitution of the subject in the 'mirror stage' is thus reduced to absurdity. This subversion also affects the spectator. Metz admits that the situation of the spectator in the cinema is closely related to that of the little child in front of a mirror, but that the two situations are not identical, since the spectator's own body is never reflected:

> For what the child sees in the mirror, what he sees as an other who turns into *I*, is after all the image of his own body; so it is still an identification (and not merely a secondary one) with something *seen*. But in traditional cinema, the spectator is identifying only with something *seeing*: his own image does not appear on the screen; the primary identification is no longer constructed around a subject-object, but around a pure, all-seeing and invisible subject, the vanishing point of the monocular perspective which cinema has taken over from painting.[36]

In *Don't Look Now*, the monocular perspective is subverted through the multiplication of images in the mirrors, though it is not dispensed with altogether. Traditionally, this device has served as a reference to the 'scopic cannibalism' of the cinema, as Metz says: "bel exemple de la dévoration scopique rendue possible et désirable par la machine-cinéma."[37] Additionally, the frame or, rather, frames of the mirrors reproduce and thus foreground the frame of the screen. The spectator of *Don't Look Now* has ceased to be the "all-seeing subject". He or she is confronted not only with the disturbing multiplication of images, but also with the problematic situation in which any 'secondary' identification, according to Metz, cannot be realised. The seeing subject ceases to be unique and identifiable, the images are identified as impossible, and the gaze no longer guarantees subjectivity. In *Don't Look Now*, "I is an other". After the scene in the bathroom, Roeg cuts back to John Baxter, sitting at the table and waiting for Laura. A close-up of his face indicates subjective images. And actually, as he stares out of the window, the reflection of the sun on the canal fades into the remembrance of their departure from home. According to Metz's suggestion, the spectator will identify with John as the seeing subject, but again, this identification is destroyed when the flashback is ended with a cut to Heather's face, "as if she shares the memory".[38]

---

[35] Cf. Metz 1991, 79-83.
[36] Metz 1982, 97.
[37] Metz 1991, 82.
[38] Salwolke 1993, 41.

'Dream Factories': Hollywood and Venice in Nicolas Roeg's *Don't Look Now*

Venetian Images

In his film, Roeg clearly associates this "cinema of the seer" with Venice. As I mentioned in the beginning, Venice is not only the main setting of the film. More than this, its twilight and fleeting reflections in the water as well as its proverbial dissolution of reality and fantasy, self and other, engenders images and collates them in a disturbing montage. Almost all the shots of Venetian sites - of canals, shutters, or windows - play with the problem of vision through a combination of light and reflection. In the sequence in the restaurant, for example, John Baxter's remembrance seems to be triggered by Venetian images: the reflection of light in the water (plate 3). And repeatedly, he detects the reflection of Christine in the water of the canals. During his search for Laura, Baxter comes to a particular place, which he is to visit several times and where he finds a naked doll lying on the bank of a canal, calling into mind his drowned daughter and the female corpse which the police had pulled out of the water. When he looks round, he sees 'nothing' other than empty façades and doves. A woman is watching him out of a window, but she instantaneously disappears as soon as he notices her. Baxter is shown in a medium shot, before the camera movement duplicates his gaze roaming from the buildings to the canals (plate 4). According to cinematic conventions, these images are clearly marked as subjective such as when Roeg cuts back to the medium shot of Baxter staring in the distance. When he cuts again, the spectator expects another subjective image. However, the Venetian scenery has turned into a white screen instead, which becomes the transparency on an overhead projector, on which a police officer is drawing a rough picture of Wendy's face. By means of these representations of Venice, the surface of the screen is made visible - a surface whose emptiness is anticipated by the 'empty' spaces Baxter finds in Venice. Faced with this blank, the spectators - like the characters - feel blind for a split of a second until new images appear. As if referring to the innumerable representations and fantasies of Venice, which supersede each other in a multi-layered palimpsest, Roeg's film turns Venetian space into an empty screen, on which images are ceaselessly projected - visions, apparitions and fantasies.

This *mise-en-abyme*, the metacinematic foregrounding of the film's materiality together with the virtuality of its images, visualises what the traditional film with its realistic mimesis seeks to hide: montage as the basic cinematic technique and the empty screen as the 'site' of the film and the site where its images become visible.[39] This strategy is repeated in the recurrent image of the 'bleeding' slide, which Baxter scrutinises after he has spilled his drink. The red liquid spreading across the slide is shown as a subjective image, when first John and later Laura Baxter look at it. When Christine dies, this shot is taken up again, but now there is no identifiable trace of subjectivity because Laura has carelessly put the slide away. The frame has disappeared and the picture fills the screen. The space of the slide has become

---

[39] Cf. Metz 1991, 75.

Plate 3

'Dream Factories': Hollywood and Venice in Nicolas Roeg's *Don't Look Now*

Plate 4

Plate 5

congruent with the focus of the camera, but through the liquid spreading into the gondola-shaped form, the surface of the slide is highlighted and the illusion of mimesis (a photograph of the interior of a Venetian church) destroyed. Instead, a palimpsest emerges, which evokes Venice not merely through the picture of the church but also through the gondola shape formed by the liquid and, last but not least, by the liquid itself, calling into mind the water threatening to flood the 'sea-city' (plate 5). Venice, in Roeg's *Don't Look Now*, is no longer the product of the Hollywood 'dream factory', but figures as a 'dream machine' itself by increasingly producing images, although these products consist mainly of nightmares. Roeg's film seems to imply that these ever-changing images do not depend on an author-subject which calls them into being and orders them. Furthermore, they cannot be contained and located at a safe distance in the holiday world of a stereotyped Venice. Instead, they have come to 'invade' England and the soothing fiction of a cosy home, an intact family in beautiful surroundings - the material of a Hollywood movie. Through the slide, 'Venice' or, rather, its semantics already figure as an uncanny presence even before Venice becomes the setting of the story. It violently disrupts the harmony and shatters the illusion.

Art and Death in Venice

Since the early twentieth century, Venice has repeatedly been associated with death - most obviously in Thomas Mann's *Tod in Venedig*. Tanner reads Mann's novella as a reference not only to its being built on "skeletons of trees", thus on death, but also as a judgement of classical art: "The City of Art is sick, the classical writer is sick - is art itself a form of sickness, so that it is not so much a matter of death in Venice as that death which *is* Venice?"[40] Roeg's film can be interpreted as transferring this idea to the classical cinema. Admittedly, many films - and particularly Visconti's *Morte a Venezia* - have shown death and decay in Venice. However, in contrast to Roeg, they have not focused on the implications of this topos for the medium of film. In other words, Venice in *Don't Look Now* is more than just the setting of John Baxter's death. Instead, the city itself figures as the agent - perhaps the only agent in the film - which distorts chronology and causality and thus subverts classical Hollywood narrative. Susan Sontag has written that "[c]inema is a time machine [...]. Movies resurrect the beautiful dead; present intact vanished or ruined environments".[41] It is certainly no coincidence that Roeg does not follow du Maurier's text, but instead has turned the tourist Baxter into a restorer of churches. His work in Venice as well as his effort to 'resurrect' his dead daughter in the fleeting vision of the red figure evoke the same interest as is found in traditional cinema. Yet Venice in *Don't Look Now* has come to resist this 'resurrection' of the past and - in the figure of the dwarf - strikes back. Heather's visions can be read as a warning against the effort, represented by Baxter, to seek for answers to (Venetian) secrets, for causal and chronological connections. No other city could have served Roeg's subversion of cinematic conventions better than Venice, "the

---

[40] Tanner 1992, 358.
[41] Sontag 1966/67, 32.

'always elscwhere' [...], provocative and elusive, definitively unreachable."[42] In Venice, "our dogged confidence that we are standing on solid ground"[43] must necessarily be disappointed. In *Don't Look Now*, Venice has become Hollywood's double and, at the same time, its antipode, a 'dream factory' whose endless production of images points to the mechanisms at the core of traditional cinema, while at the same time proposing a new aesthetics of 'seeing'.

Bibliography and Filmography:

"Eine Pfalz für Steven Spielberg". In: *Süddeutsche Zeitung*, 26 August 1998, 13.
Bordwell, David, Janet Staiger and Kristin Thompson: *The Classical Hollywood Cinema: Film Style & Mode of Production to 1960*. New York 1985.
Bordwell, David: *Narration in the Fiction Film*. Madison, Wisc., 1985.
Chatman, Seymour: *Coming to Terms: The Rhetoric of Narrative in Fiction and Film*. Ithaca, N.Y./London 1990.
Cowie, Elizabeth: "Storytelling: Classical Hollywood Cinema and Classical Narrative". In: Steve Neale and Murray Smith (eds.): *Contemporary Hollywood Cinema*. London/New York 1998, 178-190.
Deleuze, Gilles: *Cinema 2: The Time-Image*. Transl. Hugh Tomlinson and Robert Galeta. Minneapolis 1989.
Dempsey, Michael: Review of *Don't Look Now*. In: *Film Quarterly* 27,3 (1974), 39-43.
Dick, Leslie: "Desperation and Desire". In: *Sight and Sound* 7,1 (1997), 11-13.
Lauretis, Teresa de: "Now and Nowhere: Roeg's *Bad Timing*". In: *Discourse* 5 (1983), 21-40.
Maurier, Daphne du: "Don't Look Now" (1970). In: *Don't Look Now and Other Stories*. London etc. 1973, 7-55.
McFarlane, Brian: *Novel to Film: An Introduction to the Theory of Adaptation*. Oxford 1996.
Metz, Christian: *L'énonciation impersonnelle, ou le site du film*. Paris 1991.
Metz, Christian: *The Imaginary Signifier: Psychoanalysis and the Cinema* (1977). Bloomington 1982.
Nash, Jay Robert, and Stanley Ralph Ross: "Don't Look Now". In: *The Motion Picture Guide 1927-1983*, vol. 2: *C-D*. Chicago 1985, 693-694.
Neale, Steve, and Murray Smith (eds.): *Contemporary Hollywood Cinema*. London/New York 1998.
Roeg, Nicolas: *Don't Look Now*. UK/Italy 1973. Warner Home Video (UK) 1995.
Salwolke, Scott: *Nicolas Roeg: Film by Film*. Jefferson, N.C./London 1993.
Smith, Murray: "Theses on the Philosophy of Hollywood History". In: Steve Neale and Murray Smith (eds.): *Contemporary Hollywood Cinema*. London/New York 1998, 3-20.
Sontag, Susan: "Film and Theatre". In: *The Tulane Drama Review* 11 (1966/67), 24-37.
Tanner, Tony: *Venice Desired*. Oxford/Cambridge, Mass. 1992.

---

[42] Tanner 1992, 364. Cf. also the essays by Andreas Mahler and Elisabeth Bronfen in this book.
[43] Dempsey 1974, 42.

Indira Ghose

Venice Confidential

As Tony Tanner reminds us, the first city in the Bible was built by Cain - a city grounded on desire.[1] But Cain was, above all, the first murderer in the Bible, and death and crime have always been closely interwoven with the history of the city. In fact, one might assume that Venice, a city whose image is saturated with death, would have engendered an entire plethora of the genre that takes death as its central motivation: the crime novel. Surprisingly, however, most of the crime novels that are set in Venice seem to centre around quite different anxieties - above all, the anxiety of travel. Most of these novels (such as Ian McEwan's *The Comfort of Strangers*, Daphne Du Maurier's *Don't Look Now*, Muriel Spark's *Territorial Rights* and Patricia Highsmith's *Those Who Walk Away*) have tourists as their protagonists, and the role that Venice plays in their novels is that of a sinister backdrop, a mythical space inscribed with the motifs of decay, desire and deception. Nothing is what it seems in this city built on water, and those least able to read the signs are the visitors. (Of course, this is particularly epitomised in Ian McEwan's *The Comfort of Strangers*, where Venice functions as the site of sexual passion and perversion.) Sometimes the destabilisation of identity that Venice symbolises and engenders is even welcomed as a release from social constraints or from identity roles that the protagonist wishes to flee, as in the case of Patricia Highsmith's *Those Who Walk Away*. When Walter Benjamin writes of the crime novel as the perfect anodyne for the anxiety of travel,[2] however, he is referring to the detective novel, whose formula consists in fulfilling the reader's craving for danger but ultimately resolving all tensions by restoring order in the solution of a mystery.[3] For the detective novel set in Venice one needs to turn to the novels by Donna Leon as well as Michael Dibdin's *Dead Lagoon*. In the following I wish to focus particularly on the latter as a paradigmatic study in genre set in Venice. What the works of both authors have in common is the figure of a Venetian as detective. For heuristic purposes I shall be drawing analogies to the novels of Leon, concentrating mainly on two significant differences: the representation of Venice and the delineation of the authentic Venetian.

The Mean Streets of Venice

Of course, a partial explanation for the difference between the two samples of detective fiction lies in the divergent generic conventions shaping their work. Donna Leon's novels are by far the better known, and have experienced a veritable boom in Germany. Her detective fiction is what I would term of the soft-boiled variety. While

---

[1] Tanner 1992, 3f.
[2] Benjamin 1972, 38f.
[3] Cawelti 1976, 5-36.

the classic detective novel of the 20s and 30s was typically set in the drawing room of an English country house, and the sleuth who so brilliantly solved the riddle at the heart of the novel was an amateur like Lord Peter Wimsey or Hercule Poirot, the detective novel of the post-war era increasingly moved into a middle-class milieu with the protagonist transmuting into a professional member of a police force. Although Leon's protagonist, Commissario Brunetti, stops just short of being a female sleuth - an increasingly popular trend in crime fiction written by women authors - he is thoroughly domesticated in every other conceivable way. He is a family man, happily married, deeply respectful of his wife (who is intellectually superior and generally bossy), non-violent - in short, he proffers a fantasy of the domesticised male for female readerships.

Brunetti roves Venice with an erotic eye, ever eager to spot new beauties:

> [...] Brunetti never tired of studying the city, and every so often delighting himself by discovering something he had never noticed before. Over the course of the years, he had worked out a system that allowed him to reward himself for each discovery: a new window earned him a coffee; a new statue of a saint, however small, got him a glass of wine; and once, years ago, he had noticed on a wall he must have passed five times a week since he was a child a lapidary stone that commemorated the site of the Aldine Publishing House, the oldest in Italy, founded in the fourteenth century. He had gone right around the corner and into a bar at Campo San Luca and ordered himself a Brandy Alexander [...]⁴

May be this is what policemen do in Venice; this is most certainly what tourists do in Venice. In fact, my impression is that Commissario Brunetti is a tourist in drag as a detective. This would explain the enormous success of the novels with (particularly German) readerships - based on a vicarious identification with the fellow tourist Brunetti. The fact that Brunetti is presented as a native Venetian only adds to our delight: this is how we had always wished our authentic native to be.⁵

By contrast, the novel I wish to focus on is the less well-known, but brilliant novel *Dead Lagoon*.⁶ Here, too, we have an authentic Venetian as detective, one who returns to his home after long years of absence in Rome, where he is posted. But in contrast to the picture postcard facade of Venice Leon presents, Dibdin's Venice is pervaded with death and decay. Here we have a classic hard-boiled detective novel set in Venice. As various critics of the detective novel have pointed out, the hard-boiled variety is not about a mystery at all but instead is a study of American society, a cityscape, as it were, which dissects urban American life of the thirties, forties and fifties in the same clinical light as a painting by Edward Hopper.⁷ The detective is lonely figure who walks the mean streets of his city in a secret quest for self-definition. The world portrayed is usually pervaded by corruption at every level. Unlike the classic detective

---

⁴ Leon 1993, 123.

⁵ Interestingly, Leon has not permitted any of her Brunetti stories to be translated into Italian.

⁶ A series of detective novels by Dibdin have the Venetian detective Zen as their hero, but this is the only one to be set in Venice.

⁷ Jameson 1983. 122-148. Also see Grella 1988 and Cawelti 1976, 137-161.

novel, where the detective is a semiotic interpreter of clues, the hard-boiled detective is far too entangled in the plot to maintain a Cartesian distance to the signs of the city.[8] Instead, he is involved in a search for meaning. If the classic detective story defuses the fear of disorder disrupting an harmonious social order, the anxiety lurking at the heart of the hard-boiled story is that of a loss of control. In the final analysis, the hard-boiled detective is a solipsistic rebel against a corrupt society, following no code of ethics but his own. In keeping with this bleak vision, the setting transmutes from the bucolic world of the classic detective story to an urban waste land. In the case of Venice the dream of living in Venice metamorphoses into a nightmare.[9]

Let me briefly sketch the plot of the novel. The detective Aurelio Zen returns to Venice on an assignment to clear up the mystery surrounding the haunting of a crumbling old palazzo and its owner, the decrepit Venetian aristocrat Ada Zulian. However, secretly he is on quite a different mission: he is investigating the disappearance of a rich American named Durridge from an island in the lagoon for the family of the American and their insurance company. The historical backdrop of the book is the nascent secessionist movement in Venice and the entire Northern Italy. It is also the time of the Italian velvet revolution, when justice Di Pietro and other magistrates calmly set about pulling down the very foundations of Italian political society by uncovering the depth of corruption it was mired in. This was, of course, something everyone knew about, but which had never been so openly stated and above all which had never had any political consequences. In Dibdin's novel normal Italians are filled with a sense of unease at this development - as a colleague of Zen's complains, how is one to get anything done if bribes are no longer viable? Corruption was a way of life and had percolated to the grassroots of society. Thus Zen, too, is on a corrupt mission for private gain. He finds his own string-pulling impeded by the new atmosphere of fear and moral probity. In the course of the novel both strands of the plot converge on the populist leader of the Venetian secessionist movement, who emerges as Zen's counterpart.

In contrast to the idiom of the picturesque deployed by Leon in her representation of Venice, the Venice presented in *Dead Lagoon* is a city of decay and corruption, but stripped of all morbid charm. There is no mention of the famous sights, famous hotels, etc. that are such a vital setting for the other novels. Instead, we have a waste land of stone and water; picturesque pieties à la Leon give way to scenes like this: "Zen entered a small square whose sealed well had been replaced by a standpipe. The tap was dribbling water into a red plastic bucket from which a mangy cat was drinking."[10] Plastic buckets replace ancient fountains, desolate housing sites, docks and industrial wastelands take the place of opulent splendour. The novel is obsessed with mud, slime and drains:

---

[8] Stowe 1983, 366-83.
[9] see Grella 1988, 120.
[10] Dibdin 1995, 157. All further references to be given in parentheses in the text.

> The air, walled off from the prevailing breezes, was heavy with the stench of mud. An assortment of débris was visible at the bottom of the water: the wheel of a pram, a punctured bucket, a boot. A large rat slithered across the mud and hopped into an open drain. In older buildings, people still kept a heavy stone on the toilet cover to stop the creatures from getting loose in the house. (34)

One corpse is actually found in the sewage system. The most pervasive image is that of the stray cats, who multiply in a sinister way in the course of the story and represent a vicious society of scavengers. The breathtaking last few scenes of the novel are a chase set in the most desolate part of Venice:

> Santa Marta was a bleak area, one of the new quarters built on reclaimed land at the turn of the century. Disused railway tracks ran between the hulks of salvaged boats propped up on concrete blocks. In the distance were redbrick blocks of flats, built to house the dockyard workers. (333)

Not far off is a prison complex, and the scaffolding of a football stadium looms into the darkness. Even the Lido does not escape this vitriolic idiom of the anti-picturesque:

> Of all the topographical freaks in the lagoon, the Lido had always seemed to Zen the most disturbing. In summer, its vocation as a seaside resort lent the place an illusory air of normality, but in the bleak depths of February its true nature was mercilessly exposed. Here was a perfectly normal contemporary urban scene, with asphalt streets called *Via* this and *Piazza* that, complete with road signs and traffic lights. There was the usual jumble of apartments and villas, offices and hotels, the usual roar of cars and lorries, scooters, bikes and buses. Everything about the place was perfectly banal, in short, except that it was built on an isolated sandbar a few hundred metres wide between the shallow reaches of the lagoon and the open expanses of the Adriatic. (341)

If Venice is a freak city, built on an insubstantial medium, the mainland of Italy is no better. In one scene Zen, the native Venetian, is suddenly overcome by a wave of nausea and claustrophobia and feels an overpowering urge to stand on solid ground again. He heads for Mestre, but when he finds himself back in the midst of traffic, pollution and the banalities of a modern urban landscape, he can no longer remember why he had come. (173-4)

In other ways the city is one of decline and desolation, too. It is, quite literally, a dying city. The average age of its inhabitants is higher than in any other city in Europe. Most of its young inhabitants cannot afford to pay the exorbitant rents and migrate towards the mainland for jobs and flats. (35) This is, of course, one of the main arguments to fuel the secessionist campaign for a return of Venice to the Venetians. As the populist politician at the centre of the novel, Ferdinando Dal Maschio argues, Venetians have been degraded to the staff of the Disney World of Venice, paid to maintain it as a theme park for tourists.

In Leon's Venice, two Venetians discuss the same obsessive worry:

'We are a pessimistic people, aren't we?' Brunetti asked.
'We once had an empire. Now all we have,' she said, [...] 'all we have is this Disneyland. I think that's sufficient cause for pessimism.'[11]

Ironically, however, the very trope of the picturesque that Leon deploys works to facilitate an imaginative appropriation of the city by the reader and its consumption as a cultural commodity.[12] The picturesque makes for the reader's narcissistic identification with Brunetti as a fellow tourist and serves to safely deflect the anxiety of real travel. Brunetti is part of the very Disneyfication of Venice that he so deplores.

While Leon's rhetoric of the picturesque proffers a Venice as an artifact for the reader's consumption, the dark underbelly of Venice that Dibdin presents is, of course, as much a discursive construct as is the former. To be sure, the image of a decaying Venice is as suffused with dark desire and fascination as is that of an aestheticised Venice. Dibdin is in good company: there is a long history of an alternative view of Venice by travellers who point up the decay of the city - Ruskin above all springs to mind. By foregrounding the intertextual references of his novel Dibdin exposes the fictionality of Venice as a palimpsest, a site for the projection of fantasies both of beauty and corruption. The intertextual echoes that reverberate within the text are not only generic: not only Raymond Chandler, but shades of Thomas Mann's *Death in Venice* are evoked as well.

Venice Orientalised

While there is no undercurrent of sensual passion pervading the Venice of Dibdin, there are other shades of *Death in Venice*. Venice here, too, is an orientalised site, suffused by the decadence and corruption of the East that wears down the Appollonian resistance of the Northern Aschenbach, as Tony Tanner has shown.[13] The deathly disease eating away at the heart of Dibdin's Venice is not the asiatic cholera but a more recent disease - the germ of nationalist fundamentalism, which has infected Northern Italy from former Yugoslavia. (After all, another term for secessionism is Balkanisation.) It is the shadow of the Yugoslav war that darkens the Venice of Dibdin. If *Death in Venice* was written under the gathering gloom of the First World War, which was first ignited in Sarajevo, Dibdin's Venice is set against the darkness of the Balkan civil war. The very convocations of feral cats in Venice prefigure a return to barbarism. Dibdin reminds us of the easily forgotten fact that the Yugoslav war played itself out at the very doorstep of Venice. The fictive populist leader of Venice (with the telling name of Dal-matio) openly pays tribute to the ancient ties between Venice and Croatia, that former outpost of the Venetian empire, and credits Croatia for being a model for his programme of regional autonomy. Historically, this is quite

---

[11] Leon 1995, 51.

[12] For the implications of the picturesque see the collection of essays edited by Copley 1994.

[13] Tanner 1992, 352-359.

accurate - as early as 1991 there are reports of arms smuggling to Croatia via a Venetian connection.[14] The ties between Venice and the Dalmatian coast reach back to the time of their joint struggle against Turkish hegemonic policy back in the 16th. century, and Venice still boasts of its significant contribution towards defeating Turkish imperial dreams in the battle of Lepanto in 1571. What is now the Republic of Croatia has also always regarded itself as the last bastion of Western civilisation against the Moslem Bosnians or the Greek Orthodox Serbs on their Eastern flank. If the collapse of the old world order and the bloc system between East and West is at the root of the break-up of Yugoslavia, so it is the main cause for the rise of populism in Italy, coupled with the wave of globalisation sweeping the world. The Northern League, which has won up to 18% of the vote in this region, has announced that Venice is to be the future capital of the independent state of Padania. ("Venice is worth a mass", party leader Umberto Bossi is quoted as having once said.) It proclaims a programme of regional autonomy coupled with a critique of the corruption of the old party system and laced with virulent xenophobia. At the heart of Dibdin's book lies a flaming indictment of the threat of nationalist movements and of an essentialist notion of identity - which are, after all, at the root of ethnic cleansing. Nonetheless, he does not deny the attractiveness of their policies, when he makes Dal Maschio attempt to woo Zen to join their movement by arguing, "Do you want a Europe that is like an airport terminal where every language is spoken badly, where any currency is accepted but there is nothing but soulless trash to buy and fake food to eat?" (311) The choice seems to be one between nationalist fanaticism and the Macdonaldisation of the world.

Dibdin's book proved to be remarkably prescient: in May 1997 in a spectacular coup the campanile of San Marco was occupied by a separatist cell who announced the renascence of the Serenissima Repubblica. A small band of fanatics hijacked a vaporetto at gun point, drove up the Piazza of St. Mark with what appeared to be a tank and scaled and occupied the tower for eight hours. They unfurled the flag of Venice with its lion of St. Mark and in a pirate radio transmission claimed to have freed San Marco. Their operation was planned to commemorate the 200th. anniversary of the surrender of the republic of Venice to Napoleon's forces by freeing Venice from Roman colonisation. The coup was rapidly ended by anti-terrorist forces. At first there were smiles at what was seen as a youthful prank, but in the meantime the smiles have faded as a whole network of separatist cells has been uncovered, fully prepared to use violence in their struggle for an independent Venetian republic, with links to politicians, businessmen and intellectuals. Since the attack on the campanile of San Marco banners of Venice are regularly hoisted on church towers, bomb threats are made against newspapers and sometimes handmade explosives are found, none of which have detonated so far. As one press commentator, Giorgio Bocca reminds us, this was the way the terrorist movement of the 70s began.[15]

---

[14] In the following I draw on newspaper articles from the *Zeit, Frankfurter Rundschau, Süddeutsche Zeitung* and *Der Spiegel* dating from 14/11/1991 to 11/7/1997.

[15] Quoted in *Der Spiegel* 28, 7/7/1997.

It is not only the shadow of the wars of the present that falls across Dibdin's bleak vision of Venice, it is also the shadow of of the past. A key to the city lies in its history of guilt. An important subplot is the story of the daughter of the old Countess Zulian, Rosetta, who disappeared during the last days of WWII. Her spectre haunts the old palazzo together with the very real masked characters attempting to terrorise the old woman into losing her wits. Countess Zulian blames an old Fascist, Dolfo, for having lured her daughter away and having murdered her. The story of Rosetta is interwoven with that of her bosom friend and look-alike, a Jewish girl from the ghetto of Venice named Rose (here Dibdin spins out his allegory somewhat at the cost of credibility.) The truth that emerges in the course of the story is that Rosetta committed suicide in despair at the news of the impending deportation of her friend. It is the member of the Fascist party, Dolfo, who decides to save the Jewish girl and hides her in his house. Dolfo's house is crammed with treasures which, he hints, he has amassed from Jewish citizens. In defence he argues, "Ours is a history of plunder and rapine [...] And in my small way I'm carrying on that tradition." (122) In Dibdin's version of Venetian history, the splendours of Venice are grounded in a tradition of greed and guilt. It is the historical memory of the betrayal of Jewish Venetians that finally determines Zen on his struggle against the secessionist movement. When asked what the tale of Rose has to do with Dal Maschio and his machinations, he answers enigmatically, "Nothing. Everything." (324) In Mann's novel, the city's guilty secret is its betrayal of its visitors for materialistic motives - the city attempts to cover up the signs of the disease. Here, too, the hidden foundations of the city are guilt and betrayal. As Frederic Jameson has remarked, "History is what hurts."[16]

The Politics of Popular Fiction

Criticism of the detective novel has tended to condemn the genre as complicitous in the state's project of panoptical surveillance. The Marxist critic Ernest Mandel in *Delightful Murder* has pointed out that the figure of the noble bandit in early 19th. century literature and that of the policeman, a suspect figure as a minion of the forces in power, change in the course of the genre. The bandit became criminalised and the policeman increasingly ennobled. In the final analysis, despite its obsession with crime and violence, the detective novel serves to contain the threat of irrationality to bourgeois society by showing that crime never pays and by reenforcing the status of state justice. If crime represented an attack on property and the reminder of death constituted a threat to bourgeois control, both were successfully deflected by the closure prescribed by the genre. In addition to providing escapist pleasure and vicarious adventure, the detective novel functions to absolve the reader from social guilt by projecting it onto the criminal Other.

However, as cultural critics have argued recently, this analysis seems overly reductive.[17] Often the contrary is true: ambiguity about law and order is articulated and

---

[16] Jameson 1981, 102.

[17] See particularly Collins 1996.

a lack of faith in the state is expressed. Crime is shown to pay and to be all pervasive, whereas justice is revealed as contingent and unenforceable. The possibility of a happy ending is often put into question. Further, critics have argued that at its best, artifacts of popular culture often work to redefine a genre from within and destabilise it while overtly affirming and perpetuating a discourse. An analysis of popular culture is productive precisely because it is issues of social reality that are played through. Leon, for instance, clearly uses crime fiction as a platform for a crusade against the various ills of contemporary society - ranging from discrimination against homosexuals and transvestites to the mass rape of Bosnian women. The secret protagonist of her novels is not the anodyne Brunetti at all but the attractive lesbian couple introduced in the first novel who are consistently recycled in later books. Thus a popular genre is often an ideal medium to transport a radical agenda. In her plot endings cosy notions of an easy solution to social problems are firmly rejected.

Similarly, in the case of Dibdin's novel all Zen's euphoria at tracking down the culprits evaporates to give way to a sense of futility. The murder of the American turns out to be that of a Serb war criminal with American citizenship (Durrige is, it emerges, a Duric) engineered by Dal Mashio to ingratiate himself with his Croatian friends. But no charges can be made to stick. The party members are defended by one of the best and most expensive lawyers in the city. Further, the politician is protected by the head of the Venetian police, mindful of future political constellations. The very state authorities are not interested in a prosecution, as they are themselves implicated in the arms trade with Croatia. In the second plot, that of the alleged ghosts haunting the old Countessa, Zen succeeds in catching the old lady's nephews red-handed in the act of terrorising her at night (ironically in harlequin costumes of the Carnival. In an interesting sidelight, Dibdin reveals that the old Venetian aristocrat does not recognise these - the Carnival was, after all, an obsolete custom artificially resuscitated by the tourist industry in the 70s.). But this time it is the victim herself who refuses to co-operate with the police, preferring to keep her knowledge as a weapon with which to blackmail her relatives. Zen returns to Rome empty-handed. Despite the change sweeping over Italy, the old mechanisms of graft and influence-peddling retain the upper hand. Thus contradictions within society are glaringly exposed rather than glossed over.

Narrative closure is called into question, too. While the main crimes are cleared up if not punished, the minor mystery about the fate of Zen's father remains unclear. An old neighbour reveals to Zen that his father, allegedly missing in action during WWII on the Eastern front, had been spotted in the city as a tourist with an Eastern European group after the Iron Curtain came down. He had admitted to having stayed on voluntarily after having defected from the army. He showed no desire to get in touch with his old family or to return to his native city. Zen's mental turmoil at this news is exacerbated by the fact that it remains in the realm of speculation, possibly the ramblings of a senile old man. A happy end is denied in other ways, too - this, once again, vintage Chandler. There is the love interest: Zen has a brief affair with the sensual, estranged wife of his antagonist Dal Maschio. And as in Chandler's world, the woman he loves inevitably betrays him in the end

But then, the detective himself is a highly ambivalent and flawed character. In this study of guilt and betrayal, Zen is implicated in more than one way. His presence in Venice is itself a sign of his personal venality. He bears the responsibility for the death of a colleague caused by carelessly gambling with his life. His treatment of his old girlfriend appears less than chivalric (though the readers sympathies are decidedly manipulated in his favour). Most heavily of all weighs his betrayal of his old schoolboy friend Tommaso, who has become an enthusiast for the secessionist movement. Hoping to persuade him to abandon his corrupt leader, Zen follows Tommaso through the darker side of Venice all night and even lies to him about his impending dismissal from the party. Like Aschenbach, the tormented Tommaso walks to his death in the sea.

Of course, critics have also pointed to the dark side of the hard-boiled hero. A figure shaped in American frontier mythology and strongly imbued with the tough guy stance of Hemingway, he is rooted in a Puritan obsession with sin and morality.[18] His true quest is to eradicate evil. His romantic individualism is the obverse of a rejection of society and his withdrawal from all human contact is grounded in a solipsistic sense of superiority. A descendant from figures like Leatherstocking and the myth of the lone ranger, he is filled with a profound distrust of civilisation and the urban landscape. The figure of the hard-boiled detective is imbued with the cult of masculinity, and as many critics have remarked, a visceral fear of women. They are shown as a disturbing force who are always seducers and betrayers. This is echoed in the love plot in Dibdin's novel. There is a misogynist touch in Zen's attitude to women, too. Zen's girlfriend in Rome is portrayed as a shrew of rigidly feminist views, waiting to snare him into marriage in complicity with his martyr-like mother. Even the old Ada is shown as a coldly calculating old woman of intransigent class arrogance.

While this critique of the hard-boiled hero is not without validity, what interests me here is the way the figure of the loner is deployed to explode an essentialist concept of identity. The most interesting aspect in a comparison of the Venetian as detective in the two sub-genres at issue is the perspective of the detective. Whereas the Venetian is constructed as an insider in Leon's work, in Dibdin's novel he oscillates between the viewpoint of an outsider and an insider - in the words of Zen himself, "an outsider, to whom everything feels at once familiar and strange." (202)

The Authentic Native

To sum up, death pervades the city, with its opening scene set in a lagoon that is rumoured to have swallowed up another, former city of splendours and its action set in the dank wastelands of the city and the isle of the dead, Sant'Ariano, where the city conveniently disposes of its cargo of dead. (Significantly, one of Dal Maschio's slogans goes: "Venice is the heart of the lagoon ... Keep the lagoon alive." His Venice

---

[18] For a critique of the hard-boiled hero, see in particular Grella 1983 and Knight 1980, 135-167.

has long been invaded by the shadow of death.) It is a city haunted by the ghosts of the past and the spectre of an ominous future. A recurrent image associated with Venice is that of instability, shifting appearances, in a city that was built on water. As Dibdin puts it, "here everything was a trick of the light, an endlessly shifting play of appearances without form or substance. What you saw was what you got, and all you would ever get." (304). An essence that is destabilised by the city of mirages is that between self and other, the central opposition at the heart of the novel. Aurelio oscillates between a sense of homecoming and belonging and alienation from the politics of essentialism propagated by the new party. He implicitly realises that patriotism and self-love are built on the hate of others. As Dal Maschio himself puts it, "The new Europe will be no place for rootless drifters and cosmopolitans with no sense of belonging. Unless we hate what we are not, we cannot love what we are." (311-2) Further, essentialism is always grounded in an exclusion of some. The figure of the Venetian Jew Rosa stands for the price to be paid for the ideal of pure-blooded Venetians. She epitomises the eternal wandering Jew, unable to find a home either in Israel or in Venice, a stranger wherever she goes. Yet rather than being a tragic exception, she stands in for the human condition itself. As studies of the dialectics of self and other have shown, the very notion of a unified self is as illusory as that of a unified other.[19] The idea of the authentic native is a myth. The quest for nationalist essence is as elusive as Venice itself. It is instructive to compare Donna Leon's native Venetian detective to Zen:

> [Brunetti] missed this city when he was away from it, much in the same way he missed Paola, and he felt complete and whole only while he was here. One glance around him, as they sped up the canal, was proof of the wisdom of all of this. He had never spoken of this to anyone. No foreigner would understand; any Venetian would find it redundant.[20]

In this classic piece of kitsch, there we have him at last, the authentic native, so dear to the tourist's heart. By contrast, let us cut to the final scene of *Dark Lagoon*: accosted by a gaggle of tourists asking him the way, Zen gives an apologetic smile: "I'm a stranger here myself." he says (354).[21] His final betrayal is that of Venice itself. Like Judas, both betrayer and betrayed, he chooses to become a wandering Jew. He joins the ranks of a long line of visitors whose ultimate reaction to the city is flight. In effect, like Rimbaud he declares, Je est un autre: I, too, am an Other. Or as Levinas might have pointed out, the story of Ulysses returning home gives place to that of Abraham leaving never to return.[22]

---

[19] For an overview of the poststructuralist critique of ontology, see Young 1990. For an exploration of the issue of the authentic native, see the work of Bhabha, in particular Bhabha 1984.

[20] Leon 1993, 57.

[21] The line is taken from Nicholas Ray's film *Johnny Guitar* (1954), a self-conscious Western in the tradition of the film noir that turned into a cult film for the 50s. The protagonist is another loner. I am indebted to Elisabeth Bronfen for bringing this intertextual reference to my attention.

[22] Levinas 1986.

Bibliography

Primary Sources

Dibdin, Michael: *Dead Lagoon*. London 1994.
Du Maurier, Daphne: "Dont Look Now". In: Du Maurier, Daphne: *Don't Look Now and Other Stories*. Harmondsworth 1978.
Highsmith, Patricia: *Those Who Walk Away*. London 1967.
Leon, Donna: *Death at La Fenice*. London 1992.
Leon, Donna: *Death in a Strange Country*. London 1993.
Leon, Donna: *The Anonymous Venetian*. London 1994.
Leon, Donna: *A Venetian Reckoning*. London 1995.
Leon, Donna: *Acqua Alta*. London 1996.
Leon, Donna: *The Death of Faith*. London 1997.
McEwan, Ian: *The Comfort of Strangers*. London 1981.
Spark, Muriel: *Territorial Rights*. London 1979.

Secondary Sources

Benjamin, Walter: "Kriminalromane". In: Benjamin, Walter: *Gesammelte Schriften* IV, 1. Frankfurt 1972, 381-2.
Bennett, Tony/Colin Mercer/Janet Woollacott, (eds.): *Popular Culture and Social Relations*. Milton Keynes 1986.
Bennett, Tony (ed.): *Popular Fiction: Technology, Ideology, Production, Reading*. London 1990.
Bhabha, Homi K. "Of Mimicry and Man: The Ambivalence of Colonial Discourse". *October* 28 (1984), 125-133.
Cawelti, John G.: *Adventure, Mystery, and Romance: Formula Stories as Art and Popular Culture*. Chicago 1976.
Collins, Jim: *Uncommon Cultures: Popular Culture and Post-Modernism*. New York 1989.
Copley, Stephen, and Peter Garside (eds.): *The Politics of the Picturesque: Literature, Landscape and Aesthetics Since 1770*. Cambridge 1994.
Grella, George: "The Hard-Boiled Detective Novel". In: Winks, Robin W. (ed.): *Detective Fiction: A Collection of Critical Essays*. Woodstock 1988.
Jameson, Frederic: "On Raymond Chandler". In: Most, Glenn/William W. Stowe (eds.): *The Poetics of Murder: Detective Fiction and Literary Theory*. New York 1983, 122-148.
Jameson, Frederic: *The Political Unconcious: Narrative as a Socially Symbolic Act*. Ithaca 1981.
Knight, Stephen: *Form and Ideology in Crime Fiction*. London 1980.
Levinas, Emmanuel: "The Trace of the Other". In: Taylor, Mark C. (ed.): *Deconstruction in Context*. Chicago 1986.
Mandel, Ernest: *Delightful Murder: A Social History of the Crime Story*. Minneapolis 1984.
Morris, Jan: *Venice*: London 1960.

Stowe, William W.: "From Semiotics to Hermeneutics: Modes of Detection in Doyle and Chandler". In: Most, Glenn/William W. Stowe (eds.): *The Poetics of Murder: Detective Fiction and Literary Theory*. New York 1983, 366-83.
Suerbaum, Ulrich: *Krimi: Eine Analyse der Gattung*. Stuttgart 1984.
Symons, Julian: *Bloody Murder: From the Detective Story to the Crime Novel*. London 1972.
Tanner, Tony: *Venice Desired*. Cambridge 1992.
Young, Robert J.C.: *White Mythologies: Writing History and the West*. London 1990.

Rosella Mamoli Zorzi

Intertextual Venice: Blood and Crime and Death Renewed in Two Contemporary Novels

The cover of a fairly recent book, *The Nature of Blood* (1997) by Caryl Phillips, reproduces a very well-known nineteenth-century painting with a Venetian subject, *The Bridge of Sighs* by William Etty (Ill. 1). In his diary, the English painter explicitly cited Byron's famous lines - "I stood in Venice on the Bridge of Sighs/ A palace and a prison on each hand" - as the source of this oil-painting. He painted both "the palace" (to the left) and "the prison" (to the right), with that essential black-legend symbol which is the Bridge of Sighs linking the two buildings; he also painted a corpse being loaded onto a boat, at night (the scene is moon-lit), presumably to be taken out into the lagoon and thrown into the water.

This painting was not done during Etty's Venetian visit of 1822-23, but at least ten years later, between 1833 and 1835, after Etty had visited Turner's 1832 exhibition of "Venetian" paintings referring to Byron's *Childe Harold's Pilgrimage*.[1] It is therefore a visual text strictly linked to other visual texts (Turner's Venetian paintings), which are in their turn linked to literary texts (Byron's poem): Byron, in his turn, saw Venice as "the greenest island of [his] imagination", based on his previous knowledge of the city as a text created by his readings: "And Otway, Radcliffe, Schiller, Shakespeare's Art/Had stamped her image in me".[2]

This might seem a complex approach to my subject, but here indeed lies the gist of my paper: any text that was or is or will be written on Venice cannot but be a text based on previous representations of the city - both visual and literary. A commonplace truth, one could say, but a commonplace truth without which we cannot look at *any* new, or future, representation of Venice, or, more widely, of Italy, as M. Pfister has underlined[3] Such is in fact the weight of the representations of Venice, that the real city hardly counts: the physical Venice could well disappear and literary Venices would still be created[4].

One might react to this over-representation in two ways: one could in fact sympathise with the well-known view of Marinetti, who declared in his *Discorso futurista*: "Venetians! When we shouted 'let us kill moonlight!' we were thinking of you, old Venice soaked through in Romanticism!"

---

[1] Pavanello-Romanelli 1983, 160.

[2] Byron 1970, 229; see also Mamoli Zorzi 1988, 247.

[3] Pfister 1996, 4; on the subject see, among the more recent critical literature, Tanner 1992; Pemble 1995; Pemble 1988.

[4] Mamoli Zorzi 1990, 285.

Illustration 1: William Etty, *The Bridge of Sighs* (Oil on canvas, 80x50, 8 cm., Xork, City of York Art Gallery, in Pavanello-Romanelli, p. 161).

Intertextual Venice: Blood and Crime and Death Renewed

Adding that Futurists wanted to free Venice from "all the immense Romantic fantasticating" with which it had been covered up by "the poets poisoned with the Venice fever".[5]

One could instead see a further, successful, representation of Venice as one of "the works of art which are keys or passwords admitting one to a deeper knowledge, to a finer perception of beauty".[6] Pound was referring to Dante's *Divina Commedia*, but his words may be used in a wider sense. This second view would freshen up this "consumed" city for us and would also help us to survive in a city that is being quickly obliterated by mass tourism (as of course several poets already have seen)[7]: the city of words remains, in this case, the more relevant of the two.

Etty's painting is the epitome of one persisting version of the representations of Venice, that has its distant roots in the Elizabethans' twofold vision of Venice as the city of beauty and the city of corruption, as Thomas Nashe's *The Unfortunate Traveller* (1594) well testifies.

It also epitomizes the view of Venice as the city of plots and crime, of artistic beauty and woman's beauty but also of dangerous seduction, often with a clear hint at the corruption of Catholicism: one could think of Jonson's *Volpone* (1606), of Otway's *Venice Preserved* (1680), of Ann Radcliffe's *Mysteries of Udolpho* (1794), and of the Romantic attraction for decadence and decay, of Byron and Shelley in primis.

Etty's painting is just one of the many nineteenth-century paintings, sketches, lithographs that illustrated the dark and Gothic aspect of the city, which was also emphasized for political reasons by French historians such as Daru, in his *Histoire de la République de Venise* (1819). The painting presented this dark Venice to the visitor who perhaps had not yet gone to Venice, preparing his perception of the city, as so many other paintings and etchings did. Among the host of nineteenth century painters, one could name Francesco Hayez (1791-1881), with his *Secret Accusation* (1847-48) (Ill. 2)[8], where a young woman takes revenge on her unfaithful lover by denouncing him to the Council of the Ten, or with his *The Rival's Revenge* (Ill.3).[9] Or one could think of such great dramatic and melodramatic subjects as *The Two Foscari* (present also in the world of the opera), where the anguishing debate between filial and fatherly devotion and loyalty to the state is set in a rather blackish Republic: Delacroix, Hayez, Grigoletti all devoted at least one painting to the subject. Or one could mention the more overtly and intensely black story of the execution of Marin Faliero, again made popular by Byron, and painted by

---

[5] Marinetti 1973, 27. See also Marinetti's *Contro Venezia passatista*, April 27, 1910, on the repudiation of the "ancient Venice extenuated and undone by century old voluptuousness" (Marinetti 1973, 26) (my translations).

[6] Pound 1952, 154. See also Mamoli Zorzi 1981.

[7] Just one example: "They have already consumed the Doges' palace / And it goes without saying the Bridge of Sighs/ Misery and the club-footed poet made famous." I. Layton, "Piazza San Marco", 1974, 34).

[8] *Venezia da stato a Mito* 1997, n. 52.

[9] Pavanello-Romanelli 1983, n. 200.

Illustration 2: Francesco Hayez, *The Secret Accusation* (Oil on canvas, 153x120 cm., Pavia, Civica Pinacoteca Malaspina, in *Venezia da stato a mito*, n. 52, p. 233).

Illustration 3: Francesco Hayez, *The Rival's Revenge* (Oil on canvas, 54x39 cm., Milano, Accademia di Brera, in Pavanello-Romanelli, n. 200, p.164).

Illustration 4: Pompeo M. Molmenti, *The Death of Othello* (Oil on canvas, 259x335 cm., Venice, Museo d'Arte Moderna, in Pavanello-Romanelli, n. 215, p.178).

Intertextual Venice: Blood and Crime and Death Renewed

Delacroix, Hayez, or represented in the very popular etchings by J. R. Herbert.[10] One could also think of the popular subject of Othello's death, as painted, for instance, by Pompeo M. Molmenti (1819-1894) (Ill. 4).[11]

Having briefly hinted at the historically and symbolically pregnant meaning of Etty's painting, let me go back now to the book on the cover of which this painting was reproduced: a significant image as regards the "seuils", or paratexts, examined by Genette[12], even if the author had probably nothing to do with the choice of the book-cover.

The Nature of Blood is indeed a novel where the author makes use of the tradition of "black" Venice, but where he succeeds in renewing it by means of the assemblage of his materials and, of course, by the intensity of the writing. The novel mixes distant epochs and places, telling, mostly, but not only, in the first person

a. the story of a woman, Eva, who survived her imprisonment in a Nazi concentration camp, and who is trying, unsuccessfully, to go back to "normal" life;

b. the story of a historically-researched Jewish persecution which took place in Porto Buffolé, near Venice, in 1480, when the leaders of the Jewish community were charged with ritual slaughter and burnt at the stake in Venice;

c. the story of an unnamed "capitano di ventura", or "General", who married secretly the daughter of a Venetian senator, named Desdemona, and was sent to fight the Turks at Cyprus.

The three stories are not told in this succession but they are constantly shuffled one with the other or interwoven, in ways that are typical of the novels of our century. The choice of a first person narrator is essential, as the reader at times hesitates in recognizing which one of the three stories he is about to read: this is exactly what the author wants the reader to do. The reader's momentary hesitation proves that the three stories are linked by the tragedy of racism. They refract it one onto the other, enhancing its impact: racism does not change in time or space, it has manifestations different only in appearance.

It is made clear to the reader that the author is re-using pre-existing material: the historical research on the Jewish Porto Buffolé community by historian S. G. Radzik, as regards the 1480 persecution story, is openly acknowledged at the beginning of the book; the name of the General's bride clearly signals the undertext of Shakespeare's tragedy, even if the General remains unnamed. A short passage, standing autonomously, does refer indeed, with a critical approach, to

> OTHELLO: A play by William Shakespeare. Probably written between 1602 and 1604, and first performed in 1604. The principal source for the play is Giraldi Cinthio's *Hecatommiti*, a collection of stories first published in Venice in 1566, and used by a number of Elizabethan and Jacobean dramatists as source material for their plots.[13]

---

[10] Mamoli Zorzi 1990, 291; Pavanello-Romanelli 1983, n. 209.
[11] Pavanello-Romanelli 1983, n. 215.
[12] Genette 1987.
[13] Phillips 1997, 166.

Historical sources are flaunted in the eye of the reader, together with other historical references mentioned in the "Acknowledgements" - as almost always happens in contemporary novels of this kind, for instance M. Ondaatje's: in a way this brings us back to Elizabethan times, when silent borrowing was the rule, - and no one thought worse of the text for it - but of course in our time borrowings are loudly exhibited as part of the writer's gears and devices.

What is interesting from the point of view of the representation of Venice is the fact that Phillips - just as every new writer - *does* use pre-existing representations, but renews the representation of the dark love and crime city by the poignancy of the underlying and unifying theme: the nature of blood, i.e. racism, which is the central issue. The author does not hesitate to have the first-person voice of an implicit author admonish the swarthy General:

> My friend, an African river bears no resemblance to a Venetian canal. Only the strongest spirit can hold both together. Only the most powerful heart can endure the pulse of two such disparate life-forces. After a protracted struggle, most men will relinquish one in favour of the other. But you run like Jim Crow and leap into their creamy arms. Did you truly ever think of your wife's soft kiss? Or your son's eyes? Brother, you are weak. You are a figment of a Venetian imagination. While you still have time, jump from her bed and fly away home.[14]

The updating of the discourse ("Jim Crow", "Brother") underlines the destruction of temporal levels already at work in the interweaving of the three stories, to remind the reader of the pressing message of the novel on *our* racism.

The contents of the novel thus confirm and deny at the same time the view of Etty's *Bridge of Sighs*: there *are* corpses in the book (the leaders of the Jewish town burnt to death in Venice),[15] Venice *is* the Venice of secret tribunals,[16] but the story of the persecution and killing of the Jews, the racism against the swarthy captain, make the city a stage where the tragic intolerance of our own century is acted out, depriving the representation of the city from any cliché-like characteristic. The intertextual references charge the story of Eva's physical survival to the holocaust with darker echoes (the past persecutions announcing the future holocaust), and in its turn the story of Eva projects onto the story of the black General and the 1480 persecution even more bloody hues.

One other fairly recent book seems to take up the tradition of a dark Venice, in particular the Venice of decay, disease, and art which found its best-known expression

---

[14] Phillips 1997, 182.

[15] "The condemned were attached by means of a long chain to iron stakes on the scaffolding, and then the torch holders lit their torches and immediately ignited the woodpiles. The loud crackling of flames began to obscure the voice of Servadio, who now only screamed." Phillips 1997, 154.

[16] "Some six weeks later, on 22 June, the members of the Grand Council received the following order from the Council of Ten", Phillips 1997, 105, but there are many other passages regarding the secret tribunals.

in Thomas Mann's novella *Death in Venice*, but also in the works of other writers such as Maurice Barrès (*Amori et dolori sacrum. La mort à Venise*) or Gabriele D'Annunzio (*Il fuoco*). In *Night Letters* (1996) by the Australian writer Robert Dessaix,[17] a literary character writes in the first person the "night letters" to which the title refers. The narrator has discovered that he has a deathly disease - which seems to be AIDS - and he decides to live in Venice whatever life is left to him to live, not unlike Milly Theale in Henry James's *The Wings of the Dove*. One epigraph from Susan Sontag's *Illness as Metaphor* ("Illness is the night-side of life") aptly suggests the meaning of these "night" letters, written in the city of night and illness, be it Mann's cholera or present day AIDS.

We are still in the wake of "black" Venice; the place indicated as the place where the letters were written, "Hotel Arcadia", sends back to the well-known inscription, "Et in Arcadia ego",[18] where Arcadia is not only the pastoral reign of ancient Greece - the Italy of so many English and American travellers - but also the place of death.

The *Night Letters*, dated Venice April 1-20th, are presented as written in Venice, but they do not refer only to Venice. They are divided into three groups - the Locarno Letters, the Vicenza Letters, the Padua Letters - which constitute the three parts of the book. Each group refers to the specific location the title indicates, but in each the discourse constantly goes back to Venice, and to what happens to the letter-writer while he is writing his letters there. Among the "adventures" of the narrator is the acquaintance with a Professor Eschenbaum, whose intellectual and physical undertakings become part of the story, but who also represents a useful *ficelle* to create dialogue.

All sorts of material make up the "letters": travel memories (Sterne is an openly presiding star), stories told by different characters to the letter-writer ("The story of Antonietta, Baroness of St. Leger and the Golden Amulet"; "The Disappearing Courtesan"), dreams, meditations on life and death.

The trip is one of escape, after the "Annunciation"[19] of the deathly disease, but also of the decision to "live out my fantasy, to taste bliss while I could",[20] for a character who has "lost interest in ticking things off, in accumulating credit",[21] and has decided that time "is for beguiling, not for spending profitably," as Lambert Strether finally found out in The *Ambassadors*.

---

[17] The book is presented as "edited" by a Igor Miazmov, in Melbourne, 1996, who presents himself in an opening note as having worked on the letters sent from Venice to a "correspondent" in Melbourne. This seems more a "Borgesian" (invented) editor than a real one, as the presence of the editor would indicate that the writer of the letters is in fact dead. As Robert Dessaix is described as living and well, the "editor" seems to me part of the invention, referring to the destiny of the writer of the letters, not to the real author; but of course he may well exist.

[18] The motto was used by Nicholas Poussin, among others.

[19] The whole story of the doctor's breaking the news of his incurable disease to the narrator is told as an "Annunciation", with constant references to painting. The equation is between the Virgin Mary - and the unexplainable event crushing her with its weight - and the man being told of his imminent death.

[20] Dessaix 1997, 14.

[21] Dessaix 1997, 21.

The impact with the city where, in a long literary tradition, characters (and artists) go to die,[22] after celebrating decay and eros and art, is described in Byronic terms, but the relation to Byron is immediately highlighted by a note:

> It's so easy to believe in magic here in Venice. When you first see the city from the train it's like a mirage, like a vision of wild splendour some sorcerer has conjured up far out to sea.[23]

The note quotes immediately the appropriate lines from Canto IV of *Childe Harold's Pilgrimage* ("I saw from out the wave her structure rise / As from the stroke of the enchanter's wand"). If the reader vaguely imagines that the German professor's name, Eschenbaum, might echo Thomas Mann's Aschenbach, towards the end of the book Aschenbach's name explicitly comes up (and is explained in a note). At least two Elizabethan writers are used in the text, the "Notes" explicitly referring to James Howell's *Instruction for Forraine Travel* (1642) and William Lithgow's *Rare Adventures and Painful Peregrinations* (1614).[24]

More generally the story regarding the "disappearing courtesan", but also the story of Professor Eschenbaum, seem to use the traditional lore of Venice as the city of eros and crime, and act contrapuntally. The story of the "disappearing courtesan", told to the narrator by Professor Eschenbaum, is about a courtesan, Donna Scamozzi, who retires from her profession and decides to use her young daughter to obtain wealth. They move from Vicenza to Venice where a rich count Lorenzo is identified as the first "victim". The story is one of plotting and intrigue - exactly as it should be in a Venetian courtesan's story - and ends tragically, if grotesquely. Professor Eschenbaum's adventures regard his foray into a homosexual joint, and his being beaten up and robbed. In both stories the traditional background of Venice as the city of eros, crime, intrigue comes to the foreground, although Eschenbaum's adventure sounds like a present-day parody of the courtesan's story, and at the same time of Thomas Mann's novella. Eschenbaum's homosexual frequentations are a debased version of Aschenbach's passion for Tadzio, rendered in the grotesque mode of Coover's *Pinocchio*. Venice is also described as the city of Marco Polo and Casanova, whose adventures are kept in written records: texts building up the macrotext of Venice, amply used by Dessaix, reflecting no doubt, once more, the city where "the smell of death and hopelessness will never be eradicated".[25]

Even when, in a moment of pure admiration for the "golden orb" of the Customs House at the beginning of the Grand Canal, the narrator evokes the other myth of Venice, that of her wealth and commerce, the lurid Venice of whores and the Rialto usurers (the latter obviously with a Shakespearean tinge) comes in. The narrator's time

---

[22] One can think of such great artists as Browning, Strawinsky, Pound.
[23] Dessaix 1997, 55.
[24] These are the spellings and versions of the two titles offered by Dessaix; the exact titles are *Instructions for Forreine Travell* and *A Most Delectable And True Discourse, of an admired and painefull peregrination from Scotland to the most famous Kingdoms in Europe, Asia and Affricke* (Pfister 1996, 491, 499).
[25] Dessaix 1997, 130.

seems for a while in suspension in his consciousness ("Time simply crumpled. I have no idea how long I stood there - it hardly matters") and he imagines ancient Venice:

> Round St. George's Island they must have come in those days, right to the point I was now standing on, gazing east. And the breeze must have been perfumed with nutmeg and cinnamon, saffron and pepper, and scores of strange languages must have swarmed in the air. And up by the Rialto Bridge the bags of gold and silver must have been dragged from the strongrooms, the moneylenders rubbing their hands, while the middlemen, victuallers, whores and pedlars readied themselves to ply their trade.[26]

One could thus underline how the representation of Venice in this book on the one hand is adjourned only in appearance to modernity by means of the causes of one's going to it (AIDS, but basically the imminence of death); on the other hand it is renewed once more by the clever juxtaposition of different materials, without ever really abandoning the black Venice tradition.

One could also add that a number of really existing writers and critics are also part of this very "literary" book: from Indian novelist Vikram Seth, to Agatha Christie, to Simon Schama, to Bruce Chatwin, to Salman Rushdie. The game Dessaix plays is basically a game with literature but the result rings true: literature is part of our life. The city in this book is more of a literary city than an existing one, but it does achieve credibility as a city of words.

---

[26] Dessaix 1997, 112.

Bibliography

Byron: *Poetical Works*, ed. F.Page. Oxford 1970.
Dessaix, Robert: *Night Letters*. Sydney 1996.
Genette, Gérard: *Seuils*. Paris 1987.
Layton, Irving: *Il freddo verde elemento*. Torino 1974.
Mamoli Zorzi, Rosella: "Venice in XX Century American Poetry". In: Kanceff, Emanuele (ed.): *Foreign Travellers in Venezia*, Genève 1981, 61-80.
Mamoli Zorzi, Rosella: "Lord Byron e Venezia". *Ateneo Veneto* 175 (1988), 243-255.
Mamoli Zorzi, Rosella: "The Text is the City: The Representation of Venice in Two Tales by Irving and Poe and a Novel by Cooper". *RSA* 6 (1990), 285-300.
Marinetti, Filippo: "Manifesti". In: De Maria, Luciano (ed.): *Per conoscere Marinetti e il futurismo*. Milano 1973.
Pemble, John: *The Mediterranean Passion*. Oxford 1988.
Pemble, John: *Venice Rediscovered*. Oxford 1995.
Pfister, Manfred (ed.): *The Fatal Gift of Beauty. The Italies of British Travellers. An Annotated Anthology*. Amsterdam 1996.
Phillips, Caryl: *The Nature of Blood*. New York 1997.
Pavanello, Giuseppe, Romanelli, Giandomenico: *Venezia nell'Ottocento*. Milano 1983.
Pound, Ezra. *The Spirit of Romance*. London 1952.
Tanner, Tony: *Venice Desired*. Cambridge/Mass. 1992.

Judith Seaboyer

Robert Coover's *Pinocchio in Venice*: An Anatomy of a Talking Book

Given the evidence in this volume for the longstanding fascination of Venice for the anglophone imagination, perhaps it should come as no surprise that Robert Coover's *Pinocchio in Venice* (1991) is one of a flood of Venice novels written in English and published in the 1990s. Even before the English Renaissance, when Thomas Nashe invented a visit for *The Unfortunate Traveller* and Shakespeare staged *The Merchant of Venice* and *Othello*, Venice had come to serve as a trope for an urbanised, civilised perfection whose underside was a seductive - and conveniently foreign - sink for greed, lust, and deceit.[1] It was with the rise of Romanticism, however, that it truly became a key symbolic landscape for English literature. The attraction of the Other persisted, but by the end of the eighteenth century, its status as a world trading power no more than a memory and a thousand years of independence at an end, Venice became the perfect stage and the perfect metaphor for Romantic loss, and for the horror of moral failure. For similar if sometimes more self-righteous reasons it continued to be important for the Victorians - Ruskin, for example, saw in the fall of this island republic a warning for England, grown fat on the spoils of empire - but after the turn of century, while it didn't cease altogether, literary production waned. It seemed as though, as Henry James had noted, with a self-consciously disingenuous rhetorical flourish, there was "nothing more to be said on the subject."[2]

By 1902 James had published his last Venice fiction and his last Venice essay and, after 1907, he ceased even to visit. The contemporary account continued to be produced and to find a wide readership - neither Mary McCarthy's nor Jan (James) Morris's, for example, have ever been out of print - and Pound and Anthony Hecht contributed to the tradition of Venice poetry in English. What I find intriguing, though, is that in the first eighty years of the century fewer than twenty Venice fictions seem to have been published, and while they include *The Wings of the Dove* (1902) and

---

[1] Tony Tanner refers to Sir John Mandeville's prototypical and influential *Travels*, first published in Anglo-Norman French in 1356–57 and soon translated into English, and he credits a description by Sir Roger Ascham (1570) as identifying "Venice as a place, *the* place, of love, lechery, sensuality, prostitution *as well as* a place of wise rulers, and just laws" (Tanner 1992, 5).

[2] This comes from the opening paragraphs of his essay "Venice," first published in *Century Magazine* in 1882. He quickly qualified his statement by adding that when it comes to writing about Venice "the old is better than any novelty" and that "[i]t would be a sad day indeed when there should be something new to say" (*Italian Hours* 1), presumably since that could mean either that the city had been desecrated by the ill-considered and poorly executed renovation and modernisation Ruskin had warned against, or - perhaps worse - that it had been successfully saved from its gorgeous decline. For all that he considered it to have become nothing more than "a battered peep-show and bazaar" (7), he went on to write two novels and a novella and three more essays for which Venice is the focus.

Frederick Rolfe's decadent masterpiece *The Desire and Pursuit of the Whole* (1909, pub. 1934), most of them are much less substantial than these.[3]

As we approach the millennium, however, there has been a remarkable increase in the production of Venice fiction. Ten novels were published in the eighties alone and, by my count, three dozen from 1990 to 1998.[4] Some of the new writing is genre fiction - detective, historical, gothic, romance, and various combinations of these[5] - trading, sometimes to very good effect, on Venice's historical reputation for duplicity and secrecy and its ongoing popularity as a tourist and honeymoon destination. But well over half of it may be classified as literary fiction. Novelists like Ian McEwan (*The Comfort of Strangers* 1981), Barry Unsworth (*Stone Virgin* 1985), Michèle Roberts (*The Book of Mrs Noah* 1987), Jeanette Winterson (*The Passion* 1987), Robert Coover (*Pinocchio in Venice* 1991), Maggie Gee (*Where Are the Snows* (1991), Harold Brodkey (*Profane Friendship* 1994), Rod Jones (*Night Pictures* 1997), Caryl Phillips (*The Nature of Blood* 1997), and Louis Begley (*Mistler's Exit* 1998), are drawn to Venice for much the same reasons as their "popular" counterparts, but their writing is also part of a tradition of writing about Venice that is linked to a broader literary continuum that interprets and shapes culture by reading and writing cities. *Pinocchio in Venice* is paradigmatic in that it is an overt response to Thomas Mann's *Death in Venice* and at the same time it is an overtly postmodernist response to James Joyce's quintessential modernist city novel, *Ulysses*. Joyce's Dublin is not a modernist space, and Coover's Venice is not a postmodernist one: each city is something of a cultural and technological backwater. But standing waters can be rich, and Joyce sees in his city, as Coover sees in Venice, a historical matrix in which the traces of a cultural past, present, and future are held in synchronous, kaleidoscopic suspension. Joyce reworks three thousand years of Western literary history within his Dublin world in little, on a single June day in 1904. Coover constructs a similar linguistic *teatro del mondo* in fin-de-millénaire Venice, during the four days leading up to *martedì grasso*, the highpoint of carnival, and this essay will consider the renovatory effects of that construction in terms of literature and contemporary literary theory.

---

[3] It is of course difficult to trace "popular" fiction once it is out of print, and so it is difficult to confirm these figures, but I have taken account of the Marciana's eccentric Tursi Collection, a gift made to the library of modern non-Italian literature set in Venice. I thank Marino Zorzi, director of the library, for giving me access to this archive.

[4] This number doesn't include novels in translation, or those in which Venice plays only a small if significant role.

[5] Examples include Anne Rice's gothic romance *Cry to Heaven* (1982); historical novels by David Thompson (*The Mirrormaker* 1993) and Ross King (*Domino* 1995); detective novels by Donna Leon (the Guido Brunetti series, 1992-98), Anthony Appiah (*Another Death in Venice* 1995), and Michael Dibdin (*Dead Lagoon* 1994); and romances by Erica Jong (*Serenissima* 1987), Ardythe Ashley (*The Christ of the Butterflies* 1991), and Judith Krantz (*Lovers* 1994).

Venetian civitas and museal desire

The interest Venice holds for urban theorists is instructive. Despite its physical vulnerability and social instability, contemporary urban planners venerate Venice as a lost and longed for model of *civitas*, a city that grew into its ideal wholeness in response to a community's changing needs and desires, and now rests in perfect, perfected stasis. The material traces of the order of meaning by which the West has constructed itself are preserved here in a kind of time warp, and as edge cities and malls seem to sprawl out of control, flattening before them both history and the landscape which once defined the boundary between city and country, Venice, its feminised body exposed to the world's gaze, promises a meaningful story of the past. This is, of course, only one view, and writers like Coover recognise any such promise of plenitude to be profoundly illusory. He favours instead the second city of fluid meanings and border crossings discovered behind the fixed classical mask. *Pinocchio in Venice* describes in realistic detail the constructed city, the acknowledged work of art, but is determinedly, deliciously situated in its abject other. Venice is

> the last outpost of the self-enclosed Renaissance *Urbs* ...a kind of itchy boundary between everywhere and somewhere, between simultaneity and history, process and stasis, geometry and optics, extension and unity, velocity and object, between product and art,[6]

and, most uncomfortably in these days of industrial pollution and *acqua alta*, between land and water. Pinocchio's redemption follows the Lion of San Marco's carnivalesque revelation that the city as work of art is a fraud, "a kind of mask the old Queen put on to hide her cankers and pox pits." Its "true face", "dark and filthy" but nonetheless beautiful, is worn, of course, on its carnivalesque behind. The traces of this Venice, founded piecemeal by migrations of desperate refugees fleeing a succession of invasions, may still be discerned in the backwaters of Canareggio and Castello, but they are largely masked by the construction of the heroic narrative of a heavenly ordained urban utopia, and what the Lion terms "bloody glorious empire."[7]

Repetition and the death drive

Pinocchio in Venice is both a retelling of and a sequel to Carlo Collodi's children's story *The Adventures of Pinocchio*, first published in serial form in 1881-82. At the end of the original story, the wooden puppet has undergone a metamorphosis to become a flesh-and-blood adolescent boy;[8] at the beginning of Coover's, he's over a century old, and fast reverting to wood. Despite the promise of the conclusion of Collodi's story, Pinocchio's life as "a proper boy" has been a disappointment. Like many young Italians, he left behind village life for the New World, where he

---

[6] Coover 1991, 20.
[7] Coover 1991, 291.
[8] Collodi 1986, 456–61.

anglicised his name to Pinenut, got himself an education, and spent time in Hollywood as an actor and as a scriptwriter. Determined to live up to the Blue Fairy's faith in him, (in other words, driven by filial guilt), he turned his back on Californian hedonism for the cloistered and virtuous life of an academic. This act of second-stage repression ensured his lifelong misery. Now a "world-renowned art historian and critic, social anthropologist, moral philosopher, and theological gadfly"[9] and professor emeritus at an American East Coast University, he is as comically repressed and self-righteous as the puppet was irrepressibly wicked, and he is as self-deluded as ever. His quest in search of self is not over, and one by one on his journey through the Venetian labyrinth, he will repeat his old puppet mistakes - misjudgements that in his former life had led to a catalogue of trials including death by hanging, death by drowning, metamorphosis into a donkey and, by far the most painful, a series of separations from the Blue Fairy, whose maternal "tough love" included not just disappearing but regularly pretending to have died of grief because of Pinocchio's failure to behave as a dutiful son.

His plane has been diverted to Milan because Marco Polo airport is fogbound, and so he arrives in Venice by train. From the moment he crosses the threshold at Santa Lucia Station, he enters a labyrinthine space of transformation that is a dizzying pastiche of Hades, Saturnalia, mystery cycle, and *commedia dell'arte*, a wonderfully abject mixture of Dante's *Purgatorio*, Bloom's Nighttown, Prufrock's fogbound city, and Aschenbach's Venice, and he contains something of each of these travellers.

Collodi's Pinocchio was Tuscan[10] but for the kinds of reasons discussed above Coover leads him "home" not to Florence or Pisa, either of which might have stood in for his unnamed birthplace, but to Venice, a city that has no place in the original story. Pinocchio has been drawn back to his "roots" because he feels Venice holds the key to the completion of his *capo lavoro*, tellingly named "*Mamma*." In keeping with his flair for contemporary confessional criticism, it is to be

> a vast autobiographical tapestry in which are woven all the rich, varied strands of his unique personal destiny under the single predominating theme of virtuous love and the lonely ennobling labor that gives it exemplary substance...but the book's conclusion, like rectitude itself in an earlier unhappier time, continues to elude him.[11]

---

[9] Coover 1991, 47.

[10] Carlo Lorenzini was born in Florence, and he took the pen name Collodi from the Tuscan town in which his mother was born. Nicolas Perella, in his excellent introduction to his parallel text of Collodi's *The Adventures of Pinocchio*, notes that although there is some disagreement, "not a few Italian readers have claimed that the environments in *Pinocchio* bear the unmistakable character of Tuscany," and they note not just signs of "a mid-nineteenth-century Tuscan mentality" but "a characteristic recourse to linguistic provincialism and witticisms - the famous *arguzia toscana*"(Perella 1986, 1, 63). Coover produces a parodic late-twentieth-century *Venetian* mentality, and replaces *arguzia toscana* with Venetian dialect slang crossed with traditional *commedia* dialogue and carnivalesque curses and blasphemy.

[11] Coover 1991, 14.

On another level Pinocchio knows he has come home to die, and the opening pages present a *mise-en-abyme* that foreshadows the vertiginous nature of *Pinocchio in Venice*. To complete his oeuvre, Professor Pinenut is entering the body of the city that is itself "a universally acknowledged work of art" and that gave birth to his career as an art historian, and he is returning to the place of his actual birth, to complete his life, which he also happens to view as "a work of art."[12]

Venetian Metamorphoses

Two aspects of Coover's text reinforce this sense of Pinocchio's experience of the city as a kind of vortex. First, he takes up the familiar Venetian leitmotif of metamorphosis and, second, he structures his text in terms of Menippean satire, and Bakhtinian dialogism and the carnivalesque.

First, it is a literary commonplace that Venice is, like Pinocchio, the product of a metamorphosis, a magical transformation of nature into art. Byron's Childe Harold sees a fairy-tale city conjured up from the mud of the lagoon "at the stroke of an enchanter's wand,"[13] and Ruskin a city made of frost-bound breakers transfixed into glittering marble and crenellated stone set with semi-precious jewels.[14] Pound, with Dante's dark wood as well as the reality of the city's foundation on millions of piles made from Istrian pine transmuted by water into stone in mind, describes "a forest of marble,"[15] and Witi Ihimaera's Venice is a manifestation of Hawaiki, the luminous mythic Maori citadel anchored at the navel of the universe.[16] Coover's city, on the other hand, is undergoing a world-upside-down metamorphosis that will return it to the Real of its swampy origins. In San Sebastiano, the paintings and frescoes come alive to torment him, and like scenes from a macabre Disney animation, pews "[slide] apart and then together again with great clashing noises like monstrous gates," and the floor rises and falls and splits apart beneath his feet to reveal heaps of bones.[17] *Acqua alta* turns the Piazza San Marco and its surrounding buildings into a storm-tossed ship about to loose its moorings from the surrounding labyrinth and carry its ancient mariners out to sea and a delicious "watery doom."[18] As though Hell were yawning beneath it, whole sections of San Michele heave and tremble, and headstones are sucked into oblivion before Pinocchio's eyes.[19] This destruction will be hastened by a rebirth of the ruthless entrepreneurism that once made the Serenissima great. In a discomfiting burlesque of reality, Coover's Venice is being sold off to become a kind of time-share resort for the feckless rich, and there are plans for dredging "a channel

---

[12] Coover 1991, 14.
[13] Byron 1986, 4.1.
[14] Ruskin 1851–53, Vol.2, 67–68.
[15] Pound 1964, Canto XVII.
[16] Ihimaera 1986, 430.
[17] Coover 1991, 128.
[18] Coover 1991, 185.
[19] Coover 1991, 216.

deep enough for sixty-thousand-ton tankers [to service] the Third Industrial Zone, making the Veneto region the rival of Osaka, Manchester, and New Jersey."[20]

In true Romantic style, Pinocchio's human flesh is undergoing a mirroring metamorphosis, as it becomes a bundle of wooden sticks. The physical manifestations of his great age are not rheumatism or hardening of the arteries but dry rot and infestations of woodworm, and he has become so thin a friend is moved sadly to observe, "They could use you as a foldout in an anatomy book."[21] It's a nice piece of self-reflexivity that leads me to my second point.

Menippean satire, Bakthinian carnivalesque, and the dialogic

Pinocchio in Venice fulfils the broad requirements of the Menippean satire, or literary anatomy, as defined by Mikhail Bakhtin and by Northrop Frye. An anatomy mockingly dissects a wide range of abstract ideas as well as contemporary theories and issues; indeed, Bakhtin sees it as "the testing of an *idea*, of a *truth* [or] philosophical position" rather than of a particular human character or type. The menippea is the adventure of an idea; the protagonist is simply its vehicle.[22] It is structured around such set pieces as parodically erudite digressions, deipnosophistical interpolations (feasts accompanied by mock-philosophical speeches and dialogues), dialogues of the threshold, and dialogues with the dead.[23] It is marked by "a special type of *experimental fantasticality*" and representations of insanity that include "passions bordering on madness"[24] - what Frye refers to as "diseases of the intellect" and "maddened pedantry"[25] - and Bakhtin drives home the links between the menippea and the carnivalesque. For example, both are distinguished by sharp contrasts and transitions from one position to another and by ambiguous oppositions whose design is to reveal that all things are interrelated. For example, the sacred can be profaned because it carries within itself the seeds of its profanation, the fool or servant is crowned only to be decrowned, the wise man's folly is exposed and the fool shown to be wise and, just as surely as birth leads to death, ritual death leads to renewal. Since everything contains within itself the potential of its opposite, everything is ambivalent and nothing is ever final: the carnivalised world is always in a state of becoming.[26]

Frye illustrates his discussion with references to Apuleius's *The Golden Ass*, Burton's *The Anatomy of Melancholy*, Swift's *Gulliver's Travels*, Sterne's *Tristram Shandy*, Kingsley's *Water Babies*, and Joyce's *Ulysses*, all of which are intertexts for Coover. In the course of Coover's anatomy, not only will Pinocchio's body undergo a Dionysiac dismemberment, but his intellectual and professional positions within late-

---

[20] Coover 1991, 202, 203.
[21] Coover 1991, 72.
[22] Bakhtin 1984, 114–15.
[23] Frye 1957, 308-12; Bakhtin 1984, 114–19.
[24] Bakhtin 1984, 116.
[25] Frye 1957, 309.
[26] Bakhtin 1984, 124–25.

twentieth-century academic discourse will be dissected and revealed to be, like the old professor himself, pedantic, solipsistic, fraudulent, and ludicrous. From this new perspective, the puppet's turning "from bad to good" that resulted in his acquisition of human subjectivity,[27] complete with a viciously well developed superego, looks less like salvation than corruption. In order to be redeemed, he must undergo a last Dionysiac and parodically Dantean metamorphosis in the course of which not only his sins and imperfections but his hard-won human flesh will be painfully stripped away so that he may be lifted from the dry rot, the "appalling human sickness"[28] which characterises his life of the mind and returned to the grotesque bodiliness and changeful becomingness of the puppet. Pinenut will be tortured and killed so that the puppet may be reborn and, paradoxically, this process, which includes a cruelly comic purification by fire in a pizza oven,[29] will "humanize him [as] ambivalent carnival laughter burns away all that is stilted and stiff" to restore his "heroic core."[30]

As a site of the carnivalesque, Venice further suits Coover's mocking purpose in that since 1980 local authorities have resurrected carnival to keep the tourists coming during what used to be the low season. It's been a commercially successful but inevitably somewhat bloodless and uncarnivalesque exercise, but Coover's is carnival at its funniest, and blackest.[31] According to the laws of the carnivalesque as Bakhtin famously explained them, not only Professor Pinenut but also Coover and his reader will be drawn into this theatre-without-footlights. While Pinocchio is mocked as the Menippean *philosophus gloriosus*, Coover, in the masterly creation of this intellectually stunning text, takes up with brio the role of the mocked virtuoso.[32] The role of critical reader is less comfortable. As I undertake the dismemberment of this text, as I attempt to peel back Coover's textual laminations and fix the grotesque vitality of his protagonist and his "disintegrating but multilaminous island"[33] into something resembling the kind of coherence required of an academic essay, I am faced with the folly of such an enterprise. Inevitably I flatten his comic savagery and

---

[27] Collodi 1986, 456–61.
[28] Coover 1991, 285.
[29] Coover 1991, 271.
[30] Bakhtin 1984, 133.
[31] *Pinocchio in Venice* is Coover's second rewriting of Collodi's story. The first, *The Public Burning*, is also a highly carnivalised, dialogic novel, although as Jackson Cope points out, Coover could not have read or even known about Bakhtin by the time that novel was completed. The influence of carnival came to him first through literary history rather than through literary theory (Cope 1986, 72).
[32] Cope notes that Coover "exists" in *The Public Burning*, through "dozens of allusions to his former novels, to his own novelistic obsessions. "He sees him as rendered "a bit singer in his own chorale, "pushed aside by the "cacophony of views, overlapping of voices "in that text (Cope 1986, 71–72). The same could be said for *Pinocchio* except that Coover also, self-mockingly, inhabits the body of his protagonist. Pinenut teaches at an East Coast university, for example, and when, near the end of his life, he nestles into the soft bosom of the Blue Fairy, it reminds him of a cornfield in Iowa. Coover is a member of the faculty at Brown University, and by birth an Iowan.
[33] Coover 1991, 295.

revitalising power, and I find myself in the role of Menippean loquacious pedant, a figure for the contemporary theoretical obsessions that have rendered Pinocchio "stilted and stiff."

Venice is the perfect setting, too, for Coover's virtuoso exegesis of Bakhtinian dialogism. Coover places himself in a long line of literary thieves of language in the construction of his text, and raids the history of western literature, art, architecture, and philosophy, much as Venice raided the Eastern Mediterranean in its self-construction as a legible, urban text. *Pinocchio in Venice* is like the façade of San Marco, a collage of disparate bits and pieces that are nonetheless of a piece. Coover brings dozens of heterogeneous literary historical voices into dialogic collision and coexistence in a single moment in time and space, and this linguistic chaos brims with potential. In a Rabelaisian feast of scatology, profanity, and learned allusion, he takes up where Collodi left off and parodies and brings into "joyful relativity" an encyclopedic selection of western literature. In addition to the texts already mentioned, he brings to his dialogue fragments from (for example) the Christian gospels and "The Dream of the Rood," Plato's *Phaedrus*, Euripides' *The Bacchae*, Rabelais' *Gargantua and Pantagruel*, Congreve's *The Double Dealer*, Gogol's "The Overcoat," Ruskin's *The Stones of Venice*, Nietzsche's *The Birth of Tragedy*, Eliot's *The Love Song of J. Alfred Prufrock*, Pound's *Hugh Selwyn Mauberley*, Calvino's *If On a Winter's Night a Traveller*, Derrida's "Plato's Pharmacy," and his own *The Public Burning*. Such an anatomisation is a destructive process, but each text becomes part of a flexible structural frame that is grotesque in its Joycean "Here Comes Everybody" capacity to extend, incorporate, and transform. For example, Joyce, Bakhtin, and Derrida all, like Coover, engage in word play that is eccentric and communicative, and along with Dante, Pound, Eliot, Mann, and the writers of the gospels, they all expand the horizons of their own texts by writing in the margins of other people's. By means of linguistic bellylaughter, Coover skilfully brings all these texts into contact as he reinterprets them in the light of each other. It is part of a literary tradition, but at the same time it is, in the words of Coover's female *commedia* hero Columbina, "a whole new lazzo."[34] By means of this carnivalesque destruction and renewal, he offers alternative endings for a huddle of angst-ridden wandering literary heroes who haunt Pinenut's journey.

Purgatorial Venice

Coover's is in a long line of rereadings of Dante, which include those of Collodi, Eliot, and Pound. The latter is, like Dante and like Coover's Pinocchio, an exile with links to Venice, and it is interesting to contrast his response to Dante with Coover's.[35] The *Cantos* are structurally and thematically based on the *Commedia*, and *Hugh Selwyn*

---

[34] Coover 1991, 307.

[35] In political exile from Florence, Dante wrote the *Commedia* in Ravenna and spent time in nearby Venice. Unlike Pinocchio he was not able to return home. The Arsenale is said to have influenced the hellish imagery in the *Inferno*; Coover renders the whole city hellish.

Mauberley is an ironic inversion of it. In the latter, Dante's dignity is replaced by Mauberley's self-pity, an inheritance of classical, Italian, and Provençal poetry gives way to nineties decadence, and love fails.[36] Coover's pilgrim is self-pitying, and dignity has always escaped him. He throws tantrums, for example, when his university attempts to withdraw his franking privileges, or deprive him of his second office, and in the crisis that leads to the first Menippean dialogue of the threshold at Santa Lucia Station, La Volpe is able to play on his irascibility to steal first his dignity and then his precious manuscript. He blames his failure to command respect on the fact that he has never managed to look the part of the scholar philosopher. Not only does his recalcitrant nose continue to make a fool of him, but he complains that even after he "put on flesh" he continued "to look like a spindly unstrung puppet...a veritable insult to the rules of human proportion - where was the heroic frame, the hairy chest, *where - someone has a lot to answer for! - were the powerful thighs?*"[37]

Dante's *Commedia*, like Collodi's and Coover's stories, hinges on metamorphosis and the Christian drama. Coover borrows the doubled structure of the *Purgatorio* as Pinocchio undertakes a literal journey through a city that becomes the intermediate, liminal space that lies between the *Inferno* of his life as a human subject and the *Paradiso* that will succeed it. A parallel spiritual journey takes him toward a level of understanding that will enable him to discard intellectual knowledge - philosophy - in favour of love. During four days over Easter, Dante Pilgrim journeys toward Beatrice and redemption; in the four days leading to the culmination of carnival before the grim days of Lent, Pinocchio travels through Venice-as-purgatory, toward the Blue Fairy. Like Dante, he has been lost in a dark wood and he has lived a life of exile. Like Dante, he is driven by the desire to know that is underpinned by another, less worthy desire, for fame. And as with Dante the constant inspiration of his life's work has been a long-dead girl he fell in love with when they were both children, and she has since, like Beatrice, watched his every move, and marked his every error.

An abiding theme of the *Purgatorio* is reunion and reconciliation, and Dante brings together not only old friends, enemies, families, and lovers, but dispersed communities of texts. In carnivalised Venice Pinocchio is reunited with the ghosts of his past as, within the text, dozens of disparate literary voices are brought into dialogue. Dante is spiritually reunited with Beatrice, a type of Christ. Pinocchio's reunion with the Blue Fairy, on the other hand, is concerned ultimately with the body rather than the soul.

In the century that has followed the publication of Collodi's *Pinocchio*, a flourishing industry has developed that encompasses long-nosed souvenir puppets and masks hawked at shops and market stalls in Italy and in Little Italies from Toronto to Melbourne, together with adaptations in various media. Disney's 1940 animated film - a "vandal's raid" Jackson Cope notes has already been repulsed by Coover with *The Public Burning*[38] - is still widely available on video and is re-released in cinemas from time to time. Perella points out that more recently the academy has taken "this most

---

[36] Hutcheon 1989, 88.
[37] Coover 1991, 118.
[38] Cope 1986, 16.

fortunate of Italy's minor classics" to its heart, because of the subtlety of its linguistic and narrative strategies, its literary and sociocultural allusiveness, and its use of archetypal patterns and images.[39] At conferences and in scholarly journals *Pinocchio* is earnestly compared to Odysseus, Aeneas, Christ, and Dante, and even to Renzo, the working-class hero of Manzoni's revered political novel *I Promessi Sposi*.[40] (It is no comfort to be reminded I am not alone in my loquacious pedantry!)

Coover's *Pinocchio*, then, parodies as it joins a tradition of adaptation and interpretation that includes popular and academic culture. But Coover is manifestly outside the tradition, too, in that his reading of Collodi's puppet is as expansive and all-encompassing as most translations, rewritings, and interpretations have been "monolithically reductive."[41]

Perella notes that "Collodi himself was among the first to feel uneasy about [his] tale's ending...which he once told a friend he could not remember having written [though] the manuscript copy leaves no doubt." In what he suggests "may well be the story's cruellest image," the chestnut-haired, blue-eyed "real boy" eyes his discarded puppet self "propped against a chair, its head turned to one side, its arms dangling, and its legs crossed and folded in the middle so that it was a wonder that it stood up at all." He says "with a great deal of satisfaction: 'How funny I was when I was a puppet! And how glad I am now that I've become a proper boy!'"[42] "His subsequent uneasiness," suggests Perella, "betrays the ambivalent attitude he had toward his wayward, unregimented puppet and the deep-rooted sympathy he had for the free-living street kid."[43]

Coover takes advantage of Collodi's ambivalence toward his protagonist to address questions relating to the acquisition of bourgeois subjectivity and to "rescue" Pinocchio. As he does so he emphasises ambivalences in Mann's semi-autobiographical novella about artistic creativity and the role of the writer in the early twentieth century.[44] The result is a seriously funny critique, and a self-reflexively parodic study of the role of the artist and thinker in Coover's own historical moment - our historical moment - of literary and theoretical discontent. Aschenbach's earnest tones may be heard in Pinocchio's thoughts from Coover's opening pages. For example, his own great epic, *Maia* (the mother of Hermes), a "richly patterned tapestry...that gathers up the threads of many human destinies in the warp of a single

---

[39] Perella 1986, 2, 5.
[40] Perella 1986, 4.
[41] Perella 1986, 2.
[42] Perella 1986, 54–55; Collodi 1986, 460–61.
[43] Perella 1986, 55.
[44] In an autobiographical sketch, Mann states that a trip to the Lido furnished him with all the material for the novella, and that his task was merely to interpret it. Like his protagonist (and like Pinenut), he was at a literary standstill, and at a crossroads in his development (Gronicka 1964, 46; Reed 1974, 149). Like Pinocchio, Aschenbach comes to Venice because he finds himself unable to complete the work he has undertaken: "it would not yield either to patient effort, or a swift *coup de main*" (Mann 1989, 7, 8).

idea,"[45] sounds suspiciously like Pinocchio's *Mamma*. Both men have spent their adult lives striving for perfection, in the pursuit of idealised beauty and truth, and both have achieved a public dignity Mann and Coover agree to be inimical to the artistic imagination. Both doubt their intellectual capabilities, and both are physically frail; their success is a "heroism born of weakness."[46] Both are deeply dissatisfied, both are drawn with uncharacteristic spontaneity to visit Venice, and both will die there. Both see premonitory visions on arriving in the city: Aschenbach sees an old fop pretending to be a youth, and Pinocchio a crazed figure fleeing through the streets. Aschenbach will "become" the fool he despised, as Pinocchio will "become" the fleeing madman, *and* Aschenbach's fool. Each has a strange encounter with an impertinent gondolier, and each has problems with missing luggage, which lead to an immersion in the city that would not otherwise have occurred. Each contemplates his life from a deck chair on a Venetian beach, though Aschenbach's beach is the Lido and Pinocchio, whose meeting with carnival has snatched him from wealth and respectability into homelessness, occupies the no-man's-land where a derelict boatyard meets the lagoon. Both have doubts about being in Venice at all but their desire for what lies beyond the pleasure principle means neither has any intention of leaving. Both feverishly hunt an unsuitably young lover through the labyrinth, and both delude themselves as to the nature of their passion with parodic readings of Plato's *Phaedrus*. Aschenbach dreams of a Dionysiac orgy, and Pinocchio's carnivalesque rebirth depends on his becoming the object of its terrifying reality.

Homer's *Odyssey* is an intertext for Collodi, but it is Joyce's response that is most clearly heard in *Pinocchio in Venice*. Coover's text shares characteristics with Joyce's in its structure and in its details. For example, Joyce plays on his text as anatomy by devoting different sections to different bodily organs. Coover in turn devotes sections to the ear (Pinocchio's are the first of his organs to be shed, reminding us he never was much of a listener), the tongue, the intestines, the kidneys, the flesh, the skeleton, the locomotor apparatus, and the genitals. Pinocchio's famous phallic nose is the only organ to remain in good working order until the end. It continues to embarrass him almost until the moment of his death, but in true carnivalesque fashion, what was folly for Aschenbach is revealed to be wisdom for Pinocchio as he is led by the "nose" to paradise in the arms of the Blue Fairy.

Dublin and Venice are distinguished by the juxtaposition of land and water - along with the littoral, tidal space of its Bay and the Liffey, both of which are central to the narrative construction of *Ulysses*, Dublin even has a Grand Canal. Both texts reflect the liminality of their topography, subsuming earlier texts, breaking them down and bringing them together in a destructive-reconstructive flood of words. For all that both are in some respects so novelistically realistic that routes may be traced down to the narrowest lanes and alleys, both are labyrinthine, disorienting, and nightmarish. Both are filled with the hubbub of hundreds of voices - those of their protagonists

---

[45] Mann 1989, 7. Compare Coover 1991, 14.
[46] Mann 1989, 11.

competing with those of their intertexts. Both are peopled with ghosts, including Stephen Dedalus's revenant mother and the Blue Fairy (Pinocchio's surrogate mother) who, from her inception in Collodi's text, has never been able to make up her mind whether she is dead or alive. Bloom and Pinocchio each pay a visit to "Hades," represented by a cemetery.[47]

Both contain set pieces devoted to Platonic discourse in libraries: Joyce's "Scylla and Charybdis" section is set in the National Library in Dublin and Coover's chapter 21, "Plato's Prank," in the Salone Sansoviniano of the Libreria Marciana, the original Venetian state library. Pinocchio, perched between Plato and Aristotle who have been his own Scylla and Charybdis and whose portraits flank the entry to the Salone, rehearses a mock-Platonic speech to the Blue Fairy (disguised as Bluebell, a buxom college co-ed) as Phaedrus.[48]

At the end of the Cyclops section, Bloom/Jesus/Moses becomes Elijah as he escapes The Citizen to ascend into heaven amid clouds of angels - "like a shot off a shovel."[49] Pinocchio has visions of angels, too, but he escapes the carabinieri to experience a bathetic descent rather than Bloom's mock apotheosis. Ignoring Arlecchino's warning to stick to him *"like shit to a shovel,"* he is distracted by a glimpse of the Fairy, "just drifting by as though in an angelic vision." He staggers through a tiny underpass, the Sottoportego del'Uva, misses his footing, and as though "pitched from a slick shovel," he undergoes a second lustration, not in Dante's Lethe but in the "slimy ooze" of a side canal, Rio di Santa Margherita.[50]

As the end nears, Pinocchio comes to regret a life in which he rigorously repressed any impulse toward pleasure, and his snappish "No, no, ... that's not what I mean at all"[51] brings into focus echoes of Eliot's Prufrock that have been present since Pinocchio's arrival in Venice. Both men walk the streets of an unreal city in search of an elusive answer. On his arrival at Santa Lucia, Pinocchio's aged body makes its way along the platform "like a crab," reminding us of Prufrock, whose tough outer shell has protected him from pain but also from love and who, in his loneliness, soliloquizes: "I should have been a pair of ragged claws / Scuttling across the floors of silent seas."[52] When his old enemy Il Gatto, disguised as a female tourist bureau clerk, drops his key, it "clatters to the floor like a coffee spoon."[53] Both cities are wreathed in fog. It "rubs," "licks," "lingers," "slips," and "curls" about Prufrock's city and, yet another avatar of the shape-shifting Blue Fairy, it haunts Pinocchio's: "swirling," "coiling," "like teasing wisps of bluish hair," it exacerbates his short-sightedness and the descending fog of

---

[47] Joyce 1968, Ch. 6 "Hades"; Coover 1991, Ch. 19 "At L'Omino's Tomb "and Ch. 20 "The Original Wet Dream."
[48] Coover 1991, 236.
[49] Joyce 1968. 449.
[50] Coover 1991, 140, 154, 155.
[51] Coover 1991, 175; Eliot 1917, l. 97.
[52] Coover 1991, 15; Eliot 1917, l. 73–74.
[53] Coover 1991, 17; Eliot 1917, l. 51.

old age.[54] Prufrock holds up a mirror to Professor Pinenut's sorry hairless thinness and to his fussy sartorial vanity as well as to his much-regretted failure to have "dared," and his dawning realisation that he may indeed have been "obtuse," "ridiculous," "the Fool." He predicts people will say of him: "How his hair is growing thin!" and "how his arms and legs are thin!" A friend, on seeing Pinocchio's body, sighs "He's thin as a nail, he's lost all his hair."[55]

The Bakthinian loophole and the politics of bourgeois subjectivity

The text as anatomy reflected in the body-in-bits-and-pieces is reinforced by the repetitious use of that stock scene in Menippean satire, the marvellously termed deipnosophistical interpolation. Within an hour or two of Pinocchio's arrival, the first of three Menippean feasts takes place. It's a recapitulation of the dinner the puppet shared with Il Gatto and La Volpe at the Gambero Rosso, the Red Crawfish Inn, in Collodi's *Pinocchio*. The first time, because of his greed and naivety, the young puppet was tricked into parting with the gold coins that were supposed to change his life from poor to rich, from bad to good. This time, Il Gatto and La Volpe are rather thinly disguised behind *commedia* masks. Pinocchio is gulled again. To be fair, he is tempted by what he falsely believes to be a free meal, but this time he's vulnerable not because he's a poor child who would like to be a rich one, but because he's an old man who wants to belong. Again, Pinocchio eats little while his companions consume what is this time a meal of truly gargantuan proportions, but he does join them in drinking rather a lot of good local wine and grappa. Punningly foregrounding the role anatomy will play, the menu includes tripe, sweetbreads, kidneys, "pickled spleen and cooked tendons ... slick and translucent as hospital tubing ... sliced stuffed esophagus [and] calf's liver alla veneziana."[56] In carnivalesque terms, this feast is only a precursor to the one that counts.

Deserted by his companions and lost in "the snowy night" of the Venetian labyrinth, Pinocchio's digestive organs collapse under the assault of so much wine on an all but empty stomach. Other figures appear from his past as he relives the nightmare of his puppet past and the "*galantuomo*, and universally beloved exemplar of industry, veracity, and civility" is apprehended by the law for, among other things, "indecent exposure" and "polluting the environment."[57] Collodi's puppet had friends as well as enemies, however, and Pinocchio is rescued by Alidoro, the police mastiff who in the earlier narrative had rescued him from death-by-frying at the hands of a fisherman. He and his philosophical watch-dog friend Melampetta begin the process of reconstructing Pinocchio's clean and proper wooden body. As the old professor discourses, the dogs deconstruct his confessional monologue *and* his hard-won human

---

[54] Eliot 1917, l.15–22; Coover 1991, 13, 178, 258, 293.
[55] Eliot 1917, l. 117–19, l. 41, 44; Coover 1991, 68–69.
[56] Collodi 1986, 166–69; Coover 1991, 34.
[57] Coover 1991, 47–48.

body with their tongues.[58] Amidst much blasphemy and good-natured Rabelaisian punning, and with a cheerful fortitude that contrasts starkly with Pinocchio's "in spite of" heroism, they lick away his excrement, and make a start on his solipsistic metaphysics and his subjectivity. Careful as they are, "the little duck's as brittle as croccante and flaking like puff pastry"[59] so that they inadvertently lick away scraps of flesh, and an ear.[60] It is the first step toward the revelation, literal and metaphorical, of the puppet beneath ("it's the naked truth we want, the unvarnished reality!"[61] It is an example of Coover's excess-with-a-purpose, since this feasting followed by literal purgation and cleansing links *commedia dell'arte* to that other *Commedia* - the purgation and cleansing undergone by Dante Pilgrim as he makes his way through his *Purgatorio* to seek redemption in the presence of *his* dead beloved, Beatrice. His sins and imperfections, too, are slowly, painfully stripped away until he is a new man.

A third and equally astonishing *cena* is the Dionysiac cannibalism that occurs at the height of carnival. Again, Pinocchio is the feast. Wrapped in pizza dough and baked to a donkey-shaped crisp in memory of an earlier metamorphosis, he's delivered up to a maenadic throng of tourists and Juventus fans, who begin to tear him apart, and eat him. A few fingers and his feet are demolished along with the pizza dough before the *commedia* puppets rescue him and he's flown to safety behind the Teatro Malibran, by the Lion of San Marco. He's reached the heart of the labyrinth, and is one step from his destiny, the lost and longed for body of the Blue Fairy, his Beatrice, his Penelope, his Molly Bloom, his Anna Livia Plurabelle, the first object of his desire.

In order to explain how Coover creates the possibility of Pinocchio's carnivalesque redemption, it is necessary to go back to Derrida. I have mentioned that *Plato's Pharmacy*, Derrida's reading of the *Phaedrus*, is an intertext, and although his voice is not as clearly heard in this dialogic engagement as many others are, its influence is insistent. Coover reminds us that his wooden-headed puppet was born from a wooden log, and in one of a series of droll "wooden" puns that run through his text, he links log to the *logos*, word, logic, reason. This leads him neatly into Derrida's critique of the metaphysics of presence, the privileging of unity over difference, speech over writing.

The *Phaedrus* is central to Mann's *Death in Venice*. He parodically rereads that part of the dialogue which focuses on love, and the role of beauty in guiding us toward a higher realm.[62] Derrida discovers an ambivalence in Plato's attitude to the morality of writing, and also asks, again self-reflexively, whether the writer can ever "cut a respectable figure."[63] These are of course also concerns for Mann. Coover parodies

---

[58] Coover 1991, 66–78.
[59] Coover 1991, 76.
[60] Coover 1991, 99.
[61] Coover 1991, 76.
[62] Mann 1989, 70–71.
[63] Derrida 1981, 74. "Is writing seemly? Does the writer cut a respectable figure? Is it proper to write? Is it done?"

Robert Coover's *Pinocchio in Venice*: An Anatomy of a Talking Book

Mann's version of the dialogue, and Derrida's text informs the whole of *Pinocchio in Venice*.

The dialogue between Plato and Mann and between Plato and Derrida is straightforward, but it is Coover's genius that, by means of his reading of Derrida, he is able to bring Collodi and Mann, who are to say the least an unlikely couple, into jarringly disjunctive yet productive dialogue, bringing to light elements in each that allow for the possibility of new readings. The cruelly repressive aspect of Collodi's *Bildungsroman* is made to chime with Aschenbach's own repression, and Coover focuses on that repression rather than on the "happily ever after" of Pinocchio's metamorphosis into a human child. He rereads Collodi through a darkly carnivalesque lens, interweaving Aschenbach's encounter with Dionysiac passion into a reversal of Collodi's puppet's journey to create an apocalyptic voyage into the labyrinthine Real that is at once funny, and cruelly shocking.

Coover makes this link by means of Derrida's investigation of Plato's use of the word *pharmakon* and its cognates in the *Phaedrus* and elsewhere. In the *Phaedrus* it is used to refer to writing as opposed to speech as a kind of drug, and Derrida uses this to illustrate the difference that constitutes language. He argues that *pharmakon* must be translated as both remedy *and* poison, not as one or the other. Coover takes this up when he reminds us that Collodi's Fairy's gift of life to Pinocchio, which entailed his metamorphosis from puppet to human, hinged on his learning to take her bitter "good medicine" that transformed him into *un ragazzino per-bene*, which might be translated only somewhat ironically as "a bourgeois masculine subject."[64] Coover exploits the element of ambiguity in Collodi's ending to make it clear that the hand the Fairy has dealt Pinocchio is a far from straightforward one. The *Pharmakon*, as Derrida reminds us, always "partakes of both good and ill, of the agreeable and the disagreeable,"[65] and it becomes clear that the Fairy's medicine, her cruel normalising bourgeoisifying pedagogy, may have given Pinocchio life and enabled him to achieve worldly success, but it destroyed in him everything that was life-affirming.

Collodi's story is a didactic fable for children about a puppet who comes to life, but the *subtext* is the construction of a new Italian bourgeoisie. *Pinocchio* was written in the years following Unification, when it was felt that if Italy were to compete with her Northern neighbours, a hardworking bourgeoisie would have to be created from a largely peasant working class, perceived to be lazy and essentially anarchic. Collodi's text is part of that improvement project, and Pinocchio's is an instructive example of the carnivalesque grotesque body that must be excluded in the creation of the modern state. His is a lazy, far from docile, and with that famous nose, inappropriately sexual, body.

But as Perella pointed out, Collodi is ambivalent, and here we have an example of the Bakhtinian loophole that is essential to *Coover's* project. It makes possible the double movement that makes present what was absent. Coover's dialogue with Collodi

---

[64] Collodi 1986, esp. Ch. XVII and Ch. XXXVI.
[65] Derrida 1981, 99.

(via his dialogue with Derrida and Bakhtin) shows the redeemed 'proper boy' who transcends his puppet self to be an unpleasant prig who in Coover's 'sequel' grows up to be a self-absorbed if highly respected fool. It is a reading Collodi would have appreciated, and through the Bakhtinian loophole Coover constructs an alternative narrative that exposes the horror of the bourgeoisification Collodi half recommends, half resists. Everything Pinocchio does in his effort to be good is aimed at pleasing the Blue Fairy, and at regaining oneness with her. In Coover's version, Pinocchio's friends are quick to recognise that her maternal influence has been far from healthy - she is, after all, an avatar of death. Collodi's Fairy is a gruesome necrophiliac who likes to play unpleasant, spooky games with little boys, games which Coover's text reveals are designed to leave them intimidated, guilt-ridden and dependent, to say nothing of sexually perverse. Her medicine, far from doing Pinocchio good, seems to have ruined his life. It is pharmakon as poison.

Mann has said he intended the outcome of *Death in Venice* to be a shift away from his usual coolly analytical style. He had been reading Nietzsche, and considered whether a bringing together of the Apollonian and the Dionysiac might not be the key to a renewal in German art. T.J. Reed's convincing reading suggests that the ambivalences in the text, which include its ambiguous ending and its "strange mixture of enthusiasm and criticism, classical beauty and penetration, elevation and sordidness," may be attributed to the fact that he found himself unable to complete the text as he had planned it, and that it was only finished after he read Lukács's essay on Socrates. Lukács "provided a sterner, potentially moral view at a time when Mann was deeply dissatisfied with the story as he had begun it."[66]

Mann's ambivalence toward contemporary art and the role of the artist is engaged through parody in the irascible, reactionary, monologic views of Professor Pinenut. Art's endeavour must be the ceaseless striving for perfection in which eternity is what counts. History is the bit that goes wrong. Any kind of provisionality is abhorred as some kind of shilly-shallying pluralism. What the world needs is Professor Pinenut's self-righteous 'good medicine,' a good dose of absolutes.

But Pinocchio learns much through his suffering, and as he dies he rejects the self he has become in favour of the part of him he has denied. Through this acceptance Coover is able to suggest the "something more positive" Mann could not allow Aschenbach, and at the same time Pinocchio as Prufrock dares to leave behind his crab-like shell, and Pinocchio as Bloom - in no uncertain terms - renews his physical relationship with the Fairy/Molly. Like Aschenbach, and like Collodi's puppet, Pinocchio dies at the end of Coover's narrative, but this is the longed for Lacanian "second death." He is able to make a good death as the last fragments of his human body are removed, and the anarchic puppet is revealed. With great courage, and a mixture of terror, excitement, and serenity, he faces the abyss of the Real, and makes peace on his own terms with the Blue Fairy as the monstrous feminine. Before the altar of the Miracoli church, and in a blasphemous *Pietà*, the Fairy cradles Pinocchio's

---

[66] Reed 1974, 166.

broken, anatomised body, no more now than a bundle of crumbling wooden sticks. He is fit only for recycling and - recycling yet again the trope of self-reflexivity - she whispers "We'll make a book out of you!" In response to Derrida's invisible presence, to difference, and to the *pharmakon* as remedy *and* poison, the *pharmakon* as speech *and* writing, Pinocchio undergoes a last metamorphosis. "[W]ith his vanishing voice" which will not vanish because it will be part of the endless dialogue of literature that contains past, present, and future (and with a wink to Henry Louis Gates's "signifyin[g]"), he replies "But a talking book, Mamma! *A talking book* ..."[67]

The central Derridean *différance* that informs every aspect of Coover's Pinocchio's journey, and is central to my reading of it, is crystallised as the text ends not with a whimper but with Pinocchio's theft and modification of Molly Bloom's Joycean "yes ...! Good ..."[68] which brims with potential and denies linguistic boundaries as it denies Mann's tragic ending. The difference hinges in large part on the linguistic play that dances across a carnivalesque world-upside-down, and is achieved by means of a Derridean "double gesture" that refuses to simply reverse Platonic oppositions but unsettles and displaces them (as Bakhtinian dialogism doesn't merely reread earlier texts but opens them up to new interpretations), and so creates a new and productive medium.[69]

Bakhtinian theories of the dialogic and of carnival and Derrida's questioning of western metaphysics become part of the complex matrix of the grotesque body of the text that is a figure at once for the palimpsest that is the mythologised textual city of Venice and for the grotesque body of the city itself, in a process that shatters in order to reincorporate and revivify the fragmented body of western literature. Coover's text becomes an exemplum of Plato's *pharmakon* in that it is an interweaving of texts that is a remedy against forgetting at the same time as it is a risky unravelling of that history from which a new fabric may be formed.

Coover's text is not merely an engagement with *différance*; it is a seriously ludic, infinitely iterable "staging" of Derrida's questioning of the metaphysics of presence. In a neat reverse mirroring of Derrida's own practice of bringing literary texts to bear on his critique of western philosophy, Coover undermines that tradition's logocentrism by an overt inscription of philosophy - in particular a rereading of Derrida's rereading of Plato's *Phaedrus* - on the grotesque body of western literature.

Conclusion

For Coover, as for most of the late-twentieth-century writers listed in the introduction to this essay, Venice "works" as a setting for reasons that can be defined as post-Romantic - that is, the attraction to "beauty in decay" remains. But there's an extra resonance now, as Venice also becomes a figure for *global* environmental degradation.

---

[67] Coover 1991, 329.
[68] Coover 1991, 330.
[69] Derrida 1982, 329.

In terms of the city as culture, Venice stands for all we have made, and for all we stand to lose. Linked to this, it is also an object of what Andreas Huyssen terms "museal desire". Huyssen points out that we live in a period that has witnessed, paradoxically in a time characterised by the waning of history and by cultural amnesia, "a memory boom of unprecedented proportions."[70] Coover's city is a realisation of Huyssen's creative fissure that occurs between the past and the present and between historical events and their contemporary representation. It is both a productive theatre of contestation, and "an anchoring space" within millennial uncertainties that enables an engagement with the present and with the future. This does not make it a symptom of conservative nostalgia; the crumbling stage on which Pinocchio finds himself is hardly an exquisite representation meant to stand in lieu of the perfect city that is slipping from our grasp. Rather, the perfection of Venice preserved as the consummate medieval-Renaissance *urbs*, the kind of space Huysssen might term a "burial chamber" of our collective western past,[71] is smashed open, in a defiant and loving carnivalesque act of creative destruction.

Bibliography

Appiah, Anthony: *Another Death in Venice*. London 1995.
Ashley, Ardythe: *The Christ of the Butterflies*. New York 1991.
Bakhtin, Mikhail: *Problems of Dostoevsky's Poetics*. Trans. Emerson, Caryl (ed.): Minneapolis 1984.
Bakhtin, Mikhail: *The Dialogic Imagination: Four Essays*. Trans. Emerson, Caryl, and Holquist, Michael. Holquist, Michael (ed.): Austin, Texas 1981.
Begley, Louis: *Mistler's Exit*. New York 1998.
Brodkey, Harold: *Profane Friendship*. New York 1994.
Byron, George Gordon, Lord: *Childe Harold's Pilgrimage*. 1812–18. McGann, Jerome J. (ed.): Oxford 1986.
Collodi, Carlo: *The Adventures of Pinocchio*. Trans. Nicolas J. Perella. Berkeley and London 1986.
Coover, Robert: *Pinocchio in Venice*. London 1991.
Cope, Jackson: *Robert Coover's Fictions*. Baltimore, Maryland 1986.
Dante Alighieri: *The Divine Comedy*. Trans. Mandelbaum, Allen. Berkeley/Los Angeles 1980–82.
Derrida, Jacques: *Dissemination*. Trans. Johnson, Barbara. Chicago 1981.
Derrida, Jacques: *Margins - Of Philosophy*. New York 1982.
Dibdin, Michael: *Dead Lagoon*. Toronto 1994.
Eliot, T.S.: *Collected Poems: 1909–62*. London 1974.
Frye, Northrop: *Anatomy of Criticism*. Princeton, NJ 1957.
Gates, Henry Louis: *The Signifying Monkey: A Theory of Afro-American Literary Criticism*. Oxford 1988.

---

[70] Huyssen 1995, 5.
[71] Huyssen 1995, 15.

Gee, Maggie: *Where Are the Snows*. London 1992. Gronicka, André von: "'Myth plus Psychology': A Stylistic Analysis of *Death in Venice*." In: Hatfield, Henry (ed.): *Thomas Mann: A Collection of Critical Essays*. New York 1964, 46–61.

Hecht, Anthony: *The Venetian Vespers*. New York 1979.

Hutcheon, Linda: "Modern Parody and Bakhtin." In: Morson, Gary Saul, and Emerson, Caryl (eds.): *Rethinking Bakhtin: Extensions and Challenges*. Evanston, Illinois 1989.

Huyssen, Andreas: *Twilight Memories: Marking Time in a Culture of Amnesia*. London and New York 1995. Ihimaera, Witi: *The Matriarch*. Auckland 1986.

James, Henry: *Italian Hours*. New York 1987.

James, Henry: *The Wings of the Dove*. London 1902.

Jones, Rod: Night Pictures. Sydney 1997.

Jong, Erica: *Serenissima*. New York 1987.

Joyce, James: *Ulysses*. London 1968.

King, Ross: *Domino*. London 1995.

Krantz, Judith: *Lovers*. New York 1994.

Mann, Thomas: *Death in Venice and Seven Other Stories*. Trans. H.T. Lowe-Porter. New York 1989.

McCarthy, Mary: *Venice Observed*. New York 1956.

McEwan, Ian. *The Comfort of Strangers*. London 1981.

Morris, James (Jan). *Venice*. London 1960.

Perella, Nicolas J.: "An Essay on *Pinocchio*." In: Perella, Nicolas J. (ed.): *The Adventures of Pinocchio*. Berkeley/London 1986, 1–69.

Phillips, Caryl: *The Nature of Blood*. New York 1997.

Pound, Ezra: *Cantos*. London 1964.

Pound, Ezra: *Selected Poems: 1908–59*. London 1975.

Reed, T.J.: *Thomas Mann: The Use of Tradition*. London 1974.

Rice, Anne. *Cry to Heaven*. New York 1982.

Roberts, Michèle: *The Book of Mrs Noah*. London 1987

Rolfe, Frederick (Baron Corvo): *The Desire and Pursuit of the Whole*. New York 1953.

Ruskin, John: *The Stones of Venice*. 1851–53. 3 vols. London 1905.

Tanner, Tony: *Venice Desired*. Cambridge, Mass. 1992.

Thompson, David: *The Mirrormaker*. Toronto 1993.

Unsworth, Barry: *Stone Virgin*. London 1985.

Winterson, Jeanette: *The Passion*. London 1987.

INTERNATIONALE FORSCHUNGEN ZUR ALLGEMEINEN UND VERGLEICHENDEN LITERATURWISSENSCHAFT

Vol. 1: NORBERT BACHLEITNER: Der englische und französische Sozialroman des 19. Jahrhunderts und seine Rezeption in Deutschland. Amsterdam/Atlanta, GA 1993. VIII,637 pp.
ISBN: 90-5183-522-1   Bound Hfl. 260,-/US-$ 143.-

Vol. 2: EZRA POUND AND EUROPE. Ed. by Richard Taylor and Claus Melchior. Amsterdam/Atlanta, GA 1993. VIII,242 pp.
ISBN: 90-5183-521-3   Hfl. 75,-/US-$ 41.50

Vol. 3: LA NOUVELLE ROMANE (ITALIA - FRANCE - ESPAÑA). Sous la rédaction de José Luis Alonso Hernández, Martin Gosman, Rinaldo Rinaldi. Amsterdam/Atlanta, GA 1993. XII,183 pp. ISBN: 90-5183-539-6   Hfl. 70,-/US-$ 38.50

Vol. 4: FLORENT ET LYON. WILHELM SALZMANN: KAISER OCTAVIANUS. Hrsg. von Xenja von Ertzdorff und Ulrich Seelbach. Unter Mitarbeit von Christina Wolf. Amsterdam/Atlanta, GA 1993. 402 pp. Reich illustriert.
ISBN: 90-5183-622-8   Hfl. 160,-/US-$ 88.50

Vol. 5: ALFRED NOE: Die Präsenz der romanischen Literaturen in der 1655 nach Wien verkauften Fuggerbibliothek. 1. Band: Diplomatische Ausgabe des Codex 12.579 der Österreichischen Nationalbibliothek («Mauchter-Katalog»). Amsterdam/Atlanta, GA 1994. XXVI, 650 pp.
ISBN: 90-5183-633-3   Bound Hfl. 280,-/US-$ 154.-

Vol. 6: DER PHILHELLENISMUS IN DER WESTEUROPÄISCHEN LITERATURE 1780-1830. Hrsg. von Alfred Noe. Amsterdam/Atlanta, GA 1994. 236 pp.
ISBN: 90-5183-702-X   Hfl. 75,-/US-$ 41.50

Vol. 7: ZEICHEN ZWISCHEN KLARTEXT UND ARABESKE. Konferenz des Konstanzer Graduiertenkollegs «Theorie der Literatur». Veranstaltet im Oktober 1992. Hrsg. von Susi Kotzinger und Gabriele Rippl. Amsterdam/Atlanta, GA 1994. 387 pp. ISBN: 90-5183-728-3   Hfl. 120,-/US-$ 66.50

Vol. 8: LUDVIG HOLBERG: A EUROPEAN WRITER. A Study in Influence and Reception. Ed. by Sven Hakon Rossel. Amsterdam/Atlanta, GA 1994. IX,238 pp.
                             Hfl. 75,-/US-$ 41.50

Vol. 9: THEMATICS RECONSIDERED. Essays in Honor of Horst S. Daemmrich. Ed. by Frank Trommler. Amsterdam/Atlanta, GA 1995. 278 pp. ISBN: 90-5183-787-9   Hfl. 90,-/US-$ 50.-

Vol. 10: ARTHURIAN ROMANCE AND GENDER: MASCULIN/FEMININ DANS LE ROMAN ARTHURIEN MEDIEVAL. GESCHLECHTERROLLEN IM MITTELALTERLICHEN ARTUSROMAN. (Selected Proceedings of the XVIIth International Arthurian Congress/Actes choisis du XVIIe Congrès International Arthurien/Ausgewählte Akten des XVII. Internationalen Artuskongresses). Ed. by/publié par/hrsg. von Friedrich Wolfzettel. Amsterdam/Atlanta, GA 1994. VI,295 pp.
ISBN: 90-5183-635-X   Bound Hfl. 120,-/US-$ 66.50

Vol. 11: ERIC ROBERTSON: Writing Between the Lines. René Schickele, 'Citoyen français, deutscher Dichter', 1883-1940. Amsterdam/Atlanta, GA 1995. 202 pp.
ISBN: 90-5183-711-9   Hfl. 65,-/US-$ 36.-

Vol. 12: SUCHBILD EUROPA - KÜNSTLERISCHE KONZEPTE DER MODERNE. Hrsg. von Jürgen Wertheimer. Amsterdam/Atlanta, GA 1995. 221 pp.
ISBN: 90-5183-853-0   Hfl. 70,-/US-$ 38.50

Vol. 13: ALFRED NOE: Die Präsenz der romanischen Literaturen in der 1655 nach Wien verkauften Fuggerbibliothek. 2. Band. Rekonstruktion und Analyse des Bestandes (ohne «Musicales»). Amsterdam/Atlanta, GA 1995. 757 pp.
ISBN: 90-5183-866-2   Bound Hfl. 300,-/US-$ 165.-

Vol. 14: HANS CHRISTIAN ANDERSEN: Danish Writer and Citizen of the World. Ed. by Sven Hakon Rossel. Amsterdam/Atlanta, GA 1996. IX,294 pp.
ISBN: 90-5183-944-8   Bound Hfl. 150,-/US-$ 83.-
ISBN: 90-5183-948-0   Paper Hfl. 50,-/US-$ 27.50

Vol. 15: THE FATAL GIFT OF BEAUTY: THE ITALIES OF BRITISH TRAVELLERS. An Annotated Anthology. Ed. by Manfred Pfister. Amsterdam/Atlanta, GA 1996. 554 pp.
ISBN: 90-5183-981-2   Bound Hfl. 250,-/US-$ 135.-
ISBN: 90-5183-943-X   Paper Hfl. 60,-/US-$ 33.-

Vol. 16: RUSSELL WEST: Joseph Conrad and André Gide. Translation, Transference and Intertextuality. Amsterdam/Atlanta, GA 1996. 187 pp.
ISBN: 90-5183-907-3   Hfl. 60.-/US-$ 33.-

Vol. 17: VALÉRIE BAISNÉE: Gendered Resistance. The Autobiographies of Simone de Beauvoir, Maya Angelou, Janet Frame and Marguerite Duras. Amsterdam/Atlanta, GA 1997. VIII,176 pp. ISBN: 90-420-0109-7   Hfl. 60,-/US-$ 33.-

Vol. 18: DOCUMENTARISM IN SCANDINAVIAN LITERATURE. Ed. by Poul Houe and Sven Hakon Rossel. Amsterdam/Atlanta, GA 1997. X,230 pp.
ISBN: 90-420-0141-0   Bound Hfl. 125,-/US-$ 69,-
ISBN: 90-420-0123-2   Paper Hfl. 35,-/US-$ 19.-

Vol. 19: VLADIMIR TUMANOV. Mind Reading: Unframed Direct Interior Monologue in European Fiction. Amsterdam/Atlanta, GA 1997. VIII,142 pp. ISBN: 90-420-0147-X   Hfl. 50,-/US-$ 27.50

Vol. 20: TEXT INTO IMAGE: IMAGE INTO TEXT. Proceedings of the Interdisciplinary Bicentenary Conference held at St. Patrick's College Maynooth (The National University of Ireland) in September 1995. Ed. by Jeff Morrison and Florian Krobb. Amsterdam/Atlanta, GA 1997. 353 pp.
ISBN: 90-420-0152-6   Bound Hfl. 175,-/US-$ 97.-
ISBN: 90-420-0153-4   Paper Hfl. 50,-/US-$ 27.50

Vol. 21: ALFRED NOE: Die Präsenz der romanischen Literaturen in der 1655 nach Wien verkauften Fuggerbibliothek. 3. Band Die Texte der «Musicales». Amsterdam/Atlanta, GA 1997. 998 pp. ISBN: 90-420-0149-6   Bound Hfl. 400,-/US-$ 220.-

Vol. 22: CONSTANTIN V. PONOMAREFF: The Spiritual Geography of Modern Writing. Essays on Dehumanization, Human Isolation and Transcendence. Amsterdam/Atlanta, GA 1997. IX,132 pp. ISBN: 90-420-0174-7   Hfl. 50,-/US-$ 27.50

Vol. 23: YVAN GOLL - CLAIRE GOLL. Texts and Contexts. Ed. by Eric Robertson and Robert Vilain. Amsterdam/Atlanta, GA 1997. VI,249 pp.
ISBN: 90-420-0173-9   Bound Hfl. 125,-/US-$ 69.-
ISBN: 90-420-0189-5   Paper Hfl. 35,-/US-$ 19.-

Vol. 24: INTERART POETICS. Essays on the Interrelations of the Arts and Media. Ed. by Ulla-Britta Lagerroth, Hans Lund and Erik Hedling. Amsterdam/Atlanta, GA 1997. 354 pp.
ISBN: 90-420-0202-6   Bound Hfl. 175,-/US-$ 97.-
ISBN: 90-420-0210-7   Paper Hfl. 50,-/US-$ 27.5C

Vol. 25: JULIE A. REAHARD: "Aus einem unbekannten Zentrum, zu einer nicht erkennbaren Grenze". Chaos Theory, Hermeneutics and Goethe's *Die Wahlverwandtschaften*. Amsterdam/Atlanta, GA 1997. 87 pp.
ISBN: 90-420-0223-9   Hfl. 50,-/US-$ 27.50

Vol. 26: RUTH B. EMDE: Schauspielerinnen im Europa des 18. Jahrhunderts: Ihr Leben, Ihre Schriften und Ihr Publikum. Amsterdam/Atlanta, GA 1997. XV,368 pp.
ISBN: 90-420-0361-8   Bound Hfl. 160,-/US-$ 88.50
ISBN: 90-420-0351-0   Paper Hfl. 55,-/US-$ 30.50

Vol. 27: LE RAYONNEMENT DES TROUBADOURS. Ed. by Anton Touber. Amsterdam/Atlanta, GA 1998. VII,312 pp.
ISBN: 90-420-0090-2   Hfl. 130,-/US-$ 72.-

Vol. 28: IMAGES OF AMERICA IN SCANDINAVIA. Ed. by Poul Houe and Sven Hakon Rossel. Amsterdam/Atlanta, GA 1998. X,232 pp. ISBN: 90-420-0621-8   Bound Hfl. 125,-/US-$ 69,-
ISBN: 90-420-0611-0   Paper Hfl. 38,-/US-$ 21.-

Vol. 29: CONSTANTIN V. PONOMAREFF: In the Shadow of the Holocaust & Other Essays. Amsterdam/Atlanta, GA 1998. X,127 pp. ISBN: 90-420-0562-9   Hfl. 50,-/US-$ 27.50

Vol. 30: FIGUREN DER/DES DRITTEN. Erkundungen kultureller Zwischenräume. Hrsg. von Claudia Breger und Tobias Döring. Amsterdam/Atlanta, GA 1998. 269 pp.
ISBN: 90-420-0592-0   Hfl. 90,-/US-$ 49.50

Vol. 31: ÁSDÍS R. MAGNÚSDÓTTIR: La voix du cor. La relique de Roncevaux et l'origine d'un motif dans la littérature du Moyen Âge (XIIe - XIVe siècles). Amsterdam/Atlanta, GA 1998. 432 pp. + illustrations.
ISBN: 90-420-0602-1   Hfl. 140,-/US-$ 77.50

Vol. 32: ANITA OBERMEIER: The History and Anatomy of Auctorial Self-Criticism in the European Middle Ages. Amsterdam/Atlanta, GA 1999. 314 pp.
ISBN: 90-420-0405-3   Hfl. 100,-/US-$ 55.50